Sweet Tyranny

**THE WORKING CLASS
IN AMERICAN HISTORY**

Editorial Advisors
   James R. Barrett
   Alice Kessler-Harris
   Nelson Lichtenstein
   David Montgomery

*A list of books in the series
appears at the end of this book.*

Sweet Tyranny

Migrant Labor,
Industrial Agriculture,
and Imperial Politics

KATHLEEN MAPES

UNIVERSITY OF ILLINOIS PRESS
Urbana and Chicago

© 2009 by the Board of Trustees
of the University of Illinois
All rights reserved
Manufactured in the United States of America
1 2 3 4 5 C P 5 4 3 2 1

∞ This book is printed on acid-free paper.

Library of Congress Cataloging-in-Publication Data
Mapes, Kathleen, 1967–
Sweet tyranny : migrant labor, industrial agriculture, and
imperial politics / Kathleen Mapes.
    p.   cm. — (The working class in American history)
Includes bibliographical references and index.
ISBN 978-0-252-03436-7 (cloth : alk. paper)
ISBN 978-0-252-07667-1 (paper : alk. paper)
1. Migrant agricultural laborers—Middle West—History—
20th century. 2. Child migrant agricultural laborers—Middle
West—History—20th century. 3. Agricultural laborers, Foreign—
Middle West—History—20th century. 4. Rural industries—
Middle West—History—20th century. 5. Industrialization—
Middle West—History—20th century. 6. Agriculture and
politics—Middle West—History—20th century. 7. Agriculture—
Economic aspects—Middle West—History—20th century.
8. Middle West—Rural conditions. 9. United States—Emigration
and immigration—Government policy—History—20th century.
10. Imperialism—History—20th century.
I. Title.
HD1527.M54M37   2009
331.5'440977—dc22   2008041247

To my family
Dean, Dorothy, Wendy,
Rita, and Mary
and
In memory of
Peter

Contents

Acknowledgments ix
Introduction 1

1. Rural Industrialization and Imperial Politics 13
2. Contract Farming in Rural Michigan 39
3. Family Farms, Child Labor, and Migrant Families 65
4. Farmers and the Great War 96
5. Immigrant Labor and the Guest Worker Program 122
6. Mexican Immigrants and Immigration Debate 143
7. Child Labor Reformers and Industrial Agriculture 166
8. Remaking Imperialism and the Industrial Countryside 186
9. The Politics of Migrant Labor 215

Epilogue 241
Notes 247
Index 301

Illustrations follow page 64

Acknowledgments

Over the many years it took to research, write, and revise this book, I have benefited from the generous support of a number of institutions and individuals. These acknowledgments represent merely a token of my deep appreciation.

The History Department at the University of Illinois provided much-needed funding that made the bulk of the research possible. The Illinois Project for Research in the Humanities gave me both time and money to begin serious writing. Since then, a Presidential Summer Fellowship and a Nuala Drescher Fellowship from SUNY Geneseo made it possible for me to finish the book. I am thankful to all the above-mentioned institutions for helping financially support my research and writing. I am also thankful to the numerous librarians and archivists who aided in my quest to identify and locate primary sources, including Michigan State University Archives and Historical Collections; Michigan State University Library; the Archives of Michigan at the Library of Michigan; the Hoyt Library, Saginaw, Michigan; the Bay County Historical Society and Museum, Bay City, Michigan; the Bancroft Library, University of California, Berkeley; University Library, University of Illinois, Urbana-Champaign; the Rare Book and Manuscript Library, University of Illinois; the National Archives, Washington, D.C., and College Park, Maryland; the National Archives, Great Lakes Region, Chicago; and Mann Library, Cornell University.

I am deeply indebted to those who first introduced me to the historian's craft. Norman Pollack made me believe that history really does matter and that those who choose to become students of the past must do so passionately and responsibly. David Bailey pushed me to think conceptually and encouraged independent thinking. Lisa Fine stressed the importance of taking gender seriously. Joseph Spielberg Benitez and Leigh Binford welcomed me into their discussions of Marxist anthropology and the history of sugar. Most important of all, James Barrett helped to shape and shepherd this book in its earliest stages. I am deeply grateful for his support, as both my life and what would become the book went in unconventional directions. His genuinely humane approach to life and to history has influenced me deeply.

Many people have read all or parts of this book and deserve my thanks. Matt Garcia, Nils Jacobsen, and Sonya Michel read an early draft, and provided the perfect mix of honest constructive criticism and encouragement. The participants in the Newberry Seminar in Rural History and the Newberry Library Labor History Seminar read select chapters and suggested revisions that certainly helped to make this a better book. Cathy Adams, Ruth Fairbanks, Tobias Higbie, Rose Holz, Jordan Kleiman, Val Littlefield, Michelle Moran, Andrew Nolan, Glenn Penny, Randi Storch, and Caroline Waldron not only provided critical commentary on individual chapters, but friendship. I would especially like to thank Randi for continuing to listen to my concerns, answer my queries, boost my confidence, and read anything that I send her at the drop of a hat. Many of my colleagues at SUNY Geneseo have supported me as a teacher, a scholar, and a friend, even under the most trying circumstances. My three department chairs, James Williams, Michael Oberg, and Tze-ki Hon, looked out for my best interests and encouraged me to do my best, while the department secretary, Barb Rex-Mckinney, provided help whenever I asked. Tze-ki deserves special mention for reading the entire manuscript.

At the University of Illinois Press, acquisitions editor Laurie Matheson expressed early interest in this project and waited patiently as revisions took much longer than expected. She also provided very helpful suggestions as I revised the manuscript. I would also like to thank those who read the manuscript for the press, including an anonymous reader, David Montgomery, and Cindy Hahamovitch. Cindy made especially helpful comments and generously supported this book, providing a model for what it means to be in a scholarly community. Leon Fink deserves thanks for suggesting the title for the book and Janine Giordano for selflessly helping me collect illustrations at the very last minute.

Although I have thoroughly enjoyed researching and writing this book, it remains a distant second to what is and will forever be most important in my life—my family. My mother, Dorothy Mapes, has always supported me and continues to believe in everything that I do. My siblings, their spouses, numerous nieces and nephews, and in-laws provided welcome breaks from academic life. My husband, Stewart Dean Atkin, has been ever so patient over the years I have spent working on what he likes to call "the book." His love and levity have made my life meaningful and fun. Our daughters, Dorothy and Wendy, never cease to inspire me with their boundless love and seemingly endless optimism. My niece, Rita, remains a constant source of energy and humanity. More than any other person, my twin sister Mary Mapes, also a historian, has made sure that this book would see the light of day. In the earliest stages, she provided much-needed (and free) child care, taking time away from her own historical research and writing. Since then, she has not only listened patiently and attentively as I discussed the manuscript with her, but she has read through more drafts than I care to admit or that she cares to remember. Her keen insight and critical perspective have made this a much better book than it would have been. I cannot thank her enough. Finally, with a very heavy heart, this book is dedicated in the memory of Peter R. D'Agostino—fellow historian, Rita's dad, and Mary's husband. Mere words cannot begin to express how completely and deeply he is missed.

* * *

An earlier version of chapter 6 appeared as " 'A Special Class of Labor': Mexican (Im)Migrants, Immigration Debate, and Industrial Agriculture in the Rural Midwest," *Labor: Studies in Working-Class History of the Americas* 1.2: (Summer 2004): 64–88.

# Sweet Tyranny

Introduction

A year after Congress passed the 1901 Platt Amendment, dramatically restricting Cuban sovereignty, the U.S. House of Representatives convened special hearings to debate what kind of trading rights to award its southern neighbor.[1] While dozens of witnesses paraded before Congress, the majority who made the trip to Washington had come to protect the fledgling American beet sugar industry from Cuban cane sugar. One of those witnesses, Michigan sugar beet industrialist N. H. Stewart, insisted that there was a rather simple answer to the question Congress had met to decide. Repeating an argument that industry spokesmen had been making since the waning days of the Spanish-American War, Stewart protested that the issue was national and racial at heart. "I am here before you, gentlemen, to represent the state of Michigan in the beet sugar industry. As citizens of the United States . . . they ask the protection of this government . . . and that they not be ruined for Chinese, coolie, or any other labor that is brought in competition with our farmers and laboring men in the North, where they can not sleep under a fig tree or lay down on the side of their work."[2] In other words, Stewart argued that Congress should privilege "civilized" beet sugar grown by American citizens over "barbarian" cane sugar tended to by "savages" abroad—regardless of Cuba's "colonial" status.

The same year that Congress met to decide the fate of Cuba, hundreds of residents from the small town of Croswell, Michigan, population 613, celebrated in the streets to congratulate each other on their collective good fortune—the building of a half-million-dollar sugar beet factory in their town. This announcement had come after months of boosterism, in which townspeople had promised prospective investors cheap land, reduced taxes, and a more than ample supply of sugar beet. Seemingly impervious to the international debates taking place hundreds of miles away in Washington, D.C., Croswell's residents looked forward to a glorious future of higher land values, increased business, better schools, and greater access to all the material goods that modern industrial capitalism had to offer. To the men and women who took to the streets, the arrival of the sugar beet factory marked the coming of modernity itself.[3]

Just down the road from Croswell, however, a more complicated story was unfolding. Frustration and anger reigned in many of the rural communities that had already succeeded in getting factories of their own, for many of the farmers who had contracted with those factories to grow the crop complained that they had been cheated out of their just earnings. A number of farmers even argued that growing sugar beet by contract for the local factories had placed them in a position of "slavery" and warned that unless the sugar companies treated them fairly, they would simply quit the sugar beet crop and begin growing something else.[4]

And finally, even as farmers and company officials were battling over who would profit most from the crop, thousands of eastern European immigrant families were disembarking at train stations throughout rural Michigan.[5] They had been recruited by the sugar companies to work for local farmers who grew sugar beet but refused to do the arduous hand labor necessary for this gardenlike crop. Although the majority of the newly arriving families were German Russians, and considered themselves distinctly German, they would soon find themselves labeled as class and racial outcasts—Russian beet weeders. In the words of one German Russian woman who labored in rural Michigan in the early twentieth century: "We were a different people."[6]

These four vignettes from the year 1902 are not the kinds of stories one usually thinks of when envisioning the rural Midwest. When asked to describe the rural Midwest, most Americans—historians and non-historians alike—conjure up images of family farmers living in close-knit communities far from surrounding cities and international conflicts.[7] Early on, students learn to link urbanization, immigration, and industrialization as the holy triptych of modernization, leaving rural Americans either on the sidelines as more significant developments took place elsewhere, or as a relic of a past era superseded by history itself. In this grand narrative, urban industrial America overtook rural America, either with the Populist defeat of 1896, which symbolized the transfer of power from agrarians to industrialists, or with the 1920 census, which found that more Americans were living in urban areas than rural surroundings. In the words of rural historian David B.

Danbom, "To live in the countryside in 1900 was to have the sense that the nation was passing you by, leaving you behind, ignoring you at best and derogating you at worst."[8]

The stories told here call into question the traditional portrait of the rural Midwest as a classless and homogenous place untouched by industrialization and imperialism. As we shall soon see, the coming of the sugar beet industry to rural Michigan in the late nineteenth and early twentieth centuries not only remade community, class, and race relations by introducing large factories, contract farming, and migrant labor, it also helped shape and was shaped by national and international debates regarding immigration and imperialism. As a grassroots and global history of Michigan's sugar beet industry from 1899 to 1940, this book comes to terms with that history. What emerges is a complicated and compelling history about the creation of migrant labor, the emergence of industrial agriculture, and the development of American imperialism, both at home and abroad. What emerges is a history of the making of modern industrial America—one that is easily missed when the links between the countryside and cities, agriculture and industry, farmers and migrant workers, and foreign policy and domestic debates are overlooked.

Sugar

The rise of the sugar beet industry over the course of the nineteenth century represents one of the most important, if overlooked, developments of industrial agriculture.[9] Though the industry first rose to prominence during the Napoleonic era, when European nations found themselves cut off from colonial cane sugar, the most extensive expansion took place in the second half of the nineteenth century. In that period, sugar beet not only rivaled but surpassed sugar cane as the most important source of sugar in the world, with more than half of all sugar coming from sugar beet by 1884. Fifteen years later, in 1899, sugar beet accounted for 65 percent of the world's sugar. Although the rapid expansion of this industry can be partially explained by technological advances in the growing and processing of sugar beet, the primary causes were political in nature. European nations shielded their domestically grown sugar beet with high tariffs and lucrative bounties, leaving even their own colonies to compete in a world marketplace increasingly guarded by protective trade barriers.[10]

Rural reformers in the United States closely watched the phenomenal growth of sugar beet over the course of the nineteenth century from an insignificant source of sweetness to the most important source of sugar in the world. And they were more than well aware that most of the production had taken place in Europe, where state boosterism, bounties, and protectionism had fostered a large and well-supported industry.[11] Hoping to follow in the footsteps of countries like Germany, which alone produced more sugar in the 1890s than the entire Caribbean, American reformers and prospective investors hailed beet sugar as the civilized alternative to cane sugar.[12] For unlike cane sugar, which had long been closely associated with colonialism, slavery, and plantation agriculture, beet sugar was heralded for delivering rural industrialization and prosperity to family farms and rural communities. Charles Saylor, the United States Department of Agriculture's main sugar beet investigator, certainly adopted this perspective, for he celebrated the sugar beet industry as one that would not only transform local communities but also assure the United States independence in a global economy. "It brings the factory and the farm side by side. It brings farmers, laborers, and capitalists into close association and cooperation. It places supply at the door of demand. It meets the logic of modern times in the concentration of advantages and conservation of forces. It eliminates the foreign grower as a factor in the supply of our daily wants, our business methods, and the emergencies of war. The development of the sugar beet industry tends to prevent the concentration of manufacturing . . . in some sections of the country and of agricultural . . . in others. It conforms to an ideal system and simplifies the problems of our social and economic life. It is a great decentralizing power."[13] To let this opportunity pass, to stand on the sidelines as Europe continued to move forward as the world's most important sugar beet center, seemed like a risk the United States could not afford to take.

Beginning in earnest in the late nineteenth and early twentieth centuries, state officials and aspiring industrialists, buoyed by lucrative state bounties and protective tariffs, did all that they could to create a domestic sugar beet industry in the United States. As a result of these economic and political incentives, the number of factories in the United States increased from just six in 1892 to thirty-one in 1899, to fifty-six in 1903, to sixty-four in 1906. (In 1906, Michigan led the nation with seventeen factories, followed by Colorado with fifteen and California with eight.) By 1906, the amount of sugar in the United States produced from beet sugar even surpassed the amount of cane sugar raised on Louisiana's historic sugar cane plantations. Within just two decades, the sugar beet industry had become an important economic and political factor in the United States.[14]

At first glance, Michigan's sugar beet industry seemed to embody all of the virtues that Charles Saylor had identified when boosting for this industry—rural factories located next to small family farms, plenty of workers in nearby city centers, and close contact between urban markets and agricultural products. A closer look at conditions on the ground, however, reveals that the sugar beet industry in Michigan often followed a different path than the one envisioned by optimistic boosters. Rather than bring industrialists and farmers closer together in mutual harmony, class conflicts and battles erupted as soon as Michigan's sugar beet factories began contracting with local farmers to grow the crop. The very geographic interdependence of this industry—the fact that the companies depended upon surrounding farmers for an ample supply of sugar beet, and that the crop was too heavy and perishable to ship more than a few dozen miles—provided fertile ground for farmers and companies as each battled for control over what proved an elusive and ever-shifting boundary dividing and uniting the factory and the field. That this crop was grown exclusively by contract meant that those farmers who decided to grow sugar beet had no choice but to do so for local sugar factories. Unlike the other agricultural crops that farmers grew, which were transported to nearby markets and sold to the highest bidder, the sugar beet crop had to be hauled to a nearby factory with the price having been set months before the crop was even planted.

Fearing that the sugar factories were taking advantage of them, farmers from varying ethnic and class backgrounds banded together to challenge the sugar companies—the most imposing and concrete manifestation of modern industrial capitalism in the countryside. When Michigan's farmers joined to protest against the sugar companies, however, they rarely expressed a moral or ideological antipathy to either the size of the factories or the fact of contract farming. Many even welcomed the opening of the sugar factories as a chance to generate cash income and hoped that contract farming might allow them to avoid the volatility of a market that seemed so utterly out of their control. What infuriated farmers was their belief that the companies were unfairly profiting from their land and labor. This conviction led to new cross-class and cross-ethnic alliances as farmers with varying degrees of wealth and from different ethnic backgrounds forged an oppositional class identity based on three key factors: their traditional roles as laboring men, their ideals of independent landholding, and their newly emerging identities as agricultural businessmen. This multifaceted class identity provided an opportunity for these farmers to make sense of and defend the multiple roles they assumed in an economy that was both market-driven and industrially bound, and in a world where the lines between agriculture and industry, and between the rural domain and the urban realm, were becoming less and less clear.

In addition to transforming the farmers' class identity, the sugar beet industry also helped to remake the sources and meaning of rural labor. Ever since the settlement of Michigan in the early nineteenth century, farm families and hired hands had made up the overwhelming majority of the agricultural workforce. Company officials initially had hoped that farmers growing sugar beet would use traditional labor sources, including their own families and unemployed local residents. It did not take long before the arduous demands of this crop overwhelmed local labor supplies. Though some farmers used their own families in the fields, and others tried to hire children from local communities and nearby cities, these two labor sources proved woefully insufficient, forcing industry officials to respond by recruiting and transporting thousands of the nation's newest immigrants to come toil in the fields for the season, which began sometime in April or May and ended in October or November.

Considering the reformers' initial promises that the sugar beet industry would provide plenty of labor for unemployed locals, it seems somewhat ironic that this industry not only came to depend on an international labor force but that in doing so helped to transform rural labor relations for the rest of the twentieth century. The hundreds of German Russian families who first stepped off the trains throughout rural Michigan in 1901, and the thousands of Hungarians, Bohemians, Poles, and Mexicans who followed in their footsteps, found themselves not on the first step of a traditional agricultural ladder but rather on the bottom rung of a rural social hierarchy defined by class, residency, and race. In contrast to traditional hired hands, who sealed their work arrangements with a shake of the hand or a nod of the head, migrant fathers were required to sign legally binding contracts. And in contrast to hired hands, who often lived with the families on whose homesteads they toiled, migrant families usually lived quite a distance from the farmers' own homes, often in small colonies with other beet families or alone in the open countryside. And finally, in contrast to hired hands, who expected their labor to lead to independence and community acceptance, migrant families found themselves the object of community derision and disdain. For, the companies recruited foreign migrant families because they believed that women made men more stable, children made men more vulnerable, and that these foreign families would segregate themselves. This family-based migratory labor system was supposed to ensure farmers a vulnerable, seasonal, and nonthreatening yet stable workforce; migrant family labor was not merely a labor form but also a means for keeping workers in the fields and away from the local community in which they were only temporary residents.

Just as the sugar beet industry transformed community, class, and race relations on the ground, it also plunged rural Michigan into the center of national debates regarding imperialism and immigration. The fact that the United States acquired its own sugar-producing empire at the very moment that its domestic sugar beet industry was coming into its own, as well as the fact that the domestic sugar beet industry came to depend on immigrant workers as the basis of its field labor force, magnified the local and global ties as well as the political battles that ensued. Whether American consumers would satiate their ever-growing demand for sweetness with beet sugar grown at home or cane sugar raised in colonies abroad became part of a much broader debate about the shape of American imperialism and the future of immigration.

To "defend" their industry, Michigan's sugar beet industrialists continually attempted to influence U.S. foreign policy, beginning at the turn of the century, when they argued that the United States needed to protect domestic "civilized" sugar raised at home from "barbarian" slavelike sugar grown in the newly acquired empire. Fighting against the national mantra that gaining an overseas empire would provide boundless markets for American producers, sugar beet industrialists and their allies warned that the nation's own markets would become inundated with tropical products coming in from the opposite direction. As such, this industry called for maintaining high tariff rates against the newly acquired territories as a way to continue the nation's historic practice of protectionism, and thereby make sure that gaining an empire would not "endanger" farmers and workers at home. As the battle to determine what path U.S. imperialism would follow played out in the years after the Spanish-American War, the sugar beet industry continued to assume a surprising and powerful role. By the late 1920s and early 1930s, as concerns about competition between domestic sugar beet and imperial sugar cane mounted, domestic sugar beet industrialists even opportunistically spearheaded the call for Philippine independence so that they could eliminate colonial cane sugar from the U.S. market altogether.

In addition to influencing the outlines of American imperialism, the sugar beet industry also played a significant role in the development of U.S. immigration policy, especially with respect to Mexico. Beginning during World War I and continuing throughout the 1920s, a time when the nation decided to close the door to immigrants from Asia as well as limit those coming in from southern and eastern Europe, industrialists sought to keep the door to immigrants from Mexico wide open. They challenged the trend toward restrictionism by arguing that Mexican workers could be imported and exported as need be. Seemingly unconcerned with the contradiction of calling for high tariffs on colonial sugar to protect "white" American workers while also demanding unlimited access to Mexican workers so that the nation's farmers could have easy access to "cheap" labor, the sugar beet interests placed themselves at the center of debates about whether to extend the nation's immigration restrictions to Mexican nationals and whether to create a guest worker program for those whose labor they so desired.

What might at first appear to be totally distinct histories—the local story of industrializing the midwestern countryside and the United States' rise as an imperial powerhouse—converged and combined in unanticipated ways. To capture this history, this book pays special attention to the various groups and individuals who played a role, including farmers, townspeople, industrialists, migrant families, rural reformers, state officials, congressmen, presidents, and colonial interests. To avoid privileging one set of voices over the others, however, the book's chapters will usually highlight the perspectives of two or three of the above-mentioned groups and shift from the local to the national and international stage as need be. Although focusing on both the local and global parts of this history, and especially the places where the two intersected, makes this book much longer than it otherwise would have been, focusing on only one-half of the story would artificially separate a history that was very much intertwined. In the words of historian Frederick Jackson Turner, "we cannot select a stretch of land and say we will limit our study to this land; for local history can only be understood in the light of the history of the world."[15]

Taking Turner's advice to heart, chapter 1 explores both the local "roots" of industrial agriculture and the international politics surrounding sugar. In this chapter, I argue that town elites and townspeople saw the prospect of getting a sugar beet factory as the best way to "industrialize" without abandoning the agricultural base that had long fueled their local economies. Similarly, rural reformers and state officials saw the sugar beet industry as a unique means for modernizing and industrializing the countryside without creating any of the social problems already associated with these processes. However, the Spanish-American War, in which the United States gained not only an empire but the greatest sugar-producing one in the world, greatly complicated this vision. While many U.S. residents celebrated the war as an example of U.S. humanitarianism, military prowess, and economic might, and looked forward to the opening of markets abroad, sugar beet industrialists feared that U.S. markets would be overwhelmed with cane sugar from its new colonial possessions. Not surprisingly, then, the issue of sugar figured prominently in all the debates regarding the future status of the colonies (especially what trading rights to grant Puerto Rico, Cuba, and the Philippines) and the shape of U.S. imperialism.

The second chapter shifts our focus from international politics to daily relations on the ground from 1898 to 1916 as farmers and the sugar companies sought to control the relationship between the factory and the field. During these years, farmers regularly formed growers' associations and unions, demanded more for the crop than the companies were willing to pay, challenged their exclusion from the factories, and staged strategically timed strikes. In response, sugar companies tried to stave off the farmers' demands by forming trade associations, buying land, and simply threatening to shut the factories down altogether. Though it might be tempting to view these conflicts as a simple contest over who would profit most from the proceeds of this industry, a closer examination reveals a much more serious battle over contract farming in the industrializing countryside.

The next chapter highlights an issue that united the farmer and industry antagonists: finding a labor force willing to do the arduous and tedious hand labor that many farmers refused to do themselves. Chapter 3 describes the various strategies that the sugar companies and farmers pursued to solve their "labor problem," including the use of farm-family labor as well as women and children from local communities and nearby urban centers. After detailing the gendered and communal assumptions underlying these labor forms, this chapter argues that sugar companies began to recruit new immigrant families to the fields because they believed that these families would be a seasonal, self-isolating, vulnerable, and nonthreatening labor force that could be recruited when needed in the spring and then just as quickly escorted out of town in late fall. Solving the "vexing" labor problem, then, was never simply a matter of making sure that the sugar beet crop was properly tended to in the fields, but rather involved a much broader attempt to guard the meaning of belonging and community in the industrializing countryside. In addition to exploring farm labor as a problem to be solved, this chapter also looks at the numerous ways migrant families contested and reinvented the meaning of migrant labor. Although these new immigrant families were ostracized as a class apart, because they toiled in other people's sugar beet fields, as well as a people apart, for their presumed racial inferiority, they nonetheless challenged their status as racialized "beet hunkies" and "bohunks" by creating their own ethnic enclaves, by using family labor as a means of mobility, and by traveling between urban centers and rural hinterlands as opportunities arose.

Chapters 4 and 5 focus on World War I, a pivotal moment in rural America. Chapter 4 describes the increasingly contentious and sometimes violent conflicts between the farmers and the companies during the war and postwar years as each side sought to capitalize on the skyrocketing price of sugar. Though these battles might seem a mere repeat of earlier conflicts, the stakes were raised as numerous state and federal officials intervened to make sure that the nation's sugar bowls would not go empty. Rather than simply placate the farmers, federal intervention helped spur a much larger debate over the place of agriculture in modern industrial America and what role the government would play in helping to determine that status, leading farmers to demand a form of "industrial democracy" for the countryside. Chapter 5 continues the discussion of the role of the state in rural America by looking at how and why the United States Department of Labor (USDL) assumed the responsibility of labor padrone when it began recruiting workers from Mexico to meet what farmers throughout the nation had claimed was an extreme labor shortage. I argue that the USDL's labor program, which involved waiving the head tax and literacy test as well as contract labor laws, resulted in the creation of a racialized labor program that categorized Mexicans as workers but not as immigrants, much less potential citizens. In rural Michigan this perception led to that state's first repatriation campaign after the war as local residents sought to import and deport Mexican workers according to their own racist ideals as well as their alleged economic needs. This chapter also explores the response of Mexican officials, who did their best to challenge the United States' unilateral guest worker program.

This issue of Mexican labor and citizenship continued to be an important one into the 1920s as Congress wrestled over whether it would be possible to admit Mexicans as agricultural workers while making sure they did not become industrial immigrants. In other words, could the United States use its control over immigration to forge a racialized labor policy that would meet the alleged need of the nation's farmers for a "cheap" and "tractable" labor force without violating the nation's newfound commitment to immigration restriction? Chapter 6 highlights the part that Michigan's farmers and industrialists played in the 1920s debates, for these midwesterners often assumed the center stage, arguing not only that they had come to depend on Mexican labor but that Mexican labor was indispensable to the future of family farming in the Midwest. In doing so, they challenged the conventional wisdom that racialized migrant labor and family farming could not go hand-in-hand. This chapter also looks at these debates from the perspective of the Mexican immigrants, examining the numerous ways these immigrants not only challenged racist assumptions but also created geographic, economic, and social mobility in spite of their exclusion from the body politic and the larger community.

Chapter 7 turns to the other national debate about migrant labor in the 1920s: whether or not children should labor in the fields. As child labor reformers shifted their attention from industrial employment to rural agricultural labor, they pointed to Michigan's sugar beet industry as one of the worst offenders. Challenging romantic notions of the rural Midwest as a classless and homogenous place of family farmers, child labor reformers criticized Michigan's sugar beet industry as an especially egregious example of industrial agriculture and exploited child labor. They charged that Michigan's sugar beet fields were "just factories without walls" and pushed for federal, state, and local governments to outlaw this kind of labor. Michigan's farmers and townspeople responded to this criticism by claiming, somewhat disingenuously, that working in the beet fields represented an opportunity of economic mobility and citizenship for children who would otherwise be confined to urban industrial slums.

The last two chapters carry the story of Michigan's sugar beet industry through the 1930s. During the Great Depression and New Deal era, all of the issues that had troubled the U.S. sugar beet industry—farmer militancy, labor conflicts, immigration, the role of the state in the countryside, and the future of U.S. imperialism—collided with a vengeance. Chapter 8 returns to the issue of imperial politics by highlighting the self-interested ways that sugar beet industrialists used the agricultural depression to call on Congress to increase the tariff rate on Cuban sugar and to grant the Philippines independence so that they would be able to control as much of the domestic sugar market as possible. However, while the industrialists attempted to dominate the domestic market, they also had to contend with President Franklin Roosevelt, who insisted that if the sugar industrialists wanted protection from cheaper sugar abroad, they would have to adopt a more equitable relationship with the farmers with whom they contracted to grow the crop. To this end, Roosevelt pressured Congress to pass the Jones-Costigan Act of 1934 and the Sugar Act of 1937, both of which were supposed to level the playing field by forcing industrialists to share in the profits of this industry by paying farmers a "fair and equitable" price for sugar beet.

The question of labor was also increasingly politicized during this tumultuous time. Chapter 9 traces this history, beginning with the repatriation of Mexicans and Mexican Americans from the Midwest during the early 1930s. The story, however, takes a sharp turn by mid decade. Not only did the repatriation campaign come to an end, but, spurred in part by the 1934 and 1937 sugar acts, both of which promised minimum wages for sugar beet workers as well as child labor prohibitions, and perhaps even more so by the New Deal in general, sugar beet workers organized into unions and demand fairer pay and better working conditions. In spite of the workers' valiant efforts to define themselves as workers, as residents, and as citizens, by decade's end they would find themselves the subject of the "migrant problem," as a distinctly midwestern *Grapes of Wrath*.

In September 1929, on the eve of the Great Depression, *Washington Post* journalist David Rankin Barbee wrote an inflammatory article entitled, in part, "Sweet Stuff—Devil or Disturber . . . Things You never Knew about the Pernicious Influence of One of the World's Staples." Adopting a rather long historical perspective, Barbee blamed sugar for a good deal of the world's problems, beginning with original sin, recounting how "it was the sugar in the apple the serpent gave Eve that tempted her more than his sugary words did. And it was that same saccharine content that made the weak, spineless Adam taste of the fruit and smack his lips over it. Thus at the very dawn of history we see how this infamous chemical began to blight the happiness of the human race." Further describing sugar as "the corner stone of more misery than ever afflicted the human race," including the rise of the Hapsburg dynasty, the spread of African slavery, and the bringing of disease to the New World, Barbee also looked to the history of sugar to explain "American slavery, the war of secession, Mexican peonage in the sugar beet fields, and the tariff."[16] Anticipating at least some of the arguments that Sidney Mintz would make nearly six decades later in his much heralded book *Sweetness and Power: The Place of Sugar in Modern History,* Barbee was right to point out that the history of sugar is a global history and that this history can tell us much about the rise of colonialism, the spread of slavery, and the development of class relations on the European continent. Though I would in no way want to claim that sugar can explain everything, especially as to why Adam bit into the tempting fruit, much less the origins of the American Civil War, I do want to argue that a grassroots to global history of the sugar beet industry in the Midwest reveals much more than one might initially suspect. For this history is an international, national, and local history taking place in the halls of Congress, small-town streets, and farmers' fields. It is a history about the ways that nations and communities imagined and defined themselves at home and abroad; the ways that class identities were created and contested; the ways that race played out in abstract debates and face-to-face interactions; and the ways that the power of capitalism and the state transformed small towns, the open countryside, the national arena, and the global marketplace. It is to these histories that we now turn.

1

Rural Industrialization and Imperial Politics

In 1899, USDA sugar beet investigator Charles Saylor wrote a celebratory account of the newly emerging domestic sugar beet industry. He proclaimed: "[H]ere is a chance in the sugar industry to see the factory and the farm side by side.... Here is a chance to hear the hum of industry, the music which thrills and inspires the soul of man, brightens and gladdens our home, amalgamates and develops our social organism." Saylor even delighted that the rural landscape would soon be transformed by "restless volumes of smoke issuing from chimneys early in the morning and late at night."[1] Though Saylor was obviously elated with the benefits that this industry had to offer rural America and the people living there, he was equally excited about the prospect that one day soon the United States would supply its own sugar needs and begin exporting the product to nations throughout the world.

Thousands of people throughout the nation's countryside shared Saylor's optimistic musings, though with more local aspirations in mind. When town leaders in Caro, Michigan, announced in 1899 that their town of 2,006 residents would become home to a half-million–dollar sugar factory—the largest and most expensive one in the state to date—townspeople came together to mark their good fortune by parading around town with sugar beets impaled on sticks as a local band played popular tunes, including "Hail to the Chief." Fred Slocum, editor of the local newspaper, forever memorialized the event the following day with the pronouncement: "The location of this immense plant at Caro means a great deal for the town and the county—vastly more than can be comprehended by the average individual.... Among other things, it settles the question of Caro's forever remaining in the lead of all other towns in the county."[2]

The enthusiasm and excitement created by the coming of Caro's sugar beet factory was part of a "sugar beet craze" that consumed large parts of the United States in the late nineteenth and early twentieth centuries as hundreds of rural communities throughout the nation sought to industrialize the countryside by inviting sugar beet factories to their towns. During these years, Michigan witnessed the construction of twenty-three sugar factories, while at least another fifty towns and villages "boosted" to get factories of their own.[3] The Michigan Bureau of Labor and Industry, believing this was only the beginning, expected that Michigan's countryside would soon have forty factories and that this industry was "destined to lead, if not exceed, any one industry in the state."[4] In 1902 the director of the Michigan Experiment Station at Michigan Agricultural College told Congress that the lower peninsula of Michigan "will support sixty factories."[5] The *Sugar Trade Journal* was so impressed with Michigan's potential as a sugar state that it predicted, somewhat prematurely, that Michigan "would soon become a prominent factor in the sugar world."[6]

The hyperbolic rhetoric surrounding the creation of the sugar beet industry in the United States generally, and in Michigan more specifically, demonstrated the high hopes of USDA officials as well as small-town residents regarding the future of modern industrial capitalism in the countryside.[7] Agricultural professionals believed that bringing factories to rural America would not only modernize agriculture but increase the value of landholding, encourage new businesses, and spur greater consumption, thereby delivering a prosperous future to the people living in small towns and the surrounding countryside. That is, rural reformers looked forward to an era in which agriculture, by embracing industry, would be able to hold its own in a modern industrial society. Townspeople, who had long worried about falling by the wayside as urban centers and industrializing towns moved forward, certainly agreed. For them, a sugar factory offered what seemed the best means available for "industrializing" without giving up their agricultural and rural base. In this case, then, industrial agriculture was not an abstract force that slyly invaded the rural domain under the cloak of agricultural professionals and outside capitalists, but rather a highly courted guest whom local townspeople hoped they could influence and control.

The inherently global nature of the sugar market, and the fact that the United States acquired its own sugar-producing empire in 1898, the very same year that Michigan's first sugar beet factory opened its doors, would greatly complicate this distinctly local and rural vision of modern industrial capitalism. Though the townspeople who boosted for factories did so as a way to control the forces of industrialization that threatened to either sweep them away into the dustbin of history or deliver them to a producer's paradise, they had no idea that they themselves had inadvertently stepped into the center stage of a much larger drama playing out in an international arena. Whether U.S. consumers would satiate their growing demand for sugar with beet sugar grown domestically or cane sugar grown abroad was no longer just a matter of boosting for factories in places like Caro, Michigan, but rather involved a much larger battle over the future of U.S. imperialism.

The Battle of Sugar

In the USDA's very first annual progress report on the sugar beet industry, published in 1898, Charles Saylor pointed out what to him seemed a terrible waste: although the United States had millions of acres of empty land, the United States, as a nation, imported more than one hundred million dollars' worth of sugar annually.[8] This price tag not only made sugar the nation's most expensive import, it also dwarfed the total value of the nation's most important export—steel.[9] For a nation that prided itself on its agricultural superiority, the almost complete dependence on foreign sugar was clearly a problem. What made the situation ironic, however, was that nearly half of the nation's imported sugar came from Europe's sugar-beet-producing nations, nations with climates similar to many parts of the United States.[10]

With the hope of creating a domestic sugar beet industry that could rival its European counterparts, Charles Saylor pointed to what he believed to be his nation's numerous advantages—fertile soil, superior technology, easy access to its own huge market, and the abundance of empty land.[11] Saylor even thought it was "fair" to count American "ingenuity and enterprise" as one of his country's "advantages over Europe."[12] As such, he predicted that the United States would soon become one of the most important sugar producers in the world, not only selling its sugar to other nations but transforming the industry so that "the conservative foreigner will hardly recognize it as one of his original industries."[13]

Though Saylor's arrogance certainly colored his perception of American agriculture, he was right to point out that the United States represented the single most important market for sugar in the world. By the turn of the century, Americans consumed more than sixty pounds of sugar per capita, and the rate of this consumption was increasing at an average of 12 percent a year.[14]

The one hundred million dollars Americans spent collectively on imported sugar equaled more than 25 percent of the total value of goods exported by the United States.[15] Pointing to these stark statistics, USDA officials inverted the dominant economic logic of the day, which was based on solving America's economic woes by searching for markets abroad by calling for recognition of untapped markets much closer to home.[16]

Congress responded to arguments that the domestic sugar industry, if given protection, could supply the nation with its own homegrown sugar by considering the Dingley bill in 1897, which, among other things, called for doubling the tariff on sugar imports.[17] It did not take long for the bill to gain widespread support from congressional Republicans. Speaking on behalf of many of his colleagues, Senator William B. Allison of Iowa not only lamented the fact that an increasing quantity of imported sugar was coming from Europe, he asserted that the United States should "do what Europe has done" by establishing its own sugar beet industry.[18] Congressman Edward N. Dingley also described his bill as a means for fostering the domestic sugar beet industry, insisting that the "time has come" for the United States to keep the one hundred million dollars "sent abroad for the purchase of our sugar" at home for American farmers.[19] On July 24 both houses responded favorably to these arguments by voting the Dingley bill into law.

Just one year after the passage of the Dingley tariff, the concern with protecting domestic sugar beet from European competitors gave way to a much greater fear regarding the possible inundation of cane sugar from the nation's own empire. For U.S. military victory in the Spanish-American War did not just mark the United States' acquisition of a formal empire, it marked the acquisition of a sugar-producing empire. Although the question of the status of the nation's new dependencies would not be settled for years, the possibility that the nation's need for ever-more sugar would be met by Puerto Rico, Cuba, and the Philippines clearly worried an infant industry that was utterly and unashamedly dependent on protective tariffs and state support.

The USDA, which had played such a central role boosting for a domestic sugar beet industry, tried to straddle the political divide separating domestic beet sugar from foreign cane sugar by continuing to support the former while insisting that there was room in the American marketplace for the latter. For example, the USDA maintained that the ever-increasing consumption of sugar in the United States would not only make competition between colonial cane and domestic beet interests irrelevant, but that the sugar industry would not suffer the fate of so many other domestic industries: overproduction and underconsumption.[20] Even more important, agricultural professionals insisted that sugar cane produced by "coolie" and "semi-slave" labor in tropical countries, including Cuba, Puerto Rico, and the Philippines, was "languishing" in the face of competition from sugar beet produced in the "most highly civilized portions of the world" by white farmers and white workers.[21] In this scenario, agricultural professionals created a hierarchy of sugars, with sugar grown on large plantations by "peon" labor representing a backward way of life and sugar grown by white farmers and white workers representing advanced civilization. Simply put, cane sugar grown in the tropics represented the history of slavery and barbarism, while beet sugar grown in temperate climates represented the future of progressive and scientific agriculture in civilized society. It seemed inevitable that, given time, beet sugar produced in the United States would surpass the cane sugar of the world.[22]

If much of the USDA's enthusiasm for the creation of a domestic sugar beet industry stemmed from the belief that the United States could become independent from other nations—and faith regarding the ability of science and civilization to overcome the natural advantages provided by tropical climates—it also arose from a hope that the sugar beet industry was in a special position to transform America's farmers and rural America in general. For lurking just underneath all the optimism regarding U.S. agriculture lay a sinking suspicion that perhaps the nation's farmers were not on such fertile ground. The same rural reformers who hailed rural America as the place where the nation's values of equality and democracy had been born also worried that those same rural communities were becoming antiquated in a world increasingly defined by industrial development and progress. Ironically, the same agricultural professionals who trumpeted the superiority of American agriculture in comparison to the rest of the world also worried that America's farmers were being left behind by the industrial revolution taking place all around them.[23]

Rather than advocate that farmers try to turn back the clock by challenging industrial "progress," the USDA encouraged farmers to join that world by growing goods that could be raised and processed locally. And sugar beet, because it had to be processed locally, seemed like an ideal crop. But it was not only the linking of the agricultural world with the industrial sector of the economy that excited agricultural reformers; rather it was the ways that this crop would transform the farmers and the communities in which they lived. Charles Saylor insisted that because the crop required "the highest types of agricultural methods," "a new race of farmers is started, improving generation after generation."[24] Furthermore, he pointed out that because the profits of local sugar beet factories supposedly stayed in the local communities, the building of rural sugar beet factories would bring greater transportation, better schools, and more business, thereby creating "prosperous" and "civilized" communities.[25] This industry would aid farmers not only by helping them pay off mortgages and meet tax debts, but it would also, more generally, transform their small towns into "suburban" modern cities.[26]

The USDA's vision of modern industrial capitalism implicitly called into question the notion that industrial progress lay only in urban centers. However, in trying to build smokestacks in the fields, Saylor and his colleagues were not trying to remake rural America in the mirror image of urban America as much as they were trying to redefine the meaning of rural, agriculture, and industry. And theirs was a vision of modern America that promised to wed a number of supposed dualisms, including modernity and tradition; industry and agriculture; smokestacks and family farms; material prosperity and rural democracy. In other words, the sugar beet industry offered an alternative route for industrial capitalism, one that would bridge the supposed gulf separating urban industrial America from rural agricultural America. In the process, the United States would supply its own sugar, an agricultural good that had already been transformed from a coveted luxury to a daily necessity.

"Sawdust to Sugar"

State officials in Michigan found the possibility of rural industrialization intriguing. At the same time that the USDA was promoting the sugar beet industry, Michigan officials were searching for a new agricultural industry to take the place of their declining lumber industry. Long before Michigan became known as the nation's automobile capital, it supplied much of the nation's lumber, a commercial enterprise born out of the state's "natural advantages."[27] Although today we think of lumbering as an extractive industry, at the turn of the century Michiganders saw it as agricultural. Trees were a product of the soil, and their felling, instead of an environmental catastrophe, represented a way to make money and a means for clearing the frontier for future agricultural pursuits. As such, the decline of lumber represented both an agricultural and industrial loss. The soil that had naturally nurtured the great white pines would have to be planted with some other agricultural crop.

Yet it would not be enough to grow more wheat or corn, for Michigan could not realistically hope to compete with the wheat of the Great Plains, the corn of the midwestern prairies, or the specialty cheeses of Wisconsin and New York in an age of growing regional and local agricultural specialization.[28] From 1898 to 1900, the value of Michigan's wheat crop fell from $21,799,000 to $6,397,000.[29] If Michigan wanted to maintain its position as one of the nation's leading agricultural states, it needed to find a new crop to market to the rest of the nation; it needed to carve out a new niche in a world of increasingly specialized agriculture.

The sugar beet crop quickly emerged as the best candidate, for it was an agricultural product with a steady demand and little chance of overproduction, not to mention government protection in a volatile world market. To encourage the construction of sugar beet factories, in 1897 Michigan's state legislators passed a law providing a one cent per pound bounty on all sugar refined within the state.[30] State officials also supported and subsidized the sugar beet industry by tending to the agricultural side of production as well, with professors at Michigan Agricultural College (MAC) regularly distributing free seed to farmers to grow on an experimental basis and advising farmers how to plow, fertilize, cultivate, and rotate the crop.[31] To make sure that the research reached the fields, the college sponsored "soil trains" and "sugar beet institutes" where farmers could learn more about the crop.[32] The state's Land Office also promoted the beet industry by sending out "circular letters" "to as many addresses as could be secured" touting the benefits of the sugar beet industry and promising free packages of seed to interested farmers.[33] The Land Office went so far as to predict that Michigan would soon have twenty factories, representing a capital investment of eight million dollars, and that each year those farmers who grew the crop would collectively make five million dollars, while the men who worked in the factories would make almost one million.[34] The only question remaining was which towns would get the factories. Local newspapers published these reports as evidence of their need to get a factory of their own.[35]

Prospective capitalist investors and agricultural professionals also did their best to spur local interest in the newly emerging sugar beet industry by linking the end of lumbering with the rise of the sugar industry. Charles M. Garrison, a land agent of the Detroit and Mackinac Railroad and an early and avid supporter of the sugar beet industry, noted that "the question of what will become of the Saginaw Valley when all the pine is all cut is now solved."[36] News soon spread throughout the state that the land would be "reforested" with beets and that Michigan was switching from "sawdust to sugar."[37] Even USDA secretary James Wilson attempted to assuage the fears of Tuscola County residents in February 1899 by claiming that those who made money from lumber would make even more by raising sugar beet.[38] Two years later, when speaking before the Michigan State Farmers' Institute, Wilson promised farmers that they would have "cleaner and richer farms" for having "sold a manufactured product instead of a raw material."[39]

Considering all the publicity about how sugar would replace sawdust, it seems only fitting that the state's first sugar beet factory was built in Bay City—the heart of the lumber industry. Although its population of thirty thousand would seem to qualify Bay City as an urban center, this was a city in the shadow of its agricultural environs. With the lumbering industry on the decline, the men of the Bay City Businessmen's Association turned their attention to the highly publicized and much touted beet sugar industry as the key to their community's future. To ensure that their city would become the center of this new industry, Bay City's businessmen offered thirty-five acres of prime waterfront land to any investor willing to raise the capital necessary to begin construction. Lumbermen Benjamin Boutell, Nathan Bradley, and Thomas Cranage, along with newspaperman Frank Zagelmeyer, all of Bay City, took up the offer and raised $200,000. The Michigan Sugar Company began its first season in the spring of 1898.[40] Ten months later, the company announced that its first season had been a resounding success, with the factory producing 5,271,406 pounds of fine granulated sugar, and the 990 farmers who grew the 3,103 acres of sugar beet making approximately $53 an acre, half of which was estimated to be "profit."[41]

The highly publicized results of the Michigan Sugar Company's very profitable first season spurred businessmen, including more lumbering men, retail grocers, real-estate investors, and manufacturers from within and without the state, to organize financing for additional sugar factories. Even the Michigan Supreme Court's October 1899 decision to outlaw the 1897 sugar bounty did not dissuade prospective investors from channeling money into this new industry. Bay City, viewed by many as the future center of the sugar beet industry, added two new factories. Not to be outdone, Detroit capitalists raised the funds for a sugar factory in Rochester, a nearby suburb, while the residents of Kalamazoo spearheaded stock subscription drives to make sure that they too would have a sugar factory.[42]

The year 1899 also witnessed an even more important trend—the building of sugar beet factories in more distinctly rural settings. In 1899 capitalists decided to build factories in Caro, population 1,683; Alma, population 1,499; and Holland, population 6,307. In the following years, industrialists continued to build sugar factories in small towns, with these rural factories easily outpacing their urban counterparts. Between 1899 and 1903, ten rural communities would become home to sugar factories. The majority of these towns had populations with fewer than 2,500 people; the smallest town, Croswell, had just 613 residents.[43]

The building of these rural factories helped to spur a sugar beet craze throughout Michigan's countryside that was fed by aspiring sugar beet industrialists, who were looking for a good locale, and townspeople, who were eager to make sure their towns did not miss out on what they believed would be a golden opportunity. For example, in 1901 prospective investors promised the people of Sebewaing—a town of 1,243 dominated by German immigrants and German Americans—that they would build a sugar factory and arrange for the Michigan Central Railroad to extend its line all the way to Sebewaing if locals solicited four thousand acres of sugar beet and donated a site free of charge for the future factory. Townspeople responded by immediately organizing to meet those demands.[44] Similarly, when the National Construction Company hinted that it was looking to build a sugar factory somewhere in Gratiot County, the residents of St. Louis, a town of 2,503, quickly mobilized. Local businessmen donated a twenty-acre site on the Pine River, and villagers and farmers met to officially organize the St. Louis Sugar Company. To show their commitment, three hundred citizens pledged a total of $25,000 in stock and farmers promised to raise three thousand acres of sugar beet.[45]

Other towns, hoping to replicate the good fortunes of places such as Caro, Sebewaing, and Alma, did their best to attract sugar beet investors as well. In fact, although prospective investors had originally initiated the sugar beet craze by promising to build sugar beet factories as long as locals subsidized initial costs and convinced farmers to take up the crop, town boosters soon outdid the outside investors in their quest to get factories. In at least fifty towns and villages, local residents organized extensive campaigns to "sell" themselves to prospective capital investors by offering free land, reduced taxes, local stock subscriptions, and pledges from local farmers to grow sugar beet.[46] Some town businessmen even went so far as to incorporate sugar beet companies, which were nothing more than legal entities, in their towns' names in hopes of attracting prospective investors.[47]

The townspeople's eagerness to attract outside investors reflected an attempt to carve out a rural and agricultural pathway to industrialization. And the rural sugar beet factories, which they saw being built in neighboring towns, represented a space and place unlike any other in the surrounding landscape. Standing three to four stories tall, with smokestacks protruding even higher, sugar factories resembled the great factories of northern industrialized cities more than they did local grain elevators or even cheese and canning factories.[48] In comparison to these rural enterprises, the sugar factory was, without a doubt, the most capital intensive and technologically sophisticated. In 1894, the state's 221 butter and cheese factories represented a combined capital of $810,745, with each factory costing somewhere between $2,500 and $4,000 to build.[49] Even the 571 flour, grist, and feed mills in the state were worth only a combined $7,149,063.[50] In contrast, each sugar factory cost between $300,000 and $750,000 to build, and by 1906 Michigan's sugar beet industry represented a total capital investment of $10,900,000.[51]

Considering the impressive capital investment required to build sugar beet factories, it should come as no surprise that townspeople hoped that this industry would transform the social, cultural, and business milieu of their towns, believing that by meeting the nation's demand for sugar, they would in turn spur their own consumption patterns and cultural advancement. Just after the sugar factory in Caro opened its doors in 1899, the local newspaper even added a weekly column entitled "Sugar Beet Notes," where it routinely publicized the benefits of this industry to townspeople and surrounding farmers. One of the first editorials proclaimed how the building of the local sugar factory would likely double the value of land in the area and put $920,000 cash in the pockets of local farmers each year, thereby making it easier for them to pay off their mortgages and buy more consumer goods in town.[52] Similarly, when the Sanilac Sugar Refining Company began its first season, the town of Croswell, population 613, included a special eight-page supplement in the local newspaper announcing the arrival of the sugar factory as the most important event since the coming of the railroad, promising "prosperity and plenty" for both local residents and nearby farmers.[53] Escalating expectations even further, a traveler through Michigan's countryside claimed in a national journal that, "The sugar industry brings to its community prosperity, education, pianos, books, schools and good roads—which means civilization."[54]

Sugar beet industrialists, agricultural professionals, and state officials eagerly joined the choir of good news by singing the praises of this industry. They hailed the sugar beet industry as unlike any other—one that would make capitalists, farmers, and workers wealthy and healthy, bring much-needed industry to the countryside, and transform small towns and villages into prosperous centers and vibrant communities.[55] The Michigan Bureau of Labor and Industry even went so far as to describe this new industry as a godsend to farmers, claiming that those who grew the crop had been paying off mortgages, buying new farm utensils, and making their home villages prosperous places.[56] Perhaps most important of all, the bureau hailed the sugar beet industry as the only one that could end the all-too-often combative and competing interests of town and county, and of agriculture and industry, by making them mutually harmonious. "It is the one industry that combines agriculture and manufacture, two of the greatest elements that enter into the prosperity of the people."[57]

From Local to Global

Though this rural, agricultural, and intensely local path to modern industrial capitalism may have seemed like a panacea to rural professionals concerned with the declining fortunes of rural America, it also tied Michigan's small towns and family farmers closer to an international market they would find difficult to control. In what may have seemed like an ironic twist of fate to many, Michigan welcomed its first sugar beet factory the very same year that the United States gained control over its own sugar-producing empire. This did not stop the building of sugar beet factories in Michigan, which continued apace with eight in 1899 and twelve more in the years between 1900 and 1903. It did mean that what happened hundreds and even thousands of miles away would matter a great deal to those in Michigan. In the words of Sidney Mintz: "probably no single food commodity in the world market has been subject to so much politicking as sugar."[58] Though Mintz was primarily concerned with cane sugar, which he brilliantly linked to the history of European colonialism, capitalism, and slavery, his comments apply equally well to the late nineteenth and early twentieth centuries, only this time around the debate revolved around U.S. imperialism, capitalism, and protectionism.[59]

As the majority of U.S. residents hailed the Spanish-American War as an example of U.S. humanitarianism or military prowess, and very often a bit of both, sugar beet industrialists viewed the war in a different light. It was clear to these men that the United States had acquired a sugar-producing empire that threatened the very existence of their own infant industry. At the same time that their fellow businessmen were looking forward to an opening of markets abroad, sugar beet industrialists at home feared that U.S. markets would be "flooded" by products coming in the opposite direction. Not surprisingly, then, the sugar beet industrialists went to great lengths to make sure that sugar would figure prominently in the debates regarding the future status of the "colonies" and the commercial, cultural, and political ties between the metropolis and periphery.[60]

As soon as the war ended, sugar beet industrialists began an extensive public relations campaign to ensure not only *that* they would be invited to the debates, but that they would determine *what* would be debated. This campaign took place primarily in the press as well as in congressional hearings, and in both venues, sugar beet industrialists relied on constitutional, economic, racial, labor, and geographic arguments. Rather than hedge their bets that increased consumption and American ingenuity would make it possible for domestic producers to compete with colonial cane, they did all they could to safeguard as much of the U.S. market for themselves as possible. And the question that sugar beet industrialists wanted the country to ask itself as it considered what to do with its newfound global empire was: would the United States rely on sugar grown on large aristocratic plantations by "coolie" labor or would it consume sugar from small family farms tended to by white farmers and white workers? Simply put, did the United States want "barbaric" or "civilized" sugar?[61]

In raising these kinds of questions, sugar beet industrialists attempted to place the debate over imperialism in the context of a much longer history of protectionism. They reminded Republican congressmen of their party's decades-long pledge to protect home industries, complaining "we took it [the Republican Party's pledge of protectionism] in good faith, and the factories started right in, and then came the Spanish [American] War."[62] Without questioning U.S. imperialism, sugar beet interests claimed that it was unjust to sacrifice the interests of white capitalists, white farmers, and white workers to the "barbarous" cane culture of aristocratic plantations and supposedly racially degraded labor. In 1899, the sugar beet industry's national journal, the *Beet Sugar Gazette,* protested against the alleged injustice of forcing American producers in the United States to compete against foreign interests abroad, regardless of their political status, noting, "The importation of cane sugar from tropical islands, under principles of reciprocity or free trade or greatly reduced duties, awarded because they are insular dependencies of the United States, would bring into competition a product raised by coolie and debased labor that would be ruinous to the American farmer and to the production of sugar in the United States."[63]

Industry advocates went so far as to describe the admission of any sugar from "our tropical islands" on a free or reduced status as "suicidal," warning that once the United States gained control over the new island dependencies, it would be impossible for U.S. sugar beet producers on the mainland to compete. The problem was not just that U.S. producers would have to vie with "coolies and half-civilized tropical races," though as we shall soon see, this was a serious and consistent concern. The key problem was that U.S. businessmen, looking to profit from the overseas empire, would head to places like Puerto Rico, Cuba, and the Philippines and bring American "capital" and "ingenuity" with them. Domestic sugar industrialists feared that this would turn the "backward" and "autocratic" Spanish colonies the United States had just acquired into modern-day economic powerhouses with both the natural advantages of climate, soil, and cheap labor and the manufactured advantages of American enterprise, expertise, and science. Industry experts therefore protested: "If anything, the duties on imported raw sugar ought to be increased rather than lowered to meet this probable intensified competition."[64]

In their quest to protect the home industry from products coming from abroad, sugar beet industrialists had a number of important allies among those who had long fought more generally for a protected domestic market. In 1900, Edward N. Dingley, the congressman who had sponsored the Dingley tariff, responded to the prospect that his political hard work would be undone now that the United States had acquired its own sugar-producing empire by calling for a continuation of the nation's protectionist policies. In a rather dramatic fashion, Dingley warned that, "If expansion and the struggle for commercial empire means the surrender of protection, then Porto Rico had better be turned back to Spain, and General Otis and the army and navy had better be recalled from the Philippines. If the victories at Manila and Santiago mean the defeat of the fixed policy of the nation (with slight but disastrous interruptions) since 1789, they will be victories dearly bought."[65] Another important ally, Herbert Myrick of the League of Domestic Producers, also worried about the ability of farmers and workers in the United States to compete against American producers who hired cheaper labor overseas. To those unconvinced by the argument that U.S. producers needed to be protected from competitors in foreign lands, especially when these competitors were fellow Americans looking to take advantage of cheaper production costs abroad, Myrick likened protectionist tariff barriers with exclusive immigration policies. In a scathing address to President Theodore Roosevelt, his Cabinet, and Congress, Myrick asked: "if self-preservation required us to protect ourselves against the Chinese within our own borders, how much more important is it that we protect our domestic farmers, laborers and manufacturers against the products of coolie labor operated by the ablest management under all the natural advantages of tropical environment." Rather than pointing to U.S. imperialism as a first step to becoming a major world power, Myrick warned that it represented the "greatest danger" confronting "domestic agriculture, . . . labor and capital."[66]

The sugar beet industry's most obvious ally, the much older Louisiana sugar cane industry, had long depended on a protected marketplace. Furthermore, that state's politicians had never shied away from using the political arena to protect their well-known sugar industry. However, in their quest to safeguard their state's sugar from Puerto Rico, Cuba, and the Philippines, the Louisiana interests would find themselves playing second fiddle to their sugar beet counterparts. Though domestic sugar beet would not surpass Louisiana sugar cane until 1906, it was clear to both sugar cane and sugar beet interests that the former industry had largely reached its limit, while the possibilities for the latter seemed limitless. Sugar beet interests also had the advantage of hailing from more than a dozen states, giving them even greater leverage in the House and the Senate, where geographic diversity translated into political power. Finally, as we shall soon see, Louisiana sugar interests had a hard time describing the colonies' sugar industry as barbaric and their own as civilized, when they themselves had created a racist labor system that brutalized thousands of African Americans.[67]

The first extended public contest over whose sugar Americans would consume took place in 1900. In that year, the Supreme Court was asked to decide what legal status would be granted to the new territories and whether or not all the rights in the Constitution would apply to the residents of Puerto Rico, Cuba, and the Philippines. These were important constitutional questions, for up until this point, the goal of eventual statehood after a period of territorial probation had guided both U.S. ideals and practices. With the hope of influencing the Court's decision, the sugar beet interests insisted that the new territories should not be treated like the nation's previous territories and that the Constitution did not follow the flag. Perhaps the most academic of all their arguments was that constitutional precedent and theory lay on their side. Industry advocates contended that when it came to the territories and what status they would be granted, the basic issue that needed to be determined was "the meaning of the term the United States." They claimed that in making this decision, the Supreme Court could either broadly declare all inhabitants living under control of the United States as part of the union, or it could more narrowly decide that the United States included only those states already a part of the federal union. Hoping for a narrow interpretation, sugar beet interests insisted that because the nation's founding fathers "did not dream of island possessions of alien, inferior races becoming subject to the United States, it cannot be reasonably assumed that they contemplated the expansion of the constitution to such territory."[68] Sugar beet industrialists had no problem with expansionism or imperialism per se; they simply wanted all extraterritorial dependencies to be subject to the United States' trade tariffs as a means to protect their own industry.

As the Supreme Court wrestled with the legal status of the nation's newest territories, Congress was already meeting to decide if the United States would levy a tariff against Puerto Rican products and if so, at what rate the barrier would be. In this venue, sugar industry representatives largely abandoned the seeming high ground of constitutional theory and instead focused on more banal economic and racial arguments, continually referring to the Puerto Ricans as "coolies," "slaves," and "semi-slaves." Perhaps most important of all, sugar beet advocates worked hard to shift the terms of the debate from philanthropy and free markets to nationalism and protectionism. Challenging the dominant humanitarian narrative that had enveloped U.S. popular and print culture through newspapers, magazines, music, poems, and novels, they derided those who insisted that the United States had a moral obligation to help their "little brown brothers" by claiming that the United States had already sacrificed too much. When testifying in front of Congress, California sugar beet industrialist Henry Oxnard spelled out his industry's mantra by asking: "Have our taxpayers not done enough, for a little while at least? We have given our sons as a sacrifice in the case of humanity; we have incurred millions of debts. . . . There is no pressing necessity for tending alms to a people who have been thus situated for many years, when it is asked to be done at the expense of our home industries."[69]

The sugar beet industrialists' concern with Puerto Rico belied that nation's sugar-producing capabilities. Since the mid-nineteenth century, the Puerto Rican sugar industry had been in decline, hindered by both a lack of capital investment and a smaller slave population than other Caribbean counterparts.[70] Sugar industrialists even admitted that Puerto Rican sugar was unlikely to affect, much less overwhelm, the domestic sugar industry. The real concern was that if Congress allowed Puerto Rican products into the United States duty-free, it would not only violate the Republican Party's long-held principle of protection but it would pave the road for "the graver danger" of allowing other "tropical countries" to "capture our markets" and eventually undermine domestic production.[71] Herbert Myrick made this point emphatically when he testified in Congress, stating that "I say that our fundamental objection to free trade with Puerto Rico is that, in all probability, it will inevitably be followed by free trade with Cuba and the Philippines, and later all the countries to the south of us. All these tropical countries are great agricultural producers. Their capacity . . . is almost unlimited."[72] Inverting the dominant economic theory of the era—the idea that the United States' overproduction could be solved by finding markets abroad—protectionists proposed that a greater danger would come from the inundation of U.S. markets with products from abroad. They insisted that the nation's obsessive search for markets abroad not only blinded most Americans to the possibility that those markets might be more illusory than real, but that the markets at home might be much more lucrative than previously imagined. In this scenario, allowing Puerto Rican products into the United States duty-free would not only open the floodgates to cheap foreign labor but also entail redefining the very meaning of the United States itself.

In March 1900, when Congress agreed to impose a duty on Puerto Rican products at 15 percent of the current tariff schedule, sugar beet industrialists proclaimed victory.[73] Although they would certainly have preferred that Puerto Rico pay the full duty, the larger issue at stake—whether the United States would or could impose any duties at all—had clearly been won by protectionists who insisted that Puerto Rico should be treated differently than previous territories. The Supreme Court's decision in the 1901 *Downes v. Bidwell* case, issued just months later, further affirmed Congress' right to impose tariff barriers and to treat the colonies as outside of the United States.[74] In this decision, the Supreme Court declared that though Puerto Rico was not a "foreign country" because it was "owned" by the United States and hence "subject" to U.S. "sovereignty," it remained "foreign to the United States in the domestic sense" as an "unincorporated" "possession." In other words, Puerto Rico was neither free and independent nor really part of the United States.[75]

The sugar beet industry's joyous reaction to both the tariff on Puerto Rican goods and the Supreme Court's decision quickly gave way to growing concern over the question of how Congress would deal with Cuba. Now that the Court had legitimated Congress' right to impose tariffs, the issue at hand was no longer one just of principles—whether or not the United States could impose tariffs—but rather one of pragmatics: at what rate those tariffs would be set. As such, the battle shifted from constitutional questions and the framers' intent to more pragmatic imperial politics.

Domestic sugar beet industrialists and their allies had long been concerned with the prospect of competition from Cuba, not only because Cuba represented one of the most important sugar producers in the world but because American capitalists held a significant and ever-growing interest in that island's sugar cane industry. As early as 1898, when Congress initially granted President McKinley authority to intervene in Cuba, thereby officially beginning the United States' participation in what became known as the Spanish-American War, Henry Teller, a Republican congressman from the sugar beet state of Colorado, authored the Teller Resolution, which read in part: "The United States hereby disclaims any disposition or intention to exercise sovereignty, jurisdiction or control" over Cuba "except for the pacification thereof." Though most historians remember this resolution as an expression of ambivalent imperialism, an attempt to make sure that the United States would not replicate Old World Colonialism, we would do well to keep in mind that Teller also represented the economic interests of the sugar beet producers in his state, who feared competition from cheaper Cuban sugar.[76]

Two years after the passage of Teller, sugar beet industrialists and their allies were battling yet again to protect their industry from "cheap" Cuban sugar. By this time, the domestic sugar beet interests and their allies faced a contingent of opponents that included not only free-trade advocates, who had long questioned the United States' protective trade policies, but also President Theodore Roosevelt and Secretary of War Elihu Root.[77] What seemed like a simple economic issue to the sugar beet industrialists—protecting their industry from cheaper sugar—represented a very serious political dilemma for President Roosevelt, who found himself responsible not only for balancing domestic concerns and international relations but for presenting U.S. imperialism as a benevolent venture. In his first annual message to Congress in 1901, Roosevelt tried to persuade protectionists, including the sugar beet contingent, that the United States was "bound" by "weighty interests of morality and national interest" to pass commercial measures that would look out for Cuba's best interest.[78] In other words, the United States needed to open its doors to Cuban products. Making the same point, Secretary Root linked the peace of Cuba to the peace of the United States, claiming that the same issues that had led the United States to war with Spain—humanitarianism and fear that some other Old World nation might try to colonize the island—now meant that the United States had to adopt trade policies "under which Cuba can live."[79]

In spite of these impressive adversaries, domestic sugar beet industrialists not only stood their ground but, in the words of one contemporary observer, "developed unexpected strength" as the battle to determine the commercial ties between the United States and Cuba developed.[80] (Of the twenty-six "sugar" witnesses who came before Congress in 1902 to testify against free trade with Cuba, twenty of them came on behalf of the sugar beet industry, with four from Michigan, while six men came to defend the interests of the Louisiana sugar cane industry.) Insisting that Congress should maintain a full duty on all Cuban goods, sugar beet interests recycled many of the arguments they had made when trying to determine the fate of Puerto Rico. They questioned humanitarian arguments about the plight of poor Cubans and complained that their industry was being asked to shoulder too much of the burden.[81] Picking up on the testimony of sugar beet interests in front of Congress, the *Beet Sugar Gazette* criticized the "Misplaced Sympathy" directed toward Cubans, insisting that they were in no way as desperate as the American news media had portrayed.[82] Describing Cuba as a spoiled child, the *Gazette* further complained how "they [the Cubans] asked for men, and many Americans joined their army. They asked for armed assistance and the United States sent its army and navy and drove the Spaniards from the Island. . . . They now demand that the United States shall kill their own industry and buy most of their sugar in Cuba. Uncle Sam is a good-natured individual and willing to help a poor neighbor, but it seems the point has been reached where indulgence has spoiled this 'ward of the nation' and the spoiled child needs a lesson."[83]

Besides belittling Cuba as an unappreciative ward of the United States, sugar beet industrialists also asked whether opening free trade with Cuba would help the Cubans or merely allow U.S. monopolies to take advantage of the island's new dependency. This represented a shrewd political move at a time when many in the nation already associated the word monopoly with the American Sugar Refining Company, also known as the "mother of all trusts." Playing into the nation's fears about the power of trusts, Mr. F. R. Hathaway, general manager of Michigan's Alma Sugar Company, told Congress that even if it might be cheaper to buy tropical cane sugar, once the sugar trust dominated the market, it would exercise complete control of what had obviously become not just a luxury but a daily necessity.[84] Hathaway's California colleague, Henry Oxnard, offered an even more sinister appraisal of the trust. "Its object is destruction and annihilation . . . spending vast sums of money to destroy American beet sugar."[85] Even USDA officials warned against the possibility of allowing Cuban sugar tended to by the sugar trust into the United States, noting that "Cheapness is not the only thing to be looked after in political economy. We can have cheap labor if we want. We can break down the barriers which keep out the Asiatic hordes, and we can supply labor at 30 cents a day; but are we in a position to ask that our laborers be brought into such a ruinous competition?"[86]

Excoriating the trust, the sugar beet industry advanced a racial objection that pitted hard-working white farmers and white workers who toiled as "free laborers" against black, "yellow," and "coolie" workers who were only recently freed from slavelike conditions or who still toiled in semislave circumstances for "slipshod" and "unprogressive" plantation owners.[87] For example, in describing the phenomenal growth of the beet sugar industry in his state, which he credited with rising land values, improved markets, and rural prosperity, W. L. Churchill, president and manager of the Bay City Sugar Company, at first asked: "What has revolutionized the sugar markets in this short time?" He then answered his own question by detailing how "Beets are grown in a northern climate and pushed by the energy and vigor of northerners. Cane grows only in tropical climates, which is conducive to ease and indolence, a total absence of the snap, energy, and perseverance of the northerner."[88] Speaking in front of Congress, Oxnard pushed the racial argument even further, claiming that history itself revealed that cane sugar could only be grown successfully under "semi-servile coolie-labor conditions."[89] Also testifying in front of Congress, sugar beet industrialist N. H. Stewart of Kalamazoo compared Michigan's "intelligent labor" to Cuba's "Chinese or coolie or dago labor," which he alleged slept under palmetto trees and lived off dates and bananas.[90] Even the Louisiana sugar cane witnesses who came to testify often hailed the laborers toiling in the domestic sugar beet industry, after their efforts to distinguish their own labor relations from laboring practices in Cuba fell short.[91]

While sugar beet advocates proved more than adept at employing the racist ideas of the era to protect their industry, they raised the stakes when they insisted that the issue of foreign cane sugar versus domestic beet sugar was really a battle between the temperate civilized societies and the barbarous tropical nations of the world. They did so by imbuing the history as well as the future of sugar with racial significance. USDA chemist H. W. Wiley lent scientific authority to the idea that sugar cane represented barbarous culture while sugar beet represented civilized life when testifying before the Ways and Means Committee regarding the reduction of the duty on sugar imported from Cuba. Wiley tried to "enlighten" the legislators by providing a discussion of the relationship between sugar and the advance of modern civilization. He began his testimony by explaining that sugar cane's naturally high sugar content had not been affected by man, while sugar beet, a plant naturally low in sugar content, had reached "its present excellence as a sugar-producing plant" due "solely to scientific culture." He then continued by extrapolating from these facts that "the sugar cane may, therefore, be regarded as the great natural source of sugar, while the sugar beet represents what human intelligence, science, and agricultural skill can do in developing certain qualities of plants which are of utility to the human race."[92] Next, Wiley provided a brief history of beet sugar, from the discovery of the possibility of extracting sugar from the garden beet in 1747 by the German chemist Andreas Maargraf, and the expansion of the sugar beet industry in France during the Napoleonic Wars, to 1890 when the quantity of sugar beet surpassed the amount of sugar cane in world circulation. "Thus we have the remarkable fact that what at the beginning of the last century was regarded as little more than a scientific discovery, of no practical value, has come to be one of the greatest factors in the world's commerce."[93]

Wiley also combined botany, geography, race, and history in ways that must have seemed familiar to an audience accustomed to viewing the world in terms of racial hierarchies. After describing how sugar cane was more susceptible to frost than sugar beet, Wiley deduced that "Mankind, as well as the sugar beet, is also subject to environment, and is radically influenced thereby. The history of the world shows that the temperate regions produce a race which is superior in all of its qualities to that which is produced in the tropics. There fore the sugar industry which is practiced in the sub-tropics and in high northern latitudes becomes an industry of the advanced and most developed human race, while that which is practiced in the tropical regions is an industry of a less advanced and less developed race."[94] Expanding on this racial theme even further, Wiley celebrated that, "Finally the great product of a sugar industry is found in the superior race of human beings which it engenders. It fosters every branch of science. It rewards every kind of labor. It sends its favors into every department of manufacture. It requires the highest scientific intelligence. . . . It demands the best which humanity can offer and offers to humanity the best which any industry can command. To make our own sugar means not only the supply of our home market, but it means the development of citizens of superior qualities, of higher intelligence, of greater skill. No country can afford to throw away the chance to develop a citizenry of such qualifications."[95] To men like Wiley, the battle of sugar involved nothing less than the future of civilization itself.

The case made against Cuba highlights the paradox plaguing the sugar beet demand for a protected marketplace. On one hand, sugar beet industrialists and their allies insisted that because of sugar cane's natural advantages and the cheap labor used in its production, they simply could not compete. Seeming to abandon the laissez-faire Darwinian rhetoric of the day, sugar beet advocates claimed that the kind of competition they faced from tropical producers was inherently unfair. This was not competition between equals but competition between unequals, with the latter holding the advantage in a world of free trade. Still, sugar beet advocates had to be careful about suspicion that sugar beet would never be able to compete. As such, they insisted that one day science would trump nature and that at that point, sugar beet would be cheaper to produce than sugar cane. In the words of N. H. Stewart of Kalamazoo, "the American people only go forward and not backward, and inside of ten years the development of the machinery and appliances for the extraction of the sugar from beet will be so improved and increased that this country will defy any tropical country on the face of the earth."[96]

When the House voted in 1903 to reduce the Cuban duty by 20 percent, and all signs pointed to a similar outcome in the Senate, the sugar beet people proclaimed that their interests had been "sacrificed" to the sugar trust while the Cuban sugar industry had been "delivered into the clutches of monopoly."[97] They charged that the Supreme Court's ruling that the nation's new dependencies could be subject to tariffs was being squandered by Congress, which proceeded to dismantle the wall of protectionism in favor of tropical colonies. But before the industrialists could spend too much time licking their wounds, they faced the prospect of a "new danger"—cheap sugar coming from the Philippines. For, just a month after Congress voted to reduce Cuban tariffs, members started to call for reducing the rates for the Philippines as well. (In 1901, the United States granted the Philippines a 20 percent reduction. Now Congress was entertaining proposals to reduce that rate by another 50 or 75 percent.) Lamenting the possibility of Philippine sugar coming in at a drastically reduced tariff rate, industry proponents bemoaned that "[t]hese privileges," when combined with the "natural advantages of the islands" and "coolie labor," would make the Philippines as "formidable" a competitor of domestic sugar "as Cuba is now."[98] Just weeks after reluctantly conceding defeat when it came to the tariff policy toward Cuba, the sugar beet industry geared up for what it believed would be not only the biggest but perhaps the most important sugar battle of all.

Of the three colonial possessions, sugar beet industrialists feared that the Philippines posed the most significant long-term threat. Although the Philippine sugar industry was small compared to Cuba, the sheer size of the Philippine Islands, as well as the larger population, raised the prospect of a tropical sugar-producing nation unlike any the world had ever known. In fact, industrialists at the 1904 Annual Beet Sugar Convention not only voiced concern that the Philippines had enough land to produce sugar for the entire world, they also warned how Filipino laborers easily lived on wild fruits and vegetables from the land and fish from the sea.[99] The fears about competing against Philippine sugar mounted in the following months as sugar beet interests searched for ways to convince Congress to protect them from the nation's most distant colony. A few sugar beet industrialists, including Michigan's F. R. Hathaway, even packed their bags and traveled to the Philippines to witness their future competitors firsthand. After returning home, they told tales of laborers toiling in the fields for a mere fifteen cents a day and warned how it would be impossible for American workers to compete with tropical laborers abroad, especially those long accustomed to low wages, poor living conditions, and hierarchical labor relations.[100]

Sugar beet industrialists not only worked hard to depict the contrasting labor system at home ("white" farmers and "white" laborers) and abroad ("blacks" and "coolies") as a battle between civilization and savagery. They also warned that if the United States allowed in Philippine sugar at a reduced rate or duty free, the nation would, in essence, be violating its own immigration policies.[101] For many critics feared that if Philippine sugar was allowed to come into the United States, thousands of Chinese immigrants would be recruited to work in the Philippine cane fields, further lowering what was already the lowest wage scale of all the colonial possessions. Intertwining the most important questions of the day—imperialism, immigration, trade and labor—sugar beet advocates insisted that it did not matter whether American workmen had to compete against Chinese workers in the United States or in the Philippines, because the result would be the same. Speaking in front of Congress in 1906, one sugar beet advocate insisted, "The honor and dignity of labor should ever be maintained and protected against competition from servile and cheap contract labor, no matter from what source it may come, whether it be from our own territory or dependencies in the islands of the seas, or whether it comes masquerading under the guise of reciprocity."[102]

Even as sugar beet industrialists and their allies continued to repeat their racially charged arguments, they also began to come up with new reasons to explain why the United States needed to maintain a high tariff against the Philippines. Perhaps the most imaginative of all the arguments revolved around the issue of the real distance between the United States and the Philippines. Insisting that the thousands of miles separating the United States from the Philippines did little to protect the American sugar industry, Truman Palmer asked the audience at the 1904 Beet Sugar Convention to distinguish between geographic distance and commercial distance. "They [the Philippines] are far away, speaking geographically, but commercially they are closer to the United States than Omaha is to Chicago." He then explained that after taking into account current tariff reductions and shipping rates, "commercially speaking, the Philippines, with all their cheap labor and cheap cost of production, can be said to be located just outside of New York or San Francisco harbor."[103] This geographical argument was repeated over and over again in national publications to demonstrate how cheap labor, combined with shrinking shipping costs, threatened to redefine the meaning of space in the global marketplace.[104]

As further evidence that lowering the tariff duty would be unwise, sugar beet advocates pointed to the colonial practices of their European counterparts, who had not only fostered their 1,500 sugar beet factories through state bounties and tariffs but had continued to maintain high tariffs on their own colonial possessions.[105] Speaking before Congress in 1906, Bay City's own Hathaway pointed out how "Europe, with its hundred years' experience in the sugar business, and its centuries of experience in handling colonies, uniformly maintains higher tariffs than our full Dingley schedule against sugar from the Tropics, even though such sugar comes from its own colonies. Still the United States, with its seven years' experience in governing colonies and about the same in raising beet sugar, proposes to expose her own domestic sugar industries to direct competition of tropical cane sugar without any protection whatsoever."[106] Truman Palmer posed his critique of American tariff policies with a series of questions about why, "with the exception of mountainness Switzerland, sleepy Portugal and lethargic Greece," all the European countries not only produced all the sugar they consumed, but with the exception of France, maintained full tariff duties on colonial sugars. After telling Congress about the success of the sugar beet industry in Europe, Palmer insisted that "there must be some underlying economic reason for this universal action on the part of European rulers, statesmen, and political economists." Answering his own queries, Palmer pointed out that by producing their own sugar, Europeans delivered more than $200,000,000 to farmers and $100,000,000 to "home laborers."[107] The lesson to be learned was an obvious one: if European colonial powers continued to foster their domestic sugar beet industries, then surely the United States should do the same.

For those unconvinced that the United States should follow in the footsteps of their European counterparts, sugar beet industrialists asked the nation to reflect critically on its own "brief" history of colonialism. In so doing, they called into question the dominant assumption that the United States had experienced an economic windfall by gaining an overseas empire. To the contrary, sugar beet industrialists decried that the United States had lost more in terms of trade and revenue than it had earned precisely because of the strategy of reducing tariffs. With respect to Cuba, sugar beet advocates publicized that in the years from 1904 to 1907, the United States spent $135,000,000 more to buy Cuban exports than the Cubans spent to pay for U.S. imports. Furthermore, they insisted that because of the reduced tariff, the U.S. Treasury lost out on $30,000,000, money that the Cubans supposedly spent to buy products from Europe and Canada.[108] Putting the issue of trade and imperialism in an even greater global context, Truman Palmer claimed that the total value of U.S. exports in 1905 to Africa, Asia, South and Central America, as well as to the nation's colonies added up to "several million dollars less" than what the American people spent to pay for sugar alone.[109] Directly confronting the ostensible economic motives underlying U.S. imperialism—that having an empire would save U.S. capitalism—sugar beet interests insisted that it was having the opposite effect.

After what turned out to be a nearly seven-year battle over what duty Philippine sugar would have to pay to come into the U.S. market, in 1909 Congress decided on a different solution altogether. To shield American sugar beet producers from the prospect of unlimited Philippine sugar coming onto American shores, while also providing some economic "benefit" to the Philippines, Congress decided to allow three hundred thousand tons of sugar to come in duty free, with all additional sugar paying the full duty rate. When news of this compromise became public, the sugar beet industrialists and allies responded with a guarded sigh of relief. Although they would have preferred that all Philippine sugar pay the full duty, and still called for the reimposition of the full tariff against Cuban sugar, they conceded that this compromise represented the best economic and political solution possible, at least for the time being. The leading sugar beet journal even proclaimed: "We may look forward to the promotion of many new sugar enterprises in the near future."[110] The only strong criticism came from the Philippine Assembly, which passed a resolution asking the U.S. Congress to maintain trade barriers between the Philippines and the United States. Assembly members were more than aware of their nation's dependent political status, and they feared that becoming economically dependent on their colonial masters would ultimately "hinder the attainment of independence."[111] As we will later see, the assemblymen had correctly recognized the dangers of trade dependency.

Conclusion

Commenting briefly on the rather late arrival of the United States onto the imperial stage, Sidney Mintz advised that "those interested in the rise of North American imperialism could do worse than looking carefully at the history of U.S. sugar consumption."[112] The history told above certainly confirms Mintz's suggestion. The issue, however, was not just a matter of consumption but also one of production. The rise of the sugar beet industry at the same time that the United States acquired its own sugar cane empire ensured that U.S. sugar policy would be, once again in Mintz's words, a "major political football."[113] And as this high-stakes game played out, the domestic sugar beet industry tried to determine the final outcome by pursuing a vigorous public relations campaign and testifying in front of Congress whenever possible. As the "most active, best organized and most ably represented" of all sugar producers, the sugar beet industry pursued its game plan "intelligently" and "persistently."[114] Though the industry failed to win everything it wanted, it did manage to convince Congress that maintaining some kind of tariff barrier would be in the best interests of both domestic and colonial producers.

Turning from the influence of the domestic sugar beet industry on American imperialism to the influence of imperialism on the domestic sugar beet industry, the results were much less drastic than industry leaders had predicted. In spite of the sugar beet industry's almost ceremonial-like mourning of each reduction of the sugar tariff as its death knell, many of the factories continued to thrive.[115] (Between 1902 and 1906, thirty-seven new factories were built in the United States.[116]) Domestic producers remained competitive in local and regional markets even as greater amounts of colonial sugar entered the United States through reduced tariff rates. In fact, throughout the early twentieth century, Michigan maintained its position as one of the top three sugar beet states in the nation, and the number of acres devoted to the crop continued to rise in the post-1905 period, reaching more than one hundred thousand acres by 1909.

Although the reduced tariff rates for colonial sugar certainly did not destroy the domestic sugar beet industry, this does not mean that the industry remained trouble free. In 1901 the Wolverine Sugar Company in Benton Harbor, financed by Chicago interests, closed its doors after only two unsuccessful seasons.[117] Two years later the Kalamazoo Sugar Company also closed down, as did the Rochester plant near Detroit. These factories had failed not because of competition from sugar cane abroad but rather because farmers in the vicinity simply refused to grow sugar beet when they could grow equally lucrative and less troublesome fruits and vegetables, which were easily marketed in nearby cities.[118] Sugar beet companies in areas where farmers grew lots of sugar beet also experienced troubles. In the Saginaw Valley and Thumb regions of the state, so many factories had been built in such a short time and in close proximity to each other that "overcrowding" spelled the doom for many. More than half of the urban-based factories failed within the first decade.[119] When the half-million-dollar Tawas sugar beet factory closed in 1905, even the national journal *The Sugar Beet* admitted that "the only cause for its removal is the impossibility of securing beets."[120]

These failures reinforced the lesson that early twentieth-century capitalism was both local and global. No matter how much time and effort industrialists put toward protecting their market from international competitors, and no matter how much city residents or townspeople supported this industry, it was at base an agricultural and local one, and if farmers refused to grow sugar beet because of the attractiveness of other crops, or if they simply would not grow enough of this crop to make it profitable for the factories to process it, the industry could not survive. All of the optimistic boosterism in the world could not hide the fact that the ability of towns to maintain their status as the processing link between urban and rural America was utterly dependent on what farmers in the area chose to do. Therefore, it is not too surprising that Michigan's rural factories fared much better than their urban counterparts. Moreover, it is also not too surprising that local newspapers often singled out farmers when praising the beet sugar industry, promising them that they, more than any other group, would greatly prosper from it. In a lead article in the *Tuscola County Advertiser*, Robert Rutledge, a prosperous farmer, addressed his less "ambitious" colleagues on behalf of the sugar company by claiming that "it [the factory] is really the farmers' factory, our factory, for in this vicinity, indirectly if not directly, all we farmers own stock in this institution. . . . It is not often that farmers are called to decide the destiny of a mammoth institution, it is nevertheless a fact, however, that the destiny of the Caro sugar factory lies in our hands."[121]

Harmonizing the interests of industry and agriculture would prove more challenging than the sugar beet boosters had anticipated. In contrast to his 1901 prediction that the sugar beet industry would "bring farmers, capitalists, and laborers into close association and cooperation," in 1902 Charles Saylor admitted in front of Congress that "there is no royal road to success in the beet sugar industry. It is only when a factory has gotten down to a knowledge of the facts in its own locality, studied its own conditions, and so on, that it can make a success of the enterprise . . . until the farmers know just what they must do in order to get the best results, until the factory people know how to adapt themselves to the conditions of the farmers to bring out the best results, they will not get the best results."[122] It is these results, or the lack thereof, that the next two chapters will explore.

2

Contract Farming in Rural Michigan

In December 1899, Michigan sugar beet industrialists Gilbert H. Lee of Caro, W. L. Churchill of Bay City, and N. H. Stewart of Kalamazoo traveled to Omaha, Nebraska, to meet with other sugar beet industrialists from across the country. They had gathered to organize the American Beet Sugar Manufacturers' Association in order to "combat the power which is trying to crush the life of this young but promising industry . . . our new colonial dependencies."[1] Just two months later, however, when Churchill wrote to his fellow sugar beet industrialists, he had little to say about Puerto Rico, Cuba, and the Philippines. Rather, Churchill wrote to complain about a threat much closer to home—the farmers upon whom the sugar companies depended to provide an ample supply of sugar beet. He expressed alarm that they had "organized under an association known as the Michigan Beet Growers' Association" and that this association was "already strong and are daily growing stronger." He ended with the warning that the "officers of this association called upon me and made known their wants and grievances, claims that the farmers as a whole lost money on their beet crops the past year, and that they would not grow beets unless they received a fair increase in the price paid by the factories."[2]

Churchill's concern with Michigan's family farmers provided an important lesson that capitalism was not just a global phenomenon but an intensely local one as well, and that the sugar beet industrialists who ignored this reality did so at their own peril. Churchill could not have been more right. In spite of the USDA's rhetoric about the numerous ways this industry would bring farms and factories together, as soon as the state's sugar beet factories began contracting with farmers to grow the crop, farmers and company officials engaged in what seemed like a perennial war. They battled over the role of the companies in the farmers' fields and the role of the farmers, if any, in the factories. They battled over how to cultivate the crop, when the crop would be delivered to the factories for processing, and who would weigh and test the sugar beet for sugar content. Most important of all, they battled over the contract price for the beet and whether to base that price on a sliding scale, a flat rate, the refined beet sugar product, or a share of the company profits. In essence, farmers and industrialists were battling over where the agricultural side of production ended and the industrial side began in this agricultural industry.

The battle between farmers and company officials to define the relationship between the field and the factory from 1898 to 1916, the topic of this chapter, reveals a great deal about the changing role of capitalism in the countryside. However, it is essential to recognize that by the time the sugar beet industry came to rural Michigan in 1898, the "transition to capitalism," if viewed in terms of market relations and ties, was certainly a foregone conclusion.[3] For years Michigan's family farmers had produced agricultural goods that they sold in the open market, and the prices they received certainly influenced their farming practices. The decision of whether to grow wheat or to plant beans and potatoes was in large part a market-based one. And, each year, farmers relied more and more on consumer goods bought from mail order catalogs and large department stores.[4] Yet the capitalist underpinning of the rural agricultural economy reflected through market influence in production and consumption does not necessarily reveal everything about the changing socioeconomic relations in the countryside as capitalism itself changed and evolved in the late nineteenth and early twentieth centuries. By the early twentieth century, capitalism in the countryside often meant more than selling goods in the market or the introduction of new consumer commodities; it increasingly came to include the act of processing raw materials into finished, or at least semifinished, products. The face of capitalism was changing, and for farmers who grew sugar beet, capitalism had come in the form of contract farming and consolidated processing, not an open market.

When Michigan's sugar beet farmers challenged the sugar companies, they were less concerned with the elusive adversaries of the nineteenth century—markets, middlemen, and money—than with confronting industrial capitalism in their own backyard.[5] And these sugar factories, as the most visual manifestation of industrial capitalism, were hard to miss. Besides literally overshadowing all other businesses, the sugar beet factories represented a significant capital investment, costing between $300,000 and $750,000 to build. It was not just the size of the factories or the financial costs associated with building them that distinguished the sugar beet industry from most other agricultural pursuits. Rather it was the way the product itself changed hands. In contrast to other agricultural products, which were often shipped to distant places and sometimes stored for weeks and months at a time, sugar beet was an extremely weighty and perishable crop that could be transported economically only a few dozen miles and needed to be processed immediately after harvesting. And in contrast to other agricultural products, which were sold in an open market, sugar beet was grown exclusively by contract, with the price farmers were to receive having been set months before the crop was even planted. Sugar factories and farmers, therefore, were linked in ways that made it impossible for either partner to grow or process the crop without the other, leading USDA sugar beet investigator Charles Saylor to comment that "There is such a community of interest between factory and farm in the production of sugar beet and manufacture that it is really hard to draw a line of separation."[6]

Contract Farming

At the turn of the century, Michigan farms were primarily family enterprises averaging about ninety acres.[7] On these modest farms, farmers practiced diversified agriculture by growing corn, wheat, oats, hay, beans, and potatoes. They regularly engaged in the expanding commercial market that surrounded them and depended on their families and local hired hands for labor. Some even engaged in wage labor during the winter months by joining ice harvests, lumbering in the North, or working in nearby cities.[8]

Although Michigan's farmers were far from isolated from the capitalist world, growing sugar beet for the local refining factories by contract represented a new kind of farming.[9] Farmers who planned to grow the crop had no choice but to sign legally binding agreements with the sugar companies. And these contracts did not just stipulate tonnage or weight; rather, they were very specific agreements detailing the number of acres to be planted, the exact tract of land where the beet seed was to be planted, how and when to cultivate the crop, and when to deliver the harvested sugar beet to the factories for processing. Farmers were obligated to buy seed from the companies at fifteen cents a pound. Furthermore, some contracts specified that once the seed was planted in the farmer's ground, the crop legally belonged to the companies and, therefore, if it were not properly tended to, the companies claimed the right to bring in their own workers and charge the farmer for this cost. When the farmers brought their sugar beet to the factories, the companies reserved the right to reject the crop if it was spoiled, damaged, or too low in sugar content to be refined. The companies also estimated the amount of "tare" (rocks and dirt) mixed in with the sugar beet and reduced the tonnage weight accordingly. Perhaps most important of all, the sugar beet crop was priced on a sliding scale. From 1898 to 1900, farmers were paid $4.00 a ton for sugar beet testing at least 12 percent sugar and an extra 33.5 cents for each additional percentage in sugar.[10]

Although the prospect of raising a new cash crop excited some farmers, and the possibility of securing cash advances for a crop even before it was planted attracted even more, many feared putting too much time and effort into this labor-intensive crop and becoming dependent on the factories as the sole market.[11] Farmers also wondered whether the sugar beet industry was simply a fleeting fad and worried about the dangers of growing a cash crop that was worthless unless refined by nearby factories. An inspector for the Michigan Bureau of Labor and Industry found farmers "loath to promise to grow beets until they too, were assured of the stability of the enterprise."[12]

To convince reluctant farmers to grow sugar beet, professors from Michigan Agricultural College (MAC), USDA officials, elite townsmen and representatives from the sugar companies hosted mass meetings in local school gymnasiums, opera houses, town halls, and even churches—the same public spaces farmers would soon occupy to challenge this industry.[13] At these meetings, agricultural professionals pressured crowds of farmers to plant sugar beet, arguing that because the companies paid farmers an assured price for the crop, irrespective of changes in the market price for refined sugar, sugar beet was not only one of the few real cash crops they could grow but also the only one that would allow them to avoid the ups and downs of the market.[14] Furthermore, these professionals pointed out that as the overall acreage in sugar beet increased, farmers would grow less of other crops that were susceptible to market fluctuations. Speaking before a crowd of Holland-area farmers, the Holland Sugar Company representative proclaimed: "The possibilities of this new industry are beyond conception. There is no danger of overproduction in the sugar industry as is suggested in the raising of wheat, corn and the like." In other words, it would be impossible for farmers to grow too much of this crop because the United States regularly imported more than one hundred million dollars' worth of sugar from other countries each year.[15] And finally, sugar beet boosters pointed to the 1897 Beet Sugar law, which mandated that sugar manufacturers had to pay farmers a fixed price for sugar beet and allow state inspectors to oversee the weighing and the testing of sugar beet, as a way to "assure the farmer against fraud in weighting and testing" and thereby "stand between the factory and the farmer to insure absolute justice."[16]

Local newspapers also did their part to convince farmers to take up the crop by publishing glowing accounts of the industry and highlighting the experiences of individuals who had succeeded at making a profit. The *Mount Clemens Monitor* reminded local farmers that they had "been complaining for years that there has not been profit enough in the crops.... Now comes the sugar beet, a crop that the farmer is guaranteed a good price before he plants it."[17] Another small-town newspaper, the *Allegan Gazette,* promised that the sugar beet crop was not only profitable but perhaps the "most profitable" of all crops farmers might grow, because farmers could expect to receive from $70 to $80 an acre.[18] Local papers also publicized how the local sugar beet factories offered advances to farmers—sometimes as much as 50 percent of expected earnings—to help them meet expenses.[19] Contract farming, then, was described as a way to avoid the dangers of an unpredictable market, assure a steady profit at the end of each season, and gain access to much-needed credit.

Michigan's farmers responded conservatively to the barrage of publicity directed at them, with the majority choosing to plant just two or three acres. Farmers also refused to sign multiyear contracts to grow the crop and generally rebuffed the efforts of sugar beet industrialists to convince them to invest in cooperative sugar beet factories—even with the offer of paying for stock in the form of beets.[20] This represented a pragmatic decision on the part of farmers who were unwilling to become dependent on the factories. Instead of radically adjusting their farming practices to grow sugar beet on a large scale, most farmers initially grew only as much as they felt they could incorporate into their farming system. By doing so, however, they were not reacting against the factories per se or trying to forestall the capitalist encroachment; rather, they were simply attempting to maintain as much autonomy as possible in an environment in which specific industries were playing increasingly important roles. Unlike the townspeople who vigorously boosted for this industry, doing everything in their power to attract potential investors, the majority of Michigan's farmers, including native-born and immigrant as well as rich and poor, remained cautious about tying their farming practices, and hence their livelihood, to this new industry.

Sugar Beet Battles

In spite of the small acreages that farmers planted, tensions between farmers and sugar manufacturers quickly emerged. Unusually bad weather plagued the first couple of sugar beet seasons, making it difficult, if not impossible, for many inexperienced farmers to profitably grow this labor-intensive crop.[21] But bad weather was not the only problem. Many farmers chose poorly suited land, started planting too late, and, perhaps most important of all, failed to appreciate the amount of work required.[22] Farmers sometimes complained that they and their wives and children could not take care of all the acres they had contracted to grow; still others found that after calculating the cost of their own labor and land use, they actually lost money.[23] Farmers also failed to turn a profit when they could not deliver their crop to the factory quickly enough after harvesting. Sometimes this was due to a lack of available railroad cars for shipments. Other times the companies refused sugar beet shipments when their own storage facilities were filled to capacity or when the factories had to close down for repairs.[24]

Factory officials found the first couple of seasons equally difficult. Hindsight revealed that too many factories had been built too quickly and too closely together.[25] Even with the support of townspeople who did their best to pressure farmers into growing sugar beet, factory officials often found it difficult to get enough of the crop to keep the factories running for an entire season.[26] In 1899 Michigan's nine sugar beet factories hoped to contract for a total of sixty thousand acres but had to settle for half that figure.[27] The following year, many companies found that farmers refused to sign up for as large an acreage as they had the previous year, thereby forcing company fieldmen to find other farmers to take their place.[28] Moreover, because most farmers grew only very small amounts of the crop, the task of contracting acreage each year proved timely, costly, and burdensome.

State officials who had so vigorously promoted this industry looked for reasons to explain the rather disappointing start. A Michigan Bureau of Labor and Industry investigator reflected "most farmers had little or no knowledge of the industry and of course mistakes were made. . . . This want of knowledge . . . made a profit impossible."[29] A few sugar officials tried to lay all the blame on the farmers, charging that they tended to this crop carelessly.[30] Most company officials, however, realized that they would have to bear some responsibility. Indeed, because the majority of sugar companies were so busy trying to master the technological side of sugar production, they had hoped that the agricultural side would somehow take care of itself. Even state officials who often blindly supported the sugar beet industrialists chastised factory officials for leaving farmers with few instructions on how to grow the crop, noting, "The companies were very busy looking after the construction of the factories and it was next to impossible to secure agriculturalists who were sufficiently acquainted with the growing of the beets to be of any material aid to the uninstructed farmer."[31]

To confront the problems plaguing their industry, Michigan's nine independent sugar company presidents met in December 1899 to define their common interests and outline a plan to better coordinate this industry. The result was the founding of the Michigan Beet Sugar Manufacturers' Association (MBSMA), an association whose members agreed that they needed to minimize the cutthroat competition that had made the 1899 season so difficult. For, far too often, sugar companies struggling to get enough beet had raised the price they offered farmers for the crop and thereby forced all other companies to do the same or risk being boycotted by disgruntled farmers. A number of the urban companies had even "hijacked" the sugar beet of their neighboring competitors by urging farmers who had contracted with other companies to deliver the crop to their own factories.[32] To avoid such problems in the future, the sugar companies vowed to establish a uniform price, divide the available surrounding farming territories into clearly defined "company territory," and confer with one another should future problems arise.[33]

Just weeks after the manufacturers created the MBSMA, farmers throughout Michigan responded by forming local sugar beet associations and unions of their own. Farmers living near Bay City, including a significant number of first- and second-generation German immigrants, were the first to organize. Hoping to spur interest among other farmers, Bay County farmers decided to name their organization the Michigan Beet Growers' Association (MBGA) and invited all other farmers in the state to come on board. In the following weeks, farmers founded other associations, including the Alma Sugar Beet Growers' Association, which included farmers growing sugar beet for the Alma sugar factory. Even though Alma's farmers were mostly native born and better off than their Bay County neighbors, they vowed to stand by all growers as well as the other growers' associations until their mutual demands were met by the sugar companies.[34] Insisting that "the business of sugar beet growing . . . has been conducted during the past year at a loss and has been unprofitable," these newly formed sugar beet growers' associations protested that the price of $4 a ton was too low and insisted that $5 a ton would be more reasonable.[35]

The farmers who banded together in 1900 calling for higher prices went far beyond merely demanding more for their crop. They were frustrated that the sugar companies and the local press had overestimated profits and underestimated the time and labor required, and they asked for the sugar companies to spend more time and resources instructing them on how to handle the crop.[36] Farmers also questioned whether the sugar beet crop was really an assured cash crop, suspecting that the complex weighing and testing of their crop was really a way for the sugar companies to deny them just profits. Upset that the price they received for their crop was determined inside the factory walls and not in the fields, or in a more neutral place somewhere in between, farmers throughout the state demanded not only that they be allowed to bring their crop to the factory at will but that they have some influence in choosing who would weigh and test the crop to guarantee fair and honest results. Farmers in Bay County even sent a petition to then-Michigan Governor Hazen S. Pingree complaining that the manufacturers had "discriminated" against them when weighing the crop.[37] Farmers in Bay County and the town of Alma went further to ensure that their demands would be heard by preparing their own contracts and submitting them to the factory managers to sign.[38]

The speed with which farmers banded together to challenge the companies speaks not only to their common grievances but also to the possibility of successfully challenging a visible adversary. Unlike traditional markets and middlemen, which were often difficult to identify, much less challenge, the sugar factories represented very real and tangible opponents with whom the farmers had frequent contact. Each season, farmers could expect to see the company fieldmen who had first signed them up to grow the crop and then periodically visited them to make sure they were doing so according to company standards. Equally important, farmers who read the local newspapers or farm journals were repeatedly inundated with reports about "their factory" and what this industry meant to their local communities. The very visibility of the factories and their representatives convinced many farmers that this was a battle they could fight and win.

These sugar beet associations and the tactics they developed are also important for what they can tell us about the ways that farmers changed their organizational strategies as they encountered new forms of capitalism. Unlike the state's other farm organizations, most notably the Michigan State Grange and Farmers' Clubs, which focused on uplifting the farmers socially and educationally, local sugar beet associations were the first to represent farmers on a single issue: renegotiating new contracts with the sugar companies. Sugar beet farmers came together because they recognized that their immediate and long-term interests—gaining better prices and setting the terms of the contract—could not be achieved individually. Equally significant, because these associations tried to negotiate contracts for all members, regardless of how many acres tended, and because there were no price variations based on acreage, these associations tended to bring together farmers who otherwise might have had different interests based on class standing and ethnic background. In spite of rural Michigan's varied ethnic and class demographics, the sugar beet growers' associations neither explicitly included nor excluded members based on ethnic background or class status. The contracts that they signed acted as a leveler, bringing diverse farmers together to challenge a common adversary.

As the 1900 season approached and all signs pointed to yet another brewing conflict, R. C. Kedzie of Michigan Agricultural College and H. W. Wiley, chief chemist of the USDA, hosted a special conference for beet growers and sugar factory representatives at the 1899–1900 Michigan State Farmers' Institute. In the hope of bringing the two sides together, Kedzie told the crowd of farmers and industrialists that considering the challenges of growing the crop, and the difficulty of dividing the profits between the two sides, it should come as little surprise "that frictions and disputes should arise." Blaming some of the conflict on the "too great expectations of some and exaggerated disappointments of others,"[39] Kedzie then dropped his tone of neutrality and spent the rest of his talk trying to convince farmers that much of their disappointment stemmed from their lack of knowledge about the crop and how it was weighed, sampled, tested, and analyzed.[40] He advised farmers who felt that they had been cheated by the companies to turn to the courts rather than to look to MAC for help.[41] Kedzie's colleague, Professor C. D. Smith, also chastised the farmers for trying to use the college and the experiment station to aid them in their quest to win concessions from the sugar companies, denouncing the "dissatisfied growers" who had attacked "the good faith of the factory."[42]

Not too surprisingly, Kedzie's and Smith's efforts to broker a peace failed miserably. As both the sugar companies and the farmers closed ranks, however, it became apparent that it was the farmers and not the manufacturers who had more leverage. While the farmers' associations gained momentum in the early months of 1900, focusing on issues that united them, the manufacturers had a difficult time fulfilling the promises they had made to each other in late December 1899. Just a month after the MBSMA formed, its treasurer, W. L. Churchill, president of the West Bay City Sugar Company, wrote to Henry Lancashire, president of Alma Sugar Company, to complain that the association, which was supposed to be of "mutual benefit and protection" for all, was in reality a farce. Churchill complained bitterly that when his company's field agents went out to the countryside to make contracts with the farmers, not only had the price they were offering been outbid by a number of other sugar companies, but the Michigan Sugar Company, one of West Bay City's closest competitors, had been accepting sugar beet that his company had initially contracted. "With the above state of affairs, it seem[s] to me there is no concert of action or unity of action among the sugar manufacturers of Michigan; each corporation seems to be working for its own interest and advantages."[43] Churchill also warned his colleague about the ever-growing militancy of the farmers, noting that he feared that if he simply ignored them and their grievances, his company would not be able to garner enough sugar beet to keep his factory running. This prospect threatened to undermine what had already become a multimillion-dollar industry.[44]

As sugar companies approached the spring 1900 planting season, the farmers' proposed sugar strike forced their hand. The Wolverine Sugar Company in Benton Harbor, which was having a difficult time competing with the area's lucrative truck farming, was the first to give in to the farmers' demand for higher prices.[45] Once these companies caved in, the other companies feared that unless they too matched the highest price being offered, the farmers would simply abandon the crop.[46] Therefore, all of the other sugar companies followed suit and began offering the farmers $4.50 a ton instead of $4.00. The sugar companies fell like a row of dominoes and the farmers quickly claimed victory in what had turned out to be a short and rather easily fought battle.

This first battle highlighted the sugar companies' dependence on the farmers for an ample supply of sugar beet. If the farmers refused to grow the crop, as they did in areas where truck farming was more lucrative, the sugar companies faced the prospect of bankruptcy. Or if the farmers refused to grow enough of the crop to make the business cost-efficient and profitable, the industrial side of production was doomed to fail. To run a sugar beet factory profitably, industry officials had little choice but to depend on the surrounding farmers to supply them with an ample supply of beets.[47] As long as the farmers were willing to abandon the crop, and could pressure enough of their friends and neighbors to do the same, they held the balance of power. This point was made by a participant at the Michigan State Farmers' Institute, who remarked that "the farmer has his capital in his land that he can turn to a variety of crops."[48] Ironically, the fact that most farmers grew just a couple of acres, and did not yet fully depend on this crop as part of their regular crop rotation, had reinforced their bargaining power as a class.

The farmers' victory turned out to be only a partial one. Although the companies were willing to discuss prices, most refused to negotiate over when the farmers would deliver the crop to the factories or how the crop would be weighed and tested.[49] Company officials demanded that farmers bring the beets to the factories when they needed them, not when the farmers thought it best to deliver. Perhaps most important of all, they insisted that while farmers were welcome to bring their sugar beet to the factory doors, they were not welcome inside the factory walls. Drawing the line of negotiation far from the factory gates, company officials refused to treat the farmers as partners or to recognize that the value the farmers created in the fields was equal to the value the processors created in the act of processing. Having won the first battle, it was clear that farmers had yet to define the terms of the war.

Defining the Boundaries

In the years immediately following the spring 1900 victory, farmers continued to challenge the sugar companies, focusing on the control issues—the weighing and testing of the crop—that they had lost during the first dispute.[50] In fact, suspicion over what happened inside the factory walls intensified after the Michigan State Supreme Court's October 1899 ruling that the 1897 Beet-Sugar Law, including those provisions guaranteeing a minimum price for all farmers as well as state-appointed weigh- and taremen at each factory, was unconstitutional.[51]

The main problem was that farmers deeply resented the sliding-scale prices, fearing that the sugar companies were cheating them out of their money by underweighing the sugar beet, underestimating the sugar content, and overestimating the amount of tare. Farmers were also frustrated that the value of the crop was not based merely on weight or volume but rather a combination of weighing and testing that made it difficult, if not impossible, for them to understand, much less estimate, the value of their own crop. That these tests were done in a laboratory, behind closed doors, further fed the farmers' suspicion that the sugar companies were cheating them out of just earnings. Even state officials who tended to side with the companies admitted that "the chemical process by which the sweetness of the beets is obtained is most interesting, not only requiring skill, but tried, trusty and accurate employees. This work of the beets passing from the hands of the growers to the manufacturer is of the greatest importance as involving large money consideration."[52] Sugar companies also recognized the bad feelings that this process engendered, with one executive noting that the sliding price scales "caused considerable grumbling" on the part of the "farmers who could not understand why their beets were not worth as much as their neighbors' were."[53]

The farmers who had brought the companies to their knees rather quickly during the first contract dispute in 1900 found it much more challenging to bring them back to the bargaining table in the following years. After the disastrous 1900 defeat, the sugar industrialists worked more closely together to make sure that none of their fellow colleagues would give in to the farmers' demands. Moreover, the companies vehemently refused to negotiate the control issues so central to the sugar beet conflict. Raising prices was one thing. Actually giving farmers control over what happened behind the factory doors was clearly a different matter altogether.

Faced with manufacturers who refused to even talk with them, farmers adopted a new strategy that would provide them with greater protection and profits without requiring that the industrialists give up any control over what happened behind factory walls.[54] They demanded a flat rate for their crop—usually from $5 to $6 a ton—instead of the $4.50 sliding scale the factories usually offered. That is, farmers wanted to be paid $5 a ton for the sugar beet they brought to the factory, irrespective of the amount of tare, as long as the crop tested a minimum of 12 percent. By proposing a flat rate in lieu of the sliding scale, farmers tried to lessen their exclusion from the factory by making what happened within the factory largely irrelevant to the price of sugar beet. By asking for a flat price, farmers wanted their assured cash crop to have at least a minimum value.

In response to the farmers' demand for a flat rate for the crop, the industrialists decided that this time they would gain more, not less, control over the boundary dividing the factory and the field. As the 1903 season approached, the industrialists who met at the MBSMA convention not only agreed to refuse to give in to the farmers' demands but also to offer the farmers a uniform contract of $4.50, still based on the sliding scale.[55] To add insult to injury, the sugar companies announced publicly that they would "divide territory amongst themselves" and force farmers to grow sugar beet for one predetermined factory even if there were other factories in the area. Sugar companies not only refused to let the farmers gain more control over what happened behind the factory walls, they attempted to extend their power far into the farmers' fields.[56]

Farmers responded to the companies' plans as "slavery" and warned that "they will get out of the beet crop if that is done."[57] Equally important, the farmers began a new round of organizing. In Almer Township in Tuscola County, farmers adopted a resolution pledging not to raise any sugar beet unless the companies paid at least $5 for every ton of sugar beet.[58] Farmers in Gratiot County's "Union District Number 1" called for an increase to $6 a ton, and banded together with other sugar beet organizations in the Central Beet Growers' Association.[59] Likewise, farmers in Huron County met in the town of Bad Axe to form a countywide sugar beet organization and then demanded $6 a ton and "no tests," threatening not to grow any more sugar beet unless the factories met their demands.[60]

These strike threats soon translated into action as growing numbers of farmers refused to sign sugar beet contracts when the company fieldmen came around to sign them up for acreage. However, this strike, and those that succeeded it, differed from craft and industrial workers' strikes of the same time period. Farmers did not picket the factories or physically try to shut them down. Nor did most farmers even participate in the strike, which might be more appropriately called a boycott. Enough farmers did participate, making it difficult for the companies to secure the acreage they needed to make full-run campaigns. By 1903, the majority of the sugar factories found themselves without enough sugar beet and had to shut down operations early.[61] The following season, sugar companies continued to experience problems securing enough sugar beet to keep the factories running at full strength. Both the West Bay City and German-American sugar beet plants stopped operating weeks earlier than they had hoped because neither factory "has more than 60 per cent of the desired acreage, owing to the apathy of the farmers in making contracts last year." Similarly, owing to the small acreage of sugar beets, the Owosso plant near Lansing ran only thirty-one days in 1904, the "shortest [run] in its history."[62] Because the sugar companies depended on "full-run" campaigns to turn a profit, a strong minority of farmers held a great deal of power.

Considering the effort townspeople had invested to attract the sugar beet factories in the first place, it should come as no surprise that the farmers' slowdown, which began in 1901 and continued through 1904, inflamed town and country tensions. During the long conflict, farmers were castigated in the local press for trying to take advantage of the factories and trying to destroy the industry. Sugar company fieldman Mr. Thissell described the growers' associations as "a damage and a set back to the best interests of the farming community."[63] Town newspapers printed numerous articles and editorials reminding the farmers that this was "their industry" and chastising them for being so short-sighted and selfish. One editorial criticized the farmers for "allowing themselves to be influenced by irresponsible agitators to choose an inopportune time to demand an increased price for beets. . . . Farmers owe a debt of gratitude to the enterprising capitalists who risked their money in developing the sugar beet industry."[64]

As the strike wore on, the sugar companies did their best to frighten townspeople with repeated warnings that if the farmers refused to cooperate, they might have to shut down.⁶⁵ Mr. Lee, president of the Caro factory, publicly announced how his plant might not operate in 1904 because "of the attitude of the farmer."⁶⁶ These threats mobilized nervous townspeople who sought to save their "besieged" industry by rallying to help the companies contract for acreage, even promising that if worse came to worse, they would simply grow sugar beet for the factories themselves. In the spring of 1903, with the planting season just weeks away, numerous small-town businessmen's associations throughout Michigan organized various beet-growing companies to raise sugar beet for their local sugar factories.⁶⁷ For example, the businessmen of Owosso and Corruna formed the "Merchants Beet Company Ltd." and pledged to grow one thousand acres of sugar beet for the Owosso Sugar Company.⁶⁸ The Marine City Businessmen's Association, which had gone to great lengths to help its local factory secure acreage by calling meetings and giving speeches, now called on "all businessmen, farmers, mechanics, and laborers" to work together to make sure that the sugar factory would have enough acreage and therefore be "profitable and successful in every way."⁶⁹

Even as local businessmen made plans to grow sugar beet, the companies were trying to figure out ways to restructure this industry by cutting the farmers out altogether. That is, sugar company executives tried to take matters into their own hands by making plans to grow their own supply of sugar beet.⁷⁰ W. H. Wallace, president of the Michigan Sugar Company, insisted that his company "will buy land and raise our own beets, which all the factories may have to come to before many years."⁷¹ Just two months later, Owosso Sugar Company officials also tried to cut farmers out of the beet business altogether. Remarking that they no longer wanted to depend on farmers, the company hoped to solve its "farmer problem" by purchasing eight thousand acres of land in Saginaw County, where it planned to grow its own sugar beet.⁷² The following month, in April, the Peninsular Sugar Company of Caro announced that it too would grow one thousand acres of sugar beet.⁷³ Finally, Charlevoix Sugar Company president August Mueller announced that his company was looking to lease land, for "this method of coaxing each and every farmer year by year to do us the favor and grow some beets for us is disgusting."⁷⁴

By threatening to vertically integrate this agricultural industry, the companies were hoping to gain complete control over what happened not only in the factories but in the fields as well. This represented a serious effort to restructure the countryside in the interest of the industrialists. In spite of the companies' best efforts, however, these threats remained just that—threats. Few of these company farms made it past the planning stage and those that did fared poorly.

Part of the problem was that sugar beet cannot be grown on the same plot of land year after year, so to successfully grow six to ten thousand acres, each sugar company needed to acquire eighteen to thirty thousand acres of land. This kind of plantationlike landholding was simply unfeasible in southern Michigan, a state dominated by small family farms.[75] Michigan's sugar beet companies lost thousands of dollars on these company farms, demonstrating the limits of vertical integration in this particular industry.[76]

The sugar companies' inability to take over the agricultural side of production provided a harsh lesson that in this agricultural industry, the geographic interdependence tying the processing companies and the farmers together could provide the latter with a great deal of leverage. Not only did the factories fail to gain a foothold in the field, the farmers' strikes of 1902, 1903, and 1904, though by no means complete, had a taxing effect on this industry when viewed cumulatively. For example, by 1904, with all but one of the sugar company farms and the majority of the businessmen's growing association farms having failed or failing miserably, the acreage of sugar beet grown in Michigan dropped from 93,685 in 1903 to 59,634 in 1904, a decrease of more than one-third. That year only two factories anticipated a "full-run" campaign, and most factories were forced to shut down in October and November for lack of beets.[77]

The farmers' leverage in the long, drawn-out contest came from the fact that they could always grow other crops and that they only needed the cooperation of a significant minority of other farmers to force the sugar companies to the bargaining table. Conversely, the just recently built sugar beet factories simply could not afford to keep running unless they had "full-run" campaigns. Once again, the farmers' limited ties to this crop reinforced their bargaining power as a class, while the sugar companies' dependence on local farmers made it costly for them to ignore the farmers' demands.

As the 1905 season loomed, and three years after the farmers' "strike" had begun, Michigan's sugar companies finally met the growers' demands by offering a choice of contracts, including one with a flat rate of $5 a ton.[78] Company officials also tried to alleviate the growing class tension of the previous years by hailing the new flat contract of $5 as an important breakthrough. According to S. O. Burgdorf, an important investor in the sugar beet industry, "there seems to be clearly a better understanding between the farmer and the factory management. It is now realized that both are partners in the business."[79] Holland Sugar Company executive C. L. McLean claimed: "We believe that with careful, economical management, treating the farmer at all time[s] courteously and fairly, making his interest and that of the factory one, in practice as well as theory.... [E]very factory in the state can be put on a paying basis and the farmers made friends of the industry."[80] In an attempt to foster "close personal relations with every grower," the Peninsular Sugar Company promised its contracting farmers that it would give them a "fair deal" and that its weigh stations would employ men "living in the neighborhood of each, known for honesty and integrity who will give every man honest weight and fair tare."[81] Factories also began hosting "Farmer's Days" as a way to provide farmers with free refreshments, sugar samples, "beautifully illustrated" souvenir books, and cash prizes.[82]

The publicity generated by the new flat rate contracts and the optimistic predictions that the factories and farmers could be "friends" overshadowed an equally if not more important development also taking place—the rise of the American Sugar Refining Company (ASRC) as the most important sugar corporation in Michigan. The ASRC, the sugar beet industry's nemesis in the tariff hearings, had first begun to invest in Michigan's sugar beet industry in 1902, buying stock in a number of different companies.[83] Two years later, in the midst of the long-running standoff between the farmers and the factories, the ASRC decided to form a central board of control for those factories in which it held the majority of stock. Although the ASRC claimed that it had organized this board simply to make the factory operations "more economical," it was clear that the ASRC was trying to establish order in this tumultuous industry.[84] Two years later in 1906, the ASRC formally consolidated eight of Michigan's sixteen factories into one corporate entity—the Michigan Sugar Company—making it "the largest industrial enterprise in the state" with a capitalization of $12,500,000.[85]

The emergence of the sugar trust in Michigan elicited surprisingly little response from local communities that had prided themselves on getting sugar beet factories in the first place. When the ASRC took over the Peninsular Sugar Company in Caro in 1903, the local newspaper insisted that the trust was not trying to take over and that management would remain in "local" hands because "the trust cannot come into Michigan and deal with the beet growers and insure a crop. Local men who are familiar with the conditions and who are acquainted with the farmers are necessary to deal with them."[86] As the ASRC continued its monopolistic path, R. G. Wagner, president of the Wisconsin Sugar Company, insisted that the consolidation of the sugar beet industry was simply a means for simplifying management.[87] Similarly the *Grand Rapids Herald* noted that though some might be concerned that Michigan's sugar beet industry was becoming a mere "subsidiary company to the octopus," the real power lay with the farmers who could always raise some other crop if they felt that the trust would not pay fair prices.[88] This theme was repeated over and over again. According to the *Beet Sugar Gazette,* "Beet sugar production is a neighborhood industry.... [N]o trust could possibly control it."[89] One of the few critical accounts of the coming of the sugar trust, printed in the *Flint Democrat,* lamented the lack of concern in the rise of the trust, asking: "Why this lack of interest exists when this trust bids fair to be more serious in its result to the agricultural interests of the state than any other that has been formed is a mystery." The *Democrat* went on to warn that lower prices would naturally result, and even worse: "When the trust shall have become possessed of the market, which is beyond doubt its real aim, there will be no such competition, and the farmer, if he raises beets, will find himself in the fall with a lot of perishable property in the shape of beets, and only one buyer, and he can take what that one buyer offers or let them rot."[90]

Farming the Farmers

Michigan's farmers responded to higher prices and a choice of contracts by growing more sugar beet than ever before. In 1906, farmers harvested 93,984 acres, and in 1909 the long-sought goal of one hundred thousand acres finally became a reality, with farmers tending to 112,232 acres. Sugar industry profits also reached new heights, especially the profits of the newly amalgamated Michigan Sugar Company. In 1909, the profits of the eight factories controlled by the Michigan Sugar Company rose so dramatically that in June 1909 the company announced that even after setting aside $200,000 to take care of preferred dividends, it still had a surplus of one million dollars.[91] By October, the Michigan Sugar Company announced it would set aside $225,000 for dividends, put "large sums" of money into building new sheds, and still have a surplus of $1,609,000.[92] The following year, the company showed a surplus of $3,025,000 after spending $3,500,000 for labor and beets and paying the regular dividends on both the common and preferred stock.[93]

Michigan's newspapers provided plenty of newsprint space to show that farmers were profiting as well. In addition to printing sugar company profits, newspapers published farmer profits, listing the names of the most successful farmers, their total acreage, and total receipts. The *National Farmer* reported how during the 1906–1907 season, nearly thirty thousand farmers had grown ninety-five thousand acres of sugar beet, making $4,750,000 for doing so.[94] Sugar town newspapers personalized these profits by publishing the names of successful sugar beet growers. In February 1907, the month farmers usually signed contracts with the sugar companies, the *Alma Record* reserved front-page space all month long so that the Michigan Sugar Company could list the area's most profitable 250 sugar beet growers, the total acres they planted, and their total receipts.[95]

Ironically, the growing publicity regarding factory profits helped to fuel discontent among sugar beet farmers throughout the state, who now began to complain that even if they were making money, they were not making enough. In other words, they were no longer satisfied with merely making enough to cover costs and turn a profit; rather, farmers began to demand what they saw as a *fair share* of the industry's profits. And farmers, who were still paid the $5 rate they had won in 1905, felt that they were not reaping the benefits of this prosperity.[96] As early as 1907, farmers began meeting with the hope of forming a new sugar beet growers' association, and by early 1908 they not only began calling for $6 beets but also that a farmers' representative be present at the factory at all times to ensure that the farmers were not being cheated.[97] The American Society of Equity (AS of E), a radical national farm organization that had begun to establish locals in the sugar beet districts of Michigan, even organized a "Sugar Beet Growers' Department" to represent the special interests of sugar beet farmers in the state, a development that caused a great deal of excitement.[98] After the editor of the *Sebewaing Review* criticized farmers for joining the radical farm organization, J. W. Michener, treasurer of the AS of E's Sugar Beet Department, wrote back to complain. "Now Mr. Editor, don't you think the farmers have stayed at home too much to properly keep in touch with the various business transactions that is of great importance to them. Of course the trust interests don't like to have the farmers find out too much of their methods of doing business. . . . Now, really, Mr. Editor, do you think it was the sugar beets that paid the mortgages. [Or] was it the wages of the farmers' wives and children?"[99]

As discontent among farmers started to mount yet again, the Gleaner, the state of Michigan's most popular farm organization, finally decided to enter the sugar beet fight. Though rarely mentioned in the historical literature, the Gleaner was an impressive farm organization. Founded in Caro, Michigan, in 1893 as a fraternal insurance society by Grant Slocum, the Gleaner grew quickly, outpacing the more nationally recognized Grange and Farmers' Clubs throughout Michigan by the end of the first decade of the twentieth century. In 1912, the Gleaner counted 64,920 members in 1,015 Gleaner Arbors (groups), while the Grange counted sixty thousand members in eight hundred Granges, and the Farmers' Clubs a mere seven thousand members in 118 clubs.[100] Just ten years later the Gleaner would have more than eighty thousand members, mostly concentrated in the sugar beet belt of Saginaw, Bay, Tuscola, Shiawassee, Sanilac, Huron and Gratiot Counties, while the Grange's membership fell to slightly more than forty thousand, with strongholds in the Upper Peninsula.[101]

With its secret handshakes, elaborate rituals, sporting teams, holiday celebrations, and picnics, the Gleaner appealed to farmers eager for social outlets. However, the Gleaner was also popular because it offered an alternative to more conventional and conservative farm organizations. Under the direction of Grant Slocum, the Gleaner espoused a critique of the usual enemies—markets, middlemen, and money—as well as Michigan Agricultural College, the United States Department of Agriculture, and sugar beet company officials. But when criticizing agricultural institutions and middlemen, the Gleaner did not call for farmers to retreat from markets or capitalism more generally. Rather, the Gleaner encouraged farmers to wrest control of their farming, as a business, for themselves. In one of the organization's two papers, the first editorial stated that the paper's objective was to "represent the business end of farming! Always it will teach when and where to sell, how to place the farm on a business basis and run it as a manufacturer does his factory for a profit."[102]

The Gleaner organization appealed to farmers who grew sugar beet because it told them they were businessmen farmers who deserved a fair price for their product and a right to exercise some control over it. "After all is said and done," the Gleaner asserted, "farmers who grow sugar beets are entitled to every dollar the factories can pay. The labor, the uncertainty of harvesting the crop, the chances on the roads and weather, the depletion of the soil—all argue for better prices for farmers."[103] As businessmen who both "worked with their hands" and "owned their own land," the Gleaner encouraged farmers to cooperate with one another. An article entitled "Does the Farmer Get the High Price of Sugar?" concluded that, "the real producer didn't get it to be sure."[104] In contrast with the Country Life movement, the USDA, and the agricultural colleges and experiment stations, all of which pressured farmers to be more businesslike so that they could increase production, the Gleaner called for farmers to be more "business-minded," so that they could control their own destiny. And, in rural Michigan, the only way to succeed as businessmen was if farmers banded together. Individual success was dependent on communal cooperation.

Under the rubric of the Gleaner organization, sugar beet farmers developed increasingly sophisticated strategies for confronting the sugar companies. As part of its effort to spearhead farmers' organizations in all fields, in

1910 the Gleaner helped to launch a completely new Michigan Sugar Beet Growers' Association (MSBGA) and provided plenty of newsprint in its journals to publicize the organization's battles with the sugar companies. Equally important, the Gleaner encouraged farmers to see themselves not only as laborers and landowners but also as agricultural businessmen and to call for just compensation based on all these roles.[105] This multifaceted class identity was reflected in the constitution of the Michigan Sugar Beet Growers' Association, which not only highlighted how the acreage farmers devoted to sugar beet was "of equal value" to the capital invested in the manufacturing plants, but that as landowners and workers, farmers deserved "an equitable return for our land and labor."[106] This identity was also reflected in media coverage of farmer/factory conflicts. In *The Gleaner* farmers were warned that to permit the factories to "set an unprofitable price on your labor and compel you to rob your soil in order to make a profit is a reflection upon the intelligence and business ability of the farmers of the beet growing section of this and adjoining states."[107] To make sure that they received their fair share of profits, the Gleaner encouraged farmers to keep better track of the costs of farm production in "nature's workshop" by keeping account books, promising that when "the farmer learns to figure his business as do the business corporations, he will begin to realize how profits are calculated in advance."[108]

When farmers began to contest the sugar beet companies in 1910, then, they did not cultivate resentment or resistance to capitalism. Their class identity was not a throwback to a producerism from a preceding era, although the producerism ideal certainly played a role. Rather, farmers combined the producer ideal with equally important notions about their roles as laboring men and agricultural businessmen. This identity was both pragmatic and abstract; it reflected the numerous roles that farmers assumed in an era of industrial agriculture at the same time that it questioned the workings but not the structure of capitalism itself. Using the business rhetoric of the USDA and Michigan Agricultural College to demand fair and equal treatment as agricultural businessmen who worked with their hands and owned their own land, farmers transformed seemingly conservative rural identities into more militant ones.

Feeling more empowered organizationally and ideologically, and frustrated that everyone except "real producers" seemed to be making a profit, the farmers tested the companies' resolve and their own strength by trying to stage strategically timed strikes. In December 1910 the MSBGA began holding meetings in all the sugar beet counties, hoping to persuade farmers to stand together against the sugar companies this year. In an ad placed in one local newspaper, the Gleaner informed farmers that the sugar companies could have paid them $8 per ton for sugar beet and still paid out "reasonable dividends" to stockholders. The ad then informed sugar beet growers that, as it was, the dividends the companies paid stockholders were "out of this world." "And the Farmers Get the Same Old Price. . . . Will You Stand by Your Brother?"[109]

In addition to calling for a sugar beet strike, sugar beet farmers began to look for alternative strategies for challenging the sugar companies that would allow them to keep growing sugar beet without being taken advantage of by the processors. Some farmers hoped to establish cooperative sugar beet growers' associations to sell their crop collectively. For example, farmers in Gratiot County, who had traditionally contracted with the Alma Sugar Company, tried to bypass the factory as the only market for their sugar beet by forming a cooperative growers' organization.[110] Adopting an even more ambitious proposal, the Gleaner called for five thousand farmers to buy $100 in stock and another five thousand farmers to take $50, so that together they could build their own cooperative sugar beet factory and hence "break the chain of the sugar trust."[111] Gleaner officials even went so far as to take an option on some riverfront land in Pigeon, with the expectation that they could soon raise the funds to begin building.[112] Like the sugar companies' previous attempts to take over both the agricultural and industrial sides of production by buying land and raising their own beets, the farmers now tried to bridge the boundary between the factory from the field by shutting the industrialists out.

Farmers also sought to gain greater control over the relations of production in both the field and the factory, and especially the places where the two met, by looking to the state. In 1911, sugar beet growers pushed for the state to regulate their industry by supporting a sugar beet bill, which called for supervisors from the State Dairy and Food Commission to oversee the processing, weighing, and inspecting of sugar beet. The proposed bill stipulated that farmers had the right to demand "re-tests" of any sugar beet they believed had been unfairly weighed and tested. The bill also mandated that the sugar companies were legally obligated to keep records of all sugar beet tests and to make the tests available to the farmers upon request.[113]

Despite the farmers' multipronged approach for challenging the sugar companies, they failed miserably on all fronts. Though many of Michigan's farmers may have believed this was the perfect moment to force the sugar companies back to the bargaining table, they soon found that their adversaries—the sugar companies—were not about to give in so easily. In fact, their adversaries themselves had changed. In contrast to the turn of the century, when the majority of sugar companies were independent, by 1910 one company, the American Sugar Refining Company, held a controlling interest in eight of the state's sixteen factories. That is, when farmers first challenged the sugar beet companies at the turn of the century, they faced a number of newly created and independent companies trying to turn a profit in a highly competitive market. By 1910, when Michigan's sugar beet farmers tried to force the companies to negotiate, it was a matter of David battling Goliath, for they faced the challenge of forcing the hand of what was commonly known at the time as the "mother of all trusts." And this mother was not about to give in to the farmers' demands.

The difficulty of challenging the sugar beet industry was further aggravated by the steps the sugar companies had taken to gradually expand the geographical boundaries of their industry. Recognizing that geographic interdependence had provided farmers with a great deal of leverage in the sugar beet battles from 1899 to 1905, the sugar beet companies began to look for ways to make sure they would never again have to give in to a minority of militant farmers. To lessen their dependence on farmers immediately surrounding the factories, companies began building weigh stations on railway lines out in the countryside to make it easier for farmers in outlying areas to grow sugar beet. In 1906 the German-American Sugar Company in Bay City built twenty-nine weigh stations and increased its supply of sugar beets coming from those weigh stations from 8,985 tons out of 37,141 in 1906 to 39,464 out of 52,439 in 1909.[114] That same year only 20 percent of the Owosso Sugar Company's acreage was grown within an eight-mile radius of the plant, with all the rest coming from weigh stations throughout the countryside.[115]

Combined with the growing use of automobiles by company fieldmen, these weigh stations made it easier for the companies to contract with farmers farther out in the countryside.[116] Although geography still limited the ability of the companies to contract with farmers statewide, much less regionwide— sugar beet was still a highly perishable and heavy crop that needed to be processed soon after harvesting—the weigh stations allowed the companies to expand the geographic boundaries of their industry outside the area immediately surrounding the factories. Now, when farmers in the heart of the sugar beet districts refused to sign contracts, the sugar companies had the option of simply looking farther afield to find others to take their place.

The ability of sugar companies to contract with farmers over a larger territory, combined with the solid front of the newly consolidated Michigan

Sugar Company, clearly helped to undermine the farmers' community-based, grass-roots militancy that had fueled previous battles. The MSBGA, which counted thousands of members and found ample opportunity for publicity in both local newspapers and the Gleaner's publications, nonetheless had a difficult time translating rhetoric into action, especially when sugar beet farmers feared there would be thousands willing to take their place. Increasingly, many farmers were unwilling to jeopardize the profits that came with growing even just a couple of acres of sugar beet. In this way, farmers lost their greatest bargaining chip—their willingness to abandon the sugar beet crop. Though most farmers still grew fewer than four acres, and although Michigan's farmers still ran their farms as diversified enterprises, many had come to depend on the sugar companies for cash advances and often needed the cash generated from the crop, which was as much as $50 to $55 per acre, to meet unpaid expenses.[117] The farmers' affiliation with and affection for the MSBGA, as evidenced by the Gleaner's status as the most popular farm organization in Michigan's beet growing counties in the early twentieth century, did not change the fact that many felt they could not afford to give up the sugar beet crop.[118]

Just as the farmers' calls to abandon the crop failed, so too did their plans to build cooperative sugar beet factories. Farmers found it impossible to create cooperative selling organizations, much less build their own sugar beet factories. They, like the sugar companies, could not bridge the boundary separating and uniting the factory from the field. Part of the challenge was financial, for to build a cooperative sugar beet factory would have entailed raising at least $500,000. To succeed, farmers needed support from townspeople and business elites, not to mention outside capitalists. And not surprisingly, townspeople were often unsympathetic to the farmers' calls for cooperative factories. In 1911 the editor of the *Tuscola County Advertiser* wrote that while "cooperative business enterprises are ideal in theory," the farmers' plan to build a cooperative sugar factory was an "idea too absurd for discussion." Grant Slocum, the leader of the Gleaner who publicly supported the idea of a farmers' cooperative factory, was even chastised for trying to stir up "class hatred" because he "hates the town of Caro." The paper warned farmers not to be manipulated by Slocum and reminded them that the sugar beet crop was responsible for paying off more mortgages and building more homes and barns than any other single crop.[119]

And finally, although the state may have seemed like the best institution to deal with farmer/factory differences, farmers found it difficult to gain more power by looking to the state as a potential ally. The sugar industrialists were not only able to spearhead the defeat of the 1911 Sugar Beet Bill, but they succeeded in putting forward a "compromise bill" to take its place that was more to their liking.[120] The 1913 bill, which was passed, made Michigan Agricultural College chemists responsible for "rules and regulations for the uniform weighing, taring and testing of all sugar beets raised in the state."[121] However, this act did not specify what powers Michigan Agricultural College possessed to regulate this industry. Nor did it provide any protection to farmers who questioned whether they could ever really depend on Michigan Agricultural College to act as a neutral factor. According to the farmers, the college's Board of Agriculture did not include any "real practical farmers" but was instead dominated by bankers, lawyers, elevator businessmen, and, worst of all, officers of the sugar combination, the men who are "farming the farmers."[122]

Conclusion

The farmers' charge that the sugar companies were "farming" them contrasts sharply with the future that the Michigan Sugar Company had envisioned when it first opened its doors in 1898. During that year, the company began a scrapbook to memorialize its founding and to document its history. Among the various stories and news clippings was one taken from an 1897 volume of the *Louisiana Planter and Sugar Manufacturer,* which touched on the relations between the farmers who grew the sugar beet crop and the manufacturers who processed it. The article warned that, "To make this new infant [sugar beet] industry healthy, the producer, the farmer, and the manufacturer, the capitalist, must not only act in accord, they must cooperate in good faith, and the one should not mis-trust the other. Both must be satisfied with mutual agreement and both must believe in equity."[123]

That Michigan's sugar company officials included the above clipping hardly proved prophetic, for in practice there was very little cooperation, much less good faith or equity, between the farmers and the factories during the first decade and a half of this industry. During these years farmers not only organized grower associations to demand more for their crop than the factories were willing to pay, they also went to great lengths to challenge their exclusion from the factories. Sometimes the farmers even waged strategically timed strikes. In response to the farmers' militancy, the sugar companies formed an organization of their own, sought out townspeople as allies, tried to buy land, and even threatened that they might shut the factories down altogether.

They also began building weigh stations to lessen their dependence on local farmers.

These conflicts are significant for what they reveal about the changing nature of capitalism in the countryside and the kinds of social relationships that new forms of industrial agriculture engendered. The very geographic interdependence of this industry—which agricultural professionals had hoped would foster cooperation and equity—instead provided fertile ground for farmers and companies to battle over what proved to be an elusive and ever-shifting boundary dividing and uniting the factories and the fields. And, not surprisingly, the contracts, which were supposed to mediate this boundary, became the embittered battle ground. Because most of the specific contract clauses involved stipulating where the farmers' rights and responsibilities ended and where the sugar companies' began, the contracts that agricultural professionals and townspeople hailed as a new phase in farming became the contested terrain between farmers and factories. However, it was not the mere existence of the contract that engendered disagreements, but rather the distinct relations of production embedded in the text of the contract. On the one hand, the contract symbolized and codified the close and inseparable link between the agricultural and industrial sides of production. On the other hand, it also functioned as a means of drawing a line to show where the agricultural side ended and the industrial side began. That the line between the agricultural and industrial sides of production had to be drawn showed farmers that the boundary separating and uniting the field from the factory was negotiable and contestable. This not only afforded farmers the opportunity to question the assumption that the manufacturing side of production—the processing of raw materials into finished products—was more important than the agricultural side of production, it also provided the means for contesting for control: the yearly ritual of signing contracts.

When viewed from the ground up, the history of the rise of industrial agriculture in rural Michigan is not one that easily fits into the grand narrative of the decline of family farming or the rise of agribusiness—two themes that are all too often presented in the historical literature as opposite sides of the same coin. The coming of the sugar beet industry did not undermine family farming; in fact, sugar beet became an important cash crop for thousands of family farmers and tenant farmers trying to climb the agricultural ladder. Moreover, even though the sugar companies had powerful allies in the agricultural professionals who staffed the United States Department of Agriculture and Michigan Agricultural College, they could not simply or always impose their will on the surrounding farmers. Rather in this case, the ties that bound the field and the factory—the fact that the companies depended upon surrounding farmers for an ample supply of sugar beet and the fact that the crop was simply too weighty and perishable to ship more than a few dozen miles—at times provided the farmers with a great deal of leverage. Although the industrialists had seemed to triumph by 1910, refusing to negotiate with the farmers and refusing to award higher prices, this was not an easily won victory. Nor would it prove to be permanent.

Sugar beet factory with farmers waiting to unload their wagons, Bay City, Michigan, 1901. Source: Charles F. Saylor, *Progress of the Beet-Sugar Industry in 1902* (Washington, D.C.: GPO, 1903).

Polish Women harvesting sugar beets, Saginaw, Michigan, 1901.
Source: Charles F. Saylor, *Progress of the Beet-Sugar Industry in 1901* (Washington, D.C.: GPO, 1902).

Eastern European migrant families, Carney, Michigan, 1922.
Source: Elton Brainard Hill, "Sugar Beet Culture," masters thesis, Michigan Agricultural College, 1922.

Typical sugar beet workers' houses and sugar company fieldman, 1922. Source: Elton Brainard Hill, "Sugar Beet Culture," masters thesis, Michigan Agricultural College, 1922.

Cartoon highlighting post—World War I contract battles, 1920. Source: *Michigan Business Farming,* February 14, 1920, p. 453.

"Help He's a Bolshevist." Source: *Michigan Business Farming,* March 6, 1920, p. 534.

"We Put Dollars in and Get Only Cents Back." Source: *American Sugar Industry & Beet Sugar Gazette,* 1910, p. 131.

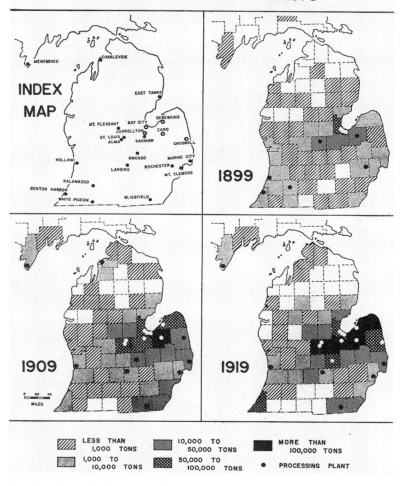

Sugar beet factory locations and production, 1899–1919. Source: John M. Ball, "Sweet Success: The Story of Michigan's Sugar Beet Industry," *Papers of the Michigan Academy of Science, Arts, and Letters* 45 (1960), p. 140. Courtesy of the Michigan Academy of Science, Arts, and Letters.

Mexican sugar beet worker standing in front of Michigan Sugar Company property, 1941. John Vachon, photographer. Source: Farm Security Administration–Office of War Information Photograph Collection, Library of Congress Prints and Photographs Division. Digital I.D.: 8c20146u.

Mexican woman and her children, 1941. John Vachon, photographer. Source: Farm Security Administration–Office of War Information Photograph Collection, Library of Congress Prints and Photographs Division. Digital I.D.: 8c20147u.

Mexican families in rural Michigan, 1941. John Vachon, photographer. Source: Farm Security Administration–Office of War Information Photograph Collection, Library of Congress Prints and Photographs Division. Digital I.D.: 8c20319u.

Mexican women standing in front of Michigan Sugar Company property, 1941. John Vachon, photographer. Source: Farm Security Administration–Office of War Information Photograph Collection, Library of Congress Prints and Photographs Division. Digital I.D.: 8c20320u.

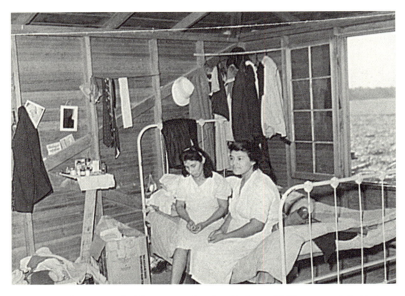

Mexican women inside company housing, Saginaw, Michigan, 1941. John Vachon, photographer. Source: Farm Security Administration–Office of War Information Photograph Collection, Library of Congress Prints and Photographs Division. Digital I.D.: 8c20321u.

Typical home for Mexican migrant family, 1941. Saginaw County, Michigan. John Vachon, photographer. Source: Farm Security Administration–Office of War Information Photograph Collection, Library of Congress Prints and Photographs Division. Digital I.D.: 8c20323u.

3

Family Farms, Child Labor, and Migrant Families

Company officials and farmers, who spent much of the first decade and a half of this industry battling over the relationship between the factory and the field, nonetheless found themselves in agreement on one fundamental issue: the need to find an appropriate labor force for this labor-intensive crop. Despite the numerous rhetorical assurances by company spokesmen that their industry would provide plenty of work for white Americans, the problem was not one of providing jobs for the unemployed but rather finding enough workers who would be willing to toil in the fields. In the first of his many sugar beet reports, even the ever-optimistic sugar beet booster Charles Saylor soberly admitted, if he were to ever write a history of the sugar beet industry, it would in large part be devoted to the "trying" and "vexing" experiences of the farmer and manufacturer at "arriving at a solution of this labor problem."[1]

At the time Saylor wrote this report, farmers throughout the country complained that agricultural workers were becoming more costly and harder to find. And in rural Michigan, the close proximity of urban centers to rural areas did make it especially difficult to attract and maintain a low-waged and dependent workforce. Farmers warned all who would listen that labor shortages might make it impossible for them to plant, cultivate, and harvest their crops. Local newspapers frequently carried stories about the "scarcity" of "desirable" farm help, with headlines like "Farmers Need Help," "Dearth of Farm Help," and "Plenty of Work and Labor Scarce."[2] A participant at the 1904 Michigan State Farmers' Institute even lamented how, "the labor problem is one of the greatest we have to solve, and it is the greatest item in our expense account."[3]

Though the cries of labor shortages often masked the farmers' real motive of finding cheaper workers, the labor question did prove especially vexing. The sugar beet crop required up to five times more labor power than the other crops farmers regularly grew, making it by far the most labor-intensive crop they might tend. And as was true with so many crops associated with industrial agriculture—like fruits and vegetables—sugar beet was not amenable to mechanization. In fact, the sugar beet crop required a great deal of patience, and attention to detail often counted more than brute strength. Equally important, the sugar beet season was extremely long, beginning sometime in April or May, when the fields needed to be "thinned," continuing periodically throughout the summer months, when the fields needed to be hoed and weeded, and winding down only sometime in late October or November after the last beets were "pulled" from the ground and "topped" with large knives. Besides being extraordinarily tedious and arduous—the workers had to toil much of the time on their hands and knees—the work was intermittent. The most serious problem confronting the farmer was that of finding a seasonal labor force that would be willing to begin working early in the spring, come back to the fields every few weeks during the summer months, and then finally return in late fall.

During the first few seasons, sugar beet industrialists adopted strategies that both reinforced traditional family labor while transforming the meaning of rural labor and rural community in radically new ways. Based on the hope that family farmers could handle the crop on their own, sugar beet industrialists encouraged them to do what many of them had always done—work together as a family in the fields. For those farmers who either could not or would not ask their wives and children to toil in the fields, industrialists suggested that they should try to hire women and children from local communities and nearby cities. It did not take long, however, before it became obvious that farm families and women and children would not be able to meet all of the labor needs of this exceptionally labor-intensive crop. In response, in late May 1901, just three years after the first Michigan sugar beet factory had opened its doors, the Peninsular Sugar Company transported a trainload of German Russian immigrant families from Lincoln, Nebraska, to the small town of Caro to "help" the farmers there. Other companies soon followed suit, and within a couple of years all the sugar companies made annual pilgrimages to cities throughout the nation to bring thousands of German Russians, Bohemians, Hungarians, and Poles to work in the fields as migrant farm laborers. Somewhat ironically, during the very same years that sugar industrialists sought to protect their industry from colonial sugar by arguing that their industry protected white farmers and white workers, they themselves were tapping into an international labor market for an ample supply of what they hoped would be a cheap and pliable labor force.

This chapter tells the story of how the sugar beet industry and family labor became both intertwined and internationalized during the early twentieth century by exploring the many forms of family and familial labor and hence the changing nature of rural labor itself. Doing so provides an opportunity to look critically at the perception of the Midwest as a place of family farms and hired hands where locals always worked hand-in-hand to make sure that the fields were tended. It also provides an opportunity to examine how ideas about class, gender, race, and residency transformed rural labor as industrial agriculture descended over the countryside. For though all those who toiled in the sugar beet fields tended to do the same tasks—weeding, thinning, hoeing, pulling, and topping beets—the meaning of the labor varied greatly for the farmers and farm families who toiled on their own land, the women and children who came to work for the day or the week, and the thousands of migrant families who arrived in the fields sometime in April or May and then left only after the last sugar beets had been harvested in October or November. By exploring these varied meanings, this chapter comes to terms with labor as the very fabric of a community in which ideas about race, class, and belonging could either create closeness and cohesion or distance and disdain. Solving the "vexing" labor problem, then, was never simply a matter of making sure that the sugar beet crop was properly tended to in the fields, but rather involved a much broader debate over the meaning of community in the industrializing countryside.

Family Farming and Commercial Agriculture

In many parts of the Midwest, commercial agriculture and family farming seemed to go hand-in-hand. This was especially true in Michigan, where most farms averaged fewer than ninety acres, and where commercial agriculture had often come in the form of labor-intensive crops like potatoes, green beans, and spearmint, which were not amenable to mechanization.[4] In contrast to midwestern wheat-producing states, where commercial agriculture often encouraged the exclusion of women and children from cash-producing crops, in Michigan farm men, women, and children continued to share most tasks, as they had done for decades. This meant that each family member was expected to do his or her part, whether that entailed feeding chickens, milking cows, picking beans, digging potatoes, or working long hours during the harvest.

The successive waves of "old immigrant" farmers who chose to make rural Michigan their home in the nineteenth and early twentieth centuries reinforced the importance of family labor. As late as 1910, Michigan ranked fourth nationally in terms of first- and second-generation immigrants residing in rural areas, with a rural population of 754,038 "native white stock" and 720,468 "foreign-born stock."[5] Many of these first- and second-generation rural immigrants, including a substantial number of German and Dutch farm families, practiced family labor, leading observers at the time to comment how the line dividing the work of men from that of women and children was even less clear in these families than in the native-born farm families living in the same areas.[6]

There were many advantages to relying on family labor in an agricultural economy increasingly dependent on commercial crops. For many of Michigan's farm families, both immigrant and native born, their ability to shift family workers to where they were needed allowed them to take part in the market culture around them while still maintaining significant control and autonomy over their farming practices. That is, by keeping work in the family, farm families were able to ease the transition toward a more commercially dependent agriculture while also making more money than would have otherwise been possible. Adopting a new crop, then, even one that was closely tied to commodity markets, did not necessarily undermine the independence of family farmers or lead to the dissolution of family laboring practices. In some cases, commercial agriculture not only depended upon but actually reinforced traditional family laboring practices.[7]

When Michigan's sugar beet companies first began contracting with farmers to grow sugar beet at the turn of the century, many company officials merely assumed or hoped that most farm families would tend to their own sugar beet crop. Sugar beet industrialists even explicitly described the sugar beet crop as an ideal one for family farmers looking to get ahead in a world of commercial agriculture. Speaking in front of Congress, Nathan Bradley of the Bay City Sugar Company lamented the financial challenges of small farmers who could "make scarcely a living" from grains because of falling prices. He then hailed the sugar beet industry as a way out of this economic dead end, claiming that farmers who raised a few acres would earn enough money not only to pay off debts and cancel mortgages but also buy goods that would improve their land, their buildings, and their homes, thereby making rural life "pleasant" for farm families.[8] Bradley's fellow sugar beet industrialist, W. L. Churchill, also publicized the sugar beet crop as a good one for families trying to make money in a world increasingly defined by commercial agriculture, describing how "the beet sugar industry requires not only the father and the mother, but the sons and the daughters and everybody they have round them to work in the beet fields; and the crop is a profitable one."[9]

Townspeople, who had so vigorously courted the sugar beet industry in the first place, did their part to encourage farmers to work their own families in the fields, even when it meant making children labor long hours, and even when this labor took place during the school year.[10] Newspapers regularly reported how families who did their own fieldwork could increase their profit margin by at least 50 percent because it cost $20 to $30 an acre to hire someone else to tend to a crop worth from $40 to $60 an acre. One newspaperman joked that "success in the sugar beets depends on first raising a sugar beet family," which he defined as "a family of ten or a dozen children about a year apart."[11] The *Alma Record* of Gratiot County went so far as to publish the names, acreage, and dollar earnings of the area's "most successful" sugar beet growers, along with photos of their homes.[12] The last photo in one of the stories featured "little Mamie Bickford," an eight-year-old standing waist high in a sugar beet field with a hoe clutched between her hands. The caption below her photo reassured the readers that though "her judgment in blocking beets with a hoe is far superior to many men," she is still "a little lady in every respect."[13]

During the first couple of decades, large numbers of farm families like the Bickfords did rely on family labor, thereby incorporating the sugar beet crop into their crop rotation without dramatically transforming their agricultural practices. From the first season in 1898 until World War I, anywhere from one-third to one-half of all farmers who successfully grew sugar beet for the factories kept all the work within their immediate families.[14] The family labor success stories so prominently reported by local newspapers, however, masked the fact that there were always equal if not greater numbers of farmers who either could not or would not grow this crop on their own.[15] Each year anywhere from one-half to two-thirds of all farmers growing sugar beet needed outside labor to help tend to their crop, leaving thousands of farm families with a severe labor shortage and the sugar companies with the threat of not garnering enough sugar beet to keep the factories running profitably.

Despite numerous signs that the labor question would become an important one, during the first couple of seasons, industry officials seemed unwilling to fully address the issue. They often underestimated the amount of work required and overestimated the ease with which farmers would be able to find hands to help them in the fields. Either way, many company officials assumed that the field labor issue was primarily the farmers' responsibility. Bay City sugar beet industrialist Nathan Bradley advised farmers anxious about meeting the labor supply to "just let it be known that a larger demand than usual will be made for help in a given locality, and the unemployed will find their way there. I do not think there will be serious trouble on that score. . . ."[16] In contrast to this kind of blind optimism, the USDA adopted a more cautious tone, warning that "it requires all the fortitude of a community to meet the first shock, when the revelation of the amount of labor to be performed in raising the beet first draw upon them [the farmers]." USDA officials pointed out how it took sixty to eighty hours "of the most tedious hard work" to thin an acre, and warned farmers that if they did not already have enough laborers in the fields, things would only get worse when they started growing sugar beet.[17] MAC professor C. D. Smith, an avid sugar beet booster, similarly advised farmers that because of the arduous, tedious, and intermittent nature of the work, finding an "army of field workers" would not be easy. He suggested to the farmers that before deciding how many acres to plant, they should make sure that "plenty" of help would be available to tend to the "customary" farm work as well as the sugar beet crop.[18]

Unlike other crops, then, sugar beet required large numbers of workers for relatively intense and short work periods over a six- to seven-month time span. In fact, farmers faced the prospect of losing their entire investment if not enough workers were readily available as needed. What farmers wanted, therefore, was an "army of workers" who could be called in at just the right time and hired as cheaply as possible.[19]

Finding a New Rural Workforce

Considering the regular use of hired hands in Michigan, this might have seemed to have been the most obvious first option for farmers who wanted to grow the crop but could not do all the labor themselves. The dearth of evidence regarding hired hands who worked in the fields, as well as the dearth of evidence regarding farmers trying to convince them to do so, provides an important clue as to how quickly sugar beet labor gained a reputation as hard, tedious, back-breaking, and unskilled work.[20]

Rather than view their labor as just a commodity to be bought and sold in the labor market, early twentieth-century hired hands expected agricultural labor to be part of an informal vocational education leading toward landownership. Moreover, many hired hands mirrored the families they worked for in terms of ethnic background, lived with the families for whom they toiled, and expected to be a part of the farm households economically, socially, and communally.[21] So even if hired hands had been offered work in the sugar beet fields, it seems unlikely that they would have tended to this new labor-intensive crop. It also seems unlikely that offers of high wages could have convinced them to toil on their hands and knees in what most saw as an unskilled, exceptionally demanding, and arduous dead-end job. Agricultural labor, like almost any other class of work at the time, had its own hierarchy, and rural wage workers resisted what they saw as a demotion of their status from farm laborer into beet weeder.[22]

Instead of trying to convince hired hands to work in the sugar beet fields, aspiring labor middlemen and sugar companies often tried to recruit unemployed urban men to toil on the land. In 1899, both the Alma Sugar Company and Detroit businessman J. C. Siven brought gangs of city workers to rural Michigan to weed, thin, pull, and top the crop for $15 an acre.[23] Businessmen living near the small town of Bath also recognized the labor shortage and saw this misfortune as an opportunity to make large sums of money. They formed the Bath City Sugar Association, which was supposed to find workers to tend to the beet fields of local farmers.[24]

Because urban industrial employment at this time was often seasonal, sugar companies and aspiring labor middlemen probably felt confident that they could lure urban men to work in the countryside for at least part of the year.[25] Recruiting city men to the sugar beet fields proved to be one thing; convincing them to stay was an altogether different matter. And almost immediately it became obvious that keeping these men in the fields would be impossible. One group of men from Detroit "disappeared at the first opportunity" when they realized the difficult and tedious nature of the work. J. C. Siven and the Bath businessmen also had a difficult time holding onto their newly recruited workers, who proved to be unpredictable, unreliable, and restless. When word of work in nearby industrial cities reached these urban men, they simply abandoned the fields en masse. The same forces that were pulling rural farm youth to the cities made it difficult for farmers to keep their urban counterparts in the countryside for any length of time.[26]

At the same time that men like Siven struggled unsuccessfully to keep their urban male workforce toiling in the fields, those who decided to recruit women and children, and more often just children, experienced a lot more success. During the first few years, farmers, businessmen growers, and sugar companies not only hired thousands of local children to work by the day, they also recruited large numbers of immigrant children from nearby cities. From 1900 to 1903, gangs of children from as far away as Detroit, Bay City, Saginaw, Lansing, Grand Rapids, Flint, and Ann Arbor regularly came to work in the countryside, some for just the day and others for weeks and months at a time.[27] In 1900, Alma Sugar Company superintendent F. R. Hathaway recruited three hundred boys from Grand Rapids to work in Gratiot County for fifteen weeks starting in early May 1900, promising that the farmers would pay them upward of $1 to $2 a day for doing "piece work." (Each boy was also required to pay $2.50 a week for room and board.)[28] In 1902 two growers recruited forty-five Polish girls from Detroit to work on their farm. They paid the girls a dollar for each day they worked in the fields and provided board during their country sojourn as well, housing them in two large tents near the Brookfield Presbyterian Church. The local newspaper described the girls as a "pretty lot of damsels who have rosy cheeks and sturdy appearances," commenting that "it is an inspiring sight to see these young ladies down upon their hands and knees pulling weeds and thinning beets with deft hands."[29] Just a year later, in 1903, the *Lansing State Journal* reported how an "army of small boys and girls" regularly crowded together in front of the city hall, waiting for farmers to come to take them out to the country for a day of weeding.[30]

The agricultural professionals who worried about the farmers' ability to meet their labor needs hailed the use of children (and sometimes women and children) as the ideal solution to what had emerged as a "vexing" labor problem. They even argued that women and children were particularly well suited physically for this work, belying the arduous nature of the toil. When Professor C. D. Smith of MAC testified before the Industrial Commission in 1901, he reported that the work was perfect for women and children who were "not strong enough to do the hard work of a farm, but able to do the light work—to thin, hoe and harvest the beets."[31] Industry representatives concurred. The Owosso Sugar Company, which hired large numbers of local children, justified the use of child labor by not only claiming that work in the sugar beet fields "is particularly adapted to child labor" but that it was "much easier for children than for adults."[32] J. F. Thissell, a fieldman for a Michigan sugar company, went so far as to maintain that the younger the children the better, for "the quicker movements of the younger ones [are] an advantage over the older, whose muscles are not so supple."[33]

Locals who supported the right of parents to work their own children in the fields also approved of the trend of hiring children to toil as wage workers, seeing little difference between traditional family labor and hiring children on an individual basis. Some communities even allowed sugar companies to recruit children directly from schools, keeping lists of potential workers.[34] Lax enforcement of truancy laws also made it likely that many children would work in the spring before schools were dismissed, and well-established "sugar beet vacations" for two to six weeks in the fall made it possible for children to work during harvest time.[35] To justify the tendency to pull children away from school when needed in the fields, one small-town newspaper described the weeding of sugar beets as a "bonanza for ambitious youngsters who are kept out of mischief and early in life learn the lesson that money does not grow on every bush."[36] Even urban newspapers sanctioned the use of child labor, with the *Lansing State Journal* admitting that "of course seeing the children carry their fathers' dinner pails, so small themselves that the pails almost touch the ground, is very strange," all the while reassuring its urban readers that the "children are said to work hard, have a good time and earn satisfactory wages."[37]

While urban readers may have felt comforted by assurances that the children who traveled to the countryside earned decent wages and had fun at the same time, some of the industrialists and farmers who spearheaded the effort to bring urban children to the fields preferred to view their labor-relations strategy as a philanthropic venture for those who would otherwise be confined to urban industrial "slums." That is, when recruiting large numbers of urban children, sugar companies and growers often claimed charitable motives. When Sanilac Sugar Company officials brought 125 boys, aged seven to fifteen, from Detroit's Home of the Friendless Orphanage to work on their experimental company farm in 1902, they tapped into the mythic association of agriculture and democracy by priding themselves on turning "waifs, orphans and homeless children from heartless parents, city slums [who were] on the general road to ruin" into "boy farmers" and "useful citizens."[38] To fulfill its philanthropic and civic venture, sugar company officials hired two women and the local reverend to oversee the "physical, spiritual, and moral welfare of these young urchins"; each of these adults was reported to have done so "as tenderly and loving as they could if they were their own children." Sugar company officials promised the surrounding community that they would maintain the strictest of discipline, not allowing the boys to use vulgar language or smoke tobacco. At the end of each season, the boys were paid $20 in cash, given a new suit of clothes, and put on a train back to Detroit.[39]

Notwithstanding the sugar companies' claims of charitable motivation, the line between economic advantage and philanthropy was always a slippery one. Ever since the mid-nineteenth century, urban reformers had looked to the countryside as an escape from the squalor, congestion, and moral decay of the nation's largest cities. That is, at the turn of the century it was still common to portray the countryside as a haven in a heartless industrial world.[40] However, in promoting sugar beet work for children as a philanthropic venture, farmers and industrialists failed to foresee that they had stigmatized sugar beet labor as an "unskilled" form of labor, not like real agricultural work. As was true in the urban industrial world, work performed by women and children was often characterized as inherently unskilled, less because of the nature of the work than because of the identities of those doing it. The claim that they had hired "idle" women and children also masked the productive roles of women and children, who were seen as a "reserve army" of laborers who would otherwise have had nothing to do.[41]

In reality, this "reserve army" of laborers turned out to be much less compliant or docile than the farmers and industrialists had hoped. Though most farmers believed that children made the best beet workers because of their "supple" backs and "nimble" fingers, actually getting the children to do the work often proved to be a difficult endeavor.[42] In addition to requiring a great deal of oversight, women and children sometimes demanded wages that rivaled, and at times even exceeded, the wages paid to adult male farm workers. In 1905, the Michigan Bureau of Labor and Industry statisticians estimated that hired hands earned an average of $27.06 a month, including board.[43] A number of the children who worked in the sugar beet fields made as much as, and occasionally more than, hired hands. For example, in August 1901, children who worked in the beet fields near the Marine City factory made upward of $1.75 a day.[44] Boys working near Owosso's sugar beet fields took home $1.50 a day.[45] In the town of Merill, farmer Archie McLeod paid two girls, both of them younger than thirteen years old, $13.69 for seven days' work.[46]

The reason for these high wages was really quite simple: a dangerous mixture of worker militancy and mobility. Whether paid by the hour, day, or row, women and children sometimes demanded higher wages. Testifying before the Industrial Commission in 1901, Professor Kedzie stated that farmers could hire women and children in Bay City to work for $4 an acre, noting that these "Pollacks" "are very efficient in doing that kind of work, and work very cheap."[47] His colleague at MAC, Professor C. D. Smith, told the commision a different story, recounting how the "Polish women" near Bay City, "adopted the American custom . . . and when they saw the supply [of labor] was limited they formed a combination" and raised their wages. He then described how women and children who were hired for 50 to 65 cents a day at the beginning of the beet season demanded anywhere from $1.00 to $1.50 a day by harvesting time. Similarly, when women and children working near Benton Harbor realized how valuable their labor was, they demanded $1.25 a day, free board, and dinner.[48] Women and children not only required more supervision than farmers were willing to provide, they could also be militant, demanding higher wages at the most inopportune times. Instead of solving the labor problem, this supposedly "docile" and "idle" reserve labor force had created new ones.

While some farmers would continue to hire local and city children well into the 1930s, even greater numbers began to look to the sugar companies to help them find a more reliable workforce that would stay put for the entire season. Farmers wanted stable workers who would not need to be supervised as closely as children. Farmers also did not want to have to pay workers more than first agreed upon, because to do so might translate into fewer profits or no profits at all. Because the farmers' greatest investment was labor, the threat of losing their workers at an inopportune time or having to pay them double or triple the amount of wages first promised, could spell financial disaster. Comparing the European and U.S. sugar beet industries, one sugar factory official noted that "with them suitable sugar beet land rents are very high and labor is correspondingly cheap, while with us the conditions are exactly reversed. Here the matter becomes almost entirely a question of labor, not of land."[49] By the start of the fourth season in 1901, the majority of sugar companies began to realize that if they wanted the farmers to grow enough sugar beet to keep their factories running full time, they could no longer rely exclusively on local solutions to the labor problem.

Migrant Family Labor

When Michigan's sugar beet companies decided to begin recruiting immigrant workers to the fields in 1901, there was plenty of evidence from surrounding states that using foreign migrant family labor might be the perfect solution. Sugar beet industrialists in Illinois, Indiana, and Nebraska had recruited immigrant families for years because, in the words of one Nebraska company official, "our success in developing an elaborate agricultural enterprise depends, in my opinion, largely upon our ability to collect these people, and especially those with large families."[50] In 1899 the general manager of the Illinois Sugar Refining Company described how the "Russian" families his company recruited from Nebraska to work in the fields were "attending strictly to their own business and doing that well." To house these families, all the company had to do was to provide tents, tables, and beds. Each family was also given a small garden plot to grow vegetables. The general manager admitted that the families worked long hours, often from fourteen to fifteen a day, and that every member of the family over the age of six actively worked in the fields. Yet he nonetheless claimed that this was a "healthful life" and that at the end of each season each family could expect to return to Nebraska with anywhere from $500 to $800 in hand and good clothes on their backs "looking hale and hearty."[51]

Various Michigan state officials supported the sugar beet industry's decision to begin recruiting foreign families from large cities as the basis of its field-labor force. Testifying before Congress in 1901, Michigan's secretary of state even went so far as to admonish his state for not taking the lead role in recruiting foreign families as farm labor, demanding, "we need thousands of families." He also outlined a racialized division of farming by noting how "the Polanders, and Russians seem to be the most effective" in the sugar beet fields while "Germans, Scotch [and] Hollanders" were preferred in "the higher grades of farming, such as dairying [and] fruit growing."[52] Though the state of Michigan would not take responsibility for recruiting migrant workers, it condoned and even commended corporate efforts to bring migrant workers into the state.

Even USDA officials, whom historians have chastised for attempting to undermine family labor, promoted the use of foreign families in labor-intensive agricultural ventures, and especially in the sugar beet fields.[53] In fact, the USDA agreed with urban reformers that the best way to address America's urban problems was to bring a number of the newest immigrants directly into the countryside as rural workers.[54] Charles Saylor recommended recruiting immigrant families who were "accustomed to the hard work and drudgery incident to growing sugar beets" and whose "entire families [worked] all day long in the beet fields."[55] Saylor claimed that in the cities only the fathers could find work, while in the beet fields these men could find work for their entire families.[56] He even went so far as to predict that the new immigrants who toiled in the sugar beet fields would be transformed from "ignorant, vicious, disease-infected classes" into future citizens. Celebrating the immigrant who bypassed the urban center to work in the sugar beet fields, Saylor insisted that in the countryside, the newcomer "acquires a good start in the world, and becomes qualified for the duties of citizenship. He and his family belong to the healthful, strong, industrial class, and soon adopt our customs, habits, ambitions, national pride, and interest, becoming excellent citizens."[57]

When Michigan's sugar beet companies began recruiting migrant families to work in the fields in the spring of 1901, just three years after the first sugar factory opened its doors, they were less concerned with Americanizing immigrants than dealing with the labor shortage confronting this new industry. For the first few years had been trying ones for Michigan's sugar companies. Farmers' worries that they could not make money growing this crop, combined with shock at the amount of work the sugar beet crop required, threatened to undermine what industrialists had hoped would be a profitable industry. A Detroit Sugar Company superintendent even linked farmers' protests with the question of labor, noting that the " 'overpersuaded' farmer is the man that loses money, gets into trouble and makes trouble for the factory. He cannot get help during the growing season, the company can do little for him, he is disappointed, and is not only hard to contract with the next year, but likely to create ill feelings among others."[58] Within just a few years, most sugar company officials had come to the conclusion that the only way they could assure a profit was to address all aspects of agricultural production—including the question of labor. Although many farm families would continue to toil in the fields and large numbers of farmers would continue to rely on child labor, growing numbers of farmers would come to depend on the sugar companies for an ample supply of labor each year. As a result, migrant family labor quickly emerged as the most important labor form in the sugar beet fields.

The rise of migrant family labor in the early twentieth century Midwest, then, was hardly some kind of preindustrial labor form that somehow managed to make its way into the modern era, or the result of poverty-stricken workers wandering the countryside in search of bread and a dry place to sleep. Rather, as historians David Montgomery and Gunther Peck have so eloquently argued, migrant labor is best understood as the product of the large modern corporations that played a central role in fostering and directing this inherently national, and even transnational, labor flow.[59] This was true in Michigan, for the creation of migrant family labor would have been impossible without the extensive resources of the powerful sugar companies. Each year, sugar beet companies spent thousands of dollars and traveled thousands of miles to places like Denver, Buffalo, New York City, Erie, Akron, Milwaukee, Toledo, Cincinnati, St. Louis, Cleveland, Philadelphia, Chicago, and Detroit—all cities where many of the nation's newest immigrants had settled—in search of migrant families who would be willing to come to the fields. Local newspapers reported on these recruiting drives with headlines like "Beet Workers Galore—Manager Martini Scours Country from Omaha to Philadelphia" to assure local farmers that their labor needs would be met.[60] In so doing, sugar companies tapped into a national labor market, which itself was created by the international flow of labor linking Old World Europe to the United States.

To induce immigrant families to come to Michigan, the companies advertised in foreign-language newspapers, put up posters on lampposts and park benches, handed out leaflets, and held meetings in stores, saloons, and on street corners, calling for families to come spend their summer working in the countryside. The companies' labor recruiters described sugar beet work as a family affair, promising high wages, free transportation, free fuel, free housing, clean running water, large garden plots, and generous credit lines at local stores.[61]

The sugar beet companies experienced so much success in their efforts to attract the nation's newest immigrants to rural Michigan that a child-labor reform advocate working for the National Child Labor Committee (NCLC) described this process as the annual spring "exodus of families from the foreign quarters of industrial centers to rural districts."[62] Each spring in the early twentieth century, somewhere between five and fifteen thousand workers traveled to Michigan's sugar beet towns, usually aboard specially designated sugar beet trains. For example, in 1902, the town of Sebewaing, population 1,431, saw the arrival of five hundred German Russians in April and another 472 German Russians the following month. The residents of Caro, population 2,006, saw two hundred migrant families enter their town in the spring of 1905. The same scenario was repeated in dozens of small communities throughout the state.[63] In 1911 one newspaper estimated that as many as five thousand workers arrived in the "Thumb" district over a three-week period.[64] In a matter of weeks, the demographic composition of rural Michigan changed dramatically, leading one newspaper to conclude that "there are today very few native white Americans who can be properly classified as agricultural laborers."[65]

For the sugar companies the arrival of thousands of migrant families promised to solve the labor problem that had riddled this agricultural industry ever since the first sugar factory opened in 1898.[66] This solution, however, also signaled a significant transformation in the sources and meaning of rural labor. In contrast to traditional hired hands who sealed their work arrangements with a shake of the hand or the nod of a head, migrant fathers were required to sign legally binding contracts. And these contracts were very specific and detailed agreements, stipulating not only that migrant families had to be available when called on to work, but the rates of pay, time of payment (three times during the season), and a hold-back clause for a percentage of each paycheck. Finally, the sugar company officials held onto the migrant families' return train tickets until the last beets had been pulled from the ground and topped.[67] As work commenced each spring, the companies demanded that both the workers and farmers sign these mutually binding agreements and refused to provide workers for farmers who would not do so.[68]

Though these contracts might seem to be simple legal documents, they in fact offer a window onto the changing forms of rural labor and the expanded role of corporations in supplying and determining the nature of that labor.[69] The companies included staggered payments and hold-back clauses in the contracts to limit the workers' mobility, to make sure that they would not leave the fields before all the work had been completed. The contracts were also designed to capitalize on the labor power of women and children. Companies recruited only large families and calculated the acreage based on the number of family members, though usually only fathers were mentioned in the contract, and usually only fathers signed on the dotted line. Women and child workers remained legally invisible. And finally, by transporting families hundreds and sometimes even thousands of miles from their homes, and holding their return tickets for them until the end of the season, the companies and farmers tried to create a disciplined and captive labor force. The main purpose of these labor contracts, then, was unmistakable: to create a controlled labor force bound by a legally binding agreement that was premised theoretically on the ideal of free labor but that in practice assured not only that most family members would work in the fields but that they would remain there over the long six-month season.

These contracts also ensured that the sugar companies would assume a great deal of control over the field-labor force. Although only the farmers and the migrant fathers signed the labor contracts, the sugar companies drew up the contracts, held them for safekeeping, and asserted the legal right to intervene should workers and farmers conflict. Furthermore, the sugar companies moved the migrant families from field to field as the crop developed and paid the migrant workers at the end of the season by deducting the funds from the farmers' own payments. And, because most migrant families worked for three or four farmers a year, the sugar company fieldmen arranged credit for migrant families at local stores and transported them from field to field as the crop matured.[70]

In contrast to the great care company officials took with respect to contracts, they expressed little interest in how to house the arriving migrant families. Certainly even under the best of circumstances, housing thousands of migrant families would have presented a significant challenge. In this case, however, neither the sugar companies who recruited the workers, nor the farmers on whose land they toiled, put much effort into coming up with plans to deal with this issue. In fact, housing the thousands of migrants was treated as an afterthought. When a German Russian woman by the name of Elisabeth Catherine Maser came to Michigan with her family in the early 1900s, the company placed her and her family in a migrant camp near some railroad tracks. The family was given a tent that was supposed to last them not only through the summer but also long into the fall. Although the companionship of living near other German Russian families eased the social isolation of migrant work, Maser's granddaughter later recounted how her grandmother suspected that "people thought of us as vagrants and tramps the years we traveled and lived in tents."[71]

In addition to tents, sugar companies and farmers housed migrant families in abandoned farmhouses, dilapidated tar-papered shanties, outdated barns, and specially built sugar beet "wagons" and "cottages."[72] One year housing came to such a crisis that one local newspaper encouraged the farmers to pressure school boards into leasing vacant school buildings for the summer migrants.[73] Migrant workers often had to endure extreme overcrowding and substandard living conditions including missing screens, windows, and doors. Long hauls to fresh water, sometimes more than a mile, aggravated these poor living conditions. Moreover, migrant families were often housed in hastily and haphazardly constructed "colonies" far from the locals in the community.[74] Undoubtedly, these varied housing arrangements must have reinforced the locals' perception that migrant families were a roving band of crop followers with minimal community ties, a newfound rural other.

A small handful of farmers expressed concern about these living conditions, not because they believed that the migrant workers deserved better, but rather out of fear that these families might not be willing to stay put. In spring 1906, just as the season was beginning, a farmer wrote an editorial to his hometown newspaper, signing it "Farmer with Experience," in which he urged his fellow neighbors to pay more attention to housing migrant families, arguing that it was necessary to provide "comfortable quarters . . . if we want them [the families] to stay." Noting the incessant complaints from his neighbors, who claimed they would plant more sugar beet "if they were sure of the help," this farmer responded by asking his fellow farmers, "What have you done? Simply kicked, or have you asked some man with a large family not to get too close to your farm for fear his unruly boys and chickens would commit some depredations." To stop the migrant families from abandoning the fields, this farmer suggested that his neighbors should provide good housing and "give your labor a suitable place for a small garden, and access to the fruit which falls to the ground and [would be] wasted otherwise."[75]

Housing, therefore, was not merely a matter of accommodation or geography. Rather, housing both symbolized and helped codify the status of migrant families within the larger community. And in this case, the geographic distance that separated migrant workers and farmers—as well as the dismal conditions in which migrants lived—provided yet another indication of the less tangible but no less important class and communal distance dividing migrant workers from the farm families for whom they worked.

"A Different People"

Just as important as the geographic distance separating migrant families from local residents were the supposed racial/national differences dividing the incoming new immigrant families from the native-born and old immigrant resident majority. That is, as new immigrant families arrived in the fields, they were greeted as both a class apart, because of the fact that they toiled in the fields by contract, as well as a people apart, for their presumed racial/national distinctiveness. This was even true for the German Russians, the first group to come to rural Michigan. From 1900 until 1910, German Russians came in such large numbers to Michigan that they were almost singularly identified with the sugar beet industry.[76] (By 1920, German Russians and their offspring living in Michigan numbered more than twelve thousand.[77]) Although the German Russians who came to Michigan considered themselves quintessentially German—during their long sojourn in Russia they maintained separate villages, ran their own schools, practiced their own religion, and continued to speak German—once they arrived in the United States they ran into a hierarchy defined by class, race, and nationality that denied their German background. Even while living in areas heavily populated by compatriots, German Russians had a difficult time asserting their German identity. Hattie Plum Williams, an early twentieth-century sociologist who studied this group in Lincoln, Nebraska, found that German Russians experienced "ignorance, prejudice, and misunderstanding" when it came to asserting their identity. "Many people who have lived in the city for years are ignorant of the fact that the mother tongue of these foreigners is German instead of Russian."[78] She also found that as the German Russians' class status rose, so too did their racial/national identity. "When a Russian German rises out of the ranks of the street sweepers, he is recognized as a

'German,' while the 'Russian' remains the lowest type of laborer."[79] Clearly, German Russians were marked as outsiders by a class- and racially-based hierarchy defined by what they did and where they had come from rather than how they defined themselves.

The same kind of assumptions about class and race continued to haunt the German Russians who migrated to Michigan, which may have seemed ironic to them because when these families first came to Michigan, the majority landed in the middle of the "German" section of the state. In Bay County in 1900, the heart of the sugar beet district, native-born Americans made up only 22.6 percent of the population, while the native-born with foreign parents made up 48 percent and the foreign-born white another 29 percent. Of the first- and second-generation immigrants, those with German ancestors were the overwhelming majority. In Huron County, where the Sebewaing Sugar Company was located, native-born whites made up only 12.9 percent of the population, while first- and second-generation foreigners, many of them German, made up 87 percent.[80]

Even though the resident immigrant farming population and the newest migrant workers shared a distant national past, these German American and German immigrant hosts did not see the newly arriving German Russian families as the newest generation of German immigrants—as compatriots to be welcomed—but rather as Russian beet weeders. As one German Russian woman recounted to her family, "In Russia, we, the German people, had been leaders and had been admired for our success and prosperity. Here in America we were considered stupid, ignorant, lazy, and dirty."[81] Equally important, throughout Michigan's beet districts, German Russian migrant workers were almost always referred to as "Russian," with little or no mention of their German background. Almost without exception, local newspapers announcing the arrival of the German Russians referred to them as "Russian." When Michigan sugar company officials began recruiting migrant families, they referred to this labor form as the "Russian Contract Labor System."[82] When farmers listed sugar beet labor as an expense, it was described as "Russian Labor."[83] And when the Michigan Sugar Company inventoried its properties in 1906, it described the shacks it built for migrant families as "Russian Cottages." Local newspapers reinforced the identification of German Russians with sugar beets by reporting that only "Russians Can Handle the Sugar-Beet Crop."[84] In 1908 a newly hired company fieldman even joked that once he started working he would "have to learn the Russian tongue."[85] The term Russian had come to mean more than a national destination—it reflected the supposed class and racial status of those doing sugar beet work. The class and racial identities had completely intertwined.

Though locals would continue to associate "Russians" with sugar beet work, and sugar beet work with the "Russians," as the migrant labor force became even more ethnically diverse in the 1910s, and especially after greater numbers of Bohemian and Hungarian families began coming to the fields, the terms "beet hunky" and "bohunk" came to be used to describe all of the various ethnic groups working in the fields regardless of national origin.[86] In this case, the issue was not that locals were ignorant about the various racial/national backgrounds of those who came to work in the fields. In fact, local newspapers often carefully identified the backgrounds of incoming migrants as they arrived. What is important is that the terms "beet hunky" and "bohunk," like the term "Russian," designated a common class and racial identity for those contract migrant workers who toiled in someone else's sugar beet fields. Economist Theresa Wolfson of the NCLC hinted at this association when she reported that the "average farmer looks upon his [sugar beet] help with contempt, probably because they are foreigners, but partly because of the work they do."[87] Her colleagues even more directly stated that "as a rule, the contract laborer occupies an inferior social position. He is slurringly called a hunkie."[88] After finding that many sugar beet migrants were "seriously sinned against by the community," the NCLC concluded that, "contract laborer families . . . are not integral parts of the community. They, parents and children, are strangers in a strange land. . . . They are only 'beet hunkies.'"[89] Frank Taussig, a critic of the sugar beet industry, described the Russian Germans toiling in the fields as an "inferior class" living in a "semiservile state," a condition he found "socially and industrially unwelcome."[90]

It is not hard to see that the heterogeneity of rural Michigan's immigrant population did not translate into ready acceptance for the migrant families who came to toil in the fields. In fact, distance and disdain much better describes the reception that migrant families encountered as they filed off the sugar beet trains and made their way to the fields. Viewing them as "indispensable outcasts," locals did their best to ignore and isolate the migrant families without insulting them to the point that they might not return the following year.[91] What emerged in rural Michigan was a kind of passive nativism, one based on a hope that migrant families would keep to themselves during the season and then leave after the crop had been harvested.

This passive nativism manifested itself most notably in distant relations between migrant families and the farmers who hired them. Farmers who contracted with the migrant families to work on their farms preferred to defer to the sugar companies when it came to transporting, housing, and even overseeing this mobile workforce. Most farmers felt little if any responsibility for the welfare of the migrant families who toiled on their land. (It took one sugar beet farmer a week before noticing that the migrant family of five he had hired to work in his fields had simply taken off.[92]) In contrast to the highly personal relations that many farmers fostered with their hired hands, most farmers expressed little if any interest in the well-being or welfare of these workers, leading the National Child Labor Committee to proclaim of migrant workers: "They are in the community but not part of it. They work for and with the farmers, but seldom enter into their home lives or have any social relationships with them."[93]

Much of what locals "knew" about migrant families they learned from their local small-town newspapers, which occasionally included accounts of migrant families in their pages. In contrast to coverage of local residents, which most often focused on such quotidian events as Sunday visiting, baseball games, and church dinners, migrant families were usually only included during extraordinary moments, such as crimes, tragedies, and untimely deaths. The message that emerged from these accounts was that migrant families were a people that might be pitied and sometimes feared, but not included as accepted members of the community.

During the first couple of years, it was not at all clear that this would be the case. Perhaps to alleviate fear about the annual arrival of thousands of migrant families, in 1901 local newspapers, such as the *Alma Record,* at first introduced migrant workers as "experienced beet growers" who had come to "help during the busy season."[94] When German Russians arrived in the neighboring town of Pigeon that same week, the newspaper there, the *Pigeon Progress,* reported how they "as a people" are "religious, industrious and natural tillers of the soil."[95] The following year, the *Sebewaing Blade* reported that of the 170 families who had come from Nebraska to work in the local fields, more than 60 percent had decided to remain in Michigan.[96] In addition to discussing the possibility that migrant families might stay, newspapers sometimes covered the migrant train ride up north, with the journeys in which migrant mothers gave birth on the road attracting the most attention. For example, after one "Russian" immigrant woman gave birth aboard the Pere Marquette train as it traveled from Nebraska to Michigan in 1902, Mr. W. H. Wallace, general manager of the Michigan Sugar Company, requested that the family name the girl Hermania Mueller Koch, promising the family a $25 gold piece in honor of their joyous event.[97] The following year, local newspapers celebrated the birth of three babies aboard the Pere Marquette, noting that the train was "making history."[98]

The "feel-good" accounts that dotted newspapers during the first couple of seasons did not last long and were soon replaced by more ominous reports about how the migrant families might not be doing the work they had been hired to do. Although the labor contracts were intended to create stable work arrangements, local newspapers told how some farmers were becoming concerned that migrant families were leaving them with substantial labor costs and little profit. As early as 1903, the *Pigeon Progress* recounted how growers in Huron County expressed displeasure with the "Russian" families the sugar company brought to work in their fields, alleging that the "Russians slighted [the work] to a great extent."[99] Just a year later, the *Tuscola County Advertiser* found that "the importation of Russians to this point from Nebraska last spring is not proving as satisfactory as formerly. . . . They are very independent and arbitrary in their actions and resent any attempt at dictation regarding the work. . . . When directed to use more care they are indignant and refuse to comply with the terms of the contract." The article then described how some farmers were even refusing to use the contract migrant families for fear that they were a "trouble breeder with the other help."[100]

Local newspapers also carried stories about how migrant families who took their labor contracts too seriously could be just as much trouble as those who did not, detailing how migrant fathers sometimes tried to sue the sugar companies and the farmers when they had not been given as many acres as they had been promised.[101] Some of these conflicts led to face-to-face confrontations. One such case took place in 1907, just as the harvest was to begin, when Hungarian beet worker Antoine Kretzler became frustrated that his former employer, John Berger, had not paid him his full wages for the previous spring. After a night of heavy drinking, Kretzler walked to Berger's house and demanded that he come outside to discuss the pay. At first Berger hesitated, for, as the local newspaper told the story, "he knew that Kretzler had not only been drinking, but possessed a large knife." After Kretzler promised to put the knife away, Berger came out and "instantly the foreigner grappled with him and in the struggle that ensued Kretzler got his dirk and stabbed Berger between two ribs just below the heart." Portraying Berger as the unlucky "victim of a murderous assault," the paper challenged the local community to track down Kretzler and give him "the punishment due."[102] In another case, with a much less tragic result, sugar beet worker Sluco Guronor and his "pretty Polish wife" insisted that they had not been paid what their contract promised, and demanded their employing farmer make up the difference. The farmer called in the Owosso Sugar Company fieldman, Arthur Carr, to settle the dispute. When Guronor and his wife asked Carr if they could take a look at the contract, Carr refused. At this point, Guronor pulled a gun on Carr, who finally handed over the contract for Guronor to review. When Carr reported the incident to the police, both Guronor and his wife were arrested and sentenced to sixty days in jail. Unfortunately, and rather suspiciously, the newspaper reporting the incident failed to mention whether Guronor had indeed been underpaid.[103]

Alongside stories detailing labor problems were more voyeuristic accounts describing family tragedies and untimely deaths, especially of young children. In these cases, local newspapers often demonstrated a fair amount of compassion for those who came to toil in the fields and who had lost so much in the process. Such was certainly the case for one "Russian" family who had come from Nebraska to rural Michigan in 1903. That summer, the mother had given birth to a son, whom she regularly brought to the fields with her. In late October, however, when the mother went to check on her son, she found that he had frozen to death. The *Sebwaing Blade* and the *Pigeon Progress* recounted the fateful events of that day without a hint of condemnation, noting instead that "to her horror [she] found that the little fellow had perished from the cold and exposure."[104] There was also a good deal of sympathy for the unidentified "Russian" parents who lost not one but two babies during the 1913 season. Without many resources, the young couple had paid undertaker George Atkins to bury the children, providing him $10 for each child. Atkins then proceeded to illegally bury the children in just six to eight inches of sand. When the children's bodies were discovered, the *Tuscola County Advertiser* headlined with the horrific announcement that "Babies Buried Few Inches in Sand." As soon as the facts emerged, Atkins was condemned by the community for his cruelty and greed while the unnamed "Russian" parents were pitied as unfortunate victims.[105]

The most common narratives locals encountered in their small-town newspapers were ones that highlighted how migrant families, like their urban counterparts, drank too much, brawled too often, and failed to conform to the middle-class standards of rural America. Although much of the potential anxiety about the annual arrival of thousands of migrant workers was alleviated by the fact that these workers came exclusively in family groups who were supposed to tend to their own needs, local newspapers periodically reminded their readers that even these family ties could not always ensure that the migrant population would keep to itself. Many of the stories carried the message that if migrant workers acted violently toward one another, they might turn this anger outward.

Newspapers ran stories detailing conflicts between and among migrant family members and fellow workers, especially those that violated sexual and gender norms of the day. In 1910, the *Tuscola County Advertiser* recounted how Polish beet worker Alex Sebedie assaulted fellow beet worker Paul Backsher's wife.[106] The following year, the *Pigeon Progress* followed the case of John Salz, a Hungarian beet worker, who was put in jail to await trial for sexually assaulting his own daughter.[107] Similarly, the *Pigeon Progress* advertised the case against sugar beet worker Martin Phester, who was arrested for assaulting a fourteen-year-old Hungarian girl who had come with her parents to work in the sugar beet fields.[108] Fights, especially those that took place after long nights of drinking, also made it to the front pages of local newspapers. More than one newspaper carried the story about how a "free for all fight" broke out among "Russian" beet workers near the town of Kilmaugh after a long night of drinking. The strife began when Conrad Roemer, an accordionist who was performing for the partygoers, refused to add to the collection plate for more "joy water." Following this affront, nearly everything and everybody in the place erupted, leaving the accordionist with "a serious cut to the head."[109] Two years later, in August 1912, the *Pigeon Progress* again reported how Sheriff McAulay was called in to put an end to a "Russian beet weeder" party, which had turned into a near "riot." When McAulay arrived to break up the party, he himself became the victim of a flying bottle and ended up with a nasty cut to the head.[110]

In the most sensational and widely reported case of this era, an entire community of beet workers came under suspicion. On April 30, 1912, 280 Hungarian families boarded trains from Cincinnati headed to the sugar beet towns of Caro and Croswell. That same day in Cincinnati, two young boys, aged four and six, disappeared after walking into the Hungarian section of town trying to find their father's workplace. After they failed to return home, police assumed that they had been kidnapped by a Hungarian family heading north to Michigan's sugar beet fields. Relaying the events of that fateful day, the *Washington Post* described how the "neighborhood was searched, and then came the stories of children being seen with the Hungarians who departed for Michigan about the time the Nichols children disappeared."[111] The story then played out like a modern-day captivity narrative, with the Hungarian beet weeders playing the role of captors and the boys the vulnerable victims. The *Tuscola County Advertiser* headlined its weekly edition with the frightening warning: "Kidnapped Children in County." Immediately, hundreds of people began searching for the boys while others reported "sightings," including one man at a train station who claimed to have seen "two such boys with a small woman, evidently a foreigner, on a train going to Toledo." Though this lead was soon proven false, Michigan Sugar Company fieldman Henry Martini promised to conduct a complete search of his migrant families in hopes of finding the missing boys. Even the father of the young boys headed to Michigan to assist in the search for his missing sons.[112]

After Martini and the boys' father searched through the Hungarian beet shacks, the latter returned home only to discover the lifeless bodies of his young sons in the feedbox of a wagon. Apparently, when the boys could not find their father at work, they decided to play in the feedbox and were suffocated when the heavy lid and clasp slammed shut. As the family mourned the untimely and tragic deaths of their young sons, The *Tuscola County Advertiser* reported that "all suspicion pointing to beet workers of the Michigan Sugar Company was cleared away."[113]

Although these newspaper accounts can be read as anecdotal pieces of evidence—for all contemporary newspapers carried stories of labor conflicts, murders, sexual assaults, drinking brawls, and kidnappings—they also point to the lowly status of migrant families within rural Michigan. If we understand small-town newspapers as collective biographies, in which the boundaries of community and cohesion as well as difference and distance were regularly drawn, the status of migrant families becomes much easier to see. Unlike local residents, whose daily joys and tragedies were regularly memorialized, including births, weddings, graduations, dinners, and visits, migrant families were usually only included during truly extraordinary events—including drinking brawls, physical assaults, tragic deaths, and suspected kidnappings. In this way, local newspapers acted as a public forum in which proper definitions of behavior were established, insider/outsider identities were maintained, and community boundaries were continually constructed and reconstructed. And this "forum" reminded migrant families that they were, in the words of sugar beet worker Elisabeth Catherine Maser, "a different people."[114]

Migrant Strategies

Though local residents tended to view all migrant workers as indistinguishable, the migrant families who toiled in Michigan's sugar beet fields did not see themselves as degraded beet hunkies. Often hailing from the same regions in the Old World as well as ethnic neighborhoods in the New World, many of the groups who worked in Michigan's sugar beet fields did their best to maintain and build on their national and ethnic ties while working and living in rural Michigan. This would not always be easy. When migrant families first arrived, they did not find large numbers of eastern European ethnic enclaves in the countryside. This was a countryside dominated by the native-born and old immigrant groups, with the Yankees, Germans, and Dutch clearly dominating rural spaces.[115] As such, the permanent institutions that historians usually associate with ethnic communities—schools, churches, unions, mutual aid societies, and political organizations—had yet to be built. Moreover, most families labored in relative isolation from other families, thereby missing out on the shared work spaces that those working in urban industrial establishments often used as a basis for community organizing. All this does not mean that community did not exist. Rather it is essential to identify the outlines of a community that was mobile and seasonal.

Ironically, the haphazard housing practices of the sugar companies and farmers provided some migrant families greater latitude to carve out their own ethnic clusters as they scrambled for housing for themselves. Some families would find themselves housed in the open countryside far from any neighbors, much less compatriots. Others were either placed next to or chose to live near other families from the same Old World backgrounds. As a result, there was a great deal of ethnic clustering in the countryside. The 1910 manuscript census, taken in early April, reveals that many migrant families who had either just arrived or who had "wintered" in the countryside often resided near other families of the same ethnic background. In many cases, two to five families lived as neighbors in the open countryside, with some of these households including grandparents, parents, and children sharing the same homes or living nearby.[116]

In addition to these small ethnic clusters, some migrant families lived in larger well-defined ethnic enclaves almost completely dominated by compatriots. For example, almost all of the thirty migrant families living together in 1910 in a small colony in Columbia Township, Tuscola County, had come from the Austro-Hungarian Empire. Twenty-six of the families identified themselves as Hungarian Maygars, while the other four described themselves as German Hungarians. All but five of the families had immigrated to the United States since 1900, with the vast majority having come in just the past two years. In Sebewaing Township, located in Huron County, an enclave of thirty migrant families included twenty-two German Russians, five Hungarian Germans, and two Germans. In nearby Brookfield Township, census takers stumbled across another migrant colony, this one with fifty-four households. Though this colony was more ethnically diverse, with twenty Hungarian German families, seven German Russians, five Bohemians, two Hungarian Romanians, and a mix of other nationalities, within the colony the different ethnic groups tended to reside next door to others of the same background. Over time, some of these migrant enclaves developed into well-known ethnic centers, identifiable by pejorative national slurs. Just two miles outside the Blissfield sugar factory, so many Hungarian migrant workers lived there that it became known as Honkey Town.[117]

These migrant enclaves provided a sense of community identity and solidarity to the migrant families who called them home. Much of the interaction involved visiting for meals and drink.[118] A German Russian woman who worked in the Nebraska and Kansas fields before traveling to work in Michigan later told her family about her days as a migrant worker living in tent colonies. She recounted having "a good time talking" with the other women, noting that "it was fun singing and dancing around the campfire at night." They usually sang songs about their "German Russian Motherland" for "Who would want to sing about backbreaking work in the sugar beet fields?"[119] Migrant families also gathered during the frequent long lulls in sugar beet work to celebrate births and marriages, thereby reinforcing the ethnic ties that brought them to the fields in the first place. Wedding festivities were usually planned so as not to interfere with weeding or harvesting and were usually held outdoors so that all who were invited could come. Sometimes the festivities lasted for days at a time.[120]

Just as migrant families refused to define themselves as beet hunkies, neither did they think of themselves as part of an aimless migrant stream, meandering from field to field with little purpose. In fact, when National Child Labor Committee investigators asked migrant families why they had come to the fields, and why they traveled back and forth year after year, the majority of the men and women responded that the fields offered opportunities not available elsewhere. They pointed out how family labor allowed them to make the best use of their most valuable resource—the labor power of all family members—and that the close proximity to urban centers offered industrial work for migrant fathers during the winter months.[121] Moreover, for most families, this was their second, third, fourth, or fifth season working in the fields and many planned to return the following year.[122] Many of these immigrants used summer work in the fields as a way to tide them over until better-paying industrial work became available or until their children were too old to work in the fields. Others hoped that they might be able to buy land someday and farm on their own. In either case, by working all family members in the fields, and by moving between urban/industrial work and rural/agricultural labor as opportunities arose, migrant families created opportunity out of exploitation.

Creating opportunity, however, would not come easy.[123] The work itself, which agricultural professionals described more like an intense form of gardening than regular farm work, was a particularly taxing kind of labor. During the early spring, when the fields needed to be thinned and hoed, men and women could be found hunched over the crop for hours at a time. As soon as weeds started to appear in spring, and periodically throughout the summer months, men, women, and children had to get down on hands and knees, carefully pulling the weeds to make sure they did not disturb the developing crop. Harvesting in the fall involved pulling the heavy sugar beets from the ground and cutting off the tops (topping them) before loading them into nearby wagons. Because sugar beet was a persnickety and perishable crop, each stage of the work had to be done on time and quickly, regardless of weather conditions, which varied from hot temperatures in the summer to driving rain and sometimes even early snows by late fall.[124]

The family labor system placed special burdens on migrant women, who not only had to make sure they completed their fieldwork in a timely fashion but also that their children, some of whom were as young as six and seven, did so as well.[125] Women did their best to fulfill their mothering roles by bringing their youngest children to the fields, and letting the younger children run around and play while trying to do their best to keep an eye on them.[126] Women also tried to combine their roles as workers and mothers by bringing their infant children, some just a few weeks old, with them to the fields. To protect the infants from the weather, which could be quite hot in summer and near freezing in the fall, mothers brought mesh netting, baskets, boxes, blankets, and tents.[127] And finally, migrant women often returned to the fields soon after their babies had been born. One woman, a mother of six children under the age of fourteen who lost two babies while working in the beet fields, bemoaned that she "Quit beets in November, in two weeks baby born—cry—cry—all the time then die." However, this woman realized the difficulty of her position. "If me don't work, what eat, guess hard work won't kill me."[128]

In addition to working in the fields and fulfilling their numerous roles as mothers, migrant women faced the challenge of trying to keep their families fed without losing all their unpaid wages to local creditors.[129] Though migrant families made up to two-thirds of their purchases on credit, many women attempted to escape the credit cycle by growing as much food as they could on small garden plots.[130] In fact, Children's Bureau investigators estimated that 88 percent of migrants had gardens, 60 percent raised their own chickens, and 41 percent even had cows.[131] The fruits and vegetables women raised, as well as the chickens and cows they tended, greatly enhanced their families' diets. Equally important, these gardens translated into more savings for families when they left the beet fields. When the line separating poverty and exploitation from opportunity and mobility was so thin, these seemingly mundane acts take on added significance.

Just like their wives, migrant men also assumed multiple roles in order to create opportunity out of exploitation. The "traditional" agricultural ladder, whereby rural men moved from hired hand to tenant farmer to landowner, often buying or inheriting land from landed family members, was not a possibility for migrant men. Migrant men who came to rural Michigan were hired as contract laborers, not hired hands, and they tended to work for farmers of different racial/national backgrounds than their own. Moreover, migrant families were not part of long-standing rural communities. As such, they could not look to local economic institutions for help. Instead, migrant men had to create their own agricultural ladder out of the resources available to them—contract family labor, rural wage labor, and urban industrial work.

Migrant men played an integral role as the heads of their families. They signed labor contracts with the sugar companies and as such represented their families legally. Migrant men also put in long hours tending to the sugar beet crop, working alongside their wives and children. When not working in the fields, for sugar beet work included long lulls that lasted for weeks, migrant men pursued other farm labor to bring in as much money as possible, with almost all finding additional wage work during the long sugar beet season.[132] During the winter months, when most families traveled to urban homesteads or nearby cities, men tended to take whatever work they could get. Of the 282 men the Children's Bureau interviewed in 1919, only nineteen failed to get winter jobs.[133] That same year, 120 of the 133 migrant fathers the NCLC interviewed had employment during the winter months.[134] These facts led even the highly critical NCLC to admit that many migrant families were "high grade immigrant laborers who had migrated to the beet fields in an honest search for work and an earnest desire to better their economic conditions."[135]

This desire for upward mobility ultimately led most migrant families to settle in urban ethnic enclaves as higher-paying jobs became available or after their youngest children left home. For most, then, the transition from migrant families to urban industrial immigrants took place only after years of moving between rural and urban labor, toiling in the fields, and patching together whatever industrial income they could. Other migrant families, and especially German Russians and Bohemians, were able to use sugar beet labor as the first step of an agricultural ladder.[136] This, however, was far from a conventional agricultural ladder. The families that managed to create a stake on the land did so by renting small farms and growing cash crops, like sugar beet, that allowed them to maximize labor power and minimize landed and mechanical resources. Most of these families also continued to toil as wage laborers in other people's fields, thereby continuing the family labor strategies that had brought them to the fields in the first place. And finally, a large number of the landed new immigrant families who rented and bought land still returned to urban industrial work during wintertime and temporary emergencies to make sure they could make ends meet, thereby continuing to blur the boundaries between landed farm family and hired wage labor.[137] Though the sugar companies had initially recruited migrant families as a way to create a seasonal class of field toilers, at least some migrant families were able to carve out their own distinct version of the agricultural ladder.

At first glance, the fact that significant numbers of migrant families ended up settling in rural Michigan appears to confirm the optimistic predictions of men like Charles Saylor, who had hoped that immigrants who found themselves in the countryside would become assimilated Americans and hearty citizens. A closer look at the settlement patterns of the new immigrants, however, reveals that even those who managed to create a foothold on the land were not, thereby, somehow magically transformed. Rather, most immigrants lived in small ethnic enclaves where they remained distant from the native-born and old immigrant majorities and reliant on fellow compatriots, using shared work, shared faith, and a shared sense of the past to bind them together.[138] As such, when Michigan State sociologist John F. Thaden studied Michigan's ethnic groups, he concluded not with a celebration of Americanization but with the recommendations that, "Rural Michigan could serve as a convenient laboratory for the study of 'Little Europes,' of little nations within a nation, for studies of traits and characteristics of transplanted Europeans."[139]

Conclusion

When writing about the relationship between gender and capitalism in the countryside, historian Nancy Grey Osterud noted that "One of the fundamental questions about agriculture in advanced capitalist societies that economic historians rarely ask is why, how and under what circumstances family farms persist, conducting specialized, market-oriented operations in a fully capitalist context rather than being replaced by corporate enterprises employing managers and wage laborers."[140] This chapter has attempted to start to answer that question, beginning with the assumption that if we really want to understand how industrial agriculture affected gender, class, and race relations and hierarchies, as well as community boundaries, we need to look not only at farm families but also at the migrant families who, over the course of the twentieth century, became an essential part of many rural economies. When we do this, we find that family labor had more than one meaning. Most important, we find that the relationship between industrial agriculture and family labor was more complex than one might initially suspect.

In the case of the Michigan sugar beet fields, the decision to recruit migrant family labor did not signal the mere extension of the traditional family labor system that had long characterized Michigan agriculture. Though farm families and migrant families often did the same tasks—weeding, thinning, pulling, and topping sugar beet—the meaning assigned to those tasks, and the larger context in which they were performed, varied greatly. Farm families who both grew and tended their own sugar beet crop usually did so on a limited basis. It was impossible to specialize in this cash crop because it had to be rotated with other crops. Therefore, even when farm women and children worked in the fields, it was never their primary agricultural occupation but rather a bitterly resented drudgery. In contrast to the hypothesis that family labor and industrial agriculture conflicted or coexisted uneasily, in this case, family labor made industrial agriculture possible.

When the sugar companies began recruiting migrant families to work in Michigan's sugar beet fields, they sought to create an entirely new labor form. They did not see migrant family labor as a new manifestation of the kind of family labor that had long taken place on family farms. Instead, the companies turned to new immigrant families with the goal of creating a captive, controllable, and compliant labor force. They wanted workers who would be willing to stay in the fields during the long season and not look for better-paying jobs in nearby industrial cities. They wanted workers who would keep to themselves. They wanted a vulnerable yet stable workforce. Recruiting thousands of migrant families to the fields, therefore, was never just a matter of solving the field-labor problem. Rather the arrival of thousands of new immigrant families as migrant laborers each year marked the creation of a new rural other defined by class, residency, and race. In this way, the sugar beet industry helped to both proletarianize and internationalize the rural agricultural labor force.

This was not a proletariat without options. The geography of the Great Lakes region—the close proximity of numerous industrial cities and rural surroundings—made it possible for migrant families to move between seasonal agricultural labor and urban industrial work. Furthermore, the seasonality of sugar beet work, and the unpredictability of much urban industrial employment, made it necessary for migrant families to shift between the urban and rural sectors. What commentators at the time, and historians since, have too often described as pointless wandering reflected the macroeconomic fact that urban and rural America were more intertwined than most historians tend to recognize, and that the men, women, and children who traveled between the countryside and the city, just like the products that shifted between them, linked these two sectors together. By moving between agricultural work and industrial employment, the migrant families who settled in urban areas, as well as those who made homes in the rural environs, created opportunity out of exploitation.

4

Farmers and the Great War

After the United States formally declared war in April 1917, Michigan's rural population eagerly joined the war effort. Many small towns sponsored Liberty Loan Drives and abandoned German-language classes in their schools.[1] The Gleaner, the most popular farm organization in the state, supported the war by selling "Gleaner Patriotic Bonds" and sending bronze medals to its "boys" on the home front. Gleaner girls dressed in red, white, and blue performed military drills to express support for relatives and friends abroad.[2] Even businesses joined in the mobilization effort, with the German-American Sugar Company changing its name to the Columbia Sugar Company to show that it, too, supported the U.S. war effort. World War I seemed to usher in an era of unparalleled community cohesion and cooperation—anything to win the war.

Despite these numerous examples of cooperation and conformity, the story of rural Michigan during World War I was also one rife with conflict. Over the course of the war and the immediate postwar years, sugar beet farmers and industrialists engaged in a series of battles that easily dwarfed those of the earlier part of the century. In 1917 and 1918, farmers demanded higher prices and warned the companies that unless they cooperated they would simply grow other crops, leaving the companies with multimillion-dollar factories and no raw product to process. In 1920 and 1921, farmers mobilized again, this time to force the sugar companies to share in the postwar price boom, or the "dance of millions" as it was known in Cuba, as the price of sugar reached historic highs.[3] Clearly, the sugar beet farmers, who had suffered a decade of defeats, saw the wartime as an opportune moment to force the sugar companies back to the bargaining table.

Although these conflicts might at first appear to be a mere repeat of earlier battles, the wartime context had changed everything. Wartime inflation, which translated into rising prices for all agricultural goods, provided farmers with the kind of leverage they had not possessed since the earliest days of this industry. Just as important, the state, which up to this point had acted mostly as a booster, now began to intervene in farmer/factory disputes to make sure that the nation's sugar bowls would not go empty. Wrapping their intervention in the rhetoric of wartime nationalism, state officials, ranging from members of Michigan's state legislature and the governor of Michigan to the head of the U.S. Food Administration, pleaded with both farmers and industrialists to put their own private interests to the side and support the larger public good by producing as much sugar as possible.

Rather than placate the farmers, the state's intervention spurred them to make even greater demands, for sugar beet farmers responded to the government's call to increase production with their own demands for "union" recognition and government intervention in the rural economy on "their side." Borrowing from the labor movement's arsenal of rhetoric, some even started to call for a form of "industrial democracy" for the countryside, arguing that the state had a responsibility to make sure that the agricultural side of the economy, and the farmers who made it possible, would not be ignored. To justify their militancy during wartime, farmers usurped the patriotic rhetoric of the era, claiming that they were the true "soldiers of the soil" while the sugar manufacturers were "sugar czars," "sugar autocrats," "sugar kings," and "sugar kaisers." Likening themselves to soldiers fighting for democracy abroad, farmers insisted that the state had a responsibility to make sure that the market functioned as democratically as possible at home.[4]

This quest to democratize the economy took place locally, in the fields and at the factories, as well as nationally, as farm groups across the country grappled with the meaning of the war and the reconstruction that they hoped would follow the cessation of hostilities abroad. Although historians have long pointed to the Populist movement of the late nineteenth century as the last great example of "agrarian democracy," progressive and radical farm organizations during the war saw this time as an opportune one to remake modern industrial America. Because so much was at stake, and because no one farm organization could legitimately claim to represent farmers nationwide, a number of competing farm organizations vied to become *the* national farm organization. In the ensuing contest, radical and progressive farm groups, including the Non-Partisan League and the less-well-known Farmers' National Council, of which the Gleaner was an important affiliate, called for farmers to join hands to push the federal government to reign in monopoly capitalism and level the economic playing field so that agriculture could be duly rewarded. By war's end, these farm groups would find themselves challenged by conservative farm organizations, best represented by the newly formed American Farm Bureau Federation, which questioned the principles of their progressive adversaries and offered their own conservative, big-business–oriented agenda.

"Forget Profits"

The outbreak of war in Europe in 1914 ushered in a period of unparalleled prosperity and profits for domestic sugar producers. For nearly two and a half years before the United States joined the Great War, Michigan's sugar beet industrialists reaped incredible benefits from the interruption of normal trade practices and the destruction of the European beet sugar industry.[5] Between the years 1913 and 1916, the price of refined sugar in the United States jumped from five to nine cents a pound.[6] These spiraling prices, combined with the ever-present possibility of a sugar shortage, translated into phenomenal profits for U.S. sugar beet companies. As early as November 1914, one farm journal predicted that Michigan's factories would "make hundreds of thousands of dollars this year" because of the war overseas.[7] This trend continued throughout 1915 and 1916 as the price of refined sugar, and hence corporate profits, reached all-time highs.[8]

The steep rise in company profits had an unintended though not wholly unpredictable effect—it enraged Michigan's farmers, who saw none of those profits coming their way. As late as 1916, the vast majority of Michigan's sugar beet growers were still taking home $5 a ton for their sugar beet crop—the same rate they had been making since 1905—while sugar companies saw the price for refined sugar nearly double.[9] The flat-rate contracts, which had been hailed as a way to protect farmers from the vicissitudes of the market, now cut farmers out of the loop as the market turned into a bonanza. Publicizing this inequity, The Gleaner proclaimed that sugar company profits had been made "at the expense of many a poor grower who lost hard earned dollars."[10]

To recoup some of these dollars, in 1917 Michigan's two largest farmer organizations demanded a share of the rising profits, with the Grange calling for $8 a ton and the Gleaner threatening not to settle for anything less than $10.[11]

Pointing to the fact that almost all prices for agricultural goods had spiraled upward, both farm groups warned that unless the companies doubled the price for sugar beet, they would simply begin growing other crops.[12] Both groups also highlighted that while the value of the farmers' lands equaled the value of the capital invested in the companies' factories, the former could be used to grow a variety of crops, while the latter would sit useless without an ample supply of sugar beet.[13] That is, the farmers' "capital" was more flexible and could be used to grow various crops, while the multimillion-dollar factories were limited to one use—processing sugar beet. Knowing "that they have been ignored in a co-partnership in which they are the principal factor," farmers hoped that geographic interdependence in an era of high farm prices would give them the upper hand for the first time in more than a decade.[14] They promised "war" if the sugar companies refused to cooperate.[15]

Sugar beet company officials, who had staved off farmers' demands for more than a decade, were not about to give in so easily. In spite of the fact that overall acreage in sugar beets had dropped from 122,000 in 1915 to 99,619 in 1916, company officials refused to talk with either the Grange or the Gleaner, much less recognize either organization as the bargaining representative of the farmers.[16] Clinging to the idea that farmer/factory disputes represented a private affair, they even rebuffed the efforts of Michigan Agricultural College professor R. C. Kedzie, who repeatedly tried to arrange a meeting so that the farmers and the companies could reconcile their growing differences.

In previous years, the companies' refusal to bargain with the farmers would have garnered relatively little attention from those outside the sugar beet districts. This defiant stance in a wartime era, however, drew the ire of public officials from Lansing all the way to Washington, D.C., who believed that the sugar companies should share their profits with the farmers. In December 1916, Fred Warner, Michigan's former governor, chastised the companies for their greed, commenting that the sugar beet growers "gave of their time, the use of their land, and all the profits to the sugar companies this year."[17] Just a few months later, in April 1917, state representative Sheridan Ford became so incensed about the companies' refusal to bargain with the farmers that he called for the state legislature to appoint a commission to investigate the growing and marketing of sugar beet, as well as the relations between the farmers and the factories more generally. He hoped that his proposed commission would be able to force the sugar companies to open their books so that "a reasonable and fair market price" could be established.[18] Clearly, Ford's resolution threatened to undermine the manufacturers' autonomy well beyond this current dispute. Never before had the state attempted to intervene in a farmer/factory dispute so boldly.

Although Ford's resolution went down to defeat in the state's conservative senate, the fact that the resolution gained as much support as it did revealed that as the war loomed on the horizon, Michigan's sugar companies lost their ability to treat farmer militancy as a private affair. What happened in the fields was increasingly viewed as a matter of national significance and not just private profits.[19] This was certainly the perspective of Michigan's governor, Albert E. Sleeper, who stepped in after the demise of Ford's resolution. To end the dispute, Sleeper invited high-ranking sugar company executives to his office for an emergency meeting, telling the executives that he himself was under pressure, having "just received a telegram from Washington asking what our resources are." Drawing on the patriotism spreading across the nation, he challenged the executives: "I do not want to say that because of differences between the sugar beet growers and the manufacturers we are not going to be able to produce our fair share." Sleeper also reminded the executives that in the previous year many farmers had "lost heavily" when growing sugar beet. He then urged them to "forget profits and, thru your patriotism, accede to the demands of the growers, and give them the price they are asking."[20]

Less than an hour after this meeting, the sugar men agreed to pay $8 a ton, the first price increase in more than a decade. However, sugar executives were quick to tell the public that this concession represented an act of sacrifice during extraordinary times and not a new phase in farmer/factory relations. "We desire to do our patriotic duty every time," the sugar companies announced. "We have yielded to the request of Governor Sleeper, altho we are frank to say, it was only because it was the Governor who asked it and the grounds upon which he put it that we have determined to yield."[21] Cloaking their statements in patriotic ideals, sugar executives refused to admit that this was a defeat for them or a victory for the growers. Equally important, the executives insisted that their concession was not the result of negotiations with the growers or recognition of their organizations but rather a unilateral gesture of generosity and self-sacrifice during exceptional circumstances.[22]

In spite of the manufacturers' refusal to admit defeat, and the fact that the growers had not been included in the governor's deliberations with the sugar executives, the growers immediately claimed victory.[23] Offering their own version of events, they contrasted their own just cause with the "haughty sugar manufacturers" who had "scorned the growers' demands" and who had been reduced to "fear and trembling." They applauded Sleeper for intervening in this dispute and looked forward to the possibility that the government would continue to do so on their behalf. The entry of the United States into the war just days after the strike had been settled seemed to assure the growers that this just might happen.[24]

"Unseat the Sugar Kings"[25]

Once the United States officially joined the war effort, the issue of sugar production and consumption assumed even greater political significance, both at home and abroad. Over the course of the spring and summer of 1917, Washington officials watched nervously as the price of sugar rose and the supply tightened.[26] Herbert Hoover, the recently appointed head of the U.S. Food Administration, even warned the nation that by the coming October the supply of domestic sugar would run out. To make matters worse, the Cuban crop was smaller than normal, and the United States faced new competition in Cuba from European countries looking to tropical cane sugar to replace the ravaged European beet sugar industry.[27]

In an effort to assure that its citizens would have an ample supply of sugar, the United States looked to its most important supplier—Cuba.[28] Rather than compete with European allies and drive prices even higher, the United States worked hand-in-hand with Great Britain to buy the entire sugar crop at a price of its own choosing and then distribute the crop as it saw fit. Instead of allowing Cuban sugar to find its "natural" price on the free market, which by the summer of 1917 had reached nearly seven cents a pound, the U.S. authorities settled on the price of 4.6 cents a pound based on the idea that this price was high enough to assure Cuban producers a profit and low enough to avoid hardship for American consumers.[29]

Not surprisingly, Cuban producers, which included a large number of U.S. corporations, complained that these price controls were unfair. Dealing with rising food and fuel prices—especially wheat and coal—Cuban leaders claimed that they could not survive with the price of sugar capped at 4.6 cents a pound. For two months the Cuban producers refused to sell their sugar to the United States at such an artificially low rate. The U.S. Food Administration retaliated by refusing to provide Cuba with the special licenses needed to import U.S. wheat and coal. Faced with little fuel and dangerously low food supplies, the Cuban sugar producers and the Cuban government capitulated—wheat and coal in exchange for artificially cheap sugar.[30] Exercising considerable pressure and cajoling, the U.S. government had basically hijacked the Cuban sugar crop.

Having seemingly solved the most significant international part of the sugar problem, Hoover turned his attention to keeping domestic sugar prices under control. To that end, in August 1917 Hoover invited 80 percent of the nation's sugar beet executives to Washington, D.C., to work out an agreement to "prevent unjust, unreasonable, unfair, and wasteful commissions, profits, and practices."[31] Offering the sugar executives a bargain he felt they could not refuse, Hoover guaranteed them a profitable margin if they would limit the price of refined sugar beet to 7 1/4 cents a pound. (The price eventually agreed to was nine cents a pound.) For those sugar companies that did not want to cooperate, Hoover threatened that "under certain circumstances, it may be advisable [for the U.S. government] to acquire the production of some sugar beet factories that cannot under the present price of beets be sold to the public at a reasonable price."[32] Using both the carrot and the stick, Hoover guaranteed the cooperation of the sugar beet industrialists.

The only problem with Hoover's plan was that convincing the industrialists to agree to voluntary price controls for refined sugar could not ensure a continual supply of sugar beet or stop the farmers from demanding more for growing the crop. Because the government set a price for refined sugar only, this left the door open for farmers to demand higher prices from the manufacturers without directly challenging the industry's voluntary price controls. Hoover immediately recognized the dilemma he faced—that is, that he could not force the farmers to grow the sugar beet crop or assure them of profits.[33] Lacking that power, he turned to patriotic appeals. In October 1917, Hoover sent out a circular letter to all sugar beet farmers, reminding them that "one of the most vital problems confronting the nation is that of procuring sufficient sugar to meet the requirement of our people and of the Allied Nations fighting our common battle. . . . I, therefore, honestly appeal to every farmer, so situated, to come to his country's aid in this hour of need. . . . It is at least the duty of every beet grower to maintain in 1918 his normal acreage of sugar beets. It is his privilege to increase the acreage to the extent that a well-balanced production of crops will permit, and in this manner effectively demonstrate his patriotism."[34]

Farmers responded to Hoover's patriotic appeals with the demand that if he wanted them to keep growing sugar beet, much less produce more, he would have to get involved in their disputes with the factories. In doing so, they used the state's involvement in the economy to press Hoover to address the "business end of farming" and not merely the "scientific side."[35] They complained that for too long the USDA and agricultural experiment stations had simply pushed them to increase production without showing any concern for the prices they received or their relations with the factories.³⁶ Now farmers insisted that Hoover had a responsibility not only to encourage them to grow more but to mediate between the competing interests in rural America, much like the National War Labor Board was doing for industrial workers.³⁷ "Mr. Hoover, here's an opportunity for you to do a good turn for both the producers of sugar beets and the consumers of sugar of this nation and it is to be hoped that you will not let this opportunity pass."³⁸ For their part of the bargain, farmers promised that if the government did more to ensure them profits, they would "mix a generous amount of patriotism" and "best of all . . . get results."³⁹ And the result that farmers most wanted to achieve was for Hoover to use his newfound authority to "Unseat the Sugar Kings."⁴⁰

"Owing No Apologies"

As the contract signing period for 1918 neared, farmers optimistically and opportunistically turned to the federal government for help.⁴¹ Rather than try to negotiate with the companies on their own, farmers invited George Prescott, Michigan's top food administration official, to set a fair price for the 1918 crop. (They also pledged to strike if they did not get the price they wanted.⁴²) When Prescott accepted their invitation, Michigan's farmers reacted with both relief and heightened expectations. Seeing this as their best opportunity to get a greater share "of the profits of the industry," they immediately demanded a $10 flat rate, and not one penny less.⁴³ The farmers also looked to Prescott to help them in their long, drawn-out battle to convince the companies to recognize their growers' associations, even asking him to force the sugar manufacturers to deduct one cent for every ton of sugar beet to fund their organization, the MSBGA.⁴⁴ Finally, they advised Prescott that the current dispute would best be resolved, and future disputes avoided, if the Food Administration would set up a commission made up of sugar beet growers, manufacturers, and a government official.⁴⁵

Company officials reacted to Prescott's planned intervention with a great deal of ambivalence. Fearful of being charged with war profiteering, they agreed to abide by whatever price the food administrator deemed fair, while also adopting the line that because they had already agreed to voluntary price controls for the refined product, they could not afford to pay the farmers more than $8 per ton.⁴⁶ Furthermore, they insisted that because only a small number of growers actually belonged to the growers' association, it would be unfair to expect them to recognize, much less negotiate, with that body, now or ever.⁴⁷

Caught between the farmers and the sugar executives, Prescott proposed a compromise price of $9 a ton, one dollar less than the farmers had demanded and one dollar more than the companies claimed they could pay. By so doing, Prescott hoped that he would be able to keep sugar prices under control, maintain company profits, and convince the farmers to keep growing the crop.[48] When news of the decision reached the sugar companies, West Bay City Sugar president Bialy penned a public letter to Prescott commending him for his efforts. Though M. J. Bialy began by sarcastically commenting how it is "not possible for us, as manufacturers, to accept the arbitrary terms submitted by the Sugar Beet Growers Committee," he thanked Prescott for the "honorable manner" with which he handled the dispute, and for his "kindly suggestion for a compromise." Bialy also accepted the $9 price, even though he and his colleagues "consider the price beyond our ability to pay, but as a matter of fairness, and if permitted to use the term patriotism, we will agree to make use of this figure."[49]

Farmers responded to Prescott's "compromise" price in a much less conciliatory manner. They refused to accept the $9 offer and insisted that they could be just as patriotic by growing other crops. Claiming that the federal government had asked them to sacrifice more than the "monied interests," farmers charged that Prescott had simply taken the easy way out by dividing between $10 and $8.[50] Instead of standing by their pledge to accept Prescott's decision, the farmers refused to grow beets for "one cent less" than they had originally demanded and warned that they would encourage fellow farmers to abandon the crop altogether.[51] To those who might criticize them, the farmers insisted that they owed "no apology to either the manufacturers, the public, nor to Uncle Sam."[52]

The farmers' response reflected a growing militancy, owing to their newfound leverage in market conditions, as well as impatience with state intervention when it did not suit their wishes. This response also revealed the limits of Prescott's power, for he could not force the farmers to grow sugar beet if they chose not to do so. Prescott's only option was to publicly scold the farmers, charging that they were acting foolishly and selfishly.[53] Not surprisingly, this public criticism infuriated farmers throughout the state. One farm journal responded: "Why Mr. Prescott should ask that the common rule of business be suspended when applied to the farm factory, is totally beyond our ken."[54] Though growers welcomed governmental involvement, it is clear that they were not willing to abandon what they viewed as their own interests.[55] Equally important, in contesting the fairness of Prescott's compromise price, farmers appropriated the era's patriotic themes—especially those of justice, liberty, and equality—to buttress their own demand for a greater, and what they saw as fairer, share of the profits. Envisioning themselves as the champions of true American ideals, farmers referred to their own farms as "farm factories," themselves as "soldiers of the soil," and the crops they harvested as "bread bullets."[56] The Gleaner Federation even described itself as "a vast army of more than eighty thousand . . . divided into more than thirteen hundred companies . . . unitedly pressing on to solve the greater problems and in the meantime reap the fruits of true cooperation."[57] Conversely, farmers described the sugar companies as the real enemy, charging that "no autocratic Kaiser ever ruled with a stronger hand of iron than have the Beet Sugar Manufacturers of the middle west and west."[58] Using wartime rhetoric, farmers questioned the justice of the marketplace and the actions of state officials who looked after the corporate interests and not their needs. In this case patriotism led to conflict, not conformity.

In response to the farmers' use of patriotic rhetoric, the sugar companies immediately went on the offensive. With the 1918 planting season just a couple of months away, the companies charged that the farmers were taking "unfair advantage" of the wartime emergency and suggested that the state's immigrant farmers had been influenced by German propaganda.[59] An editorial in the *Michigan Manufacturer,* which was later reprinted in rural newspapers, also accused farmers of trying to tear down Michigan's industries. "We observe that the farmers of Michigan, despite their continued calamity howls, their assertions that they are the salt of the earth, and that people who live in cities are tyrants, who take advantage of every occasion to put the heel of capital on the neck of labor and agriculture, are considering how to take another wallop at the industries of this state."[60] After the *Tuscola County Advertiser* editor published these charges in his paper, he received so many angry letters from farmers that he felt compelled to publicly announce that he had the best interests of both the farmers and the factories in mind. Nonetheless he also lamented that "so many agitators are speaking and writing in apparent efforts to array class against class," "that society seems tending toward a state of disruption. Some farm papers and politically ambitious farmers would make the world believe that farmers are the only chosen people of God."[61] Not content to let the editor have the final word, farmer E. A. Rolfs from Akron wrote back, asking: "Now haven't the farmers a right to ask for what is really theirs? . . . Who is taking a wallop at the farmers when they ask him to raise beets at a loss?"[62]

After a two-month standoff, and few signs that the farmers were about to give in, the sugar companies and Prescott blinked first. Faced with the real prospect that the farmers would indeed hold out and not grow sugar beet, Prescott asked the sugar companies to give the farmers their asking price of $10. In so doing, he felt he had no choice, for in 1916 and 1917 farmers had already demonstrated their willingness to grow other crops, with the result that the overall acreage of sugar beet in Michigan had already fallen to just 82,252. Capitulating to the $10 demand, the companies claimed they had done so at the government's urging and out of a sense of patriotism, but not because of the farmers' militancy.[63] W. H. Wallace, general manager of the Michigan Sugar Company, insisted that the new contract "originated from the manufacturers in conference with Mr. Prescott only, and has not been changed to the extent of one word, and [that] there was no conference at that time or since that time with the growers' committee."[64] As in previous years, the sugar companies maintained the myth that farmer militancy had little effect on their decision to raise the price for sugar beet. Patriotism, they claimed, not pressure, had produced the price rise.

The truth, however, is that a looming sugar shortage and higher prices for other crops had provided sugar beet growers with the kind of leverage they had not wielded since the earliest years of this industry.[65] Taking the government's pronouncement "Food Will Win the War" literally, farmers threatened to take up some other crop that would allow them to be both patriotic and profitable. And because contracts were signed on a yearly basis, farmers had no legal obligation to grow the crop, and neither the federal government nor the manufacturers could force them to raise sugar beet if they chose not to do so. The farmers' willingness to hold out for higher prices also reflected their sense that this moment was an exceptional one, and that what happened during the war years would set the stage for the postwar order. "Lose this opportunity, and the beet sugar autocrats will be in the saddle when the war is over."[66]

The Larger Victory

The sugar beet growers' mix of optimism and foreboding was reflected nationally as farm groups across the country viewed World War I as a possible turning point to determine whether the progressive efforts of the early twentieth century would bear fruit or wither on the vine. The very visible role of the state in the economy seemed to offer evidence to many that this indeed was a contingent moment and that perhaps World War I might offer a template for continued state intervention in the economy long after the national emergency ended. Even before the United States joined the war effort, farmers, like industrial workers, began to plan for the anticipated reconstruction of modern industrial capitalism that they hoped would follow the end of the war. That is, although most farmers generally agreed with the government slogan that "Food Will Win the War," just how this would happen spurred a serious discussion about the status of agriculture, the ties between industry and agriculture, and the role of the government in the economy.[67]

One of the most vocal contingents in this debate was the Farmers' National Council (FNC), a rather loose coalition of self-described progressive farm organizations, recognized in its own day as the most important and radical farm organization in the United States. In 1915, the FNC had set up offices in Washington as a way to translate the goals of the progressive Granges into reality.[68] By the war's end, the FNC would grow dramatically to include among its affiliated organizations not only the well-known Non-Partisan League and the American Society of Equity but also the Gleaner Federation of Michigan.[69] Working together under the structure of the FNC, these self-styled progressive farm organizations hoped to present an alternative plan to the pro-big-business agenda being offered by the USDA and the state agricultural colleges. In fact, they saw the war as an opportunity to push the federal government to use its powers to rein in monopoly capitalism and level the economic playing field. Charging that for too long, "the privileged interests have always regarded the national capitol as their private preserve," the FNC claimed that "Washington is nearly as many miles from many farmers as it is from the battlelines in France."[70] If the federal government wanted farmers to do their part in the war effort, it would have to assure them a place at the bargaining table.

In the weeks after the United States formally joined World War I, progressive farm groups set their sights on Washington to make sure that farmers would be well represented in wartime planning. Acting as head of the Michigan Gleaner Federation, Grant Slocum visited with USDA secretary David Houston, advising him that if the government wanted to increase production, it would have to tend to the "business side" of the farmer. Grant Slocum also testified before the Senate to argue in favor of a national system of minimum price supports.[71] Using slogans like "Back the Farmers' Program of Preparedness" and "Let the State get into the Game," Slocum even called on the state to establish government contracts for food when possible and/or cost-plus contracts for farmers.[72] Though these requests might seem to reflect mere wartime exigencies, they in fact highlighted the problems farmers had long faced in an increasingly industrial economy.

Over the course of the war, progressive farm organizations developed an increasingly expansive view of the federal government's proper role in the economy. In addition to calling for government contracts for food and minimum price supports for agricultural goods, the FNC pushed for government ownership of railroads and the nationalization of natural resources, including mining, timber, and water. As a way to address the places where the agricultural and industrial sectors of the economy intersected, the FNC even called for the state to exercise extreme control over the merchant marine and the meatpacking industry. Finally, the FNC also publicly supported industrial workers in their quest to gain collective bargaining rights as well as the right to strike.[73]

The council's concern with wartime practices reflected its belief that policies established during the war would set the stage for the postwar order. Although progressive farmers recognized that the wartime emergency would come to an end at some point, they, like progressives throughout U.S. society, anxiously anticipated a period of "reconstruction" after the war.[74] Less than six months after the United States joined the war effort, FNC leader George Hampton advised the nation's farmers, "In Time of War Prepare for Peace."[75] Over the war months, the FNC continually reminded farmers that the "reconstruction" plan adopted after the war would largely determine whether agriculture, viewed by many as a "decadent industry," would "be restored to its original prominence and position."[76] Just a month before the signing of the armistice, the FNC proclaimed that our farmers were really fighting for "The Larger Victory," for "Much more than defeating the Germans will have to be done before democracy is made safe for the world. We have to establish a democracy here at home."[77]

Tapping into the dominant rhetoric of the day, farmers called for the creation of a true "industrial democracy" that would include the agricultural sector of society instead of exploiting it. Rather than simply harkening back to Jeffersonian ideals of the past, progressive farm groups envisioned a new contract or covenant with the government and between the agricultural and industrial sectors of society. Rejecting the agricultural reformers' efforts to revolutionize agriculture only through increased agricultural production and scientific agriculture, farmers believed that the government needed to recognize the business interests of farmers as well as the ties that bound agriculture and industry. Rejecting romanticized notions of self-sufficiency and unbridled individualism, and refuting the idea that government intervention in the economy should be only a wartime measure, many progressive farm groups hoped that the war would set the stage for a new era of industrial agriculture. This sentiment was perhaps best expressed by the Gleaner organization, which triumphantly proclaimed in December 1917 that "the war has exulted it [agriculture] to the top of the world's industries, and there it will stay. Governments that have pleaded with the farmers to sustain production have entered a solemn covenant which they cannot and will not break even when the war has ceased and normality again rules the markets."[78]

"Patriots or Paytriots?": Reconstruction and the "Radical Minority" in Rural America

Using the ideals and rhetoric raised during the war to frame their critique of modern industrial America, farmers in the immediate postwar era continued to lay claim to the much-contested term "industrial democracy."[79] N. P. Hull, president of the Michigan Milk Producers' Association, captured the spirit of many farmers in Michigan when he protested: "We have spent the lives of our sons and billions in money to secure political democracy for the peoples of the world, but all our fighting shall have been in vain if we do not secure industrial democracy. By industrial democracy, I mean the right of the farmer and others to organize and demand profit on the goods they produce."[80] Similarly, the FNC hailed the end of the war as just the beginning of a broader contest to remake the nation. "Make no mistake. Having beaten the Hun, the world is now face to face with an even greater war. Whether Toryism or democracy shall be triumphant is now the issue, and, at least so far as this country is concerned, the farmer will decide the issue."[81] Vacillating between agricultural fundamentalism—the view that agriculture was the base of society—and a sober realization of the power of industry in the modern era, progressive farm groups looked for ways to reconstruct the nation's economy.

As the self-proclaimed leader of progressive farm groups, the FNC wasted no time publicizing its reconstruction program.[82] This "radical minority" insisted that agriculture should be placed on a "business basis" and that the farmers who tilled the land should be assured of "reasonable and equitable pay for their work." Describing farming as "a hazardous industry," the FNC called for establishing means to assess the costs of production and to make sure that farmers would not only be "protected against loss" but also "assured a fair profit."[83] To achieve these demands, council leaders suggested that the federal government adopt a system of cost-plus contracting whereby the federal government would establish minimum prices and finance the export of surplus crops overseas.[84] Farmers also called for the government to either nationalize or exert greater control over those key transportation and processing industries that linked rural producers and urban consumers, including the stockyards, refrigerator cars, cold storage plants, warehouses, meatpacking plants, and terminal elevators.[85] And finally, the FNC called for the federal government to guarantee "living wages" to workers toiling in industry, mining, and railroads. At the conference unveiling this reconstruction plan, Michigan's Herbert Baker told the audience that "without the farmers' support, toil and sacrifice the war could not have been won. But they ask no reward except that they not be robbed of the fruits of the democracy for which the war was fought. We present our Reconstruction program, not as a petition, but as the farmers mandate to all interests."[86]

To translate its postwar plans into postwar policy, FNC leaders regularly lobbied Congress, testified at numerous congressional hearings, and met with President Wilson. The FNC had even hoped to attend the Peace Conference in Paris until one of its delegates from the Non-Partisan League was barred from going because Great Britain objected to his presence.[87] This relentless attempt to shape policy at the national and even international levels reflected a growing sense that the federal government held the balance of power. Wartime experience had taught that much. Believing that up until now Washington had functioned as the private enclave of monopoly interests, FNC leaders sought to democratize the nation's capital by making their voices heard.

As the FNC and allied groups looked forward to a "reconstruction" of the economy, they found their claim as spokesmen for America's farmers challenged by the newly formed American Farm Bureau Federation (AFBF).[88] In fact, the debate over reconstruction fueled a contest among competing farm organizations' claims to represent the best interests of the nation's farmers.[89] Tapping into the growing conservatism of the postwar era, the AFBF self-consciously portrayed itself as the conservative and practical alternative to the FNC. During the first AFBF national conference, the executive committee charged the FNC with being the ally of "the radical element of the industrial world."[90] The AFBF went further, adamantly declaring: "We wish the American people definitely to understand that the FNC has no authority to speak on behalf of the farmers of this country, and any and all efforts on the part of the FNC to ally agriculturalists of America with the radicals of the industrial world is denounced."[91] FNC leader George Hampton responded to the bureau's hostility by writing an open letter inviting AFBF president J. R. Howard to a public debate. Howard responded to Hampton with his own public letter, promising him a longer response in the future. He never wrote the second letter.[92]

The reason Howard did not write a second letter is that he did not have to. Although the FNC claimed to have 350,000 members and another 300,000 sympathizers in the Non-Partisan League, it took only a few months for the AFBF to surpass these membership numbers. In March 1920, the AFBF counted more than 400,000 members, and by the following January slightly more than one million farmers in forty-three states had joined. The AFBF's national budget in 1923 was $247,000 while the FNC's was a mere $12,000.[93] In addition, the AFBF reaped rewards from its close ties to government officials and corporate officers who eagerly embraced the AFBF as a conservative alternative to the FNC. The AFBF had good reason to declare itself as the voice of the farmers, or at least a significant minority.

As much as these membership figures and budgets help to explain the growing dominance of the AFBF, the larger political climate also influenced how and why the AFBF became the most important farm organization in the nation. While progressive and radical farm groups hoped for a period of reconstruction to follow the war, Woodrow Wilson disbanded the various war agencies as fast as he could. Instead of entering an era in which the future of American capitalism could be debated, the government sought to return to normal as soon as possible. Yet, life was hardly normal. In 1919, labor unrest crested and the hypernationalism of the World War I era came home to roost as the nation became enveloped by numerous race riots and a red scare.[94] In this conservative climate, the AFBF found a relatively easy path to national prominence, while groups like the FNC and the Non-Partisan League found it increasingly difficult to compete. Even though radical and progressive farm organizations would continue to play a role in states like North Dakota and Minnesota throughout the 1920s, progressive and radical farm organizations found their hopes for a reconstructed nation dashed and their role as the voice of the nation's farmers silenced.[95]

"Reconstruction" in the Fields

At the same time that farm organizations like the FNC and the AFBF battled for the hearts and minds of America's farmers, sugar beet growers throughout Michigan emerged from their wartime experiences emboldened. Hoping to forge a new relationship between industry and agriculture, one of mutual interdependence in which small family farms and large corporations could equitably share the fruits of their industry, farmers began to demand 50/50 contracts, whereby the sugar factories and the farmers would simply split all the company profits at the end of the season. That is, instead of being paid for the raw sugar beet at a price set months before the season, the farmers wanted the factories to equally divide all corporate profits at the end of the season.[96] Farmers developed the idea of the profit-sharing 50/50 contract as a means for ensuring equity and ending future conflicts. This new tactic also represented a larger critique of contract farming and its underlying premises. The 50/50 contract challenged the idea that farmers were merely selling their raw material and that the sugar companies created use value when processing the product and therefore deserved more. To justify the splitting of profits, farmers pointed to their investment in land—equal if not more to the capital investment of the factories—and to their investments in labor—which were far greater than the factories' labor costs—to argue that they were equal partners in this venture, and as such deserved an equal share of profits. Farmers also sought to protect their own interests once the sugar beet left the fields by demanding that they be allowed to have their own weighmen and taremen present in the factories. As they had done in the early twentieth century, farmers again focused on the ever-shifting boundary separating and uniting the factory and the field as well as the distinction between agricultural and industrial production. Ultimately, the 50/50 contract represented an important vision of what industrial agriculture could look like in the twentieth century.

The farmers framed their calls for a 50/50 contract within the wartime rhetoric of rights, justice, loyalty, and equality by demanding the right to take part in drawing up agricultural contracts, the right to present their own contracts to the companies, and the right to have their own representatives oversee factory operations.[97] In the postwar years, farmers also continued their charge that sugar manufacturers, acting like sugar czars, had denied farmers their "liberty."[98] In contract battles, sugar beet farmers asserted, "It is contrary to the principles of democracy for the many to be at the mercy of the few."[99] In responding to charges that they were acting like "anarchists, bolsheviks, socialists and radicals," sugar beet farmers countered: "We stand for law and order . . . [and] know that law and order are rooted in the principles of justice and fair dealing. . . . We are loyal Americans, citizens, fighting for the welfare of our country in approved American fashion.[100] In contrast, they claimed that the sugar industrialists were "mean spirited, despicable and un-American."[101]

As farmers geared up to challenge the sugar companies in the final days of 1919 and the early months of 1920, it became clear that they would have to do battle on their own. What had been treated just months earlier as a matter of national survival and necessity, making sure that the nation would have plenty of sugar, was now viewed as a private matter by state officials who rebuffed the growers' request that they mediate the impending farmer/factory conflict.[102] This reflected Wilson's larger directive that the regulatory wartime state be dismantled as quickly as possible, for he had no intention of allowing the wartime measures to turn into a dress rehearsal for a radically new stage of state intervention in the economy.

Rather than recoil from the prospect of confronting the sugar companies on its own, the MSBGA began a massive organizing campaign to garner support from Michigan's farmers and farm organizations.[103] Ignoring the conflicts that divided farm organizations at the national level, the MSBGA courted help from the Gleaners, the Grange, the Farmers' Union, and even the recently formed Michigan Farm Bureau, which gave the MSBGA $2,000 to help in the battle.[104] From January to March 1920, the MSBGA held mass meetings throughout the state where association representatives advised farmers not to sign sugar company contracts and urged them to form local associations of their own.[105] To ensure stability and financial support, MSBGA leaders asked local groups to elect local officers, collect dues, and affiliate with county and state associations.[106]

MSBGA officers motivated local farmers by telling them that if they did not secure a place at the bargaining table now, when sugar prices remained high, there would be little chance of doing so once prices began to fall.[107] The MSBGA also highlighted the profit differential between the factories and the farmers, claiming that in 1919 manufacturers made $4 for every $1 the farmers took home.[108] Calling for a "fair division of the profits of the business," the association warned "we'll take no less."[109] Moreover, the MSBGA promised that it would protect farmers' interests and make the industry more prosperous for all by promoting intelligent production and collecting practical information.[110]

Farmers throughout the state responded enthusiastically to the MSBGA campaign. By the end of the first week of organizing in January, the MSBGA counted ten local associations and one thousand members, many in the traditional beet growing counties of Bay and Saginaw.[111] By April, just four months after the organizing drive began, more than nine thousand members had joined one hundred different locals, while state and MSBGA conventions drew between 1,500 and two thousand members.[112] Based on this impressive start, MSBGA supporters confidently warned that unless the factories met their demands, the beet crop would be down by 90 percent.[113] It seemed that the MSBGA had finally developed a sound institutional footing and support from the vast majority of farmers growing sugar beet in the state.

In addition to establishing local and county associations to work in conjunction with the state organization, the MSBGA also joined a national campaign to organize beet growers. During the first national convention of sugar beet growers held in Denver, Colorado, in December 1919, Michigan was well represented with the Gleaners, State Grange, and the Farmers' Union all sending representatives.[114] Michigan's John C. Ketchum, the MSBGA president, was also elected president of the national sugar beet growers' federation, a post he held for the next two years. With USDA and Federal Trade Commission officials as well as the U.S. attorney general looking on, the convention delegates voted the "Michigan 50–50 Contract" as the official federation contract.[115]

A week later, when the MSBGA presented its demands to the factories in January 1920, the companies charged that the growers' contract was impractical and refused to negotiate with, much less recognize, the MSBGA.[116] Speaking on behalf of the Michigan Sugar Company, general manager W. H. Wallace publicly denounced the MSBGA request as "ruinous" and warned that his company would shut down its plants before meeting the growers' demands.[117] The sugar companies also claimed that they would deal only with individual farmers because they had no way of knowing whether or not the MSBGA reflected the interests of its members or even if the farmers were really members at all.[118] In so doing, the sugar beet companies attempted to tap into the mythical individualism that they believed ultimately guided farmers' actions.

Underneath the sugar companies' intransigence, one can easily detect frustration with having been forced to give in to the farmers' demands. During the war, governmental pressure and the potential for profits had proven too much for the companies to resist. Moreover, because of generally high agricultural prices during the war, farmers had gained the ultimate bargaining tool. Now that most agricultural prices were moderating and some even starting to fall, the companies saw the postwar era as the time to rewrite the war experience and reassert their right to unilaterally write contracts and determine the dividing line between the factory and the field. In the face of growing farmer militancy, sugar companies even attempted to rewrite the immediate past by claiming that they had never raised the price of sugar beets because of farmers' demands and that they had never recognized the MSBGA as an organization. According to Michigan Sugar Company general manager W. H. Wallace, "the price has advanced from $4.00 to $12.50 per ton and none of this advance is on account of the association." Wallace even made the absurd claim that "we never heard of this association until a few years ago."[119] By denying the wartime record, the sugar companies tried to pick up where they had left off in 1915.

To counter the MSBGA, sugar companies began their own publicity campaign, promising farmers that the price of sugar would continue to rise and that under their sliding scale, farmers could expect $12 to $15 a ton, more than they could have possibly imagined just a few years earlier. The companies also went to great lengths to discredit the MSBGA, portraying its leaders as "agitators" and "traitors." Some sugar companies even claimed that the current strike was the work of "professional agitators from the West" who were in Michigan "endeavoring to stir up trouble, aided by a radical minority, who habitually attempt to promote dissatisfaction among the growers each spring."[120]

The sugar companies sought ways to divide the seemingly united farmers by trying to pit the leaders against the rank and file members. In April 1920, the Michigan Sugar Company claimed that C. E. Ackerman, director of the growers' association, had signed a contract to grow sugar beet while advising other farmers to not grow the crop.[121] Otto Pobanz, a prominent Huron County farmer, was also accused of abandoning his fellow farmers by signing a company contract. To stop this rumor, Pobanz took out an advertisement in the same newspaper that reported the accusation, declaring: "The above rumor is false, I take my stand as I have taken it before thousands of farmers, that I will not raise sugar beets nor seed until I can sign a contract which is approved by the grower committee."[122] Not content to let the matter rest, the Michigan Sugar Company bookkeeper responded by penning her own letter to the editor, charging that Pobanz had indeed signed a contract and that Thomas Price, an officer of the growers' association, had announced that all sugar beet growers were free to do the same.[123] The saga continued as Pobanz wrote to the paper again, charging that the Michigan Sugar Company was trying to "culminate me before the public, to instigate mutiny among the ranks of the grower association."[124] The next week the head of the Michigan Sugar Company wrote back, claiming that Pobanz was a "low, dirty, quibbly . . . contemptible and venomous reptile."[125]

As the conflict between the growers and the companies intensified, each side tried to define the conflict to support its own agenda. The companies claimed that the farmers' strike was no different from the labor strikes paralyzing the nation and that both should be condemned as un-American. MSBGA leaders countered that because they did not form picket lines or try to establish a closed shop, they were conducting a "strike of capital," and hence their strike differed fundamentally from the "labor strikes" rattling the nation.[126] As the strike progressed, however, more and more evidence pointed to the similarities between this strike of "capital" and the thousands of "labor" strikes disrupting the nation.[127]

By planting time in April 1920, the farmers' strike had spread from the written word out into the farmers' fields and the larger community. Farmers who had either refused to join the MSBGA or who had joined the association but still contracted with the companies were frequently labeled as slackers or sugar beet scabs. Militant growers sought out farmers who might be wavering by calling on them to "be loyal to their neighbors and to their association and to the cause of justice and cooperation everywhere" while also warning that "for the sake of their word, their honesty, their respect, and their standing in their community, they will put aside the temptation to grow beets."[128] Loyal members also promised disloyal neighbors retribution, threatening not only that they would be vilified within the community but that slackers would not be able to expect their neighbors' help when it came to threshing time.[129] Calling for every farmer to "be a man with men," growers in Bay County passed a resolution to stop loyal farmers from helping their "unloyal" neighbors.[130] One loyal local sugar beet growers' association became so concerned that its members would engage in pitched battles with a neighboring local that had voted to grow sugar beet that it passed an anti-violence resolution to stop its own members from breaking the law.[131]

By May, when it became clear that thousands of farmers had contracted with the sugar companies, and that the overall acreage would be quite large, tensions boiled over into defiant acts of violence.[132] Although the MSBGA proclaimed it would deal with disloyal growers peacefully and urged all to remain true to their pledge not to raise sugar beet, many members had their own ideas about how to handle "disloyal" farmers.[133] Militant farmers sometimes pulled their disloyal neighbors' sugar beets from the ground and smashed their beet drills.[134] Others painted their disloyal neighbors' houses yellow, a sign of disloyalty during the war that was now transformed into a sign of disloyalty to the sugar beet cause.[135] A number of farmers burned unoccupied migrant shacks and other buildings.[136] Violence escalated so dramatically that even the *New York Times* reported how "night riders" of striking sugar beet growers had been accused of burning down five farmhouses, dynamiting migrant shacks, and destroying farm tools worth thousands of dollars. The *Times* also reprinted a note that had allegedly been written by a striking farmer to his neighbor, which read: "Either quit planting sugar beets and cancel all contracts with refiners or your home will be burned, your cattle killed, your machinery destroyed, and your wives and daughters 'fixed.' We will tolerate the presence of no strike breakers in the Saginaw Valley."[137] The class tensions that had been developing for more than two decades reached a fevered pitch as farmers battled not only the companies but each other. The oppositional class identity, which had united farmers in the past, began to divide them as farmers expressed their militancy both outwardly and inwardly.

To help stop the escalating violence, the MSBGA publicly condemned all lawlessness and offered a $100 reward for anyone willing to identify the perpetrators who had burned the sugar beet shacks. However, MSBGA spokesmen also helped fuel the flames by commenting that, "No honest-to-God farmer" who had any conception "of right and justice, or who had any respect for the standing of himself and family in his community" would grow sugar beet and that those who had done so had sold "their souls for a dollar!"[138] Similarly, the editorial board of *Michigan Business Farming* also sympathized with those growers who had attacked their neighbors, noting, "I suppose that when the loyal beet growers talk of destroying the property of others who are sowing beets they only intend to retaliate for the injury done to them."[139]

The violence that punctuated the 1920 strike shows just how seriously farmers felt about the issues at stake. The rising tension and frustration that led some farmers to attack the good name and property of others shows that some farmers stood loyally by the MSBGA while others, for various reasons, decided to sign contracts with the companies. Not surprisingly, farmers in the heart of the sugar beet districts who were most dependent on the crop proved the most loyal because they had both the most to gain and the most to lose.[140] In contrast, farmers on the fringes of the sugar beet districts often succumbed to the lure of high prices.[141] Also, tenant farmers who depended upon sugar beet as a main cash crop often felt they had little choice. One of the few tenant farmers who publicly voiced his opinion, a farmer named McDonald, complained: "We are told that if we do grow beets we will be called slackers." He protested, however, that "all of us are not situated alike." To justify the fact that he grew sugar beet, he argued, "The liberty of the individual should not be taken away by the association. That is not good Americanism."[142] A farmer who identified himself as W.B.B. agreed, writing, "I don't think the farmer is getting a 'square deal' but many of us are forced to raise beets. The manufacturers know this and absolutely refuse to arbitrate the issue."[143] Though sympathetic to the goals of the MSBGA, many farmers could not afford to give up the crop in an era of falling agricultural prices.

Farmers who had begun the first postwar sugar beet battle with a good deal of confidence that they could bring the industry to the bargaining table even without the help of the state soon became painfully aware of how vulnerable they really were. In terms of overall acreage, the 1920 season turned out to be the largest yet.[144] Equally significant, what had looked like the state's most organized and militant organization fell apart as farmers nervously watched the prices for their other farm products fall and their leverage gained from the market disappear. In addition to the thousands of tenants and independent farmers who grew sugar beet, thousands of "loyal" farmers also gave in after promising themselves and their neighbors that they would not do so. Clearly, the MSBGA had lost this strike at the hands of many of its own members.

The Farm Bureau

As the MSBGA attempted to regroup from the divisive 1920 strike, the newly formed Michigan Farm Bureau (FB) burst onto the scene. Believing that their organization was the most powerful in the state, Michigan's FB leaders claimed that they should take over the sugar beet fight from the MSBGA.[145] To upstage the MSBGA, the FB began holding "sugar beet meetings" with prominent farmers throughout the state, promising them that it would avoid the "turmoil and confusion" of the 1920 strike by instituting a cooperative marketing plan whereby sugar beet growers would sign contracts with the FB instead of the sugar companies. At the end of the contracting season, the FB would then present these contracts, en masse, to the companies. The Michigan FB also promised that it would begin building cooperative sugar factories once it had raised enough capital.[146]

At first the leading officers of the MSBGA and the Gleaner greeted the FB's actions with a great deal of suspicion. When they learned that the Michigan FB had held meetings without inviting them, MSBGA leaders warned: "What the plans of the Farm Bureau may be we knoweth not, but we do know that if the Farm Bureau seeks to solve the sugar beet problem without the counsel and cooperation of the Beet Growers Association it will quite likely come to grief."[147] The MSBGA and the editor of *Michigan Business Farming* also criticized the FB's cooperative factory schemes as a diversion, noting that at the moment, farmers should be focusing on bringing the sugar companies back to the bargaining table.[148]

Just a couple of months later, MSBGA members voted to affiliate with the FB by becoming a department of that larger organization.[149] Without organizational papers it is impossible to state with certainty why MSBGA members joined forces with the Michigan FB, especially after their recent close association with the much more radical Gleaner and FNC. Perhaps MSBGA members hoped to maintain their autonomy while tapping into the financial, organizational, and political resources of the Michigan FB. Association leaders may have been impressed by the membership numbers of the

Michigan FB, which rose from 22,749 in 1920 to 97,246 in 1921.[150] Certainly, increasing numbers of farmers in the state began to look to the FB because of its perceived strength and size and close ties to state officials. Farmer O. C. Watkings, a *Michigan Business Farming* subscriber for years, concluded that "the Farm Bureau is the best yet, as they are organized under one head with ample capital to push it to a finish."[151] Sugar beet farmers in the state may have also been influenced by the fact that in 1920 the FB had successfully negotiated a contract for farmers in the Utah-Idaho sugar districts. After the disappointing and disastrous defeats of the previous years, it is also likely that growers were ready to try something new.

Almost immediately there were clear signs that the FB would indeed pursue novel strategies. In contrast to the oppositional and militant stance taken by the MSBGA, the Michigan FB publicized that the goal of its sugar beet department "is defined as one of cooperation with the sugar beet refineries rather than one of antagonism."[152] To avoid a protracted and violent strike, the Michigan FB proposed a cooperative contracting scheme, with a twist. Instead of waiting for the manufacturers to agree to a contract, the Michigan FB would put out its own contract—with the prices and stipulations that the growers wanted—and then canvass the countryside to convince farmers to sign the FB contracts. Michigan FB leaders claimed that this was the perfect solution, because it fit well with the FB's larger goal of cooperative marketing while avoiding the violent confrontations that had rattled rural communities in the past. The FB also sold the plan to the farmers by telling them it represented an opportunity to stand strong together while continuing to grow sugar beet.

The contracting scheme represented a conservative and peaceful means to ends that had so far proven elusive. It also proved to be a dismal failure. The Michigan FB began putting out contracts in March, four months after the sugar companies had begun scouring the countryside. Therefore, even though the Michigan FB claimed to have 100,000 acres signed up by early April, most farmers had simply signed both the sugar companies' and the Michigan FB's contracts.[153] That is, many of the farmers who had signed the association contract did so as a symbolic act of sympathy with the goals of the FB/MSBGA while still signing the companies' contracts to make sure they would be able to grow the crop.[154] As the season began, then, the sugar companies had two sets of contracts to choose from: the ones they had put out and the FB/MSBGA contracts. Of course the sugar companies chose their own. When Michigan FB officials presented their contracts to the sugar companies, the sugar companies refused to accept them, claiming that they infringed on the company's right to contract individually with the growers.[155] The FB's first attempt to solve the intractable issue of the contract had failed.

The magnitude of the 1921 defeat became clear when the crop finally came in six months later. Farmers had planted more sugar beet in 1921 than in any previous year. In hindsight, 1921 turns out to have been a rather poor year for challenging the sugar companies. Just as the FB was trying to mobilize sugar beet growers, the prices for most other farm products began to decline, leaving many farmers with little economic choice but to keep growing their most reliable cash crop.[156] That is, farmers kept growing sugar beet because it seemed to offer the best economic bet at the dawn of what would turn out to be a decade-long agricultural depression.[157] The FB contracts, and the strategy that the FB adopted, may also help explain the dismal defeat. The FB not only failed to come to terms with long-standing tensions dividing the farmers and the sugar companies, but it also failed to realize that the farmers and the companies did not have the same interests in mind and that "cooperation and harmony" were elusive goals. The sugar companies had triumphed once again, reversing the wartime trend.

Conclusion

Although the war had raised the sugar beet farmers' hopes about creating a more equitable form of industrial agriculture, by the early 1920s their dreams were largely dashed. In 1922, when sugar industrialists offered farmers the same $5 per ton contract that had been used in 1916, it seemed that the industrialists had succeeded in turning back the clock, thereby making the farmers' dreams for the future look more like a nightmare from the past.[158] The story seemed to have come full circle. To make matters worse, the Michigan FB turned its back on the sugar beet growers, dropping the MSBGA as a department. Left once again on its own, the MSBGA became a mere shadow of its former self, with active membership numbers falling from twelve thousand to one thousand. This precipitous decline led one farmer to comment in 1923 that, "when it comes to organizing the beet growers here he [the organizer] will have to get out a bench warrant to find the growers."[159]

Just as sugar beet farmers in Michigan failed to radically redefine their relationship to industrial capitalism, radical and progressive farmers throughout the nation failed in their quest to push the state to create a more level playing field for all sectors of the economy. Instead of pushing for a period of reconstruction to follow the war, state officials from Woodrow Wilson on down shifted their attention to returning to normal as quickly as possible. In this increasingly conservative climate, the Farm Bureau had a rather easy time superceding the Farmers' National Council as the nation's most important farm organization, as well as ensuring that its conservative, pro–big business agenda would dominate farm politics for decades to come.

Although historians have long recognized World War I as a critical time, especially with respect to race relations and labor conflicts, they have often overlooked the ways that this period represented a major moment for farmers as well as the development of U.S. agriculture. Like the industrial workers who took to the streets, farmers participated in numerous conflicts and engaged in a serious debate regarding the future of modern industrial capitalism, the relationship between agriculture and industry, and the role that the state would play in the economy at large. That the self-proclaimed progressive and radical farmers ultimately lost out on the ground and in the larger political arena should not blind us to the contentious nature of the battles or the contingent nature of the conservative victory. That is, rather than view the rise of the Farm Bureau as somehow inevitable, historians would do well to recognize World War I as a turning point, a moment when other outcomes were a real possibility, when the direction and future of the economy seemed very much up for grabs. Looking at the World War I period and farmers' actions in this context, rather than judging them by what came before and after, reveals a serious contest over the future of agriculture in an increasingly industrial economy.

5

Immigrant Labor and the Guest Worker Program

Soon after the United States formally entered World War I, the Michigan Sugar Company came up with a plan to convince eastern European migrant families to stay in the countryside year-round. It would erect "modest but comfortable houses" near the factories and sell them to "any of the beet workers who wish to take advantage of the offer on the deferred payment plan." To drum up support among farmers and townspeople, the sugar company claimed that building homes for migrant families would not only solve their looming labor shortage, it would also be a means to "Americanize" the migrant population. "It is patriotic in that it will tend to teach these people American ideals and make them stable citizens. It has its social side, making for better morals among them together with giving them home responsibility, and then there is the economic side through which they will be imbued with the habit of thrift. Having a home to work for they will be less apt to squander their money uselessly, as so often many of them do."[1]

Despite the company's initial enthusiasm about building houses for eastern Europeans—and thereby transforming them from migrants into neighbors and citizens—it soon abandoned its home-building plans and instead began recruiting thousands of Mexicans to work in the fields. In 1918, Michigan Sugar Company officials announced in one small-town newspaper that, "unable to get a sufficient number of Russians [we] were compelled to resort to the dark skin fellows."[2] The following year, the company attempted to assuage fears about a possible labor shortage by letting local farmers know that "[a]nother bunch of Mexicans were brought to the vicinity this week."[3] By

1920, the company continued its strategy by recruiting at least five thousand Mexicans to toil in the fields.

Both the plan to build houses and, even more significant, the decision to recruit Mexican workers, provides a window onto the numerous ways World War I disrupted labor relations in rural Michigan.[4] Simply put, the war threatened the migrant family labor system that Michigan's sugar beet companies had worked so hard to create over the past two decades. For the war, which had inaugurated a period of all-time high sugar prices, also created thousands of jobs in nearby industrial centers like Detroit, Saginaw, and Flint, thereby making it possible for many eastern Europeans, who had long combined urban/industrial work with migrant labor, to stay in the cities year-round. Just as important, the eastern Europeans who chose to remain in the fields were growing ever more militant, demanding higher wages and better living conditions. Therefore, less than a year after United States Department of Labor (USDL) Secretary William B. Wilson responded to the demands of southwestern growers by announcing that his department would waive the contract labor law, head tax, and literacy requirement for Mexicans coming to work in agriculture, Michigan's sugar beet industrialists and farmers began to hire Mexican workers as well. They did so, however, not with the intention of turning the newly arriving Mexicans into neighbors, much less citizens. The announcement that Mexicans would toil in the fields was not followed by plans to build them houses, and thereby transform them socially, politically, or economically. Rather, the sugar companies hoped that Mexicans would tend to the crop as needed and then return south of the border when no longer wanted.

Although the strategy of recruiting Mexicans may have seemed like the ideal solution to their labor problems, industrialists and growers would soon find that relying on a government program, which was basically a racialized labor program, would come with political costs. Perhaps most important of all, it would ensure that their "labor problem" would no longer be a private affair but rather a matter of national and even international interest. For its part, the federal government found itself acting as a labor padrone, a position that would prove much easier to assume than to abandon.

"The State as Padrone"[5]

The "labor shortage" that threatened rural Michigan during World War I was part of a national crisis as farmers from coast to coast scoured the nation in search of workers. In the South, white planters complained that the war had disrupted land, labor, and race relations as thousands of African Americans left for northern industrial employment, while those who stayed behind often bargained for higher wages and more humane working conditions.[6] Growers in the Southwest pointed to the newly signed 1917 Immigration Act, which raised the head tax and instituted a literacy test, as the reason they had lost access to their "cheap" workforce.[7] Even midwestern farmers warned that by creating opportunities in nearby cities and pulling farm boys into the trenches of Europe, the war had stolen able-bodied workers from their fields. Farmers throughout the nation insisted that if they were to answer the government's plea to grow more crops, the government would have to help them solve their wartime labor problem.

As a result of this crisis, the federal government stepped directly into rural labor issues, much as it did for the industrial sector. However, the labor problem in rural America was defined primarily as a labor shortage and not as a labor-relations problem. In contrast to the urban industrial realm, where the federal government's most significant role involved mediating wages, hours, working conditions, and union recognition so that workers and employers could resolve their differences peacefully, the various federal government agencies in rural America spent most of their time and resources trying to find a sufficient workforce. During the war, the most significant aspect of the government's rural labor policy involved the daunting task of recruiting thousands of workers to the fields and keeping them there for the duration of the conflict. Historian Cindy Hahamovitch's characterization of the "State as the Padrone" in the South during the war can be applied to the nation as a whole, albeit to varying degrees.[8]

At first, the federal government believed that the farm labor problem was merely a matter of adjusting supply to fit demand—a matter of finding enough workers to toil in the fields. In a conference held just days after the United States declared war, the USDA and the USDL planned to solve the looming labor shortage by bringing workers into areas where they were needed and transporting excess workers out of areas where labor was already plentiful. USDA county agents would determine where workers would go and in what numbers, while the USDL would locate surplus workers. Viewing the labor shortage in strict economic terms, both agencies at first naïvely believed that their main task would be largely bureaucratic and logistical.[9]

It did not take long before the federal government was forced to rethink the simple "supply-and-demand" plan for solving the agricultural labor problem and come up with more specific strategies for addressing the question, "Who Will Help Harvest the Crops?"¹⁰ And in practice these strategies tended to mesh with regional ideals and mores about race, gender, and age. In the South, where racial and labor hierarchies were closely intertwined, the USDA opted for coercive and punitive labor policies by encouraging local and state officials to institute vagrancy laws as well as "work or fight" measures for those who, because of race and class, were deemed agricultural laborers. In the Southwest, the USDL used its influence and power to help growers import thousands of Mexicans to work in the nation's "factories in the fields," and looked the other way as growers encouraged tens of thousands of Mexicans to cross the border surreptitiously. In both the South and Southwest, then, the state reinforced regional ideas about race and agricultural labor.¹¹

Relying on an idealized vision of the Midwest as a place of "white" family farms bereft of class conflict, the federal government at first thought that Michigan's farmers would be best served by developing local solutions to their labor problem. The idea here was that midwestern communities—supposedly homogenous and harmonious—would be able to "pull together" during the war. As head of the U.S. Food Administration, Herbert Hoover vested postal agents and USDA county agents with the power to recruit laborers, and in an open letter to Michigan farmers, he promised that "we can find a solution," even "if we have to turn out [our] town population into the fields."¹² Michigan's federal wartime labor administrator also publicized the local solution, claiming that "help secured near home is the safest proposition," and advising farmers, "If you need help advertise in your local paper. You may be surprised at the number of replies you get."¹³ In his new role as chairman of food preparedness, Michigan's former governor Fred Warner asked urban employers to let their men go to work on farms.¹⁴ To further help local communities meet their labor needs, the federal government also opened two new labor agencies so that local men could find out which of their neighbors needed help, and needy farmers could identify willing workers.¹⁵ Finally, small-town newspapers encouraged "city men," and especially businessmen, to come soil their hands in the fields to help their farming neighbors.¹⁶

In addition to cajoling grown men to work in the fields, the federal government turned to the nation's youngest community members to help meet wartime labor needs by establishing the Boys Working Reserve. Created and run by the Department of the Interior, the Reserve was a national program to entice millions of the nation's boys from rural and urban schools, Boy Scout troops, YMCAs, and community welfare organizations to work in the fields during the war. In Michigan, local newspapers encouraged young boys and their parents to think of agricultural labor as an extension of the war effort, with headlines like, "Boys to Help Raise Food—Will Be Enlisted and Trained as though They were Soldiers" and "Boys Will Help to Win War."[17] Reluctant farmers also found themselves deluged with pleas that they should welcome city boys on their farms, with the farm newspapers running ads promising them that, contrary to conventional wisdom, these boys "ARE NOT young aristocrats" but rather "honest and decent natural athletes whose talents could be easily transformed on the farm."[18] The propaganda went both ways: boys who went to work in the fields could be assured that they were doing a hard day's work for the good of the nation, while farmers could rest assured that the patriotic boys who came to work for them would be willing and eager to do whatever they were told to keep the agricultural home front productive.

In spite of the federal government's optimism that labor problems could be best solved locally, Michigan's farmers had a hard time finding enough workers willing to harvest the crops. Instead of heading to the nearest farm in need of help, farm workers increasingly set their sights on nearby cities, where industrial work was more than plentiful and the wages much higher. Farmers who succeeded in reversing the trend by luring urban men to their farms often found that they were not the best workers. One farmer from the small town of Ithaca complained that the "factory labor" he employed on the advice of a federal agricultural agent not only abused his horses but resisted working at all.[19] Plans to get local businessmen to toil in the fields did not fare much better. Although many townsmen promised to work in the fields as an act of patriotism, those who actually helped to harvest the crops remained a relatively small number. And finally, the Boys Working Reserve inspired more flag waving for the participating boys than profits for local farmers who were desperate for able-bodied workers. Instead of greatly augmenting their rural workforce, farmers held on to what labor they could get and worked themselves and their families harder than ever before. Those with the money attempted to mechanize what operations they could. Throughout the war, farmers continued to complain about the labor shortage.

The issue of finding plenty of workers proved especially vexing to the sugar beet industry, which had long struggled to meet its exceptionally demanding labor needs. Over the course of the war years, large numbers of eastern European families, the mainstay of the labor force for the previous fifteen years, abandoned the fields altogether. Not even the hold-back clauses and staggered payments could stop them from leaving the fields when other opportunities arose. Of all the families the National Child Labor Committee (NCLC) visited in the spring of 1918, almost one-fourth had "moved on" before the final harvest.[20] A sugar company agriculturist admitted to the NCLC investigator that the labor contract was only "a piece of paper," and "you can't make the hunkies stay if they take a notion to up and leave."[21]

Equally troublesome were the ever-more militant eastern European families who remained in the fields. Months before the United States even joined the war effort, farmers asked the sugar beet companies to include labor bonuses to stop the workers from demanding more pay, or worse yet, leaving the fields for better pay elsewhere.[22] Over the following months, field bosses continued to be troubled by the eastern Europeans who, "always wanting more money," would wait until a crucial part of the season, and then threaten to leave unless farmers agreed to pay more. In some cases, migrant families gained an additional $4 an acre.[23] By the summer of 1918, not coincidentally the same year the sugar companies began to look to Mexico for workers, farmers also became alarmed that "foreign-language-speaking agitators" were attempting to organize beet workers with the hope of instigating large-scale strikes. Commenting on the growing disquiet in the fields, one observer reported how, "the feeling of unrest passing over the entire industrial world is evident in the beet industry."[24] Fearing the worst, a year later, the *Tuscola County Advertiser* ran an article warning farmers how an "unknown person," possibly an Industrial Workers of the World (IWW) organizer, had unsuccessfully attempted to place an advertisement in the paper calling for an immediate $4 price increase per acre, threatening that "unless demands were met all workers will move away." Not surprisingly, the newspaper concluded that "strike fever possesses beet workers."[25]

Although little became of the IWW organizing effort, or any of the workers' other plans to organize, the farmers responded to the workers with little patience and even less understanding. Rather than join hands with the workers, as one might have expected based on the fact that they themselves were organizing during the war years, and that many of them belonged to progressive and radical organizations that were calling for "industrial democracy," farmers looked for ways to keep their labor costs to a minimum. In contrast to their politically charged demand for justice and equality with respect to the industrialists, when it came to their own labor relations, farmers abandoned both the rhetoric and substance of their own organizing efforts. As such, farmers had no problem asking the state to level the playing field so that they could garner their fair share of profits from the industrialists, while also expecting that same state to provide them with a cheap and easily controlled labor force.

As they struggled to keep workers in the fields, Michigan's farmers criticized the federal government, charging that its labor solutions were unrealistic and questioning whether patriotism was the best means for addressing the farm labor problem. The editors of *Michigan Business Farming* insisted that "town men of farm experience" and the Boys Working Reserve "do not in our judgment provide a remedy for the farm labor shortage or insure a steady and dependable supply of help."[26] The federal government had failed to realize that farmers in the Midwest did not want just any workers in their fields. If the nation's urban industries did not have to rely on local patriots to carry them through the war, then, farmers asked, why should they have to do so? This was particularly true for the state's sugar beet farmers, who had long relied on the sugar companies to provide them with a dependent, reliable, and cheap source of labor. At a time when the state was asking sugar beet farmers to produce more sugar beet than ever before, farmers responded back that without enough workers to toil in the fields, they would not be able to keep growing the crop.[27]

Finding a New Labor Force

In contrast to Michigan's sugar beet industrialists and farmers, who found the federal government unwilling to acknowledge, much less address, their situation, at least some southwestern growers had a much easier time convincing the government to act on their behalf.[28] Just weeks after the United States joined the war, they asked USDL Secretary William B. Wilson to waive the head tax and literacy clause for Mexicans coming into the United States to work in the fields. Heeding these demands, in May 1917 Wilson invoked a provision of the newly signed 1917 Immigration Act granting the USDL the authority to admit workers on a temporary and emergency basis. Wilson's departmental order allowed the temporary admission of Mexicans and their families as agricultural workers for six months without paying a head tax or passing a literacy test. He also waived the restrictions imposed by the 1885 contract labor law by allowing U.S. corporations to recruit Mexican workers abroad. Well aware that this policy would provoke a vigorous protest from labor leaders, politicians, and the general public, Secretary Wilson also implemented a number of restrictions to try to make sure that those workers who came into the United States would not drift into other employment and thereby undermine "white" men and their wages, or migrate permanently outside the control of the USDL. Prospective employers had to file a formal application informing the USDL how many workers they needed and the wages they planned to pay. They then had to meet the laborers at the border and chaperone them to the fields. To stop Mexicans from "drifting" to other jobs, the USDL took two photos of each worker and accompanying family members and insisted that the employers withhold a percentage of their pay until the end of the season. Perhaps most important of all, Wilson stipulated that employers were obligated to alert the immigration authorities if any Mexicans in their employ either quit or disappeared. Going much further than simply lifting immigration restrictions, Secretary Wilson tried to create a captive labor force, with the federal government promising to ensure that those workers who came would not be free to forge their own paths of mobility.[29]

In creating the temporary labor program, the federal government created a form of racialized and nationalized labor. For the initial order—and the subsequent circulars and memos that modified it—repeatedly emphasized not only the temporary nature of the program but that those who came should be confined to agricultural pursuits and that under no circumstances would they be allowed to become immigrants, much less citizens. (The occupational categories were expanded in 1918 to include mining, railway work, and construction.) Any workers who violated the program's rules were to be deported immediately. In the initial order, Wilson explicitly stipulated that none of the "temporarily admitted aliens" would be allowed to remain permanently in the United States, nor should any "engage in any other [work] than farm work."[30]

Because of the historical context—the fact that support for immigration restriction was mounting and restrictionists had finally succeeded in passing a literacy test over President Woodrow Wilson's veto—Secretary Wilson's actions prompted a number of quick and biting responses. Just days after Secretary Wilson issued the order, the House Committee on Immigration and Naturalization passed a resolution condemning his actions as a "violation of the immigration laws."[31] Wilson also received a stinging letter from John L. Burnett, the chairman of the House's Immigration Committee, who complained that Wilson's actions undermined his and Congress' efforts to control and restrict immigration. In response to Burnett's charges, Wilson acknowledged Congress' recent legislative accomplishments, but nonetheless insisted, "if you had been familiar with all the circumstances surrounding the action of the Department and the motives prompting it, you would have been satisfied that both [immigration commissioner] Mr. Caminetti and myself were prompted only by a desire to meet an acute emergency situation in such a manner as to prevent wide propaganda for the repeal of the Immigration Law before it had time to demonstrate its value to the country." Wilson further justified his action by explaining how he and Caminetti had been pushed to recruit Filipinos, Hawaiians, and even Chinese to meet the labor needs of southwestern growers. He quickly added that, "Of course, we could not yield to importunities of that kind. We have all the race problems in the United States that it is advisable for us to undertake to deal with at the present time."[32] Immigration Commissioner Caminetti echoed this sentiment when responding to criticism that the United States should only admit immigrants who would one day be "fit for citizenship" by stating emphatically that even though the current order would allow Mexicans to come into the United States as agricultural laborers, it "does not allow any one to become a resident beyond a short visiting period and . . . it opens no possibility to any one of becoming a citizen."[33]

In exempting Mexican workers from many of the 1917 restrictions, Secretary Wilson and Caminetti insisted that they were not trying to undermine the spirit of the nation's newest immigration restrictions but rather that they were attempting to solve the emergency labor problem without creating what they feared would be a permanent racial problem. And both men insisted that if a "race problem" emerged, it would be only temporary and easily remedied because Mexican workers could be easily deported. Equally important, both men were adamant that the labor program would not lead to U.S. citizenship, much less assimilation for the Mexican workers who came to toil in the United States. Or at least they wanted to believe that this would be the case.

As Wilson and Caminetti headed off opposition from within the United States, they also found themselves confronted with a critic from across the U.S. border—newly inaugurated Mexican President Venustiano Carranza. Although Secretary Wilson viewed the labor program as a distinctly domestic issue—a matter of meeting labor needs during the war—Mexican officials saw the order in a decidedly international framework. In fact, Wilson's actions put President Carranza in a difficult position. As president of revolutionary Mexico, Carranza was committed to a nationalist vision of his nation that frowned upon the migration of thousands of fellow patriots to the United States. In a nationalist effort to protect Mexicans who traveled across the border to work, Mexico's newly adopted 1917 Constitution, which accorded Mexican workers more rights and protections at home than any other Western Hemisphere nation, also mandated that all its nationals have contracts in hand before leaving Mexico. Those contracts were supposed to guarantee Mexican workers minimum wages as well as assurances regarding medical care, housing, labor conditions, and funds to return home.[34]

Mandating fair treatment in the Mexican constitution was one thing; making sure that the rules outlined in that constitution followed Mexicans across the border was clearly a different matter altogether. And in the quest to turn policy into practice, Carranza could not ignore a number of very important political and economic realities. Not only did Mexicans leave because of the absence of economic opportunity in Mexico, but they remitted valuable resources back home that helped to relieve the tensions created by poverty and revolution. In addition, the national government had limited power, much less autonomy, in Mexico, often having to defer to local and regional authorities. And finally, as the much weaker partner in an unequal relationship, Mexico was in no position to challenge its more powerful and aggressive northern neighbor.

Caught between these competing realities, Carranza did the best that he could. He asked for state and municipal governments to do their part to dissuade Mexican nationals from leaving Mexico without formally condoning or condemning their actions. For example, Carranza and his administration helped distribute a steady barrage of reports from Mexican consuls within the United States alerting potential immigrants of the difficulties they would face if they went to work abroad, warning them how they might be used as strikebreakers, paid inferior wages, or drafted into the U.S. Army, thereby leaving their wives and children "completely abandoned."[35] The Mexican Secretary of Foreign Relations also called on border state governors to discourage Mexicans from accepting the employment offers of U.S. corporations, noting that many who had previously traveled to the United States were now "penniless" and stranded at the border.[36]

In addition to encouraging Mexican consuls in the United States and border officials in Mexico to publicize the plight of exploited Mexicans, Carranza also asked local municipal officials and state governors to do all they could to administratively control the conditions under which Mexicans immigrated to the United States. In this way, Mexican officials attempted to make the United States' unilateral program bilateral in practice. In August 1917, just months after Wilson announced the wartime program, Mexican officials in Piedras Negras alerted the American consul in that city that they intended to enforce those sections of the Mexican Constitution that required foreign companies recruiting Mexican labor to provide credentials, including a copy of labor contracts to Mexican officials.[37] After these efforts proved unsuccessful, the Mexican secretary of industry and commerce, working with the Mexican foreign secretary, issued a circular order outlining in detail the rights of Mexicans working abroad. Described by historian Lawrence Cardoso as a "model contract," the order looked a great deal like the United States' own temporary emergency program, except that the specific stipulations sought to protect Mexicans working in the United States. The order mandated that

Mexicans who worked in the United States would be paid equal to community standards (and no less than $2 a day) and receive that payment in cash at least once a week. The order also demanded that U.S. companies cover the medical bills of Mexicans who fell ill in the United States and pay the transportation costs of all nationals who wished to return home, without deducting the money from the workers' paychecks. Perhaps most ambitious of all, the order called for Mexican workers who arrived in the United States to register with the nearest Mexican consul so that Mexican authorities could help adjudicate any contract disputes that might arise within the United States.[38]

Although Mexican officials failed to stop out-migration and lacked the power to force U.S. corporations to sign their contracts, their actions nonetheless infuriated a number of U.S. officials, who bristled at the suggestion of having to deal with Mexican authorities at all. The American consulate in Piedras Negras responded with outrage, complaining to Secretary of State Robert Lansing that, "It seems that Mexican authorities [are] attempting to dictate the status of Mexican laborers on American soil."[39] Howard Hopkins, chief farm service director in charge of Mexican labor, was even more frustrated with the Mexican officials who had tried to infringe upon his nation's unilateral program. Hopkins charged that Carranza and other "Jefes" had tried to interfere with U.S. efforts to recruit Mexican workers because they were "rabidly anti-American and strongly pro-German." He then complained that the root of the Mexican officials' antagonism to the United States was "jealousy and fear which manifest themselves in the hatred" of "all things American." Turning to the Mexican people, Hopkins described them as "ignorant" peons, susceptible to "false reports." Saving his harshest criticism for the Mexican border officials who had sometimes tried to stop Mexicans from leaving for the United States, Hopkins insisted that "there is no law and order in Mexico at present, each petty chief is a law unto himself and does as he pleases." Hopkins then contended that "the only way to get laborers from Mexico is in spite of Mexican officials," suggesting that if the United States advertised its labor needs or tried to work with Mexican officials, this would be "fatal" to the nation's objectives. Rather, he preferred a more clandestine strategy. "By working quietly, carefully, and intelligently we can get laborers from Mexico; if we let them slip across the river and the border." In other words, Hopkins wanted U.S. immigration officials to look the other way while encouraging thousands of Mexicans to cross the border illegally. In defending this proposition, Hopkins insisted that illegal border crossings would not lead to lawlessness within the United States, for a "strict enforcement of the rules and a few deportations early in the game will have a salutary effect for it is very important that the laborers understand that the rules will be enforced and an actual example is the only thing that they will understand."[40]

Hopkins' confidence that the United States could easily manipulate Mexicans at the border and within the United States belied the privately held viewpoints of many labor and immigration officials, who worried that they could control neither the border nor the Mexican nationals who had come to work as part of the government's wartime program. Part of the problem was that in spite of the public pronouncements and the order's regulations, Secretary Wilson had created a bureaucratic program without establishing a bureaucracy to run and oversee it. For example, weeks after the program had already begun, G. H. Harris, acting supervising inspector for the U.S. Immigration Service, sent out a memo to all immigration inspectors with only vague guidelines for making sure that the program's rules would be followed. Harris then requested each immigration district to nominate qualified individuals, who would then be responsible for keeping track of incoming Mexicans. These individuals, however, need not be official government agents. In fact, Harris advised that it would be preferable to appoint "responsible corporations, societies [and] organizations" to keep an eye on Mexican guest workers. After passing the buck, Harris applauded the efforts of one unnamed community whose war council citizens had agreed to monitor the "aliens" and "to prevent their entrance into other lines of industry."[41] Hailing this war council's actions as "most commendable," Harris advised that other war councils and miscellaneous organizations should do the same.

Few other war councils followed in those footsteps. Moreover, neither the USDL nor the Bureau of Immigration had plans for dealing with any problems. In early 1918, just months before the second wartime crop was to be planted, Commissioner Caminetti wrote to Secretary William Wilson to express his "grave" "concern and dissatisfaction" with the fact that the program he and his superior had created had seemed to open the door of illegal immigration, with thousands of "illiterate" Mexicans coming in, "with but slight chance of the Department even being able to locate and identify many of them." Even worse, Caminetti complained that although most Mexicans had come to work in agriculture, many had "drifted" into mining, railroad, and industrial jobs. Caminetti also questioned the original justification for the program, noting that what employers really wanted was an "abundant supply of labor" with which to drive down wages. Speaking about the difficulty of confining Mexicans to agricultural work, Caminetti was forced to admit that the bureau could not enforce its own rules, lamenting that "it seems that anything short of actually requiring the importers to keep the employees in compounds or in some other similar manner to exercise a constant guard over them is not likely to produce the desired result; and to permit the men to be compelled to work in certain places, it is apprehended, would verge too nearly upon peonage and duress to permit of the adoption of any plan of that kind." After suggesting that perhaps the Department of Labor could distribute better instructions and provide greater resources to immigration officials as a way to improve what he feared was already a fatally flawed program, Caminetti concluded his letter on a pessimistic note, pondering whether the initial order should be "withdrawn" and the current program "abandoned," and noting that "much more is involved . . . than the enforcement of the immigration law."[42]

Although Caminetti did not specify what he meant by his comment that "much more is involved," he was absolutely right. The problems Wilson and Caminetti faced during World War I highlight the logistical and legal (not to mention moral) challenges of creating a captive and controlled labor force in a nation ideally committed to free labor, and, with a number of very important exceptions, open immigration.

The Armistice and the Battle on the Home Front

Considering all the difficulties Wilson and Caminetti faced during the war, we can only imagine that they greeted the November 1918 armistice with a sense of relief. At least that is what their initial actions seem to reveal. For in December 1918, Secretary Wilson issued an order warning the nation's growers that the temporary admission program would be winding down and that the USDL would process orders for only three more days, which basically meant that no new orders would be granted.[43] Almost immediately, however, Wilson was inundated with complaints from southwestern growers protesting that they had held up their end of the bargain during the war by producing more sugar and that it was unjust to cut off access to the very workers who had made that production possible. Implying that the government had foisted Mexican workers on them during the war, growers claimed that they could not continue to grow sugar beet without this "cheap" and "tractable" labor force.

Fearing that sugar beet farmers might actually abandon the crop, and that the skyrocketing price of sugar might rise even higher, Secretary Wilson modified his December 1918 order on January 2, 1919 to allow growers and sugar beet industrialists to keep recruiting Mexicans to the fields until June 30, 1919.[44] After this deadline passed, Wilson extended the program "until the ratification of the treaty of peace, but no later than January 1, 1920," so that Mexicans would be available for the entire 1919 season.[45] On February 12, 1920 and again on April 20, 1920, however, Secretary Wilson again extended the wartime labor exemptions until March 1921—nearly four years after the United States first joined the conflict and two years and five months after it had ended.[46] In spite of a more than ample paper trail detailing the labor program's trials and tribulations, the ending of the war did not lead to its dissolution.[47] Unlike other wartime programs, which were disbanded almost immediately once the war ended, this one seemed to have nine lives.

The process of transforming the wartime labor policy into a peacetime fixture was met with vocal resistance and ignited a debate over labor, race, nationality, and immigration that would continue well into the 1920s.[48] Labor leaders were so convinced that Mexicans had ventured outside agriculture and thereby undermined the wages and status of white workers that in spring 1920, the American Federation of Labor passed a resolution asking Congress to bar Mexican and Canadian laborers from coming into the United States under the wartime extension.[49] For very different reasons, the Mexican government, now headed by Alvaro Obregon, also criticized the wartime extensions, threatening to "prevent by force the exodus of workmen to the United States." The Mexican government also warned potential Mexican emigrants that they would find themselves victims of "mob violence" if they chose to go to the United States.[50]

In response to criticism at home and abroad, in the spring of 1920 Secretary Wilson appointed a special commission to investigate whether Mexicans who had come to work in the states had drifted into cities to compete with white labor, and whether the temporary admission of this "class of laborers" was really necessary.[51] As the commission began its investigation, it chose not to "conduct an exhaustive survey with statistics" but rather to make an "intelligent impression" by talking with labor organizations, employment officials, local chambers of commerce, representatives of sugar companies, farmers, railroad employers, and immigration officers in ten western states.[52] In theory, the commission was supposed to be a neutral fact-finding body; in practice, committee members seemed intent to prove that the wartime provisions had been followed. When this proved impossible, the commission went to great lengths to argue that the numerous "infractions" did not really undermine the spirit of the original temporary exemptions. For example, after finding that thousands of Mexicans had indeed abandoned agricultural work for industrial employment, the commission claimed that these violations simply reflected a growing need for unskilled labor rather than a problem with the wartime labor program.[53] Similarly, the commission tried to allay fears that

Mexicans who had found industrial jobs might decide to stay in the United States and thereby transform their status from foreign worker to immigrant to citizen. Claiming that Mexican immigration is best understood as a two-way stream, one heading north and the other south, the commission asserted that "the Mexicans of our day, being descendants of a race in whose veins flow in dominating measure Indian blood, evince the same migratory characteristics that have always been a feature of the Indian race."[54] In other words, Mexicans were "genetically" destined to a life of migration. The fact that so many had abandoned the fields was not a problem to be addressed but rather a temporary aberration that would work itself out in time.

Commission members, who had been given the sole responsibility of ascertaining if Mexicans had abandoned farm labor and taken up industrial work, went much further in their final report, predicting a dismal future if the federal government cut off Mexican immigration anytime soon.[55] Insisting that the question was not whether the United States would need immigrants to work in agriculture but rather which ones and under what circumstances, the commission endorsed the idea that the U.S. government should continue to import Mexican workers because "so far as the Mexican is concerned, he presents certain economic advantages not possessed by other nationalities."[56] In other words, unless white farmers had unlimited access to Mexican workers, they might simply abandon the fields, leaving the nation's land resources to those willing to do the work themselves. In the eyes of the commission members, the future of the nation's white farmers, and the nation's long-cherished Jeffersonian ideal, depended on the existence of a cheap, racially "degraded" labor force, which would be unable to climb the agricultural ladder or challenge the dominance of their white employers.[57]

Mexicans in the Midwest

Although the commission's report gave the impression that Mexicans had worked only in the Southwest, thousands of Mexicans labored in the Midwest as well. Beginning in 1918 Michigan's sugar beet industrialists and farmers jumped at the opportunity to both supplement and replace eastern Europeans with Mexicans. The government's program, which included hold-back clauses that confined Mexicans to agricultural work, meshed well with the sugar companies' own contracts, which had long included hold-back clauses, staggered payments, and the withholding of return tickets until the end of the season. The prospect of recruiting workers who would come to toil for a few months and then leave after the crop had been harvested also appealed to farmers and sugar companies long accustomed to the yearly migration of thousands of workers. And finally, Michigan's sugar beet companies and farmers hoped that the federal government's presence would discourage Mexican workers from demanding higher wages or leaving before the sugar beet crop had been harvested.

Over the course of the war and postwar years, some of Michigan's sugar beet companies worked closely with the USDL, signing contracts with the government and pledging to abide by the program's regulations. Other sugar beet industrialists, however, like many of their southwestern counterparts, simply bypassed the government's program and recruited Mexican workers on their own by placing ads in Spanish-language newspapers in San Antonio and distributing fliers in Mexico, promising all who crossed the border that they would be transported to Michigan's beet fields. Thousands of Mexicans took up the offer to work in Michigan, making up as many as half of all migrant workers toiling in the fields.[58]

The arrival of thousands of Mexican workers in Michigan was greeted by local farmers and townspeople as a "welcomed invasion."[59] For example, in March 1920, the third season Mexicans had been coming to the fields, the *Adrian Daily Telegraph* headlined with the seemingly ominous title, "Blissfield Invaded by Mexican Army—200 Who Will Work in Beet Fields Reach Village," especially considering that the headline just two columns away read "Agua Preita is to be Battle Ground . . . American Owned Railroad in Sinolia is Being Taken over by Troops of the New Republic." However, the militaristic headline alerting locals to the arrival of this "Mexican Army" included the subheading: "Laden with Cooking Utensils They Wander About the Streets and Curse Michigan's Climate." The article detailed how these "dark tanned brothers" had been "drawn and mobilized from the warm sunny fields of the Laredo district to be shipped northwards." The incoming Mexicans were described as a people who "seemed to be proud of their linguistic shortcomings," and who, when offered cigarettes, "swarmed at the proffered package like flies after a sugar bowl." The article concluded: "When the beet season is over and the laborers have collected 'mooch money' they will return to their homes to smoke cigarettes and drink pulque and watch their wives work."[60]

The racist and jocular reporting of the arrival of Mexican migrants contrasts sharply with the other articles about farm labor in the same newspaper. For the *Adrian Daily Telegraph* also carried serious reports warning that many of the local farms would remain "idle" if willing workers were not found soon.[61] The *Telegraph* estimated that at least 1,500 workers were needed in the fields and that if they did not arrive shortly, more than ninety thousand acres would remain uncultivated.⁶² When the sugar companies began to recruit Mexican workers, then, they were attempting to meet what promised to be a dire labor situation.

In spite of public assurances that incoming Mexicans would not follow in the footsteps of their eastern European counterparts by striking and demanding more pay, Mexicans proved much less vulnerable and compliant than the state, the farmers, or the sugar companies had hoped. As soon as they arrived, Mexicans demanded respect and showed numerous signs of militancy. Even under the threat of deportation, many refused to abide by the stipulations in their contracts that they considered unfair. One of the most important sources of contention involved the wage withholding scheme that the government created to tie the workers to the fields. The general manager of the Michigan Sugar Company complained that though his company had agreed to withhold part of the Mexicans' wages, Mexican workers made this impossible by insisting that they were "competent to take care of their own money matters." The workers even refused to tend to the crop "at a critical time when the crop needed great care" unless the company handed over all unpaid wages. With few options, at least eight of Michigan's sixteen factories paid the workers their pay as they earned it.⁶³ Just as important, the contract rates for work continued to skyrocket, even after Mexicans began coming to the fields. The pay per acre increased from $21 in 1916, to $23 in 1917, to $24 in 1918, to a high of $30–35 an acre by 1920.⁶⁴ Although these wage increases did not keep pace with inflation, they were certainly much higher than either the companies or the farmers had anticipated.

The recruitment of Mexican workers also failed to solve the turnover problem. Just like eastern Europeans, thousands of Mexicans simply abandoned agricultural work or combined agricultural and industrial work during their time in Michigan. Of course, Mexicans were not supposed to leave the agricultural pursuits for which they were first recruited, under the threat of being reported to immigration authorities. Nonetheless, there is plenty of evidence that many Mexicans combined industrial and agricultural work as soon as they entered Michigan, with some families migrating to nearby Saginaw, where they found work in the Grey Iron Foundry, while others traveled to Detroit to work at Ford's plant.⁶⁵ The Continental Sugar Company, with processing plants in Michigan and Ohio, had an especially difficult time trying to keep Mexican immigrants in the fields. In May 1918, Continental recruited 348 Mexicans, traveling to the border to chaperone them to the Midwest. During the first month in the United States, however, 35 percent of the workers simply deserted the fields, presumably for better work opportunities elsewhere.⁶⁶ By January 1919, company officials could account for only 144 of the workers, whom they returned to immigration officials in Texas, noting that the "remainder of the laborers, with the exception of those herein listed as having entered the employ of other companies, have deserted and their whereabouts is unknown."⁶⁷

The problem was not just locating missing workers but persuading those who had been found to return to the fields. Writing to Truman Palmer, head of the U.S. Sugar Manufacturing Association, the general manager of the Continental Sugar Company complained that his company was having a hard time dutifully following the USDL's orders not only because the overwhelming majority of workers simply abandoned the fields to whereabouts unknown, but because the immigration officers he had called upon for help insisted that they "had no authority nor instructions to assist us in the maintenance of the instructions of the department." Equally maddening, when Continental officials finally located "deserters," the local police refused to help and claimed to have "no authority to arrest nor [to] prosecute."⁶⁸

Clearly, the wartime labor program had not worked as either Secretary Wilson or Commissioner Caminetti had hoped. Not only had the federal government failed to figure out ways to keep track of and control workers, company officials found it impossible to keep workers toiling in the fields when much higher paying industrial labor beckoned. Creating temporary migrant guest workers in a Department of Labor circular was one thing. Actually ensuring that the workers who came to toil in the fields would conform to the circular's mandates was clearly an altogether different matter. In spite of the numerous violations over the course of the war years and postwar years, none of the above-mentioned actors had much interest in publicizing the breakdown of the war labor program. Rather, as sugar prices rose even faster than labor costs, sugar beet industrialists and growers desperately clung to their field workers, all the while doing their best to keep labor problems hidden from public view.

This strategy worked remarkably well—that is, until the onset of the depression during the winter of 1920–1921 left thousands of Mexicans stranded with few resources and even fewer opportunities.⁶⁹ Just days before Christmas in 1920, John Clark, a regional U.S. commissioner of immigration, wrote to his superior warning him that his office was being inundated with reports "of public charge aliens from Saginaw, most of whom are Mexicans." Clark continued by recounting how "during the past sugar beet season, the Michigan Sugar Company brought to this state in the neighborhood of 3,500 of these people for work in the beet fields. With the advent of winter, and the general slump in industrials, these Mexicans are out of work, and are miseraly equipped for the climate." He then told the story of two Mexican couples and their children living together in a boxcar because they had nowhere else to go.[70] Similarly, the commissioner in Detroit also reported that when Mexican families lost their winter jobs, they could not survive off the earnings made from sugar beet work.[71] Other stories warning of destitute Mexicans poured in from all over the state, including Owosso, Lansing, Detroit, and even the small sugar beet towns of Sebewaing, Caro, and Croswell.[72]

Immigration officials blamed the sugar companies for the desperate plight of Mexicans, claiming that the companies had failed to abide by the wartime labor agreements. Officials were especially frustrated with those companies that had legally circumvented the federal government's immigration program by sending circulars and fliers into the interior of Mexico and then hiring Mexicans after they crossed the border.[73] Immigration officials claimed that the sugar companies had induced thousands of Mexicans to enter the United States illegally and then reneged on their promise to pay for their transportation home.[74] The Port Huron immigration commissioner was especially infuriated. Writing to his superior, he pointed out that the Michigan Sugar Company had brought in five thousand Mexicans but that only a small number had actually departed. "Personally, I feel that the Michigan Sugar Co. is at least morally responsible for the situation as we find it today. I reported to you that many of the laborers recruited at San Antonio were given to understand definitely that at the close of the beet season, the Michigan Sugar Co. would furnish transportation back to Texas, and that the Sugar Co. declined to do their part for the simple reason that they had not signed the agreement."[75] Equally important, U.S. immigration officials warned that if the companies did not act now, the Mexican workers would "scatter to the four ends of the earth" where they could not keep track of them.[76] Even the Mexican consul of Chicago complained that the Michigan Sugar Company had recruited Mexicans to come to Michigan based on promises that it now refused to fulfill.[77]

In spite of governmental and community pressure, the sugar companies often refused to return the Mexicans whom they had recruited. One sugar company executive claimed that his company did not have the funds to return its workers to the border because the Mexican families had insisted that the company not withhold their wages.[78] Though it is true that many Mexicans had demanded their wages in full, the company's refusal to transport Mexicans back to Mexico was not just a matter of who would pay the return fare. Perhaps more important, the sugar company officials did not want to let go of their Mexican workers for fear that they might not be able to recruit them to the state again. The prospect of losing their labor force in 1920 was a scary one, for the 1920 season had been the most profitable to date for the sugar companies, and they had little reason to believe that 1921 would be any less profitable, but only if they could assure militant growers that there would be enough workers to tend the crop. Hoping to cash in on the postwar sugar prices, sugar companies asked a Michigan congressman, known as "Sugar Joe Fordney," to pressure immigration officials to allow them to keep Mexican workers through the upcoming 1921 season. Immigration officials politely refused Fordney's request.[79]

With the sugar companies refusing to pay for Mexican workers to return home, philanthropic church groups and municipal and state authorities took matters into their own hands and sponsored what would be the first of many repatriation campaigns. The Saginaw County government, motivated by a mixture of racial nativism and fiscal tightfistedness, returned hundreds of families who had become public charges.[80] In February 1921, Saginaw's mayor, Ben Mercer, applauded his city for being the first in the county to "demobilize the army of Mexicans who have become a burden on the taxpayers."[81] The St. Vincent de Paul Society of Detroit, which spent more than $11,000 to send back hundreds of Mexicans to the border, preferred to see its efforts in a more humanitarian light.[82] According to its annual report, "The Society, made aware of the pitiable conditions, both spiritual and material, prevailing in the Mexican colony in Detroit . . . undertook to defray the expense of any worthy Mexican desiring to return to his own country." To make sure that the Mexicans it helped were "worthy," the society conducted a "thorough investigation" of each case and invoked the "invaluable assistance" of the Mexican consul in Detroit. When the society's own funds failed to meet the transportation expenses of the repatriation efforts, leaders appealed to the bishop of Mexico, who forwarded an additional $12,000 to cover the costs.[83]

Conclusion

Though we do not know exactly how many Mexicans and Mexican Americans were transported to Mexico during the winter of 1920–1921, the repatriation efforts revealed that Michigan's urban and rural residents alike saw Mexicans as a labor force that could be recruited and excluded at will, not potential immigrants to be assimilated. Though the motivation of the groups involved in transporting and repatriating Mexicans varied from punitive to humanitarian, the message was basically the same: Mexicans were welcome as long as they were working in the fields and self sufficient, but once they became public charges, or once locals feared that they might become public charges, they were expected to leave.

It should come as no surprise that local residents would react this way. When Secretary Wilson initiated the wartime labor program, he did so with the confidence that Mexicans could be easily imported and exported as needed and that under no circumstances would they be allowed to become immigrants. That is, the United States' unilateral guest worker program defined Mexicans as workers but not as future neighbors or citizens. The repatriation campaign that followed further reinforced the development of a two-tiered immigration policy—one based on labor and race and the other based on immigration and future naturalization.

The World War I experience, however, highlights the difficulty of trying to create a captive and controlled labor force in a nation ideally committed to free labor and, with important exceptions, free immigration. Unless the United States was willing to adopt draconian measures to track and detain Mexican workers, it simply could not keep them confined to agricultural pursuits or assure that they would leave when their contracts expired. In spite of Wilson's and Caminetti's claims that the temporary immigration program was the best means to maintain legal restrictions on immigration while ensuring that labor shortages be addressed, the line between guest worker and immigrant could be a blurry one. And for a number of Mexican immigrants, crossing the line from temporary worker to permanent immigrant only required walking out of the fields and finding work in nearby urban industrial centers.

6

Mexican Immigrants and Immigration Debate

Two years after passing the historic 1924 Johnson-Reed Act, which severely curtailed the number of southern and eastern Europeans coming into the United States and made it virtually impossible for immigrants from Asia and Africa to enter at all, the U.S. House of Representatives held hearings to discuss a bill to amend that act to include the Western Hemisphere.[1] The hearings, however, focused on only one aspect of immigration, as indicated by the title, "Seasonal Agricultural Laborers from Mexico." During these hearings, Roy Orchard Woodruff, a Michigan congressman who opposed the bill, read a prepared statement about the important role Mexicans played on his state's farms. To convince his fellow congressmen that the Mexicans who had been working in Michigan did not create any "race problems," Woodruff told them that when 3,500 Mexicans met for three days to celebrate "Mexican Independence" in the small town of Shepherd, a town of one thousand whites, there was not the slightest disturbance. "It was the most orderly meeting of its kind" ever seen. But before Woodruff could continue his statement, Congressman Albert Johnson, one of the main architects of the 1924 act and chair of the current hearings, interrupted him, asking: "Now, did you say that Shepherd has become a sort of a Mexican village?" Woodruff quickly replied: "No; there are not Mexicans living there at all. They just assembled there for the purpose of celebrating this particular holiday." When asked by Johnson whether any Mexicans stayed in Michigan during the winter months and "become reconciled to the surroundings," Woodruff claimed, "Not to any extent. I have not known of any who remained during the winter. The Columbia Sugar Co. when the season is closed, gets them together and returns them to the Mexican border. I do not know whether under the law you can compel them to go or not, but I have never observed a single Mexican family around that part of the state in winter time."[2]

This encounter between Woodruff and Johnson demonstrates that the repatriation campaigns of 1920–21 had not stopped the sugar beet industry from looking to Mexico for labor. As early as 1922, Michigan's sugar beet companies began recruiting Mexican workers, and by 1927 Mexicans and Mexican Americans would make up 75 percent of the labor force. The encounter between Woodruff and Johnson also demonstrates that the issue of immigration restriction had not been completely resolved with the passing of the 1924 act. In fact, the Johnson-Reed Act, which did not apply to the Western Hemisphere, fueled the flames of restrictionists, who believed that the bill's restrictions had not gone far enough and that Congress had created a new immigration problem while solving the old one. In the words of one of the most famous nativists, Madison Grant, "it is not logical to limit the number of Europeans while we throw the country open without limitation to Negroes, Indians and half breeds."[3]

Believing that the newly built immigration wall allowed "unworthy" immigrants to continue to enter the nation, men like Albert Johnson of Washington and John Box of Texas began a campaign to shut what they referred to as the "back door." They convinced their fellow congressmen to hold hearings in 1926, 1928, and 1930 to consider various bills to modify the 1924 Immigration Act to include either the Western Hemisphere as a whole or Mexico alone.[4] Recycling much of the racial nativism of the pre-1924 era, avid restrictionists, including eugenicists, labor leaders, patriotic society members, and congressmen, warned that Mexicans, like the "hordes" of southern and eastern Europeans who had come before them, could not truly assimilate into American society. They charged that Mexican immigrants posed a particular threat to the nation because they were "docile," "indolent," and "backward." Restrictionists raised the peril of allowing in a "race" of agricultural workers who would not only undermine white men and wages but also U.S. agriculture—one of the celebrated foundations of American democracy. These nativists went even further by arguing that Mexicans were part of a "racially mixed" population who would undermine the racial stock of the nation. At a time when the nation was attempting to harden its racial boundaries—the Supreme Court had just ruled that Japanese and Indian immigrants were ineligible to naturalize because they were not "white"—Mexican immigrants seemed to pose a particular threat.[5]

As they labored to build a legal wall between the United States and Mexico, the restrictionists faced a well-organized and vocal contingent of anti-restrictionists—including sugar beet interests, cotton growers, ranchers, perishable food producers, railroad executives, and their congressional supporters—who called for an open border with Mexico by using the same kind of racial arguments that had led to the restriction of immigrants from southern and eastern Europe. There was no need, they argued, to put Mexico under immigration quotas because Mexicans did not come to the United States as immigrants but rather as a racially degraded labor force. Furthermore the anti-restrictionists maintained that the issues that usually concerned Congress as it debated immigration restriction—assimilation and citizenship—need not worry those involved in the current debates. In fact, in the same year that Congress considered the 1926 bill to restrict Mexican immigration, a congressman from Michigan, J. Bird Vincent, introduced his own bill to allow the federal government to import Mexicans as agricultural workers and return them after the season was over. His reasoning was quite simple: the United States could end its immigration dilemma if it initiated a labor policy that would both alleviate the fears of the restrictionists regarding the creation of a permanent peon class and also meet the needs of American agriculture.

As the debate over restricting Mexican immigration unfolded in the nation's capitol, Mexicans continued to make their way to Michigan's sugar beet fields.[6] Turning from Congress to the rural communities in which Mexicans worked, we find that the small town of Shepherd was not such an anomaly, and that Mexicans, much like eastern European migrant workers, had their own reasons for working in the fields. For the thousands of Mexicans who worked in rural Michigan, labor in the sugar beet fields was an avenue of geographic, social, and economic mobility when the road to political mobility was blocked. The second half of the chapter will explore that part of the story.

Immigrants or Workers?

When the anti-restrictionists showed up in Washington to defend an open border with Mexico, they labored under the shadow of the nation's most recent immigration restrictions. For although the anti-restrictionists agreed with the racist arguments of their opponents regarding immigration restriction generally, they sought to distinguish the current debate from those that had taken place in 1921 and 1924. To convince Congress that allowing Mexican immigrants into the United States did not threaten the idea of immigration restriction more generally, sugar beet interests often began their testimony in front of Congress with explicit and vigorous endorsements of the nation's immigration barriers.

For example, Harry Austin, the national spokesman for the sugar beet industry, told Congress that his industry wholeheartedly supported both the principles behind and the existing legal framework of immigration restriction. "I am sure that I voice the sentiment of our producers when I say that we have no desire to break down the immigration walls which the committee labored so many years to build up."[7] However, even as sugar beet spokesmen jumped on the nativist bandwagon, paying homage to the newly built immigration walls, they also told Congress that these laws had cut them off from their traditional labor source, southern and eastern European immigrants, forcing them to look elsewhere for agricultural workers.[8] Pointing to the sugar beet industry's difficult position, L. J. Dickinson, an Iowa congressman from a sugar beet district, insisted that the two sides of the immigration debate had potentially reconcilable interests. He stated simply: "I would like to see the two conflicting views worked out on a line where we may preserve that which is necessary in the restriction of immigration, and at the same time help out a labor situation that is very critical."[9]

These anti-restrictionists sought to distinguish the current debate over immigration restriction from the 1921 and 1924 contests by arguing that immigration from Mexico was qualitatively different than immigration from Europe. T. S. Crapo, a Michigan farmer, defended the sugar beet industry's battle to stop the application of the quota system to Mexico by contending that "if restriction of immigration were in any way basically interlocked with the placing of the same rules on Mexico, as upon over-the-seas countries, then the Michigan sugar-beet industry, should stand aside. But it seems to me that for many reasons—some of them unalterably physical reasons—that the Mexican border demands special treatment." To make sure that Congress did not misconstrue his request, he ended with the statement that "if anyway can be thought of which will enable them [the farmers] to avail themselves of Mexican labor for the next few years without impairing the general restriction principle, I think they are entitled to such recognition on the part of Congress."[10] In other words, Congress should discuss the issue of Mexicans as workers rather than Mexicans as immigrants in the traditional sense of the term.

When sugar beet industrialists and their supporters argued that the border between the United States and Mexico should remain open, they also made it very clear that they did not envision a process whereby Mexicans would follow in the footsteps of European immigrants. In a seeming reversal of previous opinion, the Michigan sugar beet industrialists who had frequently described eastern Europeans as "beet hunkies" and "bohunks" now hailed them as "very desirable citizens" who were using their labor in the fields to become both "landowners and citizens."[11] Conversely, they claimed that Mexicans came only to work and not to stay, so the issue was not really a question of immigration but rather a question of labor and race. In defending the idea that it would be possible to confine Mexicans to the beet fields, Michigan representative Woodruff angrily stated, "I do not want to see a condition brought about whereby these aliens come in under the guise of agricultural labor and are permitted to drift into our cities and compete with our skilled labor."[12] A few sugar company representatives went so far as to argue that Mexicans were racially suited to field work, with one asserting that because the average Mexican "descended directly from the Indian" he has "by nature the inherent traits of that race. He is fundamentally rural. He prefers the outdoor life to the confinement of industrial pursuits."[13] To address fears that Mexicans might climb the agricultural ladder, midwestern witnesses insisted that Mexicans would never compete with skilled farm laborers or attempt to buy land and begin farming on their own. After lauding eastern Europeans as a "desirable class, in so far as they become landowners and citizens," Holland—St. Louis plant manager S. R. McLean asserted that Mexicans had no desire to become landowners.[14] Similarly, farmer F. H. Ross told Congress that, "I do not believe that there is any Mexican who is ever going to own a farm."[15]

When describing Mexicans, sugar spokesmen pointed to their own experience with them in the fields. And here, it is important to remember that the question of whether Mexicans would work in sugar beet fields in the Midwest had already been answered. Midwestern sugar beet companies had recruited Mexicans since World War I, when USDL Secretary William B. Wilson allowed the admission of Mexican agricultural workers and their families for six months without paying a head tax or passing a literacy test. Although many Mexicans were repatriated when the depression of 1920–21 hit, almost immediately sugar beet representatives began to recruit Mexican workers once again. In fact, as Congress debated whether or not to expand the quota system to include Mexico, sugar beet industry officials continued to recruit Mexicans in ever greater numbers. According to USDL investigator George Edson, by 1927 Mexicans made up at least 75 percent of the fifteen to twenty thousand migrant beet workers in Michigan's fields. When midwesterners were questioned about what might happen if growing numbers of Mexicans came to the fields, they could respond by citing their own experiences, what they already knew to be "true."

Playing into existing congressional perceptions, sugar company officials told Congress that when Mexicans initially came to work in the fields, local farmers believed that they were lawless, lustful, and lazy by nature. Roy Orchard Woodruff testified that "when they first brought the Mexicans into the farming communities of my state, everybody looked upon them with apprehension. . . . The people of the country had been led to believe that Mexicans were a worthless and dangerous lot, a lot of brigands, and the housewife on the farm was scared to death."[16] S. R. McLean, the manager of the Holland—St. Louis Sugar Company, likewise testified that "on my first trip down there, when we shipped out some 500, I rather thought that a Mexican was a greaser and could not be trusted. Our farmers in the North were very doubtful as to their efficiency as beet labor and wanted to double-bar their doors at night for fear of attacks by morning."[17]

The witnesses then told how they soon discovered that Mexicans were not a threat to their social order but rather the perfect labor force—one that was pliant, docile, tractable, hardworking, lawful, self-isolating, and temporary. Noting only three cases of "disorderly conduct" among the four thousand Mexicans his company brought to Michigan, L. B. Tompkins insisted "these people [are] clean, peaceable, and law abiding. . . . They are courteous and respectable to our women, much more so than our American men are to the Mexican women."[18] Even more revealing, Representative Woodruff told his fellow congressmen that it took only a few years for Michigan's residents to recognize that "the Mexican is a real acquisition to the community." He quickly qualified this statement by adding, "I do not mean by that that he is a man who will become easily assimilated, not by any manner of means, but people have learned to know that he is not dangerous: he attends to his own business, does his own work, and does it well. As far as I know, when that work is finished in the fall, the Mexicans have left my district."[19] According to the anti-restrictionists, Mexicans were desirable because they would not stay or assimilate—they could be manipulated to come and go just like the agricultural crops themselves. There was no need to create an immigration barrier, no need to draw a tight boundary between the United States and Mexico, because the Mexicans who came north would eventually return home.

The argument that Mexicans would not assimilate or adopt U.S. citizenship was developed into a racist "homing" theory that Mexicans "naturally" returned to Mexico at the end of each season.[20] This theory was repeated over and over again, even when evidence to the contrary emerged. For example, when speaking in front of Congress in 1926, Holland—St. Louis plant manager S. R. McLean was forced to admit that many of the Mexicans his company had recruited were not returning south, and that some had even begun to "winter" in the countryside in between beet seasons. McLean even acknowledged that it was possible, hypothetically speaking, that Mexicans could one day buy land. But he nonetheless assured all that "there is nothing to fear.... These Mexicans wish to drift back to their kind. They do not wish to stay over or stay out in the county, but wish to drift back."[21] What made Mexicans such a unique "class of labor," then, was their alleged lack of initiative toward landholding and industrial work, their docile, courteous, and tractable "nature," and perhaps most important of all, a vaguely defined "homing instinct" that would eventually pull them back to Mexico. According to the sugar beet industry, Mexicans made the perfect nonimmigrant workforce.

While sugar beet industry spokesmen spent a good deal of time trying to convince Congress that Mexicans were the perfect migrant labor force, they also went to great lengths to hail the benefits of their industry to American agriculture and America's white farmers, warning Congress that if Mexican immigration was cut off, this important agricultural industry would soon disappear. In this case, the midwestern witnesses were in a special position. Pointing to the fact that the midwestern sugar beet industry depended on thousands of family farmers, the majority of whom had small farms, the sugar beet industrialists, farmers, and supporters hailed this industry as no ordinary one but rather the "basis of modern agriculture," where the best of industry and agriculture and American corporatism and family farming had come together in an unprecedented manner. They insisted that cutting off Mexican labor would leave family farmers without the workforce that they needed to grow the labor-intensive crops that had become a mainstay on many farms. "In my part of the state," T. S. Crapo warned, "The sugar beet has been the instrument which has made it possible for innumerable families, who love the land, to maintain their residence on the land."[22] Farmer E. G. Rust stated simply that, "If the Mexican laborer is barred from coming into this country, the farming business in my section is down and out."[23]

Sugar beet interests also hailed the sugar beet crop for encouraging diversified agriculture and bringing prosperity and jobs to those rural communities lucky enough to get sugar beet processing factories. Some even argued that if farmers grew more sugar beet and less corn and wheat, the agricultural marketplace would improve for all farmers, and this prosperity would, in turn, help to halt the rural exodus that threatened the future of American agriculture.[24] And finally, many tried to convince the audience that this was not an industry of a few special interests, or merely the agricultural sector of the economy, but rather one in which the whole nation had a stake. When chairman Albert Johnson questioned Minnesota farmer August Andresen about whether the United States should import sugar made by others or import others to tend to the sugar beet crop in the United States, Anderson replied: "We should look to the salvation of the biggest industry in the United States—agriculture—which is the basis of everything."[25]

It might at first seem strange that the witnesses would put so much effort into proclaiming that the sugar beet industry represented the marriage of Jeffersonian agriculture and modern industry. However, in portraying the sugar beet industry as the second coming of Jeffersonian agriculture, albeit in a modern form, sugar beet farmers and industrialists were both anticipating and responding to the assumption that cheap "peon" labor like Mexican labor necessarily undermined white family farmers and that the two were inherently incompatible, especially in a place like the Midwest. Michigan sugar beet interests believed that Michigan represented a case where family farming and industrial agriculture as well as white family farms and racially degraded workers coexisted harmoniously. Not only did they challenge the idea that "non-white" agricultural labor led to plantation agriculture or corporate-dominated farming, they argued that the future of independent family farmers in a place like Michigan depended on whether or not they would have access to Mexican workers. The flip side of this new world of agriculture was that Mexican workers would have no agricultural ladder. Sugar industrialists and farmers justified the lack of opportunity for the newest agricultural workers by turning to their racist assumptions. Because Mexicans as a "race" were already "degraded," employing them to work in the fields, where opportunities for advancement were few and mobility was always physical and not financial, did not contradict the Jeffersonian ideal but made it possible in a new world of industrial agriculture.

The sugar beet industrialists who journeyed to Washington to testify against the restriction of Mexican immigration had hopes of accomplishing much more than simply keeping Mexican labor unrestricted. They reminded Congress that during World War I the federal government had temporarily suspended the head tax and literacy test for Mexican agricultural workers and had actually helped to recruit and regulate the nation's agricultural labor force. Reversing the terms of the current debate, Representative J. Bird Vincent and other supporters of the sugar beet industry argued that the immigration issue and the potential "Mexican Problem" could be reconciled if the federal government would once again assume responsibility for directing the flow of Mexican workers into the country. The answer to the "Mexican Problem" then was not to shut off immigration but rather to control it, to have the state use its powers to implement a labor policy. To achieve this end, Michigan Congressman Vincent introduced his own bill during the 1926 hearings to give the secretary of labor the power to admit Mexicans into the United States as temporary laborers without paying head taxes or passing literacy tests.[26]

Sugar beet interests defended the idea that the federal government should lift immigration barriers and actually help them recruit workers by pointing to European nations that had solved their agricultural labor problems by looking to neighboring nations to supply cheap and mobile laborers who could be imported and exported as needed. In 1928 Harry Austin told Congress that the German sugar beet industry had been successful because the German government encouraged and regulated the seasonal migration of thousands of Poles and Lithuanians to work in the fields. When John Box of Texas protested that "both of those races are white, high-class white," Austin admitted that, "Yes. But they had a permit to come into the country to stay a certain length of time. At the end of that time, when the harvesting was over, they were shipped en bloc back to their country. Now that has worked very successfully in Germany, and we [the sugar beet industry] have been trying to find out whether there was some way by which there could be some government regulation established here that could work out that system with Mexican and other labor."[27] Two years later, Michigan industrialist T. G. Gallagher went even further, suggesting that the United States Department of Labor could develop a system of fingerprinting, photos, and work cards for Mexican workers. When restrictionist congressmen objected that this would create a permanent "peon class" of workers, a "perfectly foreign body, living here in our midst, with no purpose whatsoever to become assimilated or educated and part of our citizenship," Gallagher admitted there was a danger in "leaving it [immigration] uncontrolled." However, he attempted to assuage his adversaries' fears by proclaiming that "I can not see any reason why they [Mexicans] can not be registered and controlled. I see no reason why we could not apply to a department or office of the Government on the border to get us sufficient beet labor."[28] Congressman Dickinson of Iowa made a similar proposal. Once again trying to distinguish the current debate from what had taken place in the early 1920s, Dickinson began by insisting that "I am not here asking this committee to liberalize the immigration law." He then continued with the statement, "I have long been a convert to the fact that if you let us bring Mexican labor here, under bond, that bond requiring that the Mexican labor be returned to Mexico at the end of the season, you would do a great service for the sugar-beet industry of northern Iowa." When asked by chairman Johnson whether that would violate the nation's peonage laws, Dickinson replied, "being an agricultural type of people, you might make an exception in their case."[29] Looking backward to World War I, and somewhat prophetically forward to the Bracero program of World War II, sugar beet interests argued that when Congress decided immigration issues, it should consider not only race but labor and geography as well.

The underlying premise of these proposed immigration/labor programs, and in fact the hearings as a whole, was that Mexicans were not only members of a distinct nation-state but members of a separate race—a race of people put on the earth to toil in the fields of others. The assertion that the racial status and nationality of Mexican workers was "conjoined" or "conflated," and hence inseparable, was perhaps the most important part of the argument.[30] When confronted with the fact that a number of Mexicans were already U.S. citizens, many anti-restrictionists quickly changed the topic. To admit that the term "Mexican" was a national term and not a racial category would have involved confronting the notion that Mexicans' racial and national identities were not one and the same. Midwesterners had little interest in distinguishing between Mexican as a nationality and Mexican as a race. The whole crux of their argument for continued Mexican immigration, albeit as Mexican workers, was based on the idea that these identities would not separate—that no matter how long Mexicans worked in the United States, they would not assimilate and would eventually return to their "roots." This conflation of race and nationality not only made Mexican immigrants forever "Mexican," it also had the effect of making suspect the very American nationality of thousands of Mexican Americans within the United States.

If judged by their ardent campaign to have the immigration quotas extended, the restrictionists failed. The decision not to amend the 1924 Johnson-Reed Act to include Mexico, however, had nothing to do with either cultural pluralism or racial tolerance, much less racial inclusion. Both sides in the debate held strikingly similar racist views of Mexicans.[31] The difference that divided the two was whether it would be possible to turn Mexicans into nonimmigrant workers—whether it would be possible to use immigration policy to create a tier of second-class, noncitizen migrant workers.

Although the restrictionists and anti-restrictionists viewed this issue in purely domestic terms, the Republican administrations of the 1920s recognized the foreign policy implications of singling out Mexico for quota restrictions. Mexico was not only one of the United States' most important trading partners in the Western Hemisphere but also a vital junior partner in the United States' aspirations to create a real Pan-American coalition. Moreover,

Republicans were sensitive to the concerns of Mexican officials who feared unjust discrimination against their nation. However, when Mexican officials proposed that the two states should work together to create a labor program in both nations' interests, the Republicans turned a deaf ear. Hoover threatened to veto any bills creating quota restrictions, should they come across his desk, and he refused to consider the possibility that the issue could be resolved by joint cooperation or administration. Instead, he instructed State Department officials to work behind the scenes to stop Congress from passing any bills to include Mexico in the 1924 Immigration Act, while relying on administrative means—stricter interpretations of the 1885 Foran anticontract labor law and increased use of the head tax and literacy test—to control Mexican immigration.[32] The net effect of this policy, or lack of a policy, not only gave the United States the greatest flexibility when addressing Mexican immigration, it also reinforced the assumption that questions of Mexican immigration were really labor questions after all.

From Washington to Michigan

The national debates regarding immigration restriction shed little light on the experiences of Mexicans in the Midwest. Turning from the floor of Congress to the beet fields where Mexicans worked, we find that the racist rhetoric developed by both restrictionists and anti-restrictionists masked a much more complex reality. Although the sugar companies recruited Mexicans to work in the fields believing that they would be docile, the immigrants developed their own strategies of survival and mobility that defied the racist logic propelling the debate over the "Mexican Problem." Rather than conforming to some ideal "class of labor," Mexican immigrants in the Midwest often combined agricultural work and urban industrial work, usually with the hope of abandoning the fields altogether. Instead of returning to Texas at the end of the season, as many anti-restrictionists insisted they did, large numbers of Mexicans chose to settle in places like Chicago, Saginaw, and Detroit. As such, the sugar beet industrialists and farmers who claimed victory in Congress for helping to block the erection of immigration walls had a more difficult time claiming such a victory when it came to making Mexican immigrants conform to the racialized notion of a "class of labor" that they had developed in the hearings.

Throughout the 1920s, as the nation's leaders debated the future of Mexican immigration in the United States, sugar companies continued to recruit Mexican workers. They put out fliers and posters, placed ads in Spanish-language newspapers, and employed labor recruiters in cities near the U.S.-Mexican border.³³ In Texas Spanish-language newspapers, the companies promised Mexicans secure employment, plenty of work, free housing and garden plots, free transportation to and from Michigan, and perhaps most important of all, lots of money. The Michigan Sugar Company lured families by promising "secure employment for you and your family," a choice of sugar beet towns, and "not [any] trouble getting pay."³⁴ The Columbia Sugar Company assured families that they would get "all the acres they wanted," work and live in a rural community "where Mexicans are respected," and that the company would "protect their rights."³⁵ That is, recruiters depicted work in Michigan's sugar beet fields not simply as a way to make money, but as a different kind of life than most Mexicans could expect in Jim Crow Texas.

Each year in the 1920s thousands of Mexican families, many of them recent immigrants to Texas, answered these ads. (In fact, Texan officials became so concerned about the large numbers of Mexicans and Mexican Americans that Michigan's sugar beet industry recruited each year that in 1929 the state legislature passed a law, the Emigrant Agency Act, that created heavy licensing fees for out-of-state labor recruiters.)³⁶ As soon as the journey north began, many families began to realize that the labor recruiters and the sugar companies made false promises and misrepresented the terms of the contracts.³⁷ Cesario Hernandez, president of the Circulo de Obreros Católicos, charged that the sugar beet industry abused Mexican workers more than any other industry. He explained how most Mexicans, signing contracts that they could not read, often believed that they would be given free room and board while in the United States and then transported home for free.³⁸ After arriving in Michigan, however, many found that the free transportation was not at all free. To recoup the costs of recruiting and transporting Mexicans, many sugar companies automatically deducted $5 per person to cover the expenses.³⁹ Mexican families were transported to the fields in April and early May, weeks before their work would begin, in order to ensure an adequate labor supply at just the right moment. But because the sugar companies paid the families only three times during the season, with the first payment coming sometime in July, most Mexican families found that they had to rely on the sugar companies' advances or credit at local stores to make ends meet.⁴⁰ In addition to being pressured to buy blankets and tools from the sugar companies at nonnegotiable rates, Mexicans complained that they were forced to buy goods from those stores where they could get credit. One of the labor recruiters for the Michigan Sugar Company, Dr. Morris, admitted that too often storekeepers pressured Mexican families to purchase goods they either did not need or could not afford. Many families had trouble keeping track of their purchases because store owners regularly refused to show them their "tabs." Weeks before they had set foot on the fields, many workers already found themselves in debt.[41]

The sugar companies who had promised Mexican families that they could work "as many acres as they want" often refused to give Mexican families more than 7.5 acres per person, even though it was generally accepted that skillful sugar beet workers could easily handle ten acres and the very skillful up to fifteen acres. The companies justified the practice of giving Mexican families less acreage than European immigrants by claiming that Mexicans were incapable of tending as many acres. The real reason was that the sugar companies often recruited more families than would actually be needed.[42] This meant that when it came time for divvying up acreage, a very serious venture that would in large part determine whether a family would make money, break even, or remain in debt at the end of the season, the companies often assigned each family fewer acres than it could handle, and less than had originally been promised.

The labor contracts Mexicans signed also shifted most of the risk onto their shoulders. The contracts show that growers and companies wanted the best of both worlds—they wanted a captive and an expendable labor force adjustable to production levels. Labor contracts in the 1920s included clauses voiding the contract in cases where the crop failed to develop fully.[43] If workers decided to leave the fields early, perhaps because they did not get as many acres as they expected, or because they hoped to find better-paying work elsewhere, they not only forfeited the withheld wages and any wages that had not yet been paid, but they could also be held legally responsible for any labor costs the farmers might incur when hiring additional workers.[44] Furthermore, the contracts gave farmers the legal right to charge workers for work that did not measure up to the farmers' or companies' standards.[45] Families who had traveled hundreds of miles, with few resources, could potentially find themselves without work and in debt if the weather, natural disasters, or diseases ruined the crop. Even those who worked from planting through harvesting sometimes found that after being charged for transportation, supplies, and accommodation, they had no money left.[46] Such contracts made a mockery of the ideal, much less the reality, of "free labor."

For some families, simply getting their just pay could prove an insurmountable barrier, further exposing the limits of "free labor" in the labor contracts they signed. Using the contract clauses detailed above, growers sometimes laid off their beet workers in the middle of the season if the sugar beet crop did not develop, and then confiscated withheld wages for not finishing the work.[47] Even families who completed the work sometimes found it difficult to collect wages. According to Charles G. Benjamin, Detroit's Mexican consul lawyer, Mexicans frequently complained that sugar companies cheated them out of their just wages.[48] Moreover, because the companies often doled out payments, even though technically the farmers had hired the workers, migrant workers who disputed their pay were faced with challenging multimillion-dollar corporations, a case of David battling Goliath. When Santiago Ortiz and his sons left the beet fields for higher-paying work in a nearby foundry, the sugar company refused to pay him or his sons for two months worth of work unless they returned.[49] Even families who had little choice but to leave the fields ran up against unsympathetic sugar companies. In the early 1920s, the Diaz family contracted to work, but after only a couple of months, Mr. Diaz died of a heart attack in the fields. Left alone with her children and fearful that she could not make ends meet, Mrs. Diaz decided to go to Chicago with friends who were heading there for better-paying work. When Mrs. Diaz explained her situation to the sugar company fieldman, hoping to collect wages for the weeks she and her family had already spent in the fields, he refused, leaving Mrs. Diaz not only bitter and angry but broke.[50]

In spite of the fact that the contracts weighed heavily in favor of the farmers and the companies, and in spite of what must have seemed like overwhelming odds, sometimes Mexican immigrants did challenge the sugar companies. In the late 1920s, Edmund G. Lopez, a Mexican American tailor and notary public, was instrumental in helping some Mexican families bring suit against the sugar companies for "cheating them out of thousands of dollars, allocating garnishment for exorbitant grocery bills and refusing to make final settlement."[51] The Comisiónes Honorificas, a Mexican philanthropic society created by the Mexican consulate, also made some efforts to assist Mexican workers in getting their last paychecks and even promised to investigate discrimination in the fields.[52] In the end, it seems that little came out of this investigation, except to reveal the relative weakness of the Mexican state in the Midwest as well as the limits of working through the legal channels that the farmers and the corporations controlled. For Mexicans working in places like Michigan, mobility would have to come through some other, less-formal means.

The difficulty of challenging the sugar companies was compounded by the fact that when Mexicans first began working in Michigan's sugar beet fields in the late teens and early 1920s, they did not find well-established Mexican communities. Moreover, the nature of sugar beet work, which frequently included living out in the fields far from others, often meant that Mexican families were isolated both from other Mexican families and from the surrounding communities. Many Mexican families lived in portable wagon homes that were moved from field to field as the crop progressed.[53] Others were housed in abandoned farmhouses, dilapidated barns, and even old chicken coops, with few neighbors. Isolation was a regular feature of the sugar beet labor system.

But isolation did not stop Mexicans from forming friendships and building their own communities where the joys of life could be shared and the hardships softened.[54] The long lulls in sugar beet work afforded Mexicans time to maintain contact with family members and friends while also forging new friendships and ties with other Mexicans in rural Michigan and in nearby cities. Using cars bought with money made in the fields, Mexicans journeyed to share meals, celebrate births, and mourn deaths. Mexicans working in the beet fields also traveled to visit compatriots in nearby cities, where they played billiards, attended movies, and went dancing.[55]

In addition to these informal gatherings, Mexican sugar beet workers gathered regularly to celebrate Mexican Independence Day. Throughout the 1920s numerous small towns in Michigan, from Shepherd to Elkton to Pigeon, were "transformed" for two to three days a year into temporary "Mexican villages."[56] During these festivals hundreds and sometimes even thousands of Mexicans gathered for days at a time to pay homage to the Mexican flag by singing patriotic songs, dancing, listening to speeches, and competing in athletic events. Rural newspapers throughout Michigan gleefully reported on these celebrations, commenting on how all in the community were welcome. For example, in 1924 the *Pigeon Progress* told its readers how two hundred Mexicans came to Pigeon for a two-day celebration of Mexican Independence Day, which included speeches, music, dancing until four in the morning, and a parade down Main Street. After describing how the town hall had been "handsomely decorated with the national colors of Mexico," the *Pigeon Progress* noted that "the crowd was very orderly and all enjoyed the affair, Americans as well as Mexicans."[57] In the following years, Pigeon continued to be the site of Mexican independence celebrations, and each year the local newspaper was filled with descriptions of how Mexicans celebrated their "own" identity.[58] To the locals, then, these festivals provided evidence that the Mexicans who came to work in their fields were not only nonthreatening but that they would forever remain Mexican.[59]

The Mexican consuls also viewed these festivals as a way to create and foster a Mexican national identity among Mexicans who had traveled so far from home. In fact, the Mexican consulate helped to fund and plan for these celebrations by creating Comisiónes Honorificas in Saginaw and Port Huron.[60] The Mexican consulate also created Mexican Patriotic Committees in rural Michigan to make sure that Mexican children would be taught "the language, the culture, and the traditions of the land from which their fathers came" long after the parades had ended.[61] In these ways, the Mexican state went to great lengths to make sure that Mexicans would be Mexicanized during their stay in the United States.

Though the Mexican state was primarily concerned with making sure that its nationals would develop a national Mexican identity, the Mexicans who participated in these independence festivals did so as a way to celebrate membership in both their local and national communities. That is, the Mexican Independence Days created a sense of national affiliation while also reinforcing the community ties that Mexicans were beginning to forge in rural Michigan.[62] As such, these very popular events helped to cultivate both local and national identities and perhaps even fostered the transition toward becoming Mexican American.

Just as these annual celebrations symbolically marked inclusion in a larger national community as well as a local one, individually Mexicans also went to great lengths to maintain ties to family and friends in Mexico by sending money to relatives and saving money with the expectation of buying land or homes in Mexico.[63] Workers also maintained ties to Mexico by choosing not to become naturalized American citizens. According to University of California sociologist Paul S. Taylor, many made this choice not only because of their "patriotism" and strong "emotion[al] attachments" to Mexico but also because of a keen understanding of their lowly status in the United States.[64] George Edson described the way many Mexicans resisted being what he described as "de-Mexicanized" by willfully choosing to maintain identity and ties with Mexico.[65] One Mexican with whom Edson spoke "express[ed] contempt for a piece of paper that a man can buy for $5 and can change his whole character."[66] Others expressed ambivalence toward naturalization because they doubted if "a piece of paper" would really affect how native-born Americans would see them. Implicitly recognizing that their racial and national identities were conjoined, many Mexicans were well aware of the fact that race mattered in the United States, and becoming "American" involved much more than just changing political allegiance or status. After interviewing sugar beet worker Marco Alonzo in Saginaw, Edson commented that Alonzo believed that because "white folks mistreat the Negro ... he is sure that American citizenship would mean nothing to a Mexican."[67] Another Mexican living in the Midwest complained that "We Mexicans don't care much where a man is from. . . . But when some Pole, Belgian or what not looks down on us as foreigners and claims that he is American because our skin is dark and he is white, we don't like it."[68]

Many Mexicans who chose to maintain close ties to Mexico by sending back money, opting not to naturalize, and fostering a sense of Mexican nationalism even while living in the United States, also carved out a future in Michigan by looking for jobs in nearby cities and settling there. By the late 1920s, sociologist Paul S. Taylor found that growing numbers of Mexicans chose to "winter" in the Mexican colony of Chicago rather than return to the Southwest or Mexico.[69] George Edson estimated that though 90 percent of Mexican "greenhorns," those who had been in the United States less than a year, returned to Mexico or Texas at the end of the sugar beet season, after two or three years most Mexicans decided to stay—with 50 percent moving to nearby cities at the end of the season, 15 percent remaining in the countryside, and just 35 percent returning to Texas.[70] When asked about the tendency of Mexican migrant workers to "drift" to the cities, Mrs. Larsen, a Chicago social worker, explained, "The sugar companies offer them free transportation and what they consider to be fairly good pay and wages and many of them when they do get here either do not find jobs or on hearing they can get $6 a day in the factories come to the cities."[71] A number of Mexicans even refused to wait until fall to leave the fields, opting instead to give up their hold-back payments in order to get better winter jobs in nearby cities.[72]

Despite the assurances of sugar beet industrialists that Mexicans could be easily controlled and that they naturally preferred "agricultural work," many Mexicans simply disembarked at train stations on the way to Michigan, never making it to the final destination. Dr. Morris, a labor recruiter for the Michigan Sugar Company, complained that the sugar companies experienced "a good deal of trouble due to the fact that a great many of the Mexicans disappeared when they got up as far as Chicago and Toledo."[73] Edson estimated that up to 10 percent of all Mexicans who took up the sugar companies' offers of free transportation to the fields abandoned the trains somewhere between Texas and Michigan.[74] Similarly, the *Pigeon Progress* described how "scores of Mexicans, especially this year, signed up to work in the beet fields only to get free transportation from Texas and as soon as they were brought to the factory centers hopped the next train or bus out to seek work in nearby city factories."[75] Even Mr. Terrazas of the Mexican consul lamented that "the lowliest class" of Mexicans who signed up with the sugar companies did not plan to stay in the fields: "Their real intention is to come to the cities. They take advantage of the free transportation offered by the sugar companies."[76] To the frustration and chagrin of the sugar companies and locals alike, at least some Mexicans took the sugar companies' offers of "free" transportation literally.

For some Mexicans mobility could be expressed in the very physical act of "jumping train"; for others the first step toward controlling their own mobility, and creating the means for other opportunities, involved the act of purchasing a used car.[77] As soon as Mexicans arrived, used car salesmen followed, encouraging them to purchase cars on the deferred plan. By the late 1920s so many Mexican migrant families were purchasing used cars on credit that the sugar companies instructed car dealers not to sell cars to their workers, warning that Mexican men could not be counted on to pay off any outstanding bills.[78] The sugar companies also threatened newly arriving Mexican field workers that if they planned on buying a used car, they would not be able to get credit advances from the sugar company or local stores.[79]

The extreme lengths to which some sugar companies went to stop Mexicans from buying cars revealed a recognition on their part that for almost all Mexican families, toil in the beet fields was not the final destination but rather a means to other ends. And the end goal for many families was industrial work in a midwestern city. Owning a car gave Mexican families the possibility of commuting from nearby cities to the fields and scouting out work possibilities elsewhere.[80] Cars were also a means for maintaining community ties and a very important avenue for economic mobility. Considering the numerous options that car ownership offered to Mexicans, it should come as no surprise that in the late 1920s, up to 50 percent of all Mexicans in Detroit either owned or shared ownership of a car.[81]

The state of Michigan, as one of the most industrialized in the nation, did offer Mexicans numerous opportunities. The close proximity of Chicago, as well as other cities like Gary and Indiana Harbor, made industrial employment a realistic goal for many. (In 1927, just ten years after the sugar companies first began recruiting Mexicans to work in the fields, Edson estimated that 20,900 Mexicans lived in Michigan and another 29,050 in Chicago.)[82] When sociologist Paul S. Taylor and his researchers traveled to the Midwest to investigate the living and working conditions of Mexicans, they found that thousands worked in factories and industrial pursuits and that many, and perhaps even a majority, had first come to the Midwest via the sugar beet fields. According to Edson, from the beet fields "they drift into factories and mills in the cities, and they begin staying through the winter."[83]

When Mexican immigrants sought industrial labor in midwestern cities, they not only found jobs but also a distinct place in a fluid and changing racial continuum—whiter than the newly arriving African Americans from the South but also not as white or "unruly" as southern and eastern European immigrants. The supposed "in-between" status that so troubled immigrant restrictionists who feared that Mexicans represented a "hybrid" or "mixed" race proved to be a bonus in the eyes of midwestern industrial employers negotiating an increasingly complex racial landscape. For many of the industrial employers who hired Mexican workers often claimed to have done so as a way to displace or replace southern and eastern Europeans, whom they believed no longer worked as hard as they used to or who had become too demanding and disruptive. A bedding factory superintendent who hired Mexicans admitted that he preferred them over Italians, because "the Mexicans don't have to be driven as much as the others."[84] A coke by-products company executive offered a similar endorsement of Mexican laborers, noting that in comparison to Italians, Croatians, and Serbs, the Mexicans proved to be "cleaner in purpose and about their work" and more "anxious to learn English and to get ahead." Perhaps most important of all, the executive believed that "the Mexicans follow directions; they are tractable."[85] A Chicago paymaster also extolled Mexican immigrants as better than their southern and eastern European counterparts, noting that Mexicans "do the work and say very little." In contrast, he complained that "the Italians are always suspicious and think we are trying to cheat them out of time and money.... The Greeks were always fighting, drunk, and kniving each other."[86] And finally, a rolling mill superintendent, whose department included a large number of Mexicans, endorsed the trend of hiring even more, noting that they "are the best class of labor we get now. They are better than the colored or the south Europeans.... If the American people will just treat them right, we'll have a fine class of people and a fine class of labor."[87]

Many industrial employers sought out Mexicans as a racial buffer between the nation's southern and eastern European immigrants and the growing numbers of African Americans who had started to migrate to the Midwest during World War I. That is, industrialists believed that by hiring Mexicans they could remain on the white side of the color line. The seeming ambiguity of Mexicans' racial identity helps to explain why at least some industrialists chose to hire Mexican workers. According to the doorman at the Sanger's Biscuit Company in Chicago, "Our Mexicans are white. Yes some of them are dark just like the niggers. I wouldn't want to live among them. I want to live among white people. No, there's no prejudice against them."[88] Similarly, an official for Wisconsin Steel highlighted his company's use of Mexican labor on racial terms, stating that when he hired Mexicans he purposely picked out the "lightest among them. [I]t isn't that the lighter-colored ones are better workers, but the darker ones are like the niggers. . . . [I]n order to minimize feelings of race friction and keep away from the color line as far as possible, I employ only the lighter-colored Mexicans."[89] The employment manager of a steelworks plant explained his company's hiring practices, noting that "The Castilian Mexicans are more intelligent than the darker Indians."[90] And finally, yet another steel plant manager insisted that he had no trouble distinguishing among Mexicans of supposedly different racial backgrounds. "You can tell those with negro blood. They seem to be thicker through the temples and duller."[91]

As many industrialists defended their practice of hiring Mexican workers by choosing only the "whiter" applicants, others questioned whether it was possible or appropriate to describe Mexicans as either white or black. A Chicago Chamber of Commerce official insisted that, "The Mexicans are lower than the European peasants. They are not white and not Negro; they're Mexican."[92] In the same vein, when asked about the racial status of Mexicans, another Chamber of Commerce official insisted that, "No they are not regarded as colored; but they are regarded as an inferior class. Are the Mexicans regarded as white? Oh no!"[93] And finally, even USDL investigator Edson held a highly ambivalent view, weighing in on the question of Mexicans' supposed racial identity. He noted that "Opinion as to just where the Mexican belongs on the scale of humanity is hard to crystallize. The composite idea appears to be that he is a white man unwashed."[94] Later, however, Edson warned about being fooled by the light-colored appearance of some Mexicans. Speaking of physical difference between twins, "one golden haired and blue eyed" and the other a "Yaqui," Edson insisted that, "They are just alike inside . . . they are both Mexicans and however much the conflicting blood may quarrel in the entrails of this metamorphing race, it is Mexican blood, and the Saxon who thinks he finds in the fair Mexican a nearer cousin than in the darker one is making both hate him."[95]

Regardless of the racist motives of the employers who hired them, Mexicans who found industrial jobs did the best they could to hold on to them. The iron foundry in Saginaw employed five hundred Mexicans in 1928, and of the fifteen who were originally hired in 1918, ten still worked there. Similarly, Mexicans who got jobs at Detroit's River Rouge plant only reluctantly gave them up, with Mexicans having one of the lowest turnover rates in the plant.[96]

By the late 1920s, Mexicans could be found working in Chicago's stockyards and steel mills, in Flint's Buick plant, at Ford, Briggs Manufacturing Plant, Inland Steel, Wisconsin Steel, Gary Tube Company, and other places. Almost all of the personnel managers Taylor and his researchers interviewed commented that the majority of the Mexicans they hired had worked in the beet fields, and that the fields continued to be an important source of labor.[97]

The lure of industrial urban centers was not just better-paying jobs with more prestige but also greater participation in the emerging Mexican colonies. By the late 1920s, both Chicago and Detroit were home to growing Mexican American communities. In 1928, Chicago had at least thirty-five Mexican societies offering financial, social, recreational, and cultural support.[98] Though many of these societies would come and go, they still provided an institutional base for the Mexican American community. Equally important, Mexicans in Detroit and Chicago had ample opportunity to visit with compatriots at pool halls, ethnic grocery stores, and restaurants. And finally, urban settlement made it easier for Mexican and Mexican American children to attend school regularly.[99] Considering the social, cultural, and economic advantages urban centers had to offer, it should come as no surprise that most Mexicans who settled in the Midwest chose urban destinations.

For many the path from rural fields to urban centers proved more circular than linear.[100] Although Mexicans often claimed that sugar beet work was only for "greenhorns" who did not know better, in fact, throughout the 1920s many Mexican families continued to combine urban industrial work with field work because, in the words of George Edson, even "[industrial] employment is often irregular" and Mexicans are "laid off during slack times and hired for short term and temporary."[101] For many families, the beet fields acted as a safety net when they lost jobs in industrial centers. Even "experienced" Mexican families traveled back to the beet fields when there were few alternatives. For example, Mrs. Maria S. Montano lived in San Antonio when she saw an ad from the Michigan Sugar Company in *La Prensa*. Lacking money, Mrs. Montano, her husband, three children, and a brother-in-law went to work in Michigan. After working from April to July, the family left the fields and moved to Saginaw, where her brother-in-law and her three boys found jobs in the Central Foundry. In 1924, she went to Detroit with her husband, who worked in the River Rouge plant until he was laid off. Eight years after they first had come north, Mrs. Montano and her husband were back in the beet fields trying to make ends meet.[102]

Conclusion

In 1928 Congress was debating once again whether or not Mexico should be included in the Johnson-Reed Act of 1924. Yet in many ways, the debate over immigration restriction as applied to Mexico was an oxymoron. On one side, the restrictionists believed that Mexicans could not be immigrants—that they could not become assimilated to the nation as had millions of immigrants before them. The question for them was one of maintaining boundaries—racial and physical—between the United States and Mexico. On the other side of the debate stood anti-restrictionists, who not only felt that Mexicans should be allowed to come into the United States as workers but that the whole debate would come to an end if Congress would use its immigration policy to create a labor policy. And their solution hinged on coming up with an immigration policy that did not treat Mexicans as potential immigrants but rather as workers who could be imported and exported at will. The debate over Mexican immigration, therefore, revolved around whether or not it would be possible to keep Mexicans coming into the United States as agricultural workers while making sure that they did not become industrial immigrants. Anti-restrictionists insisted that the United States could create a racialized labor force that would meet the needs of U.S. agriculture without violating the racist spirit of the nation's newly established immigration restrictions.[103]

In spite of the serious nature of the issues discussed, immigration and labor historians have tended to overlook these debates, preferring instead to focus on the 1921 and 1924 immigration acts as *the* answer to immigration anxiety and racial nativism in the United States. Historians who focus on Mexican immigration, however, have found that the 1921 and 1924 acts instigated, rather than ended, a debate over the meaning of immigration, labor, race, and nationality that continued long past 1924.[104] This was also a debate that extended far beyond the Southwest, much less the border, for even a cursory review of the witnesses who came to testify in front of Congress in 1926 and 1928 reveals the very national nature of the Mexican immigration debates. Of the thirty-four witnesses who testified before the House in 1926 regarding "Seasonal Agricultural Laborers from Mexico," twenty-two came on behalf of the sugar beet industry and nine of those called various midwestern states home. Two years later, eighteen of the fifty-six witnesses spoke for the sugar beet industry, while eleven of the witnesses hailed from the Midwest. Unlike the southwestern witnesses, who had a difficult time shedding their association with corporate farming, the midwesterners who came before Congress were able to play upon the traditional association of the Midwest with family farming. In fact, the sugar beet contingent, with a strong midwestern presence, attempted to appease adversaries and appeal to the general public by arguing that thousands of family farmers in the Midwest had come to depend on Mexican migrant labor to perform the stoop labor that they no longer would do. They argued that the presence of thousands of Mexican migrant workers, then, did not undermine the independent family farm; rather, they insisted that their much-needed labor made it possible to maintain family farming in an age of modern agriculture.

The thousands of Mexican immigrants who had not been officially invited to take part in these debates nonetheless challenged the racist arguments held by both the restrictionists and anti-restrictionists. By moving between rural agricultural work and urban industrial employment, and by settling in urban centers as soon as long-term jobs became available, Mexicans lived lives that belied the argument that they were merely seasonal laborers following the crops until the winds directed them back home to Mexico. By settling in the Midwest, and by creating communities within the United States, Mexican migrants became immigrants, and defied the racist motives of those who had recruited them in the first place.

7

Child Labor Reformers and Industrial Agriculture

During the same years that sugar beet industrialists sparred with immigration restrictionists over the growing numbers of Mexicans working in Michigan's sugar beet fields, they also faced criticism of their labor practices from an altogether different source—child labor reformers concerned with the extensive use of child labor in the fields.[1] Unlike the restrictionists, however, who vilified Mexican immigrants as a threat to white workers, not to mention the family farm, the child labor reformers who focused on farm children and eastern European migrant children portrayed them as the victims of their parents who made them labor in the fields and the industrialists who made it possible. Beginning in 1918 and continuing throughout the following decade, child labor reformers charged that the sugar beet industrialists had exploited the nation's children by encouraging farm families to use their own sons and daughters in the fields while also bringing in thousands of eastern European migrant families. (As we shall later see, child labor reformers tended to ignore the growing number of Mexicans in the fields.) To publicize the plight of these children, the National Child Labor Committee, the nation's most important child labor reform group, published dozens of articles and sponsored numerous studies, while the Children's Bureau (CB) conducted a thorough investigation of the beet children of Michigan.[2] In 1923, the editor of the National Child Labor Committee's (NCLC) journal, *The American Child,* responded to inquiries about his organization's focus on child labor in Michigan's beet fields with the declaration that, "if beets seem to predominate in this and our recent issues, it is for the very good reason that beets now predominate in our interests and our efforts. . . . Yes, we are steeped in beets—almost to the exclusion of everything else. But so are thousands of children."[3]

This growing concern with agricultural child labor represented a crucial shift in the movement to reform child labor.[4] Before World War I, child labor reformers focused almost exclusively on children who toiled in the nation's industries and urban centers. The NCLC, which had been created in 1904 to highlight the problem of child labor and lobby for state laws, protested the use of child labor in mines, mills, and factories.[5] Joining the NCLC in 1912, the Children's Bureau, an agency within the Department of Labor, dedicated much of its limited resources to exposing the dangers faced by children who toiled in the nation's most industrial establishments.[6] As a result of their efforts, the first two federal child labor laws of this period—the Keating Owen Act of 1916 and the Pomerene Act of 1919—specifically targeted children working in factories, quarries, mines, and mills.[7] Although the Supreme Court would later declare these child labor laws unconstitutional, the first in 1918 and the second in 1922, a combination of other factors, including state child labor laws, increasing mechanization, the rise of scientific management, and growing public sentiment against industrial child labor, led to falling rates of industrial child labor.[8] Yet before either the NCLC or the CB could celebrate, both organizations grew troubled by what they came to believe was an equal if not more serious problem—the growing numbers of children laboring in "industrial agriculture."[9]

When describing the children caught in the throes of industrial agriculture, child reformers included the untold thousands, if not millions, of children who toiled on their hands and knees in the nation's tobacco and cotton fields, cranberry bogs, truck farms, and sugar beet fields.[10] In categorizing this kind of labor as industrial, child labor reformers developed a nuanced definition of industrial agriculture that highlighted the "industrial" nature of the labor, which was marked by monotony, tediousness, strain, and repetition, as well as the changing social relations of production, which seemed to be heading toward ever-higher rates of sharecropping, tenant farming, and worst of all, migratory farm labor. Unlike rural reformers, then, who hailed industrial agriculture as the harbinger of a more efficient means of agricultural production that would make it easier to reconcile the agricultural sector of society with the needs of urban industrial America, child labor reformers pointed squarely at the rise of industrial agriculture as the culprit causing many of rural America's problems.[11] In the words of an NCLC official: "We have been attempting, by means of facts, to show industrial large-scale agriculture as it really is. We have been attempting to tear aside the false halo which surrounds it and to make people realize that this form of work constitutes a menace to the children of the country, and through them to the nation."[12]

Convincing the public—much less industrialists, growers, or migrant families—to abandon child labor would prove a daunting task. Since the early twentieth century, children made up a large part, and sometimes even a majority, of the workers who toiled in the sugar beet fields. Equally important, the debate over child labor was never simply a matter of deciding when and where to abolish child labor. Nor was it simply a matter of figuring out the legal and moral rights of parents, as well as the state's ability to intervene and mediate parent-child relationships. Rather, the debate over child labor involved nothing less than confronting the nature of labor in industrial agriculture.

Defining Industrial Agriculture

As child labor reformers began to grapple with the "evils" associated with industrial agriculture, they found themselves caught between two contradictory perceptions of American agriculture. For the early twentieth century represented a somewhat curious era in which, on one hand, many Americans worried that rural America was suffering from social, economic, material, cultural, and even spiritual backwardness and stagnation. This perspective helped give birth to an entire movement, the Country Life movement, whose practitioners sought to diagnose and treat the supposed ailments underlying rural America's problems. On the other hand, an entire contingent of sentimental reformers, mostly urban residents, looked to rural America as a salve to the alleged social decay and moral degradation accompanying urban industrial corruption. Armed with an ahistorical and idealized vision of rural America, these reformers embraced the modern romantic ideal that the countryside was somehow fundamentally different than the urban industrial realm, and that the children who toiled on the land, like the generations before them, would be duly rewarded by the regenerative power of the countryside.[13]

Rather than side with either of these seemingly opposing viewpoints, child labor reformers pointed to the numerous ways modern industrial society had already transformed rural America.[14] That is, they directly confronted the myth that all agricultural child labor was good for the children, because it built their morals and character, and good for the nation, because it ensured future generations of hearty and wholesome citizens. They also disputed the nation's idealized vision of rural America as an almost timeless place that embodied the nation's most virtuous values and appealing traditions. Instead, child labor reformers counseled the public that the social problems they associated with industrial America were not confined to the nation's big cities, and that their nostalgic rural America had long since passed.[15] Chastising the American public for failing to come to terms with the changing nature of agriculture, the NCLC proclaimed: "It is exactly the mistaken idea regarding the wholesome benefit of rural work which is responsible for one of the most serious and far reaching child labor evils we have."[16]

Child labor reformers recognized the challenge of convincing the public of the dangers of industrial agriculture in a nation historically wedded to the idea that children who toiled on the land grew to be healthy and wholesome adults. In fact, the NCLC saw its campaign in a long historical trajectory, noting that the nation's current views about agricultural child labor still reflected the Puritan idea that there was "no greater sin than idleness."[17] Even though this assumption had come to seem increasingly cruel and shortsighted for those children caught in the cogs of the industrial revolution, it continued to hold sway well into the twentieth century for children toiling in agriculture. As a result, the NCLC lamented that though cities and states had begun to recognize the "evils" of industrial labor, with respect to agricultural labor "our statue books are practically blank. Its evils simply do not exist for us."[18] The unwillingness of states and cities to acknowledge, much less address, the issue of child labor in agriculture frustrated child labor reformers, who only had to look as far as the nation's 1920 federal census for ample evidence that the most serious child labor problem could be found in the nation's countryside rather than its urban centers. Of the 1,060,858 children under the age of fifteen that census takers counted as regularly employed, the majority, or 647,309, toiled on the nation's farms.[19]

To demonstrate the "evils" of industrial agriculture, child labor reformers asked the public to distinguish between "good old fashion farm life" and the "rise of modern industrial agriculture." Describing the former as one of the "most cherished traditions of our country," the NCLC celebrated "the joys of a farm up-bringing, of the God-fearing, hard-working father and mother whose healthy, happy children play their part in the farm life by helping them with daily chores." The NCLC even went so far as to assert that this tradition had created many of the nation's "finest" men and women, who themselves credited their "sterling qualities of character" to their childhood experiences on farms. The NCLC warned, however, that "modern, industrial agriculture child labor presents a different story from the old-fashioned helping out on the farm." Unlike traditional child labor, which was characterized by a variety of tasks suited to each child's physical needs, taking place under the supervision of parents whose primary goal was to lead their children toward interesting and remunerative work as well as a "reasonable standard of living," child labor in industrial agriculture was marked by monotony, physical harm, and dead-end jobs leading nowhere but down.[20] Of the hundreds of thousands of children working on farms in industrial agriculture, the NCLC asserted that most were not just helping their parents to complete chores but rather had become "regular contract laborers" who worked exceptionally long hours instead of attending school.[21] Grace Abbott, chief of the Children's Bureau, insisted that because of these disturbing facts, migrant child labor could not be compared with the traditional farm child labor that led to a "sense of family solidarity" and "real training."[22] Abbott's colleague Nettie McGill similarly stated that for the child toiling in industrial agriculture, "his work is mere drudgery."[23]

The reformers' fears that child labor in industrial agriculture harmed children was part of a much broader concern that industrial agriculture also threatened to undermine the rural Midwest as a supposedly classless and homogenous place of family farms where hard labor on the land and communal ties in the countryside fostered equality and democracy. For the women of the CB discovered that in those areas where specialty crops had become dominant, a sign of the growing industrialization of agriculture, one also tended to find high rates of tenancy and contract farming, increasing control by a few corporations, and the replacement of hired hands with migrant laborers.[24] Owen Lovejoy of the NCLC similarly lamented how tenants and transients were taking the place of landowners and hired hands.[25] As such, Lovejoy credited industrial agriculture with creating "a silent but gigantic migratory revolution" involving not just the rural to urban migration of farm sons and daughters but also the "annual migration of more than a million families with their three million children of school age—a moving not only from one state to an adjacent state, but for a thousand miles across the country, or even from southern Texas and Mexico to Colorado, Minnesota and Michigan and back again!"[26] The conferees at the joint National Child Labor Committee and National Conference of Social Work meeting in July 1926 agreed, concluding that child labor in industrial agriculture, knowing "no geographical limitations," could be found in the beet fields of the Midwest and West, the cotton fields of the South and Southwest, and the truck farms and canneries up and down the East Coast.[27] Clearly, the child labor problem was a national one.

"Factories without Walls"

Considering the child labor reformers' concern with the plight of child labor and the future of the family farm, it should come as little surprise that Michigan's sugar beet industry quickly became one of their favorite topics. Of all the regions that reformers investigated, the Midwest occupied a special place in the nation's historical imagination. Unlike southern plantations, which had long been tainted by various forms of un-free and semi-free labor such as slavery and debt peonage, as well as southwestern "corporate" farms, which seemed to have been founded on industrial labor relations from the beginning, the Midwest was supposed to be that place where those who worked hard would be rewarded with economic independence and close-knit communities. Child labor reformers who ventured into Michigan's sugar beet fields, however, claimed to have found not a bastion of Jeffersonian agriculture but rather its modern-day perversion. Instead of buying the land and tending to the crop, the industrialists contracted with local farmers to raise sugar beet, encouraging them to exploit their own wives and children by working them long hours in the fields. Just as worrisome, reformers pointed out that the industrialists had initiated a massive influx of foreign migratory families to toil on the farms of those families who either could not or would not do the work themselves. The NCLC declared that because the sugar beet industry was controlled by "comparatively few hands," promoted a system of "contract farming," and paid migrant laborers on a "piece rate basis," it alienated farmers from their land and divorced workers from their own toil, making the fields a "factory without roof or walls."[28] Similarly, the CB castigated the sugar beet industry for importing large numbers of migrant workers who not only toiled all season long on land that would probably never become their own, but who had little chance of becoming a part of the rural communities in which they were only temporary members.

To convince the American public that the sugar beet industry was a form of industrial agriculture was one thing; to convince them that the work children actually did in the fields was the same as industrial work was quite another matter. To do so, child labor reformers spent a great deal of time actually comparing and contrasting industrial labor with sugar beet field work as a way to highlight the denigrating nature of this agricultural labor. Bertram Mautner of the NCLC emphasized how sugar beet work "is characterized by a degree of standardization, strain, and repetition of minute processes in monotonous succession. The fact that it is hand work as distinguished from machine operation in industry does not make it less mechanical."[29] Likewise, the CB described how toiling in the beet fields was "as monotonous and repetitive as many factory processes."[30] Playing on the public's view that industrial factories had employed young children because of their physical attributes, Nettie McGill explained that the sugar manufacturers also believed that children were "the most effective workers" because of their "active" and "nimble" fingers.[31] She further claimed that the conditions under which children toiled differed little, if at all, from those of "factory hands" except for the fact that the boys and girls toiling in the fields worked much longer hours than their factory counterparts.[32]

When documenting the similarity between child labor in large industrial factories with child labor in the beet fields, both the NCLC and the CB spent a great deal of time and resources detailing the work processes to demonstrate that it was not whether the children tended to machinery that mattered but rather the actual movements involved that made their toil industrial. Employing a scientific management strategy, child labor reformers studied and timed each work step to demonstrate that, in practice, little divided industrial from agricultural work. To literally illustrate this industrial argument, in 1926 the NCLC printed a series of articles in which it provided sketches comparing child labor in cotton mills with child labor in the beet fields, concluding that "the evils of industrial agriculture stand out with peculiar clarity when placed besides those of an occupation which the public, for years, has generally acknowledged."[33] In the sketches, the NCLC divided each page in half, printing an illustration of a child in a cotton mill next to a sketch of a child in a beet field. In these paired images, the NCLC highlighted the similarities in work processes, even pointing to equivalent body postures and hand and head movements. The point to be made was clear. Although cotton mill kids worked in huge factories with expensive and high-tech machinery, and sugar beet kids worked in the fields with their own hands and crude implements, the work was basically the same. Complementing the NCLC's arguments, the bureau published detailed tables and charts that broke down the work process, not only step by step but also by the children's ages, their families' economic status, and time spent in the field to demonstrate the inherently "industrial" nature of this work.[34]

When highlighting and illustrating the industrial nature of the work children performed, the CB and the NCLC also detailed the health risks involved in the fields. For, an important part of the argument that sugar beet labor resembled industrial labor hinged on proving that the work itself led to injuries, accidents, and diseases that threatened the well-being of the children.[35] In a scientific manner, bureau field investigators conducted hundreds of physical exams to ascertain the kinds of physical ailments sugar beet labor induced in the nation's "beet children." Researchers found that there were many diseases and deformities, "invisible to the eye" but still quite dangerous, that could be traced directly to their work in the fields. Of the 1,022 children examined during one Children's Bureau study, only five did not suffer from some sort of physical defect or disease.[36] In addition to the CB's highly empirical approach, which focused on the "invisible" health hazards, the NCLC made a practice of highlighting dangers that were easy to publicize and visualize, such as cuts resulting from topping beets.[37] Though it is unlikely that children actually did much topping, the committee published numerous illustrations and posed photos showing young children shrinking under the weight of heavy knives as they tried to cut off the tops of five-pound beets. These visual images tended to show children standing alone, in dreary and darkened rural landscapes, the victims of their families, the farmers, the industry, and even the nation's consumers, who enjoyed the fruits (or sugar) of their labor.[38]

Critiquing the Social Relations of Production

In addition to committing significant time and resources detailing what happened in the fields as children thinned, weeded, and topped the sugar beet crop, the CB and the NCLC also described and analyzed, as well as counted and critiqued, the larger social relations of production. Both organizations explored how industrial agriculture affected farm families and traditional family labor; migrant families and especially the mothers; housing conditions and home life; school attendance of both farm and migrant children; and the status of migrant families in local farming communities. In doing so, both groups revealed a broad agenda that touched on the power of corporations, the prerogative of parents, and the role of the state in rural America.

In their quest to document how the sugar beet industry affected rural America, reformers included in their studies not only migrant families but also farm families whose children toiled in the fields. Of the 681 families the NCLC interviewed during its 1922 investigation, 407 were grower families, while 274 were contract migrant labor families.[39] The CB also interviewed 192 grower and tenant families in its 1922 survey of 511 families who used child labor in the sugar beet fields.[40] Justifying the inclusion of farm families in its studies of industrial agriculture, the NCLC argued that because the company "controls at all times the sugar beet crop of the growers," these farmers were "really working for the company."[41] Without challenging the traditional labor of farm families, child labor reformers tried to convince farm families that toiling in the sugar beet fields for long hours would ultimately undermine their families and their communities. As evidence, they pointed to the fact that even though farm children tended to fewer acres than their migrant counterparts, they still missed up to one-third of school time, which translated into delayed educational development.[42]

Somewhat ironically, the reformers' decision to include farm children in their studies revealed that some farm families had been able to use their labor in the sugar beet fields as a stepping stone, moving from migrant wage workers to tenant farmers to landed farmers. The CB found that forty-one of the 150 farm family owners and fifty-two of the seventy-two tenant farmers it interviewed had been contract laborers before getting their own land.[43] NCLC investigators discovered a similar trend, with 28.7 percent of all growers they talked with having spent at least a few years tending to the crop as migrant contract laborers.[44] (These figures exaggerate the numbers of former contract laborers who rose to landed status because neither the NCLC nor the CB included farm families who did not use their children in the fields. A statistical profile of all growers and all migrant families would reveal that though some migrant families had indeed created an agricultural ladder, the overwhelming majority of farmers had never been migrant laborers.) Rather than celebrate this mobility, however, both the CB and the NCLC tended to scold these families for having taken advantage of their young children instead of tending to their greater needs. It was bad enough that children worked long hours in unhealthy conditions. It seemed even more troubling to the reformers that the children laboring in the fields worked alongside their parents, who were supposed to support and protect them.[45] Armed with a middle-class vision of familial relations in which fathers worked, mothers stayed at home, and children attended school, reformers sympathized little with the newly minted farmers, sometimes even underestimating the economic necessity of child labor by describing children's work in the fields as merely adding to a family's "savings." Owen Lovejoy, an executive member of the NCLC, complained that lots of the eastern European migrant families had even bought farms and pianos by working their youngest children long hours in the fields. The NCLC even claimed to have found parents who bought a $10,000 farm from the hard-earned money of their ten-year-old daughter.[46] Instead of applauding the success of migrant families who had created an agricultural ladder, NCLC officials chastised them for maintaining "old work habits" and for possessing a relentless drive to gain land, even at the cost of their children. "Thrift and economy are splendid characteristics and should always and everywhere be encouraged, but unfortunately much of the Old World idea when transferred to this country becomes nothing more than a grabbing after wealth."[47]

The CB investigators, who often sympathized more fully with migrant families, also could not transcend their own middle-class assumptions or come to terms with the migrant families' own ideas about family labor. CB investigators especially condemned those families who managed to use family labor as a form of mobility. Sounding quite a bit like her NCLC counterparts, one CB investigator found a German Russian couple that had just recently become owners because they worked their children, aged nine to fifteen, for fifteen hours a day, leaving only five minutes for breakfast and the same for lunch. The apparent "greed" of this family was matched by yet another German Russian migrant family that worked their children, aged eight, ten, twelve, and fifteen, in order to buy a "car and a new house."[48] The CB criticized these "excessively thrifty" families who "eager to 'get ahead' at any cost drove their children hard."[49]

Though the reformers certainly expressed frustration with migrant families who had moved into the rank of family farmer by using child labor, they worried even more about the far greater number of eastern European migrant children who were continuing to toil in other peoples' fields and who showed little sign of ever climbing any agricultural ladder. (Strangely, while both the NCLC and the CB noted how growing numbers of Mexicans were coming to the fields, only rarely did either group highlight the changing composition of the migrant labor force, preferring instead to focus on eastern European migrants.) In contrast to their farm children counterparts, migrant children worked even longer hours and tended to greater acreage, thereby missing out on even more schooling. To make matters worse, much worse in fact, child labor reformers noted that when children toiled in the fields, so too did their mothers. NCLC representatives highlighted how migrant family labor made it difficult for these working mothers to fulfill their traditional female duties, especially their maternal and familial roles. In its 1919 and 1923 studies, the NCLC profiled migrant women who had been forced to neglect their children, claiming "beet working mothers await maternity with little or no considerations for themselves or for the unborn child."[50] Investigators then reported that many mothers returned to the fields shortly after giving birth, bringing their young children and babies with them.[51]

Children's Bureau reformers also expressed concern that nearly half of grower mothers, 75 percent of tenant mothers, and 80 percent of migrant family mothers worked in the fields alongside their laboring children.[52]

However, CB investigators recognized that women's work in the fields was often necessary to family survival and not just a "matter of helping out."[53] In a much more sympathetic tone than the NCLC, the CB not only described how women could be found toiling alongside their children, but how many of them felt guilty about having to leave their youngest children sitting in open fields or at home with older siblings, where almost anything could happen. The bureau also discussed how migrant women attempted to take care of their children while working, recounting how they placed their youngest children in baskets or boxes alongside the fields while they themselves finished their own work. Ultimately, however, the CB concluded that the mothers' attempts to both work and watch their children proved impossible, and that it was the children, and not the work, that suffered.[54]

The reformers' view of migrant fathers was a bit more ambivalent, sometimes portraying them as victims of the industry while at other times criticizing them as household heads who had decided to bring their families to the fields in the first place. Sara Brown, an NCLC investigator, derided migrant families, noting the most important reason migrant families headed to the countryside was to "work without restrictions for all members of the household, young and old and small and larger."[55] Another NCLC reformer elaborated how families chose to travel to the countryside "not because it is more healthful but because they can use their children there at an earlier age than they can in the cities."[56] The NCLC even argued that the growing number of child labor laws curtailing child labor in urban industrial establishments had helped to create the migratory flow of family labor to the countryside.[57]

Considering the NCLC's somewhat critical view of migrant fathers, which vacillated between sympathy and criticism, it should come as no surprise that when investigators tried to give "voice" to migrant men, they often presented them as greedy and foreign. In a 1920 study of child labor in the beet fields, investigators recounted hearing the following comment: "The three of us (meaning father, mother, and 23-year-old son) in beet is jes' three that makes no money, but with the chillins is seven, that's better."[58] Writing for the *Missionary Review of the World*, Sara Brown claimed that one beet father told her that, "In the city jes' men and the woman works, chillins go to school; in the country chillins work too, more money, go to school jes after work."[59] Another father was reported to have said of his three children, aged seven, nine, and eleven, "they do acres jes' the same like two mens."[60]

The CB, like the NCLC, also asked migrant fathers how they felt about using their children in the fields. In a much different tone, perhaps even masking the workers' foreignness by understating their accents, the bureau presented fathers' motives as emotional and confused. The CB found that fathers often felt torn, and some even heartbroken, at the prospect of working their children in the fields. One father described how his children cried when he told them that they would have to return to the fields.[61] Other fathers vocalized their concern that beet work was hard, especially for women and children. One young man stated how it was "too hot; such work not for kids," and "so hard work not good for children."[62] The CB also acknowledged that many fathers were well aware of the health risks involved in beet work, including one who complained that "fall is the meanest time.... Women are wet up to their waists and have ice on their laps and on their underwear."[63] Still another father noted, "Beets are harder work than working in the steel mill. The children don't get fresh air" as they should have and instead stoop "in the dust and crawl on their knees all day."[64]

In addition to exposing the difficulties that migrant men and women faced in the fields with their children, reformers also went to great lengths to detail the horrible physical state of sugar beet homes and shacks, highlighting especially the overcrowded conditions and the lack of windows and screens. They also worried about the moral and social influence within these homes, contending that "a pathetic indifference" and "lack of interest" in the home itself had developed among the migrant families who came to Michigan year after year. "An attitude of 'what's the use' has crept into all of their relationships, and as a result children have been deprived of much that is their right during their most impressionable years."[65] The home, then, embodied the dangers of migrant labor just as much as what happened in the fields.

NCLC reformers asserted that the supposed familial indifference and apathy that migrants expressed toward their own home life also extended into the communities they temporarily entered. Sara Brown was particularly concerned about the effect of migrant labor on sugar beet communities, warning that the "most deadening influences" could be found within the migrant family who "has no sense of belonging to the community—no interest—no responsibility—no part in its government."[66] This concern with the domestic and civic lives of migrant families quickly turned into a fear of the families themselves. Some NCLC investigators even expressed alarm that migrants had begun to settle in rural Michigan communities, transferring the "balance of power" from local residents into "the hands of people who have not yet acquired a full understanding of American institutions and standards of living ... people not always in harmony with American ideals."[67] Reflecting the nativist sentiment that had captured much of the nation, these reformers worried about the future of American democracy and whether it was compatible with the changing composition of the American population. Committee reformers feared migrant families not only because of their "migratory work patterns" but because of their ethnic and foreign identity.

After establishing the fragile domestic lives and community ties of migrant families, the committee turned to an even more pressing issue—the fact that these foreign workers were raising children who would be American in legal status, but not in manners, mores, or mentality.[68] Although both the NCLC and the CB found rather high rates of naturalization among migrant parents, with more than half of all foreign-born migrant fathers having taken out citizenship papers, reformers nonetheless asserted that far too many migrant parents had little interest in raising their children to be good American citizens.[69] In a less nativistic and nationalistic manner, bureau women also wondered how children who spent their days toiling in the fields and caring for younger siblings were supposed to gain an understanding of the duties of citizenship.[70]

To protect migrant children from the labor in the fields, both the NCLC and the CB called for the enforcement of compulsory school laws. (The same laws would apply to farm children.) This solution reflected a faith in the ability of the educational system to transform migrant children into future citizens and ambivalence about whether their parents would pull them out of the fields voluntarily. The CB, with its focus on the child, decried that migrant children worked in the fields while American children attended schools, noting that "Such a segregation emphasizes social and economic differences between the children of American and those of foreign born parentage whose isolation is great under the best of circumstances, and who are particularly in need of association in the schools with children from English-speaking families and families in which American standards prevail."[71] The NCLC hoped that the enforcement of existing school laws would not only protect the children but also safeguard the future of society. According to NCLC executive Owen Lovejoy, it was not just "in the interest of the child" but "also in the interest of our general American welfare" that migrant children have access to education. Calling for an even more intrusive role for the state than the CB, Lovejoy demanded: "The State itself must become a super-parent and see that the children receive from the State the protection they are unable to get from the domestic circle."[72]

In addition to calling for the establishment and enforcement of compulsory school laws, both the NCLC and the CB pushed for the creation of state laws that would limit the number of hours that migrant contract children between the ages of twelve and sixteen worked and completely prohibit contract children under the age of twelve from working at all. Both organizations even went so far as to implore the state of Michigan to pass housing and sanitation laws to assure minimum living standards for migrant children.[73] There were limits, however, to what they believed the state could do. For bureau officials insisted that the issue was not just getting children out of the fields and into local schools, but also getting their mothers out of the fields. Bureau reformers assumed that if women and children did not work in the fields, migrant fathers would soon make enough to support the whole family.[74] The CB even hoped that sugar companies might abandon their strategy of recruiting entire families once it realized that "children as beet field laborers do not reduce the labor costs to the beet grower or to the sugar company, inasmuch as they do the work no better than adults and are paid on the same basis."[75] Unfortunately, this perception reflected a naïve ignorance of the fact that sugar companies and farmers made thousands of dollars off the labor of the children, not to mention a disregard for the mix of poverty and opportunity that had motivated migrant families in the first place.

The Battle over Child Labor in Michigan

Shortly after the NCLC and the CB published their 1923 reports, the sugar beet industry found its labor relations in the national spotlight as national magazines and newspapers repeated the reformers' charges that this "monster-industry" had created "agricultural child slavery" and "twentieth-century serfdom."[76] (In fact, the NCLC noted that its 1923 study of Michigan's sugar beet industry had "aroused more interest than any single field report heretofore issued.")[77] For example, in March 1923, the *Christian Science Monitor* carried a lengthy article detailing the phenomenon of child labor on Michigan's sugar beet farms. Endorsing the NCLC's call for ending migrant child labor, the newspaper not only described child labor as "contract peonage" and the "cruelest form of peonage," but also "abject slavery" for its denial of "the rights and privileges vouchsafed to free Americans." Laying blame equally on the sugar companies, sugar growers, and migrant fathers, the article warned about the dangers of robbing children of their right to "grow and live and be educated" and challenged the public that it could no longer "disclaim interest in or responsibility for the conditions disclosed."[78] Likewise, the *Chicago Daily Tribune* headlined its articles on Michigan's sugar beet industry with the less than flattering titles of "Work Babies in Michigan Fields, Survey Shows: Children of 5 Imported by Sugar Beet Farmers" and "Toil Cripples Child Workers in Beet Fields."[79] The latter article charged Michigan industrialists with "infant exploitation" and hiring "baby toilers," describing sugar beet work as "worse than in the textile mills and in the tenement workshops" and "almost as arduous as work in a steel mill."[80]

Using the 1923 NCLC report, *The New Republic* took license to carry a semifictionalized story about an eleven-year-old boy named Wlad Czylowitz who had come from Poland to the United States with his family five years earlier. According to author France Williams, who put together this account, immediately after arriving, the Czylowitz family began working in the sugar beet fields of Michigan. The Czylowitz family, however, was not an ordinary one. "Wlad is only an incident in the Czylowitz family; there are eight or nine others—it is sometimes hard to keep track of them." This ever-growing family lived in a two-room wooden shack that had most recently been used as a cow stable. Almost everybody in the family worked in the fields, except for Wlad's four-year-old sister, the "housekeeper" of the family, who tended to her one- and two-year-old siblings. Focusing mostly on Wlad, the story described how his working years showed most visibly in his two shortened fingers, which he had allegedly cut during his first season working in the fields. But, according to Williams, Wlad's scars ran much deeper, for here was a young boy who in all likelihood would someday be an American citizen and yet, "strange as it may seem, Wlad possess not a vestige of a social conscience." A boy to be pitied, Wlad would soon be a man to be feared.[81]

Considering the national attention that the child labor reformers' reports attracted, it should come as little surprise that many of Michigan's elected officials feared that the unwanted publicity might "blemish" their state. In an attempt to counter the bad press, in 1923 the state legislature created a special legislative committee to study the issue of child labor in the beet fields. The committee included congressmen and press representatives—almost all of whom hailed from sugar beet areas. Hardly a disinterested group, the men traveled throughout Saginaw, Gratiot, and Isabella Counties for two days to determine for themselves the real extent of child labor and to assess whether the reformers' charges were true. Rejecting the statistical methods of the reformers whose studies they sought to discredit, the committee decided that the best strategy for assessing the use of child labor was to travel through the countryside and visit with the farmers who were charged with hiring children.

The majority of the farmers whom the committee members interviewed claimed that they did not employ children—they simply hired parents who brought their kids along. Those who admitted that children "helped the parents in the fields" insisted that the boys and girls were never injured while working, that they never worked during storms, and that they had plenty of time to "attend school" and "play." Farmers also claimed, contrary to the CB's findings, that "children of beet weeders [do not] work earlier, longer or harder than the children of owners of farms."[82] Myron Hall, a prominent farmer, insisted that migrant children "appear in better health in fall than in the spring," thereby concluding that "life in the country" seemed to be "beneficial."[83] J. M. Hornbacker, a sugar company labor agent who had recruited workers from Omaha and Chicago since 1918, not only asserted that migrant housing was better than urban housing and that migrant children received "equal educational advantages" but that many migrant children proved themselves to be "good ball players, boxers and athletes."[84] The migrant families who had risen to the status of landowners offered a similar defense of child labor. John Ruppal, who had come from Russia sixteen years earlier, and who had worked his eight children in the fields, claimed that they "work and go to school" and that none had ever been injured from working in the fields.[85]

Sugar beet officials and Michigan farmers also defended child labor by playing into the same romantic assumptions of child agricultural labor that reformers had tried to undermine—that rural America represented a wholesome and healthy retreat for the nation's urban children. In fact, both factory officials and farmers described sugar beet labor as a summer "respite" for children who would have otherwise been held captive in the "dirty," "vile," and crowded "tenements." The sugar companies even argued that urban kids actually benefited from working in the fields, which was healthy and rejuvenating, in contrast to factory work, which they described as unhealthy and degrading. L. R. Stewart, manager of the Caro plant of the Michigan Sugar Company, told the state committee that kids "are taken from the tenement districts, where the children are cooped up in squalid houses sometimes many stories high, and where it is seldom the younger ones ever reach the ground." He then recalled how two years earlier, when a train full of migrant families arrived in Caro, "Hardly had the train been brought to a stop when the youngsters began to pile out of the coaches and to run to the first grass they had ever seen where they rolled around and kicked up their heals in perfect delight."[86] Another local newspaper printed similar stories of children escaping the "squalid city" to "see grass and flowers for the first time."[87] Farmer Joseph Fargett of Bay County defended child labor by stating that "he [the child] is a lot better off there than if he was in the city doing mischief or getting crippled up by machines or sticking his nose where he has no business."[88] Underestimating the amount of work children did, and playing into an idealized vision of rural America, sugar beet industrialists and farmers insisted that there was nothing industrial or exploitive about sugar beet work.

After touring various sugar beet districts and finding "the physical appearance" of the migrant children in Sebewaing, Caro, and Akron "fully equal to that of other children" in their school rooms, the state held hearings in the capitol in which NCLC representatives from New York were charged with exaggerating the extent and dangers of child labor in the beet fields. The state then rather abruptly ended its investigation.[89] Without denying that migrant children worked in the fields as common practice, the investigators nonetheless concluded that children simply helped out their parents when needed. Therefore, in its final report, the state committee officially "acquitted" the state of Michigan from the charges brought by the NCLC and the CB. The final report also charged the NCLC with "acting in bad faith" toward the citizens of Michigan, warning that the "propaganda" the NCLC spewed out would rebound to the benefit of Cuban, Puerto Rican, and Philippine "cane interests" overseas. The committee went even further, recommending that the state attorney general "draft a bill to present to the next legislature to regulate the solicitation of contributions within the state by organizers which are willing to solicit in the name of reform and at the same time spread unfair and unjust propaganda."[90] In other words, sugar beet supporters in Michigan hoped to end the current controversy by simply making it illegal for reform groups to publicize the state's child labor problem

Local newspapers from sugar beet districts gleefully reported that "charges of a misuse of child labor in the beet fields of Michigan brought about by the labor [NCLC] committee seems to have fallen flat."[91] This self-ordained "acquittal," however, did little to end the controversy regarding child labor. In the following months, child labor reformers kept up their vigorous public campaign. In October 1923, Owen Lovejoy spoke before a tuberculosis association in Flint, charging that the local sugar beet industry not only forced young children to work and live in unhealthy conditions but also deprived them of a proper education.[92] That same month, state social workers joined the discussion, devoting an entire day of their annual meeting to address the issue of child labor in the beet fields. The participants that day were an impressive bunch, including Lovejoy of the NCLC, who had spearheaded the child labor campaign; Michigan state representative Charles Culver of Detroit, who had led the state's sugar beet investigation; former Representative Geret Dieckema, who was now acting as president for the Holland—St. Louis Sugar Company; and current State Labor Commissioner Carl Young.

While both Culver and Dieckema used the forum to deride the NCLC, calling its report a "tissue of lies" that had been funded by Cuban sugar cane interests who wanted to destroy Michigan's sugar beet industry, Carl Young defended the NCLC's findings, chastising the "powerful" folks in Michigan who continued to deny what they know to be true.[93] A year later, Young continued to criticize his state's 1923 investigation for "white-washing" the truth and called for yet another investigation into child labor in the beet fields, predicting "if all the facts were told Michigan would be one of the worst-offenders."[94] John J. Scannell, secretary of the Michigan Federation of Labor, likewise questioned the integrity of the state's 1923 investigation, characterizing it as run for and by the sugar companies, "who wish to make money" by exploiting child laborers.[95]

As the charges of child labor continued, a number of farmers abandoned their romantic defense of child labor and instead insisted that child labor was not a problem because it was "mostly foreign children [who] worked in the fields."[96] Highlighting the fact that most migrant families were now coming from Mexico, a phenomenon that the NCLC and the CB rarely mentioned, locals found a new rationale for their laboring practices. An editorial in the *Saginaw News Courier,* later reprinted in small-town newspapers throughout rural Michigan, argued that child labor was not a problem because the companies "import a limited number of outsiders, most of them Mexicans."[97] Some farmers even tried to turn the debate on its head, arguing that the problem was not the harm it caused children, but the fact that these kids did not do good work in the fields.[98] In an attempt to mobilize farmers against the sugar companies, C. E. Ackerman, a former Michigan Sugar Beet Growers' Association president, added to the debate by arguing that it was the farmers who suffered most. "Are we going to . . . give them the right to go into foreign countries and get cheap labor under contract which they will control and bring into out midst to deteriorate our farm community life and bring ourselves such charges of working children and even five year old babies, as charged by the NCLC, or will we Say No."[99]

To Ackerman's chagrin, he found few supporters. When a proposed child labor amendment to the U.S. Constitution was being debated in 1924, Michigan's farmers continued to scoff at the idea of outlawing child labor, as did much of the nation. To them, the issue was much broader than the series of questions and concerns that had been raised during their state's sugar beet investigation. As a result, rather than rely on romantic arguments to defend child labor, they claimed that all federal regulation, and especially a constitutional amendment, "would destroy local self-government," "support a rebellion which menaces our civilization," and "give Congress not only parental authority ... [but] create a centralized government far removed from the people. ... [I]t would place in the hands of Congress a power to destroy our agriculture ... [and] enslave the child to the Republic."[100] One of Michigan's main farm journals, otherwise progressive on many issues, likewise proclaimed that the proposed Twentieth Amendment "is not a child labor amendment, but an exclusive grant of power to the Congress, which directly and by implication confers control over the labor and education of all persons under eighteen to an extent not now possessed by any state of the Union."[101] The state of Michigan, like most others in the nation, refused to ratify the child labor amendment, leaving the issue of child labor to Franklin D. Roosevelt's New Deal.

Conclusion

In turning to child labor in the beet fields, both the National Child Labor Committee and the Children's Bureau expressed alarm that large sections of rural America no longer resembled the Jeffersonian world of independent small family farms where fathers, mothers, and children toiled together on their own homesteads. They lamented how the expansion of industrial agriculture in rural America was remaking the nation's rural communities into a twin image of the urban industrial realm. Rather than preparing children for a future of independent farming or even skilled industrial work, industrial agriculture promised to confine them to the lowest ranks of society. Moreover, it seemed that the costs of creating a modernized agriculture, in which cheaper and more abundant food would be available to the nation's masses, were being paid by those least able to afford that bill.

What made child labor in the sugar beet fields especially troubling was that almost all of the migrant families were recent immigrants for whom migrant family labor represented not an extension of the traditional family labor of the family farm but an inversion of its best attributes. Instead of leading to economic mobility, community cohesion, and enhanced morals and values, child labor in industrial agriculture undermined the children, their families, and the larger society. To reformers, then, industrial agriculture was an evil not only because the work was monotonous, mechanical, and dangerous, or because children worked in "factories without roofs or walls," but because of the particular social relations of production. What we find is that early twentieth century child labor reformers vacillated between sympathizing with migrant families as victims of the industry that recruited them, the farmers on whose land they toiled, and the communities in which they were only seasonal members, while also fearing that these families might be so stigmatized and stunted by their labor that they would never be able to assimilate and Americanize as had previous generations of immigrants.

During the 1920s, then, the sugar beet companies' greatest threat came not from farmers—who remained relatively quiet during this decade—but rather from immigration restrictionists and child labor reformers who criticized the migrant labor system upon which the sugar beet industry had been built. Strangely, however, these labor critics seemed blissfully unaware or uninterested in each others' campaigns. In fact, it would be easy to read the congressional immigration hearings regarding the fate of Mexican immigrants and the child labor reformers' reports and not realize that they were talking about the very same fields. Restrictionists did not care whether the Mexicans toiling in the fields were adults or children; they were concerned about race and citizenship. The child labor reformers, perhaps hoping to elicit as much sympathy as possible, saw little benefit in publicizing the fact that the children toiling in the fields as contract laborers were increasingly coming from Mexico rather than eastern Europe. At least that is what their relative lack of commentary regarding this significant shift in labor seems to suggest.[102] Even if the restrictionists and child labor reformers had somehow joined hands, it seems unlikely that the outcome would have been very different for either camp. In spite of the work of the NCLC and the CB, child labor and migrant family labor remained the norm in the sugar beet fields. The reformers fell short of convincing two essential constituents that child labor was not in their best interest—Michigan's farmers and the general public. Perhaps equally important, child labor reformers also failed to fully confront or address the mix of poverty and opportunity that explained the migrant families' labor practices.

8

Remaking Imperialism and the Industrial Countryside

A year after Michigan sugar beet industrialist T. G. Gallagher traveled to Washington, D.C., to protest the restriction of Mexican immigration, he journeyed to the nation's capital yet again. This time, however, his concern was not with keeping the door open to Mexican immigrants but rather closing the door to Cuban sugar. To buttress his argument that Congress should raise the tariff on Cuban sugar coming into the United States, Gallagher asked the nation's elected representatives if they had recently consulted the preamble to the U.S. Constitution, noting, "It says in the preamble to the Constitution of the United States, as I remember it, that we must provide for the common defense and insure the general welfare of the people of the United States, and it did not say anything about Cuba in that preamble."[1] He then predicted economic disaster if Congress refused to act, warning that "unless adequate relief is extended" it will be "impossible for the industry to carry on."[2]

The late 1920s had been economically devastating for the domestic sugar beet industry, which found it difficult to make ends meet, much less turn a profit, as the worldwide price for sugar began a freefall. However, the agricultural depression, which certainly threatened this industry, also presented a golden political opportunity for the industrialists to achieve what they had failed to win at the turn of the century—a protected market unencumbered by foreign countries as well as colonial producers. When Congress convened special hearings in 1929 to consider ways to provide farm relief, sugar beet industrialists and their allies demanded that the tariff on Cuban sugar be raised and that the amount of Philippine sugar coming into the United States be limited as well. As soon as it became clear that Congress would not limit trade between the United States and a country under the U.S. flag, sugar beet industrialists began calling for nothing less than the complete independence of the Philippines as a way to protect American producers. Holding hands with a number of unlikely allies, including the racially motivated American Federation of Labor, which wanted Philippine independence to stop the migration of Filipinos into the United States, as well as many Filipinos themselves, who had long demanded independence for their homeland, sugar beet industrialists led the charge calling for the end of American colonialism. What had begun ostensibly as an economic discussion—providing relief to America's farmers—turned into a national debate regarding the past, present, and future of American imperialism and the place of the United States in world politics.[3]

At the same time that the sugar beet industrialists were doing all they could to reserve the domestic sugar market by transforming U.S. colonial relations, they were also trying to figure out ways to remake their industry at the local level. Simply hoarding the domestic market would not necessarily lead to the kinds of profits industrialists had come to expect. For how much sugar companies profited each year depended not only on the price of refined sugar in the global marketplace (plus the tariff rate) but how much they would have to pay local farmers to keep growing the crop. And, somewhat ironically, the flat-rate contracts that had proven so lucrative when the price of sugar remained high had now become a liability as the price of sugar plummeted. On the ground, then, the industrialists looked for ways to try to convince farmers to keep growing the crop while also shifting the burden of lower prices for refined sugar onto their shoulders.

The ability of the sugar men to control their industry either globally or locally was never entirely in their own hands. As the industry's demands for a protected market grew louder, so too did the Roosevelt administration's insistence that this industry needed to be reformed. President Roosevelt was deeply ambivalent about the domestic sugar beet industry, fearing that its tactics threatened the nation's colonial and foreign policy while its relations with farmers and workers made a mockery of agrarian ideals. When Congress began to debate whether to add sugar beet to the Agricultural Adjustment Act (AAA), the president himself warned the industrialists that they had better share the fruits of this industry with the farmers on whose land the crop was planted and the thousands of migrant workers who tended to the crop as it matured. The arrival of the New Deal, marked by the passage of the Jones-Costigan Act of 1934, which added sugar beet to the commodities covered by the AAA, as well as the 1937 Sugar Act, which replaced Jones-Costigan after the Supreme Court ruled the AAA unconstitutional, promised to transform the industry at both the global and local levels.[4] In addition to providing production quotas for domestic producers and the Philippines, Cuba, Puerto Rico, and the Virgin Islands, these acts also stipulated that industrialists who hoped to partake in a share of the sugar market would have to pay the farmers who grew the crop a "fair and reasonable" price and that any farmers who felt aggrieved by the companies could look to the USDA for help. On paper, then, both sugar acts had the potential to remake the global marketplace as well as class relations on the ground.

Depression as Opportunity

Anyone traveling through rural Michigan in 1929 would have found plenty of evidence that what was soon to become known as the Great Depression had already descended on the sugar beet industry. After losing $611,000 in 1928, the Michigan Sugar Company, the largest and most stable sugar company in the state, was forced to close four of its eight factories for the 1929 season.[5] These plant closings did little to stop the bleeding, as the company lost another $441,200 in 1929.[6] What had once been one of the state's most lucrative and capital-intensive industrial enterprises had become a mere shadow of its former self.

The industry's economic difficulties stemmed in part from the fact that the sugar companies had been caught too many times in the late 1920s and early 1930s trying to meet minimum price guarantees for the sugar beet crop, only to watch nervously as the price of refined sugar fell. That is, the flat-rate contracts, which had allowed the sugar companies to pocket increases in prices during good years, now left them carrying all of the economic costs. To spread the risks of a volatile market, the companies decided to abandon minimum price guarantees for sugar beet and begin offering the 50/50 profit-sharing contracts that farmers had demanded during the highly contentious World War I years. Instead of paying farmers a base price for the raw materials they brought to the factory, the companies would simply divide the "net proceeds" from the processed sugar at the end of the season and give half to the farmers. What had previously been a farmer strategy to force the sugar companies to share industry profits during a time of high sugar prices had now become a company ploy to spread the risks of this industry in hard times. When promoting the 50/50 contract, the sugar companies even usurped the rhetoric that the farmers had used decades earlier, hailing the introduction of the 50/50 contract as "the most nearly ideal of any farm crop marketing contract used in the U.S.," making "the producers of the raw materials partners in fact with the producers of the finished product."[7] Industrialists promised that it was "Our Obligation" "to approach this harvest season with a full sense of responsibility to our beet growers for the time, labor and capital involved in producing sugar beets in the field."[8]

To further convince farmers that the days of wrangling over prices and profits were over, sugar beet company officials invited farmers to join the newly created Farmers and Manufacturers Beet Sugar Association (F&M). Industrialists had created this organization in 1932 as a cooperative farmer/factory organization where the two sides could work together. When promoting the F&M, the companies repeatedly publicized that the purpose of this organization was to "promote friendly relations between the growers and manufacturers to harmonize their interests and to adjust their disputes and differences."[9] Describing an end to the class conflicts and mutual suspicions that had characterized farmer/factory relations since the first season, the F&M promised to represent the farmers' and processors' mutual interests as well as foster mutual understanding and cooperation. Pointing to the F&M, the companies announced that "a new day [had] dawned" in the sugar beet industry and that from now on, farmers could feel confident that the companies would look after their best interests.[10] In other words, industrialists hailed both the 50/50 contracts and the F&M as a way to ensure that both "partners" would share equally in the fruits of their labor.

At the same time that the sugar companies adopted 50/50 contracts and initiated the F&M as a way to restructure their industry, townspeople also worked hard to galvanize support for their local factories. Based on the optimistic assumption that the industry would return to health if more farmers began growing the crop again, local newspapers tried to convince them to keep planting sugar beet. In Caro and Sebewaing, the local chambers of commerce sponsored numerous "Sugar Beet Days" with free meals and entertainment to help the companies kick off their contracting drives.[11] Local newspapers also reminded neighboring farmers that the factories provided much-needed cash income to them, thousands of jobs for men in the community, and business to local merchants. A 1929 *Tuscola County Advertiser* article entitled "Your Help is Wanted" reminded Caro readers how their own local factory contributed more than $28,000 in taxes, paid local farmers $500,000 for beets, and distributed $220,000 to the 1,300 migrant workers who toiled in the fields.[12] Reviving the local sugar factory seemed the best way out of the Depression.[13]

The townspeople's efforts to save their neighborhood factories reflected their perception that the causes of the sugar beet industry's economic woes were local and hence could be solved locally once farmers realized their mistake. In reality, however, the roots of the Depression were global in nature, a fact not lost on the sugar beet industrialists. After World War I, the sugar market represented a bubble waiting to be burst. When sugar prices reached an all-time high at nineteen cents a pound in May 1920, producers worldwide expanded production dramatically, hoping to cash in on the economic boom. Not surprisingly, this soon led to overproduction and falling prices, with the world price returning to less than five cents a pound by December 1920. Prices continued to tumble during the next few years, reaching 3.1 cents a pound in 1925. In spite of attempts by European sugar beet states and some Latin American countries to limit the amount of sugar traded on the world market, production continued to rise as prices went in the opposite direction. With the exception of a slight reprieve in the late 1920s, prices continued to plummet, reaching just 1.74 cents a pound in 1930. Two years later, the free market price finally hit rock bottom at a mere half cent per pound.[14]

Although U.S. tariff barriers shielded domestic producers from the worst of these price drops, they could not completely protect sugar prices in the United States. By May 1932, the price of sugar in the United States fell to less than three cents a pound.[15] In the ensuing search for the cause of these price declines, domestic producers began to point to Puerto Rico and the Philippines, which had increased sugar imports into the United States. For example, imports from Puerto Rico, which came in duty free after 1902, rose dramatically in the 1920s and early 1930s, from 349 tons a year in 1922 to 739 tons by 1933, a 112 percent increase. Imports from the Philippines, which came in duty free after 1913, expanded even more significantly, increasing from 240,000 tons in 1922 to 1,160,000 tons by 1933, an upsurge of 243 percent. Equally important, by the 1930s, more than 90 percent of the sugar produced in the Philippines was being shipped to the United States.[16] The sugar beet industry's turn-of-the century warning about the Philippine sugar industry seemed to finally be coming true.

It did not take long for sugar beet industrialists and their agricultural allies to realize the political opportunity afforded by their economic misfortune.[17] Moving quickly to politicize the question of sugar production by making it part of a much larger debate regarding the impact of American imperialism on domestic agriculture, farm groups called on Congress to take action. As early as 1929, Nebraska sugar beet farmers had already begun to ask Congress to "curtail sugar production in the insular possessions and restrict Philippine importations" in order to "insure a better price for beets."[18] That same year, the American Farm Bureau Federation charged that the Senate had a responsibility to create trade policies that would make it possible for "the American farmer to maintain an American standard of living on the farm," insisting that it was an "idle gesture" to keep raising duties on foreign farm products while allowing "our so-called colonies or dependencies" to trade "duty free."[19]

As the concern over falling agricultural prices mounted, newly inaugurated President Herbert Hoover instructed Congress to hold a special session in 1929 to consider the possibility of raising tariff duties.[20] Hoover had hoped to provide a slight adjustment in tariff rates as a way to provide agricultural relief to the nation's farmers, who had suffered from a decade-long depression. But when it came time for Congress to discuss how to help domestic sugar producers, the debate over the sugar tariff turned into a much broader discussion than just providing relief to farmers. In the words of the *New York Times,* the sugar discussion "embraced this country's relationships to Cuba, to Latin America generally and to the Philippines."[21]

Much like at the turn of the century, when Congress first considered what to do with its global empire, sugar beet industrialists and various allies not only began a vigorous and extensive public relations campaign in newspapers and magazines, they also descended on Washington en masse.[22] More than a dozen of the fifty witnesses who testified in front of Congress in January 1929 did so on behalf of the U.S. sugar beet industry.[23] Five months later, sugar beet industrialists were once again more than amply well-represented. In fact, so many sugar beet industrialists showed up in Washington that Tennessee Senator Pat Harrison commented, "If certain captains of sugar companies would spend one-hundredth part of their time back home trying to run their businesses efficiently instead of remaining here in Washington appealing constantly for increased tariff rates, their business would be in better shape."[24]

During the hearings, sugar beet industrialists and their allies from the American Farm Bureau Federation and the National Grange insisted that American farmers should be encouraged to produce as much as possible. Boasting that sugar beet was no ordinary crop, they described how it had transformed American agriculture for the better by encouraging scientific farming, agricultural diversification, and rural industrialization. To head off criticism that raising the duty on sugar would only help to bolster factory profits, sugar beet industrialists and farm leaders described the sugar beet industry as "essentially a farm enterprise" with the factories "serving as adjuncts to the farms."²⁵ Ignoring the numerous farmer/factory conflicts that had rattled this industry since the turn of the century, witnesses also painted an idyllic picture of rural America, describing the 50/50 contracts as a "unique" cooperative arrangement making "the farmer a partner of the beet sugar mills."²⁶

In addition to highlighting how an increased tariff would aid America's farmers and rural communities, sugar beet interests questioned whether the United States still "owed" anything to Cuba and the Philippines. Insisting that the United States' duty to its own citizens, that is, to its own workers and farmers, should take precedence over any historically mandated obligation to those in its empire, the United States Beet Sugar Association insisted that "Our obligation rests upon Congress to protect American citizens engaged here at home in the production of an essential food commodity."²⁷ Protecting American farmers and workers meant protecting an American standard of living from cheaper labor abroad. According to Stephen H. Love of the United States Beet Sugar Association, it was simply unfair to pit America's workingmen against Cuban workers who live "in misery, in houses of palm trees, lacking even the most elementary things of modern life." He even charged that Cuban workers toiled under a labor-relations system that "approach[es] slavery."²⁸ Reading from the Farm Bureau's 1928 convention resolutions, W. R. Ogg, an American Farm Bureau representative, also demanded that the United States needed to be protected "for the benefit of our own citizens" and that Congress had a moral responsibility to ensure that farmers would enjoy the kind of returns that guarantee them an "American standard of living."²⁹ Ogg then introduced a brief endorsed by various farm organizations that not only criticized any tariff policy that might harm "American high standards and the welfare of the consuming public" but also chastised "the foreign capitalists whose investments are in these cheap labor foreign fields."³⁰ According to these witnesses, the question of what sugar Americans would consume was really a question of what kind of labor system Americans wanted to promote—one that provided an American standard of living at home or one that took advantage of poorly paid and servile labor abroad.

In spite of the effort by agricultural interests to determine the topic and tone of the tariff debate, the sugar beet growers and industrialists who testified in front of Congress often found themselves in the hot seat, forced to answer questions about *their* use of Mexican labor. Anti–high-tariff congressmen jumped at the opportunity to highlight the hypocrisy of an industry calling for protection from foreign labor abroad while depending on foreign labor at home. As such, the sugar beet witnesses who had come to Washington expecting to rail against the injustice of having to compete against cheap labor abroad found their own foreign labor strategies at the center of the debate.

This was certainly the case for Michigan sugar beet grower James N. McBride, who began his testimony by declaring: "The bringing in of the foreign labor is a godsend to us."[31] In response, Senator Tom Connally of Texas asked McBride: "Isn't the chief object of the tariff to protect American labor against foreigners? And do you want to keep up the tariff and then bring in this labor from abroad too?" Perhaps sensing that this was an argument he could not win, McBride responded defensively: "They have only been there for a few years, and they are getting opportunities they have never had before in their lives."[32]

Later that day, when industrialist Fred Crawford testified on behalf of the Michigan Sugar Company, he also faced hard questions about his industry's use of Mexican labor. When asked why his company recruited Mexican labor in Texas, Crawford responded that Mexican people looked forward to working in Michigan's beet fields as "a vacation period," explaining that had he been given the opportunity to head north as a young man, "I would have traded my soul for the privilege of doing so."[33] After his incredulous cross-examiners questioned whether Michigan's sugar beet industry recruited Mexican workers because whites refused to do such demanding, low-wage labor, Crawford, a native Texan, insisted that race played no role in his industry's labor strategy. While admitting that Michigan's native-born white residents generally refused to work in the beet fields because of the possibility of earning higher wages in the auto industry, he insisted that he could recruit twenty-five thousand "Anglo Saxon Texans" to toil in the beet fields if he wanted to. When asked why he did not, Crawford insisted that it was "custom" for his industry to use Mexicans.[34] However, Crawford contradicted his own argument that race played no role in his industry's labor strategy, by warning that "if we can not get the Mexican, we are going to pull the colored people out of the South and take them out of the cotton fields."[35]

The national press, which was highly critical of the sugar industry's political maneuverings, wasted no time in pointing out the blatant hypocrisy of domestic producers demanding higher tariffs for Cuban sugar and limits on Philippine sugar to protect an American standard of living while at the same time relying on thousands of Mexican immigrants to toil in the fields. Rephrasing the congressional testimony of one witness, the *New York Times* asked "in view of what beet sugar growers said about their dependence on Mexican labor, the question seemed to be whether Mexicans or Cuban workers were to be given the most consideration."[36] Similarly, after questioning whether the increased tariff would actually help sugar beet growers, the *Washington Post* pointed out that sugar beet districts already depended on Mexican labor, and that if the industry continued to expand, it would import even more "alien labor."[37] And finally, *Washington Post* columnist and critic of the sugar beet industry, David Rankin Barbee, made no attempt to veil his contempt for the beet industry, or his own racist assumptions, when he charged that the industry depended upon "the cheapest class of labor known to this continent . . . Mexican peon labor," adding that this particular labor form "is not allowed in any civilized country on earth—except the United States."[38]

In addition to chastising the sugar beet industry for its hypocrisy regarding the issue of Mexican labor, critics also pointed to the industrialists' crass opportunism of using the call for farm relief to remake American colonialism, with little or no concern for anything but their own industry's survival and prosperity. As the first round of hearings was just beginning in January 1929, newspapers chided the sugar beet industry for abandoning any pretense to principle in order to protect its own profits.[39] After witnesses testifying against raising the sugar tariff rightly predicted that an increased duty would create economic and political mayhem in Cuba, which the United States would then be forced to address, a *Washington Post* letter to the editor warned that if Congress bent to the wishes of the sugar beet industry, Cuba might "slip into anarchy or go Bolshevik."[40] Just two months later, the *Washington Post* pleaded with Congress to act with "statesmen-like consideration" during the upcoming tariff session questioning "whether the domestic sugar industry is justified in asking for a high tariff to be obtained at such great risk."[41]

The sugar beet industry's other demand—that the amount of sugar coming from the Philippines should be limited as well—elicited even greater responses of disapprobation. President Hoover, who had initiated the tariff proceedings, was concerned that the tariff battle in Congress might upset foreign relations and further invigorate the independence movement in the Philippines. Though Hoover was willing to concede a minor adjustment of the tariff with respect to Cuba, he refused to entertain the possibility of limiting sugar from the Philippines as long as that country remained under the American flag. That is, Hoover feared the hypocrisy of keeping the Philippine people under American tutelage while not allowing their products in duty free, especially in the context of the United States' self-proclaimed mission of benevolent imperialism.[42]

As Hoover's representative during the tariff battle, Henry L. Stimson, former governor general of the Philippine Islands and soon to be secretary of state, loudly sounded the administration's warning that Congress would do great harm if it tried to interfere with free trade between the Philippines and the United States. Speaking to reporters in Washington, D.C., Stimson insisted that, "We have promised them self-government, and in order to be capable of self-government they must be economically capable. They would not be if we went back on our policy of free trade."[43] Speaking a month later before the Committee on Ways and Means, as secretary of state, Stimson repeated his objections, noting that limiting the amount of sugar would not only be viewed as "a betrayal of trust by the United States," which had claimed benevolent intentions in taking over the Philippines, but that it would inspire "widespread criticism" throughout the world, thereby undermining U.S. commercial relations.[44]

The theory that limiting free trade between the United States and the Philippines would spur revolutionary sentiment throughout the Far East garnered a great deal of attention nationwide. Largely adopting the administration's perspective, the nation's most influential newspapers predicted a dangerous future of colonial revolutions if the United States abrogated its duty to the Philippines by bending to the will of sugar beet interests. (Estimates at the time indicated that 61.6 percent of newspapers opposed Philippine independence, 19.7 percent favored letting the Philippines go, and 18.7 percent remained neutral on the subject.[45]) The *New York Times* was especially critical of domestic sugar beet producers who demanded protection regardless of how it might affect the welfare of the Philippine people. The problem, however, was not just the fate of the Philippines. According to a *Times* editorial, premature independence in the Philippines would spur a "bloody revolution" in India and destabilize the Far East more generally, thereby undermining "world peace." As such, the newspaper concluded that the United States had a "moral obligation to continue to exercise control over the [Philippine] islands, at least until the Filipino people have shown they are capable of self government."[46]

In spite of the beating that sugar beet interests and their agricultural allies endured from administration officials and the national press regarding their reliance on Mexican labor, and their alleged callous disregard for foreign policy, over the course of the tariff debate they grew increasingly emboldened. Many began to demand that if Congress refused to limit the amount of duty-free Philippine sugar allowed into the United States as long as the Philippines remained a colony, then perhaps the United States should try to figure out a way to let go of its sugar-producing empire. Soon thereafter, what had been largely a rhetorical demand took a more tangible form as a number of representatives and senators authored various independence bills. For example, in an effort to appease both his pro-imperialist Republican colleagues in the Senate, as well as his high-tariff constituents back home, Michigan Senator Arthur Vandenburg sponsored a bill calling for tariff autonomy for the Philippines, to be followed by full political independence once economic independence had been established.[47] His fellow senator from Utah, William King, went one step further by calling for complete and immediate independence for the Philippines.[48]

The domestic sugar beet industry's vocal and well-organized demand for higher tariffs on Cuban sugar and limits on Philippine sugar placed both Cuban and Philippine interests on the defensive, scrambling to make political arguments that might sway an increasingly protectionist Congress that was looking for a way to address the economic concerns of an ever-isolationist public. Largely financed and controlled by American capital, the Cuban industry had become almost completely dependent on the U.S. market in the years following the Spanish-American War. With a reduced tariff rate of 20 percent, Cuban sugar had largely supplanted almost all other foreign sugar coming into the United States. This coveted position, however, was clearly threatened by Philippine sugar, which came into the United States duty free after 1913. As Philippine sugar imports increased in the 1920s and early 1930s, sugar imports from Cuba declined. In fact, while Philippine sugar exports nearly tripled from 1922 to 1933, Cuban sugar exports fell by more than 54 percent.[49] This translated into a significant loss in revenue for Cuba's sugar industry, from an average of 150 million a year from 1900 to 1929 to an average of just twenty-five million by the early 1930s.[50]

Both the Cuban and the American capitalists who dominated the Cuban sugar industry did their best to convince Congress that any tariff increase would not help domestic sugar producers but rather "foreign" producers in the Philippines.[51] Cuban sugar advocates also challenged the idea that Cuba should be treated any differently than sugar producers within the United States. In the words of a prominent Havana merchant, "Cuba is economically as well as financially a part of the United States."[52] U.S. citizen Herbert C. Lakin, president of the Cuba Company as well as member of the American Chamber of Commerce of Cuba, made this point even more forcefully. "Undoubtedly you have been told that Cuban producers have no rights because Cuba is an independent foreign country. Even if that statement were true, it would have nothing to do with the case, because 75 percent of the Cuban production is in the hands of Americans, who, as a matter of fact, have more money invested in Cuba than the total American investments in the Philippines, Hawaii, and Porto Rico."[53] Though Cuba was technically a foreign country, the fact that American capital dominated the island, and the fact that the United States had fostered close economic and political ties, created a strong basis for hope that Congress might favor Cuban interests over those of the Philippines.

For their part, the Philippine sugar interests, which included far fewer Americans, played on the fact that the Philippines were legally part of the United States. This argument was an important one considering that American capitalists had not invested heavily in the Philippines, due in part to the prohibitive land laws passed in 1902 at the behest of sugar beet industrialists.[54] These legal land limits, combined with the geographic distance between the United States and the Philippines, had deterred American capitalists from looking to the Philippine sugar industry, especially when easy profits could be made much closer to home in Cuba and Puerto Rico. When Congress convened to decide what to do about the question of sugar production and consumption, it faced the paradox, well stated by Carlisle Bargerson in the *Washington Post,* of "whether it [Congress] should continue to favor the Philippine industry in United States territory, but largely owned by foreign interests, or the Cuban industry, in a foreign country, but heavily involving American financial interests."[55]

After a long and contentious battle, Congress finally succeeded in passing the 1930 Smoot-Hawley Tariff Act. In its final version, this act represented a partial victory for domestic sugar interests, defeat for Cuban sugar interests, and a temporary reprieve for the Philippine sugar industry. Congress raised the duty on Cuban sugar from 1.76 cents per pound to 2 cents per pound, thereby making home-grown sugar more competitive within the U.S. market. Congress refused, however, to set any limits on the amount of sugar coming into the United States from the Philippines, contending that it would be unfair, unjust, and unwise to limit the sugar from the United States' own colony from entering the colonizer's market. As such, Congress tried to provide economic relief to the sugar beet industry without imperiling America's imperial presence in the Far East.[56]

The Sugar Beet Industry and Philippine Independence— Graduation or Expulsion?[57]

Though the Philippines had been spared from the domestic sugar beet industry's attempt to limit exports to the United States, the question of whose sugar Americans would consume was still very much open for debate. Months before the Smoot-Hawley bill officially passed both houses of Congress, Senator Hiram Bingham initiated hearings before the Senate Committee on Territories and Insular Affairs to discuss the topic of Philippine independence. Rather than represent the political will of the Philippine people, the independence talk reflected the political power of agricultural interests in the United States. According to a *New York Times* editorial, "The zeal of converts in Congress to Philippine independence knows no bounds. Hardly a week goes by without some new bill, or rider, designed to give the Filipinos the blessing of liberty and the American sugar growers, dairy interests, and rope makers freedom from competition by Filipino farmers."[58]

As the Senate began hearings in January 1930 to consider the possibility of granting independence to the Philippines, a host of pro- and anti-independence witnesses lined up to convince the members of their particular political viewpoint.[59] The most powerful anti-independence witness, Secretary of State Stimson, once again laid out the administration's strong objection to what it regarded as irresponsible and premature independence, claiming not only that independence would prove "disastrous" to the Philippines and U.S. interests abroad but that the sugar beet industry was acting selfishly for demanding that the Philippines should be let go.[60] The agricultural interests who came to represent the pro-independence side of the debate, however, denied they were economically selfish. After reading the Farm Bureau's most recent resolution calling for Philippine independence, Chester H. Gray defended his organization's demand by insisting that America's farmers were motivated by historic and humanitarian reasons as much as if not more than economic self-interest.[61] By history, Gray was referring to the fact that all U.S. presidents, from William McKinley to Herbert Hoover, had promised that one day the Philippines would be set free. Gray even drew parallels between the United States' own independence movement against Great Britain and the Philippines' pending independence, noting that the longer the Philippines remained under direct U.S. control, the more its economy would grow dependent on U.S. markets. As such, he asked: "Shall we grant them independence now, when it is politically and economically possible to have independence granted, or shall we delay it for another 25 years, when economically it will be impossible to grant independence?" Claiming the mantle of morality, Gray insisted: "We think the kindest way to treat them is to grant them independence when they can economically bear it."[62] Dropping any pretenses to kindness or morality, Gray's fellow agriculturalist, Frederic Brenckman of the Grange, criticized unlimited Filipino immigration as the importation of a people "who can never be assimilated" and the importation of Philippine products as the importation of an "inferior and un-American standard of living."[63]

As the agricultural witnesses made their case in front of the Senate, they were joined by American Federation of Labor representative W. C. Hushing. Although the AFL had previously adopted a neutral position when it came to the question of sugar tariffs, now that the debate had shifted to independence for the Philippines, the AFL jumped in on the side of the sugar industrialists. To explain his organization's support of independence, Hushing at first pointed to the AFL's historic critique of U.S. imperialism as a violation of the nation's democratic ideals. Quickly, however, Hushing turned to more contemporary arguments, which revolved around racist immigration politics rather than ideological objections to imperialism. Reading from the AFL's 1928 convention proceedings, Hushing likened the recent increase in Filipino immigration to a "cheap labor" "cancer in American private and public life, destroying American ideals and preventing the development of a nation based upon racial unity."[64]

Strangely, the group most closely identified with demanding Philippine independence—the sugar beet industry—remained conspicuously absent from the 1930 independence hearings, a fact not lost on anti-independence witnesses. When John Switzer, the director of the Philippine-American Chamber of Commerce, came to offer testimony against independence in early February, he began by warning the Senate that "we must not be carried off our feet by selfish interests at home or by overzealous sentimentalism in the islands."[65] He explicitly charged that domestic sugar interests "have been back of the agitation for Philippine independence . . . in the guise of liberating the Filipinos from American oppression." He then chastised the sugar beet industry for attempting to impose trade restrictions on Philippine products, and for demanding "complete and immediate independence."[66] At this point Senator Hawes asked Switzer: "Where do you get that? . . . No witness has appeared here representing the sugar interests." To which Switzer responded: "No and they are not likely to, Senator." After Switzer's brief quip, Hawes then pointed out how representatives from the nation's largest farm organizations had appeared, but "so far nobody has appeared here representing the sugar people. I notice that you put the whole onus of this thing on the sugar people." At this point, Switzer not only defended his charge that domestic sugar interests had propelled the independence talk, he insisted that they were unlikely to appear before the committee because "the sugar people are beginning to realize that they have overplayed their hand."[67]

Although one sugar beet representative would show up two years later to testify in front of the House when the Committee on Insular Affairs took up the question of Philippine independence, Switzer was basically right.[68] The sugar interests had, for the most part, remained absent from the congressional hearings they themselves had helped to instigate. The low profile of sugar beet interests did nothing, however, to take their industry out of the national spotlight as, in the words of one contemporary, the "real driving force behind independence."[69] In fact, newspapers nationwide continued to castigate this industry for acting selfishly and thoughtlessly.[70] Highlighting the "purely selfish reasons" of the sugar beet industry, the *Wall Street Journal* advised, "If one digs into the currently professed sympathy for the aspirations for independence of our 'little brown brothers' it will be found that much of it is a cloak that covers the American sugar beet."[71]

The national press was not just troubled by the economic selfishness of the domestic sugar beet industry. Rather, following the lead of the Hoover administration, which regularly warned about the foreign policy impact of Philippine independence, the national press provided plenty of newsprint to publicize the feared international reverberations that would follow Philippine independence. In an August 1931 editorial, the *New York Times* worried that simply letting go of the Philippines, which it characterized as a "ward," would lead to "permanent disgrace and a deadly loss of reputation and influence in the East."[72] An editorial in the *Christian Science Monitor* by Senator Hiram Bingham expressed fear that premature independence in the Philippines would not only prove "disastrous to the Filipinos" but also harm U.S. interests in the Far East.[73] To highlight this danger, the *New York Times* reprinted large parts of a speech by Newton W. Gilbert, president of the Philippine-American Chamber of Commerce, in which he warned that independence would not only destroy the Philippine economy and initiate a return "to poverty and disease" but that it would "kindle a flame in the entire Orient which might result in a devastating war between the yellow and brown men on the one side and the white man on the other."[74] And finally, after pointing to what it feared might be the very real possibility of revolutions in Java, the Dutch East Indies, India, and Indochina, the *Wall Street Journal* asked: "Would we be justified in lighting such a torch for sentimental reasons, or even for the sake of our sugar beets?"[75]

Overshadowed by the domestic debate that was largely driving the independence dispute in the United States, Filipino politicians did their best to make sure their voices would be heard. As soon as Congress announced that it would be addressing the issue of Philippine independence, the Philippine legislature sent a delegation to the United States to speak on its behalf. Largely adopting the nationalist rhetoric that had undergirded domestic Philippine politics for more than three decades—immediate, absolute, and complete independence—the Philippine representatives applauded the movement to finally set their country free. Philippine House Speaker Manuel Roxas thanked the United States for its "noble and disinterested guardianship." He described the pending Philippine independence bills before Congress as a "monument to America's unselfishness" and predicted that by giving the Philippines its independence, "America shall have rendered its greatest contribution to civilization, mankind and enduring world peace."[76] When questioned whether the Philippine people would be willing to forgo the American sugar market for political independence, Roxas bravely responded that "we would stake our very lives on independence."[77]

This public bravado masked a deep unease with the fact that the movement behind independence was being pushed by those whose primary concern was to kick out Philippine sugar, and that independence might indeed cut the economic ties between the United States and the Philippines. Moreover, there was little disagreement that if the domestic sugar industry succeeded, the Philippine sugar industry, not to mention the Philippine economy, would be devastated. So once it became clear that any independence bill that was likely to pass both houses of Congress would include strict limitations on immigration and sugar exports, Philippine consternation assumed a more public face. In early December 1932, as Congress debated various independence bills, the *Manila Tribune* warned that the proposals for independence "will mean the ruin of our sugar industry." Special correspondent Aura Smith of the *New York Times* largely concurred, noting that "what has been held up for years as the culminating glory of American altruism may shortly be achieved as the final selfish blow at a competitor."[78]

What Filipinos hoped to achieve was political independence and continued economic ties for as long as it took their economy to adjust itself to a free market. Therefore, when Roxas testified in front of House members in 1932, he adopted a more cautious tone, pleading with House representatives that when the United States granted the Philippines independence, it should make sure that the close economic ties that had been forced upon his nation not be cut too quickly or too severely. Roxas even suggested that Congress might try to limit the amount of Philippine products coming in, or adopt a reduced tariff rate as it had done for Cuba, instead of automatically imposing a tariff duty that would all but ensure that Philippine products would be kept out of U.S. markets altogether.[79]

In December 1932, just as Congress was about to recess, and after a good deal of debate and deliberation, the House and Senate finally agreed to what they believed would be historic legislation—the Hare-Hawes-Cutting Act. This legislation provided for Philippine independence after a ten-year transition period, during which Filipino immigration to the United States would be limited to fifty persons a year, thereby fulfilling labor's demand that immigration be restricted, and duty-free sugar imports would be limited to 850,000 tons a year, thereby answering the domestic sugar industry's demand for relief from Philippine sugar. To prepare the Philippines for the day when all Philippine products would be forced to pay full duties, an export tax would be assessed for all products coming into the United States from the sixth through the tenth years, beginning at 5 percent and increasing 5 percent each year thereafter until the tenth year, when the rate would reach 25 percent. With full independence after the tenth year, the tariff rate would jump to 100 percent. And finally, to ensure that the United States would be able to maintain a military presence in the Far East, the act called for the establishment of military bases and for U.S. officials to maintain a great deal of control over the islands during the transitional independence period.[80]

What many had hoped would represent a historic moment of U.S. benevolence was instead perceived by large numbers as the ultimate act of selfishness. The day after Congress passed the Hare-Hawes-Cutting Act, the *Washington Post* carried an editorial from the *St. Louis Dispatch* heralding the act as "Fake Independence," charging that "instead of proceeding from a whole-hearted desire to give them liberty, it arises from a desire to restrict Philippine immigration and products, particularly sugar. The hand is the hand of Uncle Sam, but the voice is sugar."[81] Two days later the *Washington Post* carried another article, this one describing the independence act as an "Independence Joker."[82] Instead of signaling a new enlightened phase in America's supposed "benevolent" imperialism, independence marked the hard reality of protectionism in a global age.

Like the national press, President Hoover charged that the independence bill represented a violation of American history and principles. In his presidential veto, he repeated the argument that administration officials such as Secretary of State Stimson had been making for years. He insisted that the issue of Philippine independence involved a "responsibility to the Philippine people, responsibility to the American people and responsibility to the world at large."[83] Hoover charged that the current independence act not only abrogated the U.S. responsibility to ensure that the Philippines not fall into "economic and social chaos" but that it placed the United States at greater risk in a "world already sorely beset by instability."[84] In addition to highlighting the ensuing political, social, and economic chaos that Hoover feared would overtake the islands, and the danger this would pose to American officials in the Philippines as well as American foreign policy interests more generally, he also took time to castigate the farm interests that had helped propel Philippine independence forward. After highlighting the fact that the United States provided the main market for more than 80 percent of Philippine exports, Hoover proclaimed: "We are trustees for these people and we must not let our selfish interests dominate that trust."[85]

In spite of Hoover's strident and passionate veto, both the Senate and the House voted to override the veto by a margin of 66–26 and 274–94, respectively.[86] However, for the act to take effect, it also had to be approved by the Philippine legislature, a possibility that looked increasingly unlikely even before both houses passed the bill. Considering the Filipinos' loud and long-historic demand for independence dating back to 1898, it would have seemed that they would have jumped at any independence bill, as long as it meant that the United States would hand over sovereignty. However, 1932 was not 1898, and much had changed. Because of the free-trade policy the United States had instituted over the protests of many elite Filipino leaders in 1913, the Philippine economy had become increasingly dependent upon U.S. markets. In 1899 U.S. products accounted for only 10 percent of imports to the Philippines. By 1929, this figure had increased to more than 60 percent. The economic ties in the other direction proved even more dramatic. In 1899, the Philippines exported approximately 20 percent of its products to the United States. By 1929, that figure had grown to 75 percent, and by 1934 the rate would rise to 90 percent.[87] And of all the products the Philippines shipped to the United States, sugar was clearly the most important, counting for 63 percent of all exports by the early 1930s.[88] By the time Congress voted to grant independence, the question of independence involved more than political aspirations and nationalist ideology—it also revolved around the politics of an imperial economy, which had tied the economic well-being of the Philippines to the United States. This was an ironic twist, considering that imperialists at the turn of the century had predicted that the Philippines would become an "Oriental Trading Post" whereby the United States would gain a foothold in the Far East and a way station to the fabled Chinese market. Instead, as U.S. colonialism in the Philippines unfolded, the United States ended up creating a traditional colonial model, whereby the colony supplied raw materials to the colonizer.

The issues of trade and immigration figured prominently in the Philippine reaction to the Hare-Hawes-Cutting Act. On the one hand, Washington delegates Manuel Roxas and Sergio Osmena encouraged their fellow countrymen to accept the legislation as perhaps the best deal they could expect under the current circumstances. This represented a realistic understanding of the politics propelling independence within the United States. On the other hand, Manuel L. Quezon, Osmena's political rival and future president of the Philippines, insisted that the act did little but "to close American doors to Filipino labor and Philippine products."[89] He charged that the act represented "a triumph for Cuban and beet sugar interests and American labor" rather than a victory for the Filipino people who had long demanded independence.[90] Following Osmena's lead, five thousand Manila residents gathered to protest the act as an "unjust and insulting" effort to restrict immigration and sugar exports.[91]

When the Philippine legislature formally rejected the independence act in October 1933, it issued a formal resolution stating the reasons for rebuffing the United States' offer of gradual independence, specifically citing the limits on immigration and the trade provisions as well as concerns about the establishment of military and naval bases as the main reasons.[92] This response, however, did not mean that the Philippines had given up on achieving independence. Shortly after President Franklin D. Roosevelt's inauguration, Quezon traveled to the United States in the hopes of lobbying for a new independence act that might address some of the immigration, trade, and military issues that he and others had found so offensive. Quezon had also hoped that the incoming president, who had said very little about Philippine independence during the presidential campaign, might be amenable to a revised independence bill. Once in office, Roosevelt responded to Quezon's call for changes in the independence act with the warning, "if you insist upon better economic considerations, you may get your independence in twenty-four hours."[93] When Quezon met with Millard Tydings, the new chair of the Insular Affairs Committee, he had no better luck. In fact, Tydings cautioned Quezon that Congress had grown even more parochial and protectionist since the passage of the first independence bill, and that if Quezon and his countrymen were not careful, they might find themselves having to agree to an independence bill with even less-favorable economic terms. Tydings also warned Quezon that the latter's well-publicized statements that the Philippines would prefer immediate and complete independence to what Congress had offered was a gamble Quezon could not win. "You want to play draw poker, but I'm playing showdown."[94]

As Congress discussed whether to vote on a revised independence bill, it became obvious that the revisions would be minimal and that the interests that had pushed independence—mainly the sugar beet and labor factions—would see their lobbying efforts duly rewarded. The Tydings-McDuffie Act Congress passed in March 1934 differed little from its predecessor, except for the fact that it did not guarantee the United States military bases but rather delayed the decision until after full sovereignty returned to the islands. Otherwise, the act maintained the same limits on the number of Filipino immigrants, as well as the amount of duty-free Philippine sugar allowed to come into the United States. Rather than celebrate the momentous occasion, then, a *New York Times* editorial stated: "Even from the American point of view the Independence Bill has self interests written all over it. The obvious desire was not so much to set the Filipinos free as to prevent their sugar from coming into this country.... The most powerful interests behind the bill in Congress were the beet sugar industry ... together with the opposition on the Pacific Slope to all forms of immigration from the Orient. Thus the measure had its birth, not in a generous impulse of human liberty and love of self-government, but in that kind of perverted 'nationalism' which is now raging like a pestilence over the whole world."[95]

In spite of the obvious prejudices embodied in the Tyddings-McDuffie Act, this time the Philippine legislature accepted Congress' action, though certainly with a great deal of ambivalence if not outright trepidation. The *Philippine Free Press* called it "a pyrrhic victory," noting that "One more such victory and we are undone."[96] Quezon, who reluctantly supported acceptance of the act, and who was associated with this phase of independence more than any other Filipino politician, instructed the Philippine legislature to accept the act but not to do so until after the anniversary of the Battle of Manila Bay had passed, to make sure that it would not be seen as part of the long-fought nationalist struggle for sovereignty.[97] Based on President Roosevelt's pledge that any "injustices" could be worked out later, Quezon hoped that he would be able to negotiate better terms in the following years.[98]

The New Deal on the Ground

Just two months after Congress passed the Tyddings-McDuffie Act granting the Philippines gradual independence, it also passed the Jones-Costigan Act, which added sugar beet and sugar cane to the AAA as basic agricultural commodities. At first glance, these two historical developments might appear unrelated. By adding sugar beet to the list of basic agricultural commodities covered by the AAA, the Jones-Costigan Act was supposed to stabilize the domestic sugar market, provide bonuses to farmers who agreed to the government's production limits, set up a bureaucratic framework where farmers and industrialists could address and resolve their differences, and generally increase profits to both farmers and the industrialists. (Jones-Costigan even provided minimum wages and child labor provisions, two issues that will be discussed in the next chapter.) As such, the Jones-Costigan Act fits nicely with the AAA program that had already been created to deal with problems in the cotton, tobacco, and rice fields of the nation.[99]

A closer look at the Jones-Costigan Act, however, reveals the ways that the question of sugar production differed from most other agricultural crops. First, sugar was not a surplus crop domestically. That is, American producers were not even coming close to meeting domestic consumer demand, so limiting sugar production in the United States would not lead to better prices or do anything to end the agricultural depression. Second, because most of the sugar Americans consumed came from Cuba and the Philippines, Congress could not hope to provide relief to domestic producers without addressing imperial production. Therefore, when Congress passed the Jones-Costigan Act in 1934, it included production quotas for Cuba, Puerto Rico, Hawaii, and the Philippines as well as domestic producers, making this part of the New Deal international and domestic.[100]

Much of the impetus for addressing the problematic sugar market came from the U.S. Tariff Commission, which had been created by Congress in 1916 as an impartial body that would be able to take the tariff "out of politics" and ensure objective and intelligent means for establishing trade policies.[101] After studying the issue of sugar in 1933, the commission recommended that the United States would do well to adopt a system to control sugar production rather than to continue to rely on tariffs that had so far proven not only highly political but ineffective.[102] Newly inaugurated President Roosevelt heartily agreed with the commission's assessment. In fact, Roosevelt was especially concerned that the 1930 Smoot-Hawley Tariff had not only failed to stabilize the domestic sugar market but that it had led to economic and political chaos in Cuba. (After the passage of Smoot-Hawley, Cuban sugar exports to the United States fell from an average of 4.2 million short tons in 1929 to 1.8 million short tons in 1932.[103]) Therefore, in 1933, the Roosevelt administration authorized the USDA to host a number of sugar meetings, inviting representatives from both the beet and cane industries to try to figure out a way to address the perennial sugar problem.[104]

After much politicking and debate, Congressman Marvin Jones of Texas and Edward Costigan of Colorado proposed amending the 1933 Agricultural Administration Act to add sugar beet and sugar cane to the list of agricultural commodities the AAA had the power to regulate. Coming from sugar states, both men had a vested interest in protecting domestic sugar. However, both men also realized, as did many others, that the traditional solution of higher tariffs had failed to effectively stabilize the domestic sugar industry or deal successfully with the very important foreign relations surrounding sugar. In place of high tariffs, Jones and Costigan proposed to establish a quota system, whereby the USDA secretary would provide production quotas for mainland producers as well as Hawaii, Puerto Rico, the Philippines, the Virgin Islands, and Cuba. All other sugar would have to pay the full duty to gain entry to the U.S. market. The goal, then, was to divide the market and balance the interests of domestic and colonial producers, thereby keeping mainland sugar cane and sugar beet growers content without damaging the United States' supposed benevolent relations with its colonial interests. In addition to establishing production quotas, both men also proposed establishing a processing tax on sugar processors so that mainland sugar beet and sugar cane growers could be given a more equitable share of their industry's overall profits. In this way, Jones and Costigan hoped to address sugar politics at both the grassroots and global level.[105]

Although President Roosevelt supported the idea of adding sugar beet and sugar cane to the AAA, he was concerned with the potential international ramifications of Congress' actions. In particular, Roosevelt feared that if Congress restricted foreign sugar too severely as a way to appease sugar beet interests, it would further aggravate an already unstable situation in Cuba, which had fallen into social, economic, and political chaos since the 1930 tariff hike, and undermine U.S. relations with the Philippines, which was now on the road to independence. Speaking before Congress in 1934, Roosevelt insisted that any sugar bill needed to "increase returns to our own farmers, contribute to the economic rehabilitation of Cuba, provide adequate quotas for the Philippines, Hawaii, Puerto Rico and the Virgin Islands, and at the same time prevent higher prices to our own consumers." He also warned domestic sugar interests against trying to use the proposed sugar bill as a way to establish dominance over the U.S. market, insisting that the main goal should be to stop "the further expansion of this expensive industry."[106]

Sugar beet industry officials objected to Roosevelt's insistence that the interests of foreign nations should be taken into consideration or that sugar production in the United States should be limited in any way. They even charged Roosevelt with plotting to destroy the domestic sugar beet industry, for they wanted the sugar bill to act as a protectionist and nationalist measure. Reminding Congress that sugar was not a surplus crop and that farmers could expand sugar production without coming close to meeting domestic demand, sugar beet interests attempted to turn the debate into one of American sugar versus foreign sugar, and American farmers and laborers versus "coolie" labor abroad. For example, Charles M. Kearney, president of the National Beet Growers Association, testified before Congress using polemical language. "Our many thousands of beet farmers, together with their families ... must not be told that the right of remote tropical labor supersedes the rights of those who have pioneered and reclaimed the soil of the United States."[107] Playing on patriotic ideals, Kearney told Congress that when the United States imported foreign sugar, it upheld the "rights" of foreign labor at the expense of American farmers.[108]

In defending their industry, sugar beet interests could not deny that tropical sugar cane was cheaper to produce than domestic sugar beet. Instead they recounted, yet again, the innumerable benefits their industry brought to American farmers, small towns, and even the nation as a whole. Speaking on behalf of Michigan's growers and processors, C. R. Oviatt, a sugar company official, described the sugar beet industry as "most desirable" because it depended on both "agricultural and industrial employment" and by so doing brought together the best of the urban and rural worlds, thereby creating a true "community of interests."[109] Oviatt insisted that in a time of "staggering depression," this industry had "rescued" thousands of locals from joining welfare lists.[110] Oviatt also stressed how the recent introduction of the 50/50 contract had allowed this industry to make "a real partnership in fact as well as principle" out of previous enemies, the farmers, and the sugar companies.[111]

Costigan, who had helped author the 1934 sugar legislation, went to great lengths to convince recalcitrant sugar beet industrialists that the proposed bill before Congress was the best deal they could expect and that it offered the only tenable solution to a long-standing problem. In a March 6 radio address, he claimed that the sugar beet industry would be "best served" by a more "orderly and centralized" means of controlling both sugar production and sugar marketing. He continued with the argument that the nation's long-standing policy of raising the sugar tariff had not only wreaked havoc on Cuba, delivering that nation "into the agonies of starvation and revolution," but that it had done little for domestic sugar producers, who found Cuban sugar replaced by sugar coming in from Puerto Rico, Hawaii, and the Philippines. As such, Costigan heralded the pending bill as the most constructive means to "save and promote our domestic sugar industry in the history of the country," noting it is the Rooseveltian "new deal experimentally applied to sugar." Finally, Costigan promised that his bill would leave "sugar out of politics."[112]

Costigan's plea that sugar interests take the high ground at first fell on deaf ears. Michigan's sugar beet industrialists and allies did not want to see politics taken out of the sugar question. For more than three decades, they had been able to protect their expensive and uncompetitive industry by politicizing nearly every issue related to it—including labor and markets. In fact, many of Michigan's representatives hoped that the recent passage of the Tyddings-McDuffie Act would be just the first step in kicking all sugar, whether foreign or colonial, out of U.S. markets altogether.[113]

After a good deal of debate and deliberation, not to mention a fair amount of arm twisting, Michigan's sugar representatives reluctantly agreed to support the Jones-Costigan bill, including Senator Arthur Vandenburg and Congressman Roy Woodruff. The latter commented that "a gun has been put at our heads . . . we must accept."[114] It did not take long, however, for both men to realize that supporting the legislation represented a shrewd political and economic move. As the bill made its way through both houses of Congress, it not only provided for basically the same production quota already promised to the Philippines under the Tyddings-McDuffie Act, thereby simply reaffirming what had already been established, but it set domestic sugar beet quotas at levels that far exceeded past and present production.[115] Perhaps just as important, domestic sugar producers were promised 30 percent of any future increases in sugar production, thereby further ensuring them that *more* and not *less* sugar would be produced in the United States.[116] In contrast, the Cuban share of the market was cut dramatically, from an average of 53 percent in 1925–29 to about 30 percent with Jones-Costigan.[117]

Even though sugar beet industrialists and their allies in Congress would not completely give up on the possibility of making all "foreign" sugar subject to the highest tariff duties, the 1934 Jones-Costigan Act, and the 1937 Sugar Act that replaced it, represented a significant foreign-policy victory for the domestic U.S. sugar industry. In the words of one of the industry's critics, Jones-Costigan not only "nationalize[d] and regimentize[d]" the U.S. sugar market, it "divorced" that market from the world market, creating a "new order in the sugar industry."[118]

The Sugar Acts on the Ground

Though most of the public wrangling over the sugar acts revolved around just how much of the market would be granted to domestic, foreign, and colonial producers, both acts also included a number of provisions that had the potential to dramatically transform farmer/factory relations on the ground. To assure an "equitable division" of the profits of this industry, both sugar acts called for the USDA secretary to establish "fair and reasonable" prices for the sugar beet crop after thorough investigations and public hearings.[119] Furthermore, the Jones-Costigan Act called for growers who believed that the processors had not offered them a fair price to file a statement of protest with the secretary of agriculture, who would then investigate the complaint and offer a settlement.[120] Industrialists who refused to cooperate with the USDA were threatened with having their "allotments" adjusted or revoked.[121] In contrast to the rhetoric underpinning the 50/50 contracts and the F&M, which claimed that the industrialists and the farmers were simply "different players on the same team," the sugar acts were premised on the idea that the two sides in this industry, the farmers and the companies, might not always agree, and that in fact their interests might diverge. In this way, the sugar beet legislation threatened the cooperative vision the industry had just attempted to create over the previous decade.

Taking into account the strong language of both acts, as well as the fact that the last time the federal government intervened in farmer/factory conflicts during World War I the companies had found themselves having to meet the growers' demands, many sugar beet industrialists viewed the acts with a great deal of trepidation. Industrialist Fred Crawford went so far as to predict that the "sugar business must decline under this new law."[122] Industrialists not only feared that government intervention would translate into greater profits for the farmers, and less for them, but that it would embolden farmers, who would look to the federal government as an ally in their disputes with the sugar companies.

Just as many industrialists feared federal intervention, many farmers welcomed it as providing an opportunity to challenge the sugar companies.[123] In 1935 growers for the Caro, Sebewaing, and Blissfield factory districts broke away from the company-controlled F&M to establish their own separate and independent organizations.[124] Caro farmers explained that the F&M "had been thrust upon us" and that it was now "time for them [the sugar companies] to know that the farmers of Michigan have come to the conclusion that they can run their own businesses." In fact, when F&M officers tried to attend one of the Caro farmers' meetings, the farmers told them to leave, shouting that "no white-collared fellows" were welcome. Farmers even charged that the companies were "blood suckers" and "parasites" who had "been in the farmers' pockets long enough."[125] Sensing that the time was ripe to start organizing the rest of the state's sugar beet farmers, the Farmers' Union began hosting statewide meetings, inviting disgruntled farmers—those who had been the "goat" of the companies "long enough"—to demand a contract that would cover the costs of production and provide an assured profit.[126]

The companies responded to what looked like growing farmer militancy with a multipromotional relations campaign to undermine the farmers' class identity and to convince them that instead of looking to each other or to Washington to solve their problems, they should cooperate with the industrialists. To stop the farmers from challenging them or identifying with the state, industrialists did their best to disparage the sugar acts while also assuring farmers that only they, the sugar industrialists, would continue to represent the farmers' best interest in the battle against foreign sugar. This represented a somewhat odd response, considering that the sugar legislation afforded the sugar beet industrialists greater quotas than they could possibly fulfill. However, this strategy helped to foster an "us" versus "them" mentality in which the "us" meant both farmers and industrialists and the "them" included all those "trying to tear down the domestic industry." To make sure that they would have the ear of all sugar beet growers, in October 1935 the F&M began publishing a free journal, entitled the *Sugar Beet Journal,* to be distributed to all sugar beet growers in the state. This journal, which claimed to represent the promotional arm of both farmers and industrialists, simply touted the industrialists' interests and encouraged the farmers to see those interests as their own. In the very first issue, the editor opened with a plea to farmers and industrialists to work "harmoniously" with each other to solve their "mutual problems" and to "combat any force or factor which might operate to the detriment of their industry."[127] After recounting the contentious past, Frank Oberst, the vice president of the F&M, encouraged farmers to recognize their "reciprocal dependence" warning that a "house divided against itself" was surely doomed to fail.[128]

Though past history would certainly lead one to believe that the time had come for yet another farmer/factory showdown, this time around farmers found it difficult to battle their industrial adversaries. The militant rhetoric of some farmers masked the fact that the majority had come to depend on the sugar beet crop and were either unwilling or unable to stop growing it. Instead of mutating into action, militant rhetoric remained just that, rhetoric. Equally important, and somewhat ironically, the sugar legislation that industrialists had vilified and feared ended up handing them unheralded power as they learned how to use the legislation to their advantage.[129] Although technically the AAA programs were under the tutelage of the USDA secretary, decentralization characterized the practice of the legislation as sugar beet industrialists assumed important posts in the agency that actually ran the program.[130] On a day-to-day basis, this meant little "governmental interference" and local control. And in this case local control meant factory control. After the AAA determined the amount of sugar that each of Michigan's sugar companies could process, it was up to the factories to contract with farmers to grow sugar beet, which in effect handed them the power to decide which farmers would receive the government's $1.13–$1.90 per ton bonus. Companies used this power to continually remind farmers that the right to participate in the sugar program would be based on "past production" and that if they decided not to grow beets one year, or to grow fewer acres than usual, they would risk losing their acreage allotments and their government benefits to new growers.[131]

In a less obvious way, the government bonuses, which raised the price farmers took home, also helped the sugar companies convince farmers to grow larger acreages of sugar beet. As a result of the sugar program, farmers who grew sugar beet did see their take-home pay increase.[132] The small-town newspapers publicized the benefits these acts brought to local communities and farmers, regularly reporting on the amount of the benefit checks farmers would receive. The *Pigeon Progress* highlighted how "Beet Contracts Guarantee Parity," a long-term goal for many farmers and farm organizations.[133] The same newspaper announced that "Michigan's Growers Get Millions From AAA."[134] Though less well publicized locally, the sugar legislation also ensured industrialists greater profits, as sugar beet companies, which had losses in 1932 and 1933, saw their profits rise dramatically between 1934 and 1939.[135]

Perhaps most important of all, the sugar legislation did basically nothing to empower the growers to challenge the industrialists, even though the language of both acts would lead one to think otherwise.[136] When growers turned to the USDA secretary to help them garner higher prices, as the 1934 Jones-Costigan Act told them they had a right to do, the USDA turned out to be a reluctant mediator, much less an advocate, for assuring that growers and processors would share equally in the benefits of this industry.[137] Growers from the Blissfield sugar plant who traveled to Washington, D.C., in 1935 for help were told that "Washington could act as a third party in our dispute with Great Lakes, but that they had no power to enforce, under the present law, any decision that might come out of a formal hearing."[138] During the yearly USDA sugar hearings to establish a "fair and equitable" price for sugar beets, the USDA proved equally unresponsive. USDA representatives refused to address the farmers' complaints that the price of seed was too high, that the sugar companies unfairly tested tare and sugar content, that the companies had used the 50/50 contracts to their advantage, and that the companies disciplined militant farmers by sending their sugar to outlying markets, even though both a former sugar executive and the USDA's own investigator publicly stated that the allegations were true. Instead, the USDA simply adopted the industries' contract offer over the growers' protests.[139]

Rather than create a level playing field, or work to the growers' advantage, the sugar acts ended up giving the sugar companies the kind of power they had always sought. In direct contrast to the World War I era, in which federal intervention had empowered the farmers, this time around federal intervention worked to the industrialists' advantage. Not only did the USDA refuse to negotiate farmer/factory conflicts, but by making government bonuses contingent on past production, the New Deal undermined what had always been the farmers' greatest bargaining chip—their willingness to abandon the crop. In the late 1930s, as fewer farmers grew ever-greater acreage, they proved less willing to risk the chance of losing their lucrative sugar beet contracts by challenging the sugar companies. Ironically, the 50/50 contract and continual federal oversight, two demands that farmers had made during World War I as a way to democratize the industry, ended up handing the sugar companies more power.

Conclusion

As the decade of the 1920s waned, the domestic sugar beet industry looked like it was on the verge of collapse. Plummeting prices and growing imports from the Philippines threatened to undermine what had once been a lucrative industry. Taking advantage of the context, the sugar beet industrialists turned their misfortune into opportunity, using the farm depression as a pretext to ask Congress to revisit a question it had seemingly answered nearly three decades before: Would the United States allow colonial products to compete with domestic products? Not without a great deal of politicking, the sugar beet industry got an answer more to its liking. In addition to raising the Cuban sugar tariff in 1930, two years later Congress passed an act granting the Philippines gradual independence, with the expectation that at the end of the ten-year period, Philippine sugar would no longer find a free market in the United States. Though it would take two more years, and another congressional act, before the Philippines would begin its ten-year transition to independence, it appeared that the sugar beet industry had finally succeeded in its decade-long quest to claim the domestic market as its own.

Cutting the economic ties between the United States and the Philippines, however, would not turn out as easy as the Tyddings-McDuffie Act had implied. Just as the ink was drying on that act, Congress passed the Jones-Costigan Act, which was premised on the idea of dividing the U.S. sugar market between domestic producers and colonial interests as a way to balance both domestic and foreign policy concerns. Though domestic sugar interests protested the inclusion of "foreign" and "colonial" sugar as unfair and unjust, the legislation guaranteed them a greater share of the domestic market and encouraged the growing of ever-greater amounts of domestic sugar in the following years. Unlike other New Deal agricultural programs, which sought to limit domestic production, the sugar acts ensured that domestic growers would plant even more sugar beet in the future.

In addition to addressing foreign policy, the New Deal sugar acts seemed to fulfill what farmers had been demanding for decades—a more equitable division of profits. For the USDA secretary pledged to act as a broker in possible disputes, threatening to revoke the sugar quotas for those companies that refused to cooperate. In practice, however, the USDA did little to transform farmer/factory relations. Though the price farmers earned for growing sugar beet certainly increased, neither the Jones-Costigan Act, nor the 1937 Sugar Act, provided farmers with much leverage with which to challenge the dominance of the sugar companies. The yearly hearings to establish fair and equitable prices turned into pro forma meetings in which the USDA simply adopted the industry's recommendations. When farmers did turn to the USDA secretary to represent their interests, he proved an unwilling and unhelpful ally. Rather than remake the sugar beet industry, both sugar acts reinforced the power of the corporations, while making it more difficult for the farmers to exert autonomous control.

9

The Politics of Migrant Labor

As the Great Depression spread across the Midwest in early October 1930, Detroit resident W. H. Davis took pen in hand to write a letter to Henry Hull, the Commissioner General of Immigration. In the letter, Davis complained about Mexicans as the root cause of unemployment in "his" city. Davis even went so far as to describe Mexican immigration as "alien bootlegging" and suggested that to solve this problem, the government should begin to issue "citizenship cards" and that "possession of such cards would show a person entitled to employment when they apply for work."[1]

Davis's letter hints at the numerous ways the Great Depression transformed the question of Mexican immigration and the status of Mexicans and Mexican Americans in the Midwest. In contrast to the 1920s, when the debate over Mexican immigration in the Midwest was confined largely to the halls of Congress, in the 1930s the discussion moved to private homes, small-town streets, and city halls, making the issue of Mexican immigration as much a matter of local scrutiny and debate as a concern of national and international policy. Equally important, in contrast to the 1920 debates, which had centered on whether to include Mexicans in the national origins quotas, the current "crisis" involved local and municipal authorities, working hand-in-hand or with the approval of federal immigration personnel, to organize a "voluntary repatriation" back to Mexico. Although the repatriation of thousands of Mexicans and Mexican Americans from Michigan in 1931 and 1932 would do nothing to end that state's economic woes, it did blur the line between legal and illegal immigration, turning all persons of Mexican descent into noncitizens and nonresidents who took jobs and relief from "real" citizens and "real" residents. In this way, the repatriation campaign worked to exclude Mexican immigrants and Mexican Americans from the larger American political body and the local communities in which they lived and worked.

If the repatriation campaign marked the exclusion of Mexicans and Mexican Americans, the coming of the New Deal held out some promise of inclusion. The Jones-Costigan Act of 1934 and the Sugar Beet Act of 1937 made it possible that all sugar beet workers, regardless of race or citizenship, might be recognized as workers by the state. These acts not only empowered the secretary of agriculture to intervene in disputes between growers and workers, they also required growers to abide by child labor prohibitions and minimum wage provisions. Unlike all other agricultural workers, whose only inclusion in the New Deal was as wards of the state, the laborers toiling in the sugar beet fields were recognized as workers with some rights. Rather than simply rely on the state to define and protect their interests through the sugar acts, however, many sugar beet workers also looked to other parts of the New Deal labor policy—especially the right of workers to organize and bargain collectively—to define their rights. Whether or not Michigan's sugar beet workers realized they were excluded from these parts of the New Deal matters less than the fact that by joining unions and participating in strikes, they tried to make them apply in practice.[2] As such, the New Deal had the potential to remake the ever-shifting capital, land, and labor boundaries defining rural America—offering some chance of social and economic citizenship for those who thinned, blocked, pulled, and topped sugar beet.

Depression and Repatriation

Throughout the Midwest millions of people experienced the full force of the Great Depression. By 1931 unemployment in Chicago and Detroit reached a staggering 40 and 50 percent, respectively.[3] Loss of jobs was often followed by evictions and foreclosures as residents failed to earn enough to make their mortgages or pay their rents. The closing of banks and the downfall of insurance companies and mutual aid societies dealt yet another blow to residents already hard hit by economic deprivation. Even the churches and municipal welfare offices that had traditionally helped the poor found that they could not keep up with the requests of those in need.[4]

As months of depression turned into years, a number of self-proclaimed white "citizens" tried to explain the economic disaster around them by pointing to the thousands of Mexicans and Mexican Americans who had settled in the Midwest, as well as those who migrated between southwestern homesteads and midwestern seasonal jobs. Linking race and citizenship with the right to work and the right to relief, many of these "citizens" charged either that Mexicans were taking the jobs that rightfully belonged to white Americans or that Mexicans were taking relief that should only be doled out to deserving "citizens." Some made both arguments at once. When Chicago resident John Hammerstein wrote to President Hoover, he admitted that "I suppose you don't know the hardships that are being caused in Chicago by the coming of vast hordes of cheap Mexican laborers to this city." While complaining that many "poor" and "sick" Mexicans took up beds at the Cook County Hospital, Hammerstein also told Hoover that thousands of "hard working men" were losing their jobs to Mexicans who willingly worked for lower wages. To solve this problem, Hammerstein pleaded with Hoover to "request Congress to pass a law [to] restrict their coming into the country."[5] When Michigan resident Arthur A. Caulkett wrote to Hoover, he simply asked: "May I inquire as an American Citizen, who is responsible for the deplorable and flagrant violation of our Immigration Laws? In regard to the Mexican Peon." He then suggested that the majority of Mexicans in his state were "to[o] illiterate to be eligible for citizenship" and that "if their [there] was two million less Mexicans in our country, there might be two million more American men have[ing] jobs."[6] And finally, Albert Bauaski, an unemployed steel worker from Gary, Indiana, wrote to Commissioner Hull to complain about the large number of Mexicans working in the Calumet region around Lake Michigan. Calling for Hull to rid the country of "noncitizen outlaw Mexicans" Bauaski charged that "because they will work cheaper than an American will, that's the reason there is so many out of work. The American has to walk the streets and a Mexican is working that's not justice toward the American citizen."[7]

Although the rants of men like Hammerstein, Caulkett, and Bauaski might at first appear to be isolated cases of disgruntled malcontents looking for someone to blame for their nation's collective misfortune, they in fact mirrored national thinking at the highest levels of government. In 1930 President Hoover publicly charged that Mexicans took jobs away from American citizens and promised that he would try to figure out a way to deport as many as possible as one way to address the economic depression.[8] Following through on Hoover's pledge, in October 1930 newly appointed USDL Secretary William Doak publicly announced that his department would work with local officials nationwide to expel the "four hundred thousands illegal aliens" whom he charged were taking jobs from their rightful owners—American citizens.[9]

Encouraged by Doak's announcement, dozens of municipal authorities throughout the United States began a massive repatriation of thousands of Mexicans and Mexican Americans to Mexico.[10] For example, in September 1931, Saginaw city welfare officials and police joined hands with Detroit's federal immigration commissioner, John L. Zubrick, "to drive from the city aliens who entered the country illegally." That the actual deportation of three hundred Mexicans included only fifty who had entered the country illegally mattered little to local residents who celebrated the departure. The *Saginaw Daily News* endorsed the action, noting how a good number of the repatriates had been on the city's poor list, while others had taken jobs that "rightfully belong" to legal immigrants and U.S. citizens. Zubrick himself commended the repatriation, describing how Mexicans "have little to contribute to a community and frequently take much from it."[11]

A year later, in 1932, Michigan's state and municipal governments discussed ways to expand the previous year's deportation campaign into a "voluntary repatriation" effort covering not just the state's larger cities like Detroit, Flint, Grand Rapids, and Saginaw but also the state's smaller cities and towns, including Port Huron, Mt. Pleasant, and Blissfield.[12] When the Saginaw City Council met in October 1932 to discuss whether to pay for the "voluntary exodus" of one hundred poverty-stricken Mexican families, Arthur J. Webster, a representative of the State Welfare Department, pleaded with the city council to "act quickly" before the "problem worsened." The city attorney similarly recommended the repatriation of Mexicans and Mexican Americans who might become public charges or those who had already become "indigent" as a way to save tax funds over the long run. The only cautious voice in the crowd came from Saginaw's mayor, George Phoenix, who pointed out that of the hundred families to be returned to Mexico, only seven actually received aid from the city and that the total cost added up to only $384.30.[13] Nonetheless, Mayor Phoenix pledged to support repatriation as long as surrounding communities did the same, pleading "If they make a general cleanup around us I'd be in favor of it. They say they are going to, and I'm with them if the rest do it, but not Saginaw alone."[14]

In their quest to expel Mexicans and Mexican Americans from their communities, men like Zubrick, Webster, and Phoenix found what might at first seem a rather unlikely ally in Detroit Mexican Consul Ingacio L. Batiza. In fact, Batiza took a leading role in encouraging Michigan's municipal authorities and the governor to provide funds to send destitute Mexicans back to their homeland. Like other consulate officials, Batiza was concerned about the deteriorating economic plight of the Mexican nationals he had been appointed to oversee and hoped that voluntary repatriation would offer a way to lure them to return home, where they could take part in building their nation.[15] In a handbill he distributed throughout Michigan, Batiza called for "all the Mexican residents in the region, without distinction as to their beliefs" to "take advantage of the opportunity" to return to Mexico. He warned that there was little "hope of amelioration in the near future" and that for "their own interest" Mexicans should return to Mexico as soon as possible.[16]

Working alongside Batiza, Mexican artist Diego Rivera also played an important role in the Detroit repatriation campaign. At the behest of the Detroit Institute of Arts, Rivera had come to Detroit in 1932 to paint what would become his world-famous "Man and Machine" mural. While in Detroit, Rivera grew increasingly concerned about the economic plight of his compatriots who had lost the kinds of industrial jobs he himself was depicting in his soon to be revealed mural. As a leftist, Rivera called for Mexicans to return to Mexico, where he hoped that they would form workers' cooperatives rather than stay in the United States, where he feared they would languish in the "evils of capitalism."[17]

In contrast to Rivera, who supported voluntary repatriation as part of a larger critique of capitalist inequalities, Michigan newspapers publicized and celebrated the repatriation campaign as the final chapter in a failed experiment of assimilation and upward mobility. On November 13, 1932, just days before a trainload of "voluntary repatriates" was scheduled to leave from Detroit, the *Detroit Free Press* carried a story by journalist Clarence E. McConnell, who recounted how Mexicans, "rural people of simple wants," had come into Michigan by the thousands during the past ten years. Erasing from the historical memory the World War I recruitment of Mexican immigrants, McConnell wrote how Mexicans first "swarmed" into Michigan in 1922 at the behest of the sugar companies, thereby creating "one of the most significant racial movements in history." McConnell claimed that respected sociologists had viewed this movement with "extreme apprehension," owing to their knowledge that Mexicans were an "unassimilable group." McConnell then highlighted how many Mexicans abandoned the fields for higher-paying jobs in urban factories—that is, until the onset of the Great Depression devastated both agriculture and industry. "The happiness of the homeland, where life among the peasants is usually a continuous song and unemployment does not mean unhappiness, was in sharp contrast to the misery of attempting to live through a northern winter on scant rations and very little fuel." To those who might bemoan this exodus, McConnell consoled his northern audience that the thousands of Mexicans returning home would be "laden with some of the new-found Northern comforts," including radio sets, electronic washers, and sewing machines.[18] In other words, northern readers could be reassured that "one of the most significant racial movements in history" did not end in racial conflict but rather in a consumer cornucopia.

When other newspapers reported the actual departures, they repeated the themes that McConnell had highlighted. After 430 Mexicans and Mexican Americans left from the sugar beet towns of Mt. Pleasant, Bad Axe, Sebewaing, and Saginaw in late November, the *Saginaw Daily News* wistfully reported that the "hardy souls who have gone far away in search of the pot of gold at the end of the rainbow" were now returning to Mexico after realizing that "perhaps, after all, the promised land was right at home." Though admitting that the United States had brought "suffering" and "privation and hunger," the newspaper reassured its readership that in the "sunny southland," Mexicans would return to a kind of "peace and comfort that escaped most of them here."[19] In an accompanying story, the newspaper even managed to turn the event into a blissful affair, recounting how the train ride to Mexico would be a "honeymoon" for beet workers Donaquin Martinez, nineteen, and Jane Negrette, fifteen, who had "delayed their special train by nine minutes in Mt. Pleasant by going to the Isabella County court house to get married."[20]

Though Michigan's newspapers memorialized the repatriation as a joyous event that ended a sorrowful sojourn, the Mexicans and Mexican Americans who left the Midwest for Mexico seem to have been a great deal more ambivalent. The Depression years had taken a toll on the Mexican American community, economically and socially. Despite charges that Mexicans were hired over "citizens," Mexicans and Mexican Americans were often the first to be fired.[21] Equally important, the migrant workers' strategy of combining agricultural labor in the sugar beet fields with industrial employment in urban centers became increasingly difficult as many of the sugar beet companies closed their doors in the late 1920s and early 1930s. As such, when Batista and Rivera advertised the repatriation program, painting a rosy picture of what Mexicans and Mexican Americans could expect to find in their "homeland," approximately five thousand signed a petition asking to go south.[22]

Whether they did so out of an optimism of what Mexico had to offer or a grim knowledge of what awaited them in Depression-era Michigan is not entirely clear. What we do know is that of the original five thousand Detroit residents who signed up to return to Mexico, only about eighteen hundred actually left. Moreover, from the very start, the entire voluntary repatriation effort was mired by allegations of bad conditions on the trip heading south and even worse conditions to be found across the border. After the first train left Detroit in November 1932, those on board the train complained that they did not have enough food and that they had been forced to sleep all night without heat or light.[23] During the cross-country journey, some also began to question whether they wanted to leave the United States. For example, after a trainload of repatriates from Michigan arrived in San Antonio in November 1932, at least a dozen of the families asked permission to leave the train, claiming that they had "changed their minds" about returning to Mexico. Railroad officials refused to allow the families to leave the trains, insisting that they did not have the authority to grant the request. Two young men who decided to defy the railroad officials by jumping through a window as the train was leaving Laredo were later captured and forced to return to Mexico.[24]

Considering the sugar beet industry's historic role as the most important employer of Mexicans and Mexican Americans, one might expect that company officials would have had plenty to say about deporting and repatriating their field labor force. The historical record, however, reveals a conspicuous silence. In contrast to the 1920s, when industry officials objected loudly and publicly to any proposal to limit Mexican immigration, this time around industry officials said very little. One of the only public comments came from sugar company executive Fred Crawford, who, rather than protesting repatriation, hailed it, telling his local Kiwanis Club how "approximately 30,000 of Michigan's unemployed men were given jobs at better than average wages in the sugar beet industry of the state this season and not a single Negro or Mexican was imported for work this year."[25] Crawford's words may have played well in front of his anxious audience; however, they probably did not reflect the true feelings of the vast majority of sugar beet industrialists or growers. Most industrialists and growers were biding their time, hoping that once the economy improved, the national spotlight would shift elsewhere and that their labor practices would no longer be a matter of public discussion.

The New Deal in the Sugar Beet Fields

Any hope that sugar beet industrialists and growers may have had that the repatriation campaign would end the public's concern with their labor practices was dashed less than a year later during national hearings to consider whether sugar beet should be added to the AAA. At the hearings, representatives of both the National Child Labor Committee and the Children's Bureau showed up to describe the historically poor working and living conditions that migrant workers faced and to highlight how these conditions had only worsened in the early 1930s, with wages falling by approximately 50 percent.[26] Trying to achieve what had so far eluded them, both groups insisted that any legislation to help sugar beet farmers and industrialists should also provide "decent" wages, improved working conditions, and child labor laws for beet workers.[27] Clearly the arrival of the New Deal provided these groups with the opportunity to push for legislative victories that their earlier campaigns had failed to achieve.[28]

After the first round of hearings revealed the hardships migrant beet workers regularly endured, President Franklin Roosevelt, who was not shy about expressing his frustration with this highly political industry, took a personal interest. He ordered his secretary of labor, Frances Perkins, to appoint a committee to work with industrialists, growers, and the public to devise a plan to transform labor practices in the beet fields.[29] Following Roosevelt's directive, Perkins described sugar beet migrant labor as a "social problem" that could no longer be ignored and appointed National Child Labor Committee leader Courtney Dinwiddie to head what became known as the Dinwiddie Committee. Recognizing the significance of this development, the *New York Times* heralded the formation of the Dinwiddie Committee as the first "move" to include "field as well as factory work in the recovery program."[30]

The Dinwiddie Committee strongly condemned the current conditions in the fields, highlighting the fact that children worked under great pressure, that migrant families often lived in tents and shacks, and that families currently earning $12 to $13 an acre probably needed $24.50 an acre to earn a "living wage."[31] To ensure that those who toiled in the sugar beet fields would see their labor more fairly rewarded, the committee called for farmers to pay workers at least $20 an acre and to stop allowing children under the age of sixteen to work in their fields. The committee also urged Congress to make the growers' bonus payments contingent on meeting these labor standards, arguing that those who benefited from higher prices should share the proceeds with their laborers.[32] These recommendations not only called for a significant wage increase but involved transforming family labor and granting unprecedented authority to the USDA to regulate labor, in labor's interest.

Sugar beet industrialists and their allies responded with indignation to the Dinwiddie Committee's recommendations and Roosevelt's insistence that labor be included in the sugar program.[33] During discussions over the child labor provisions in the Jones-Costigan bill, Michigan Senator Arthur Vandenberg even lobbied his fellow congressmen to drop the minimum wage provisions and greatly water down the child labor prohibitions, arguing that "labor laws" would hurt Michigan's farmers, and not help them as AAA programs were intended to do. In other words, Vandenberg saw the AAA as a farmer program and resented the fact that migrant workers' interests would even be mentioned, much less addressed. Fellow Senator Robert Wagner challenged Vandenberg by arguing that minimum wages and child labor limits were necessary for protecting migrant workers and that farmers could certainly afford to pay labor more considering they were to receive generous benefits through the AAA.[34]

After much deliberation and debate in both houses of Congress, sugar was added to the AAA with the labor provisions intact. The 1934 Jones-Costigan Act prohibited child labor under the age of fourteen and limited the working hours of children aged fourteen to sixteen. The act granted the USDA secretary the authority to fix minimum wages, but only when disputes arose, and only after holding public hearings "at a place accessible to producers and workers." The act also called for farmers to pay their workers "promptly" and "in full" before collecting their benefit payments as a way to deal with the historic inequalities embedded in staggered payments and hold-back clauses. Finally, the act granted the USDA secretary the authority to adjudicate any labor disputes should they arise.[35]

The Sugar Act of 1937, which replaced the Jones-Costigan Act after the Supreme Court ruled the AAA unconstitutional, continued the labor sections of its predecessor, in spite of attempts by congressmen to strike them.[36] In fact, when Congress met to hammer out the specifics of this new bill, Roosevelt reminded the sugar beet companies and the farmers that if they expected continued protection through quotas and benefit payments, they had better abide by the minimum wages and child labor stipulations that had been a part of Jones-Costigan. In Roosevelt's words, "an industry which desires the protection afforded by a quota system, or a tariff, should be expected to guarantee that it will be a good employer."[37] Congress followed Roosevelt's advice by not only continuing the labor provisions but actually strengthening them. The 1937 Sugar Act once again prohibited child labor and made the "fair, reasonable and equitable" minimum wage determinations mandatory. That is, instead of just granting the USDA secretary the authority to set minimum wages when disputes arose, the new law mandated that the secretary establish minimum wages in all sugar producing regions before the season began.

The significance of both the 1934 and 1937 sugar acts should not be understated. By insisting that the laborers' interests be considered when redistributing income, and by making the farmers' payments conditional upon minimum wage and age regulations, Congress had granted sugar beet workers a status not given to other agricultural workers. The only inclusion for the majority of agricultural workers in the New Deal came through the Resettlement Administration and the Farm Security Administration, which treated them more as wards of the state than as workers with rights.[38] Moreover, by recognizing that the interests of the processors, farmers, and laborers might not overlap—that in fact these interests often collided—the sugar legislation challenged the myth that rural agricultural labor relations were different than urban industrial labor relations. The 1934 and 1937 acts held out the promise of both recognizing and remaking rural class relations.

Whether or not that promise would come true hinged on the question of how the state would determine "fair and reasonable," much less "equitable," wages. In trying to devise a strategy for addressing this issue, William T. Ham, chief of the Tenure and Labor Relations Section, and Joshua Bernhardt, chief of the Sugar Section, spelled out a number of options for establishing the wage rate. In a memo to President Roosevelt, they acknowledged his personal "desire" to improve the wages and working conditions of laborers in the sugar beet industry as well as his hope to "afford full protection to the right of laborers to an equitable share of the total income of the industry." Ham and Bernhardt even wrote that considering Roosevelt's objectives, it might be possible that in determining fair, reasonable, and equitable wages they could simply grant a disproportionate share of the farmers' bonuses to the workers, who were currently surviving on barely subsistence wages, as long as the former could be assured of a yearly 6 percent return on the sugar beet crop.[39]

After spelling out this proposal, Ham and Bernhardt suggested that it would be better to come up with a formula that would take into account the growers' income as the basis for the workers' minimum pay, with the understanding that this would provide "equitable" wages.[40] Though this plan appeared to achieve the legislation's mandate for an "equitable" division of profits, whether these wage rates were actually "fair and reasonable" was clearly another issue. The problem with this solution was that "equitable" did not necessarily mean the same as "fair and reasonable," especially considering this industry's historic policy of paying low wages to migrant families. Even Ham and Bernhardt readily admitted that, "whether or not these wage rates are 'fair and reasonable' depends to some extent upon their profitableness of sugar beet production for growers."[41] Rather than determine a minimum wage based on the idea that workers deserved a living wage, or more than a mere subsistence existence, Ham and Bernhardt ended up institutionalizing the historic low earnings of the workers while giving the appearance that they had somehow radically remade grower-labor relations. This principle for determining wage rates also ignored the fact that workers' yearly earnings depended on a number of factors, including the number of acres workers were assigned, and not just the dollar value listed in the labor contract.

Even though Ham and Bernhardt had devised a general principle for establishing minimum wages, the 1937 law still stipulated that wages could be set only after the USDA held hearings in which all interested parties were allowed to participate. In theory, then, the growers, the sugar companies, and the laborers would be given an opportunity to present their own arguments and evidence for determining "fair and reasonable," not to mention "equitable," wages.

From the very beginning there were numerous signs that the minimum wage hearings would not create a level playing field for all sides. Part of the problem was timing, as hearings were usually held in January and February, months before most out-of-state migrants traveled to the Midwest. Equally important, the USDA held only a couple of hearings each year, in places like Detroit, Toledo, and Saginaw, which made it difficult for resident beet workers to attend. Not surprisingly, though growers were usually well represented, with the sugar companies and growers' associations publicizing the hearings to make sure that a large number of their representatives attended, workers often did not even know about the public forums until long after the fact. Michigan sugar beet grower Florence Brooks admitted that few workers testified at the hearings, noting that this absence "is probably due to lack of knowledge and information on the part of the worker, a lack the grower is not at all anxious to have filled."[42]

During the hearings, growers resisted almost all attempts to raise the workers' wages, insisting that because workers only toiled for about sixty days, it was unfair to expect growers to pay a living wage for the entire six-month growing season.[43] Growers also hampered the USDA's efforts to figure out how much they earned each year—a crucial part of the wage-making decision because the workers' minimum wage was supposed to be based on the growers' earnings. For example, after labor representatives at the 1937 wage rate hearings in Toledo, Ohio, complained that the growers were trying to get them to work for $15 and $16 an acre, USDA officials repeatedly asked the growers to provide evidence of their own profits or lack thereof. The growers, however, refused to cooperate. According to Stanley White, a state official who attended the hearing, the growers "evaded the efforts . . .

to learn what proportion of the benefit payments ought to be earmarked for the workers" and refused to explain how they had come up with wage rates. White suspected that growers had set the wage rate "just at the point where labor would be attracted."[44]

Laborers and their representatives who managed to make it to the wage hearings clearly encountered a well-organized and militant contingent of growers and industrialists more than willing and able to challenge them on every count.[45] When Samuel Issard, an AFL representative of the Agricultural Workers Union, asked at the 1937 Toledo hearings for workers to be granted a flat rate of $21.50 an acre, and that the USDA eliminate the sliding scale "bonuses," he found his requests ignored.[46] The following year, when unionists Issard and Albert Markva demanded $24 an acre, Fred Bodesiler of the Blissfield Beet Growers Association charged the labor witnesses with using the hearings for "labor agitating."[47] When labor witnesses requested an increase of $1.50 an acre in 1939, "growers asked for reductions averaging the same amount."[48]

When making his final minimum wage determinations, Agricultural Secretary Henry A. Wallace proved far more receptive to the growers and the companies than the workers. In 1937, Wallace raised workers' wages by 15 percent, based on the "anticipated average federal payment to growers" of $1.91 per ton.[49] What this meant was that most workers would average $17 to $18 an acre.[50] In 1938 Wallace set the minimum wage rate at $18 an acre, with $11 for spring work, a guaranteed $7 per acre for harvesting, and a bonus of $1 for every ton more than seven.[51] By the time it came time to determine a minimum wage for the 1939 season, the USDA Sugar Division announced that "it would deem the 1938 wage rates satisfactory for 1939 unless evidence to the contrary was submitted justifying changes."[52] After laborers protested that this wage scale was unfair, state sugar officials warned that they might have to decrease workers' minimum wages if the farm profits dropped. To add insult to injury, the USDA then invalidated the minimum guarantees for topping, "at the request of the growers," and adopted a sliding scale instead.[53] The following year, USDA officials yet again refused to increase the minimum wage rate in spite of the fact that laborers at both the St. Paul and Detroit hearings "expressed a general dissatisfaction with existing wages." In justifying this decision, government officials pointed to "the uncertainties affecting possible returns to growers for the 1940 crop."[54]

The effect of the nation's first experiment with setting a minimum wage for agricultural workers can best be described as unsuccessful. In contrast to the "living wage" rate of $24.50 that the Dinwiddie Committee had recommended, the USDA never established wage rates of more than $19 an acre. Perhaps most significant of all, legally set minimum wages became de facto maximum wages for most sugar beet workers.[55] The USDA's minimum wage determinations also demonstrated that it was not possible to establish "fair and reasonable" wages merely by setting a minimum wage amount. How much workers earned each year depended on a number of factors, including the overall acreage, the labor supply, and pay for unfinished work.[56] Not only did workers rarely have enough acreage, but some companies continued to enforce hold-back clauses.[57] Some growers even refused to abide by the minimum wage scale, compelling the USDA to issue repeated warnings that it was illegal to pay below the state's mandated rates.[58] Ironically, then, the government-mandated minimum wage scales ended up protecting growers' profit margins rather than addressing the underlying inequalities in this industry.

The other mandates of the 1934 and 1937 sugar acts—prohibiting child labor under age fourteen and limiting to eight per day the number of hours children between ages fourteen and sixteen could work—had mixed results. Initially, neither the farmers nor the industrialists seemed to take the prohibition seriously. In early June 1935, Agnes Anderson, a self-titled "Farmers wife," wrote to John E. Dalton, chief of Michigan's Sugar Section, to ask whether the notice he had sent to all Michigan sugar beet growers outlining the child labor prohibition of the 1934 sugar act would be enforced. "Is this merely a formality or do you actually expect the growers to comply with these regulations[?]" Mrs. Anderson then went on to complain about fellow farmers and industrialists who were not following the labor rule, writing that factory fieldmen had told her that up to 75 percent of all thinning was being done by families with children under the age of fourteen. As such, Anderson asked: "How are you going to know who uses child labor?"[59]

In response to the complaint, government representatives investigated the situation and found that Mrs. Anderson's charges seemed to be justified.[60] To try to ascertain the extent of the violations, questionnaires were sent to all area sugar beet growers asking them whether or not they were using child labor.[61] Considering the voluntary nature of the questionnaire, it is hardly surprising that only two farmers admitted to using children under the age of fourteen.[62] The sugar companies proved equally deceptive. A Monitor Sugar Company executive informed a government official that he found only a "few cases" of child labor in an area covering just less than nineteen thousand acres.[63] A Children's Bureau 1935 investigation revealed a dramatically different picture. Although nationally the percentages of children under fourteen working in the fields had fallen from 42.6 to 18.8 percent, in Michigan the decrease was much less dramatic, with the percentage of children working in the fields decreasing from 49.4 to 33.5.[64]

The continuing high rates of child labor in Michigan pointed to the most serious problem with the child labor provisions: without dramatically raising the minimum paid per acre, there was little chance that migrant families would be able to afford to pull their children out of the fields, even if they had wanted to do so. Compounding the financial issue was the fact that the strong language in the legislation was never matched by enforcement on the ground. In practice, local production control committees showed little interest in enforcing guidelines that had come from Washington or taking the time to inspect what was happening in the fields.[65]

Labor Militancy

In spite of Roosevelt's hope that minimum wages and child labor prohibitions would rectify past injustices, both the 1934 Jones-Costigan Act and 1937 Sugar Act had relatively little practical benefit. Sugar beet workers quickly learned to question the USDA's promise that the inequalities embedded in labor relations could be solved through the AAA. This does not mean, however, that beet workers abandoned all hope in the New Deal. Like thousands of agricultural workers throughout the nation, Michigan's beet workers looked to other parts of the New Deal—that is, they looked to the right of unionization and collective bargaining—as the path toward better wages and working conditions. That sugar beet workers, as agricultural workers, were excluded from Section 7(a) of the National Industrial Recovery Act, as well as the National Labor Relations Act, mattered little to them as they tried to make these laws applicable in practice.[66] In doing so, beet workers challenged romantic notions of agricultural labor as somehow different than industrial labor.

The first organized labor union in Michigan's sugar beet fields emerged in 1935 when four hundred men and three hundred women from the Blissfield factory district, including Mexicans, Mexican Americans, Hungarians, Bohemians, and Romanians, joined the AFL's Agricultural Workers Union (AWU) Local 19994.[67] The union's list of demands demonstrated a keen understanding of the fact that winning a living wage depended on more than simply increasing the price they were paid per acre. In addition to asking for a $23 per acre flat rate, the union wanted growers to stagger their plantings so that workers would be able to tend to as many acres as possible. Union officials also insisted that the sugar companies' fieldmen do a better job distributing the available acreage equally among the workers. That is, the workers wanted to make sure not only that they would be paid a fair wage per acre but that they would have enough acreage each year to make a living. To protect themselves against the industry's practice of importing large numbers of migrant workers to depress wage scales, the beet workers also insisted that the growers agree to a "closed field" agreement stipulating that, "No outside help is to be employed as long as local labor is available." The AWU contract also demanded an end to all discrimination in the fields by prohibiting any favoritism or discrimination owing to "color and creed."[68]

When Local 19994 presented its list of demands to the Blissfield Beet Growers Association in 1935, the organization the growers themselves had created to challenge the sugar companies, it faced a formidable opponent. Although the growers had created this organization as a way to counter the growing power of the factory-dominated F&M, they showed few signs that they would be willing to negotiate with the workers. Never before had the growers been asked to deal with a worker union, and they had little intention of doing so now or in the future. To reinforce the message that they were not going to raise wages, much less meet Local 19994's other demands, the growers responded to the AWU by offering the workers $14 an acre—$1.60 less than workers had earned the year before—and insisting that harvesting work be done on a sliding scale system, a system that workers charged was a "form of the speed up."[69]

As the growing season drew closer, and tensions between the growers and workers worsened, Fred Schmidt, the president of Local 19994, looked to the state to help labor's cause. Schmidt asked USDL Secretary Frances Perkins to send a mediator to settle the dispute, pleading that if she failed to do so, "Strike will be declared. Looks like Civil War if strike is declared. Please take action immediately."[70] Perkins responded to Local 19994's pleas by sending conciliator J. E. O'Conner to negotiate an end to the dispute. After O'Conner came to the fields, the growers agreed to increase their wage scale to $18 an acre and offered to recognize the union. The workers, perhaps sensing that the state might be in their favor, continued to insist that they would not work for less than $21.50 an acre. It did not take long, however, for the tables to turn, with the laborers lowering their demand to $20 an acre. Still, the growers refused to budge from their initial $18 offer. Somewhat exasperated, O'Conner then proposed a compromise price of $19 an acre, which the workers immediately accepted, and the growers rejected. Feeling that they had little choice, 80 percent of the fourteen hundred members of Local 19994 voted to strike.[71]

Although the farmers who made up the Blissfield Beet Growers Association had resisted O'Conner's compromises, they decided to meet a number of the union's demands after it became clear that the workers would indeed go on strike. They agreed to pay workers a rate of $19 an acre and to recognize the right of the union to establish a "closed field." Furthermore, growers pledged that if additional workers were needed, they would look to the union to meet that demand.[72] However, the growers refused to distribute acreage equally among all workers and insisted on keeping contract clauses allowing them to let go of workers in cases where the crop did not pan out. Perhaps most significant of all, and in direct contrast to the provisions of the 1934 Jones-Costigan Act, the contract the union signed recognized the Great Lakes Sugar Company as the ultimate arbiter in case of future disputes.[73] In spite of the bitterness of the negotiations, for its part the AWU pledged to help the growers of the Blissfield Beet Growers Association, who were in the midst of their own battle with the sugar company to negotiate a better contract.[74]

The successful unionization efforts of Blissfield Local 19994 paid off handsomely. The contract made Blissfield workers the highest paid beet workers in the state and led to decreasing rates of child labor in the fields.[75] Perhaps just as important, the average number of acres tended by families in Blissfield increased to thirty-six, while families in nonunionized areas tended an average of only twenty-eight.[76] This acreage increase is all the more dramatic considering that in the unionized southern fields surrounding Blissfield, child labor fell to 12 percent.[77] Because of the higher wage per acre and the greater number of acres they tended, families in southern Michigan earned an average of $600 a year while their counterparts earned only $400. In explaining these regional discrepancies, Elizabeth Johnson of the Children's Bureau concluded that "it is significant that Southern Michigan was the only area surveyed in which the sugar beet laborers had a collective agreement with the farmers of the area and through it some control over the number of beet workers hired."[78] Clearly, collective bargaining and unionizing brought results that *minimum wage scales and unenforced child labor provisions could not.*

The "Blissfield contract," as it came to be known, was hailed as a model for all other aspiring agricultural unionists. The contract showed agricultural workers that even though they were not afforded the legal protections provided to industrial workers, it was still possible to gain organizing rights, in practice, by banding together. Spurred by the successes of Local 19994, the AWU national committee began organizing union drives throughout Michigan's countryside, even traveling to the small towns of Lakeville and Merrill. Beet workers in Alma and St. Louis, two very important factory towns, took steps to organize AWU locals of their own.[79]

Unfortunately, the heightened expectations following the 1935 victory were not matched by success in the fields. Even Local 19994 suffered serious setbacks in 1936 as it found itself having to battle the Great Lakes Sugar Company after company officials decided to take over negotiations with migrant workers, for fear that the Blissfield Beet Growers Association had set a dangerous precedent by negotiating with the workers. The company offered workers a sliding scale contract of $15 an acre and eighty cents a ton for harvesting. Commenting on the stingy contract offer, the *Rural Worker* reported how the Great Lakes was "trying to sign up growers independently of the Blissfield Beet Growers Association. It is an attempt to break down both the Union and the Beet Growers Association." The paper then insisted that union members would not be fooled by the company's shenanigans and that they would work with the growers in their battle with the company if the growers agreed to pay them a fair wage.[80] Albert Markva, who succeeded Fred Schmidt as president of Local AWU 19994, even expressed sympathy with the growers, whom he claimed would be "willing to give better wages if they can make a better settlement with the company."[81]

In spite of Markva's hope that workers and growers might be able to work together to challenge the sugar company, the union's attempt to negotiate a contract in 1936 came to naught. To make matters worse, the Great Lakes Sugar Company increased its annual recruitment of workers from Texas as a way to try to keep wages down and the union back on its heels.[82] In the following year, 1937, the situation continued to deteriorate. When the union asked for a flat rate of $21.50 an acre, the company offered $8 an acre for spring work and a sliding scale for harvesting,[83] thereby reducing worker wages still further to just twenty cents above the USDA secretary's state-mandated seventeen dollar minimum.[84] Hoping to stem the downward spiral, Local President Markva once again looked to Frances Perkins for help, claiming that the union's demand of $21.50 was "still way below the living wage this year." He also pointed out that the Great Lakes Sugar Company had recently started to bring in large numbers of laborers from Mexico. Perkins promised to try to help the sugar beet workers in their battle to win higher wages by sending O'Conner to the fields. However, by the time O'Conner finally arrived in Michigan, the Great Lakes Sugar Company fieldmen had already succeeded in "forcing the labor to sign cheap contracts." Michigan's Governor Frank Murphy had just recently aided the striking Flint auto workers, but efforts to convince him to intervene failed.[85]

In 1938, Local 19994 tried yet again to get the growers and the sugar company back to the bargaining table. However, this time, when union officials approached the company about negotiating a labor contract, Great Lakes Sugar Company officials told them they would have to consult with the newly formed Great Lakes Growers Employment Corporation. The Great Lakes Sugar Company had created this corporation as an independent legal entity to recruit workers and set their wages. Though this employment corporation was little more than a piece of paper, with Great Lakes continuing to call the shots, legally it moved the question of labor relations from a three-way relationship between the sugar manufacturers, the growers, and the workers, to a two-way relationship between the labor corporation and the workers.[86]

When leaders of Blissfield Local 19994 met with the new labor corporation, they asked for either a twenty-three-dollar minimum per acre or the eighteen-dollar minimum as stipulated by the 1937 Sugar Act, as long as the growers also agreed to give the workers half of the cash benefits they received from their government bonuses.[87] In doing so, the union was explicitly criticizing the 1937 Sugar Act, which gave benefits to farmers but only a paltry minimum wage to workers. When the employment corporation refused to grant either demand, an estimated nine hundred workers threatened that they would walk off the fields. Labor conciliator J. R. Steelman, whom Frances Perkins had sent to the fields to head off the looming conflict, wrote to his boss complaining not only that the beet growers had refused to negotiate with the union, but that they had started to "import" Mexicans "to do the work of local citizens."[88]

As the workers prepared to strike, the Great Lakes Sugar Company warned the townspeople and farmers of Blissfield that it might simply have to shut down for the upcoming season. This was no small threat, considering that the sugar factory was the most important tax contributor in town, the most important employer, and also the most important cash crop for area farmers.[89] Recognizing the importance of this one factory to the livelihood of their town, four hundred of Blissfield's businessmen and farmers saw it as their responsibility to confront the "wild catters" who "raised devil."[90] Businessmen and farmers banded together in a vigilante group, self-titled the Lenawee Protective League, and pledged a secret oath to patrol the countryside and drive out all "radical factions" of striking workers. The sheriff, who deputized the businessmen and farmers, and assumed the rank of supreme commander, organized the men into sixteen "motorized companies" of twenty-five men each. They pledged to "maintain peace in the Blissfield sugar beet fields in the face of labor trouble" and to "protect men who wanted to work." Characterizing the AWU Local 19994 as radical "outsiders," the vigilantes vowed to "fight fire with fire."[91]

The furor of the legally ordained vigilantes frightened AFL labor leaders, who quickly sought ways to relieve the mounting tension. Unsure of how far the vigilantes might go, the AFL of Toledo, Ohio, sent labor leader Francis J. Dillon, who immediately adopted a very conciliatory tone. While calling for growers and refiners to give the workers a "just share of the profits of this industry," Dillon also promised the community that the AFL would not call for a strike under current conditions. He tried to appease the vigilantes by saying, "I thoroughly appreciate my responsibility, not only to our members, but the growers, refiners and to the community," adding that, "I have in my mind . . . no definite formula to cure all evils." Dillon even went so far as to sympathize with the vigilantes, confessing that, "I assume that if I had been born and had lived in this farming community I, too, perhaps would view the situation as you do and perhaps be prejudiced against union representatives who come preaching new doctrine and a new program." And finally, in a desperate attempt to tap into an ideal vision of rural community, Dillon called for farmers, "men who till the soil," "to join with the AFL, not in arousing class hatred, but that we together may unite as our fore fathers did, sit down in our town halls, before our firesides and in our homes and give our thoughts to social and economic problems."[92]

Though Dillon's words may have helped to stop class warfare, they did nothing to bring the growers, the company, or the newly created labor corporation to the bargaining table. His conciliatory rhetoric frustrated and alienated hundreds of sugar beet workers, who felt that the AFL had sold them out. Union members who had voted to strike unless they were granted their demands were particularly outraged when union officials pressured them to settle for the eighteen-dollar minimum, once again the same minimum rate stipulated by the USDA. Dillon's suggestion that they could meet in the town halls, or in the growers' homes by their firesides, ignored the social and economic distance between most beet workers and growers.

Dillon defended his actions by admitting that this year would not be remembered "for what we achieved but for what we have averted . . . no class hatred . . . and no poor devil will be killed."[93] Even USDL conciliator Robert Pilkington, who had traveled to the fields at Secretary Perkins's request, admitted that he felt powerless when he tried to negotiate a settlement, and like Dillon, he encouraged the workers to accept the growers' original offer of $18 an acre. He commented how the companies and the growers were working together to destroy the union and had used the USDA's minimum wages as "justification to deny collective bargaining rights to workers."[94] That is, the sugar growers and companies pointed to their compliance with the Sugar Act's minimum wage provisions as a way to avoid bargaining with the workers.

The lesson of 1938 was a pretty obvious one. The New Deal held out a great deal of promise for sugar beet workers, for on paper the sugar acts seemed to confer certain workers' rights—the right to a minimum wage and child labor prohibitions—that all other agricultural workers lacked. However, by granting sugar beet workers minimum wages but not collective bargaining, the sugar acts left them at the mercy of the USDA, the growers, and the industrialists. This represented a defeat for the workers, who found their valiant efforts to be recognized as workers, and their right to organize, rejected.

Migrant Labor as a Problem

What should have been celebrated as a community victory—the defeat of the striking workers—instead added to the public's growing perception that migrant labor was the problem. Rather than focus on the "labor agitators" or "outside radicals" as the cause of the problem, many of Michigan's residents began to vilify the sugar companies for creating a labor form that exploited both the laborers who had come to toil as well as the communities in which they worked. Though some locals, especially those affiliated with religious groups, tried to address what they saw as the migrant labor problem by publicizing the poor living and working conditions of migrant families and looking for ways to remedy the migrants' immediate circumstances, most locals tended to view the poor wages and living conditions among migrant labor as a menace to their communities and sought out ways to end this labor form once and for all.

Church groups were among the first to try to define and address what would soon become known as the migrant problem. In the sugar beet town of Caro, the Remington Methodist Church began inviting Mexican and Mexican American residents to church services in the late 1920s, providing Spanish hymn books and having a Mexican beet worker who was fluent in both Spanish and English translate the services for his compatriots. Reverend Van Dorn, who had initiated the overture, hoped that through his efforts Mexicans would learn about "the flag, the evangelical faith, and the Constitution."[95] By the early 1930s, a number of Catholic churches followed Van Dorn's lead, though probably more out of fear of losing Catholic souls to Protestant competitors than interest in what Mexicans had to say. In 1933 the Catholic Church, which had generally ignored Mexicans and Mexican Americans, started to offer Spanish-language services in rural Michigan. Father Joseph Munoz of Flint began traveling to the small town of Pigeon to provide services, confession, religious instruction, and first communion to Mexican and Mexican American residents.[96] The priest of Alma's Catholic church also brought in a Spanish speaker "to preach in various places in his factory district where colonies of Mexican beet workers prevail."[97]

In addition to offering religious services, some church groups provided real material help to impoverished migrant families.[98] In 1936 the Methodist church in Mt. Pleasant, run by Reverend McKenzie, began a program to offer recreational and handicraft instruction to Mexican children and encouraged their parents to maintain garden plots near the church.[99] Similarly, Helen White of the Homes Mission Council (HMC) joined in the effort and set up eight-week "migrant day camps" in Mt. Pleasant and Alma to offer meals and day care. The children who came to these camps were taught Bible verses and Bible songs and shown how to wash their bodies and teeth. As tempting as it may be to therefore disregard the HMC's efforts as a selfish manifestation of cultural imperialism, it is important to acknowledge that the organization offered valuable services not available elsewhere. Equally important, the HMC was one of the only organizations in Michigan to publicly endorse the beet workers' right to unionize.[100]

In contrast to the religious groups, who sought to tend to the very real material and perceived spiritual needs of migrant families, most Michigan residents focused on the alleged health dangers migrant workers brought to Michigan. In the spring of 1937, the residents of the small town of Owendale awoke to the warning that Jesus Ayala, a Mexican sugar beet worker who had previously worked in their town, had escaped from the nation's leper home in Carville, Louisiana.[101] When fifty cases of malaria emerged in Kalamazoo County that same year, it was explained as "a result of the Mexican influx." In addition, the public was warned that "the malaria danger" would persist "so long as migration continues."[102] In August 1938, one of Bay City's newspapers even published reported sightings of two Mexican families, supposedly carriers of Shiga dysentery, who had moved from Bay City to the lakeside town of Ludington.[103] When a case of "tropical shanghai fever" struck the sugar beet town of Owosso just two months later, migrant beet workers were blamed for the outbreak, even though no direct evidence linked them to the virus.[104] According to one self-proclaimed "citizen," "Mexicans from Texas have latent diseases that are very difficult even for the best of North climate doctors to recognize."[105]

Rather than challenge the association of migrant workers and disease, Michigan health officials reinforced the belief that those who came to toil in the fields brought dangerous health problems with them. In 1937, Saginaw

County health officials announced that though Mexicans made up only 2 percent of the overall population, they took up one-quarter of the beds at the Saginaw County Hospital. Shortly thereafter, the health commissioner of the Saginaw County Department of Health announced that of the 374 Mexicans he examined for tuberculosis, 174 tested positive.[106] These "facts" confirmed the "citizens'" fears that however much they attempted to draw a boundary between themselves and the migrant population, migrants still posed a threat to the larger community.

As the public concern about migrant labor mounted, the state of Michigan's Bureau of Labor and Industry decided to investigate the conditions of workers in the sugar beet fields, and more specifically, "the problems created by the families brought from Texas." In direct contrast to Michigan's 1923 sugar beet "investigation," in which the state exonerated itself of all charges of child labor, the Labor and Industry's May 1938 report cited plenty of "problems arising from the importation and employment of beet field workers" and sought to "get the sugar beet processors and growers and various governmental agencies to plan improvements."[107] A Michigan Rural Teachers' Association official spokesman went so far as to report that the committee had found "conditions [which] were said to be a disgrace to humanity."[108]

To address the numerous problems they unearthed, Labor Commissioner Robert Krogstad, who headed this investigation, invited sugar beet industrialists and growers as well as representatives from Michigan's Departments of Health, Public Welfare, and Emergency Relief "to plan improvements among the problems arising from the importation and employment of beet field workers."[109] The committee members quickly drew up a list of recommendations, some of which certainly would have improved the lives of both resident and migrant beet workers if they had been implemented. They called for all sugar beet families to be "furnished" with no less than ten acres so that they could earn a "reasonable" income, to be paid a fixed rate per acre on a monthly or semimonthly basis, and to be provided with contracts printed in both Spanish and English. To make sure that families would not become destitute before work began, the committee asked for the companies and the growers to make sure the families were "suitably clothed" and fed, and that they not be overcharged for items purchased at local stores. Other recommendations called for the sugar companies and growers to provide local school authorities with the names and locations of children who had come to the fields, pay for any necessary school supplies needed by the migrant children, and help attendance officers make sure that the children actually made it to school.[110]

Though these recommendations reflected the committee's willingness to criticize the sugar beet industry and its labor relations, the committee's other recommendations were premised on the idea that the migrant workers themselves were really the problem. The committee called for growers and sugar companies to hire "from the ranks of the unemployed in various counties" and to keep records of all workers, including "evidence of citizenship." To make sure that the labor preferences for "local" and "American" workers were followed, the committee insisted that all those recruiting migrant labor should register with the state's Bureau of Labor and Industry. With respect to the question of health, the committee called for any migrant workers found to be suffering from tuberculosis or any other communicable disease "hazardous to public health" to be returned to their respective homes at the expense of either the growers or the processors. And finally, and perhaps most important of all, the committee recommended that at the end of the season, all migrant beet workers "must return to the[ir] former residence" and those who insisted on staying would find that "no relief will be extended them by any welfare agency" in the state.[111]

Within a couple of years, some of the Labor and Industry Committee's recommendations did become public policy, but mostly those that "protected" the broader "public" from the migrants rather than those that would have safeguarded the workers. Rather than institute a state minimum wage per acre or stipulate that the industry provide a minimum number of acres per person, the state adopted those proposals that focused on issues related to citizenship, relief, and health. Beginning in 1938, the state called for workers to be "secured from local unemployed in preference to imported Mexican laborers" and for strict records to be kept on the nonresidents working in the fields. Perhaps one of the most revealing parts of the state's demands concerned the question of relief. Stated simply, state relief agencies declared that all migrant beet workers would be denied relief, something that had often been standard practice but never official policy. In fact, local welfare agencies began cooperating with the sugar beet processors by turning over to the companies any migrant applicants so that they could deal with them directly. The only two recommendations looking out for the workers' best interests—a call for employers to provide "sanitary housing" and to make sure that all children under the age of sixteen attended school—were left conspicuously vague.[112]

The state's most ambitious proposal for dealing with the "migrant problem" revolved around the issue of health. The state mandated that sugar companies and growers should shoulder the financial burden of returning to Texas individuals infected with any communicable diseases, and, even more important, that this industry should establish a system for testing migrant workers for disease long before they were allowed to come into the state. The program, which began in 1939, involved the Michigan Commission of Health, with the "approval and cooperation" of the Texas Health Department, setting up a screening center in San Antonio, Texas, to test prospective sugar beet workers for tuberculosis, gonorrhea, and syphilis. Workers who "passed" the examination were provided with photo identification cards as evidence of their right to register with an employment agency and to toil in Michigan's beet fields.[113]

Taken together, the state adopted those recommendations that assumed migrant workers were a threat who might undermine public health and public welfare. What *did not* become public policy—the right to decent and timely pay as well as enough work to keep busy during the long season—were those recommendations that recognized migrant laborers as workers with rights. The call for hiring "citizens" over migrants tended to reify the tie between the right to work and race that had been a public issue since the repatriation campaigns of the early 1930s. Furthermore, by denying migrant workers the right to relief, Michigan's communities denied that they had any obligation to the welfare of migrant beet families, only a right to their cheap labor. And finally, by associating Mexican bodies with the outbreak of communicable diseases, the state reinforced the assumption that Mexican and Mexican American migrant workers were a foreign and alien element that threatened the health of the entire community. The fact that relatively few of the Mexicans and Mexican Americans tested in Texas for tuberculosis actually had the disease— only eighty-one out of 4,271 in 1939 and 156 out of 5,753 in 1940—should have led to the conclusion that the higher rates of tuberculosis among sugar beet workers had more to do with their living and working conditions in Michigan than some inherent susceptibility to disease. However, the damage had been done, as the perception of sugar beet workers as a health menace had already taken hold in the public imagination.[114]

Conclusion

In spite of the attempt by state officials to address the "problems" associated with migrant labor, the local and state media continued to highlight the sugar industry as a corrupt one. In June 1938, the *Pigeon Progress* announced the arrival of a "tattered army of more than 5,000 Mexican peasant laborers imported to the state's sugar beet fields," detailing how the "dismal list of acute human problems which followed in the trail of the invasion last summer appeared likely to reappear this year in spite of conferences and hearings between the beet growers and the state Department of Labor."[115] A year later, another Michigan newspaper reported how "Want, poverty, misery, and terror stalk the beet fields like four gibbering ghosts, haunting the days and nights of the inarticulate Mexican laborers who have been brought so far from their homes to the strange northern land to work in strange fields."[116]

Whether one ascribed to the view that migrant workers were "Mexican peasants" who created problems for rural Michigan or victims who could only expect "want, poverty, misery and terror" in an unfriendly north, migrant labor was seen as a problem. The politicization of migrant labor on a national scale began during World War I and the 1920s as the nation's political and economic leaders debated whether it would be plausible or palatable to try to import Mexican workers, and whether or not the nation's newest immigration restrictions should apply to the thousands who crossed the southern border to work and live in the United States. By the late 1920s and early 1930s, these questions assumed an urgent form as communities throughout the United States sought to repatriate their "alien" Mexican and Mexican American residents as one way to solve the Great Depression. By linking the right to employment and the right to receive relief with perceived citizenship and race, communities throughout the United States blurred the lines between legal and illegal immigrants, turning all Mexicans and Mexican Americans into "outsiders." Or, in the words of one Indiana resident, "noncitizen outlaws."[117]

The perception of migrant labor as a problem, however, is not the only story to be told of the 1930s. During this decade, the passage of the sugar beet acts, which accorded all sugar beet field workers, regardless of race or citizenship, certain basic rights—the right to a minimum wage and child labor prohibitions—held out the promise that migrant workers might be recognized as workers. Even more important, during this decade thousands of sugar beet workers banded together to demand the right to organize into unions and the right to bargain collectively, in spite of the fact that New Deal legislation providing workers with these rights expressly excluded them. The fact that migrant families found themselves defined as the migrant labor problem, as a threat to the health and well-being of Michigan's communities, must have seemed both ironic and disheartening to the men and women who had battled so valiantly to be recognized as workers, as residents, and sometimes even as citizens.

Epilogue

In 1937 Paul S. Taylor, the sociologist who had spent two decades interviewing and writing about migrant workers in the United States, proclaimed: "Migratory labor is a proletarian class, not a people with a developed culture. It is forced to till the soil for others. It lives in material poverty. To a large extent indispensable, nevertheless it is commonly exploited and substandard. It slips through stable and often rich communities of which it is never an accepted part. It offers a breeding ground of social unrest.... It lends itself readily to the development of a form of agriculture which is not a way of life, but an industry. Thus it becomes an unwitting instrument in the breakdown of the traditional American ideal of the family farm."[1]

Three years after Taylor penned these words, dozens of witnesses traveled to Washington, D.C., to speak on the issue of the "Interstate Migration of Destitute Citizens." Congress had convened this public discussion to highlight the hardships that had become an indelible part of American culture through books such as John Steinbeck's *The Grapes of Wrath*. Almost all the witnesses who testified agreed that migrant labor represented a bane on society. P. D. Beck, the midwestern regional director for the Farm Security Administration, reported: "Here in the Middle West, our agricultural press and daily newspapers are raising the question whether or not we must make a choice between family-sized farms or, as one part put it 'Grapes of Wrath.'"[2] Beck then warned: "In terms of internal defense and human welfare, the Nation cannot afford to permit existing trends to continue and to permit a vast group of migratory, land-less, job-hungry, ill-clothed, and ill-fed people, physically and mentally ill, to develop."[3] Following Beck, Works Progress Administration workers from the state of Michigan similarly cautioned: "[W]e have found that the Joads of California had counterparts in Michigan. The thousands of migrant families entering this area have a very real effect on the social and economic life of local communities."[4]

The nation's newfound discovery of migrant labor in the late 1930s masked a much longer and more complicated past. In fact, by conceptualizing migrant labor as a problem, the men and women who testified at the 1940 congressional hearings divorced migrant labor from history. That is, instead of understanding migrant workers as workers, and as part of a much longer historical transformation of the countryside, they simply vilified migrant workers for undermining the family farm while also portraying them as victims of a greedy capitalist system that privileged profits over people. These themes have become all too familiar to the general public and historians alike, many of whom blindly accept the proposition that the rise of migrant labor was not just a sign of the downfall of the family farm but one of its main causes. What remains, then, is a romantic and ahistorical view of the family farm as a place based on community and democracy where locals pulled together to try to ward off the modern world encircling them. What is lost in such a narrative is the fact that *both* the family farm and migrant labor are part of a much broader history, a history of industrialization, imperialism, the state, class conflicts, and racial battles.

Coming to terms with this past is important not just for our understanding of what has come before but also for grappling critically with some of the most important issues facing the United States at the dawn of the twenty-first century. And, the three main themes developed in this book—the creation of migrant labor, the development of industrial agriculture, and the politics of imperialism—certainly continue to affect us. The point of looking backward is not that the past provides clear-cut lessons to be applied, as if history can act as a manual or guidebook for future action. If we think that the past offers unambiguous answers to the questions of our own day, we will be sadly mistaken. The past has never been a simple dress rehearsal for the present. What the past can do, however, is force us to recognize the limitations of our own understanding, to caution us in our confidence, and to encourage us to think more reflectively and critically.

Anyone even faintly acquainted with the nation's first guest worker program during World War I, or the debates over Mexican immigration that divided Congress in the 1920s, cannot help but note the similarities between those previous eras and our own. Like their predecessors of the early twentieth century, who debated whether or not it would be possible or politically palatable to create a class of agricultural workers, contemporary critics and proponents of President George W. Bush's proposed guest worker program recognize that his proposal involves much more than answering the question of who will provide labor to keep American agriculture competitive and the nation's food supply cheap. The immigration debate of the early twenty-first century is really a discussion about the meaning of citizenship and national boundaries in a global economy in which both capital and labor seem to know no bounds. Perhaps this helps to explain the rather strange bedfellows, in which liberals like Senator Edward Kennedy, who want to offer a humane path to citizenship to those who have already built lives in the United States, find themselves holding hands with corporate interests, whose main concern lies with maintaining a cheap and servile underclass willing to toil for the lowest possible wages. On the other side, labor groups concerned that the creation of a second class of workers in the United States will further drive down what are already declining wages and working conditions for the nation's lowest paid find themselves on the same political divide as cultural conservatives, whose ostensible effort to preserve the middle class, the English language, and American culture (whatever that may be) masks, barely, a nativist and xenophobic agenda.

The nation's previous large-scale guest worker programs during World War I and World War II should cause us to pause, to question whether it is really possible to address, much less solve, the alleged security and legal issues raised by the presence of millions of undocumented immigrants in the United States, while at the same time meet the supposed need for cheap labor by bringing in hundreds of thousands of temporary guest workers. Will Bush's proposed solution, including its mandated "'touch back" provision and stiff fines really create a "path to citizenship" for those already here? Or will those who come to toil as guest workers find themselves marked as outsiders only here to provide cheap labor? Will the proposed security measures allow the United States to physically "secure" the geographic border between itself and Mexico when economic and emotional ties continue to pull in both directions? Perhaps only time will tell, but the past seems to suggest that we should not be too optimistic.

The second major theme running through this book, the rise of industrial agriculture, has also garnered ever-greater public attention over the last couple of decades. Today, industrial agriculture conjures up images of monoculture, government benefits, antibiotics, fossil fuels, synthetic fertilizers, genetically modified food, giant feedlots, processing plants, homogenized grocery stores, and overly processed foods. More often than not, the first concern is with the consumer; second, the environment; third, the family farm; and last, if at all, the workers toiling in the fields and processing plants. In other words, much of the concern with industrial agriculture stems from fears that what we are eating may be causing us more harm than good.[5]

Contemporary critics and historians looking to explain the roots of the current state of agriculture often begin with the post–World War II era, when global conglomerates like Archer Daniels Midland and ConAgra, and government policies promoting and rewarding monoculture (especially corn), combined with advances in science and technology to transform America's farms and rural communities. While the above-mentioned developments are certainly important (and probably the most important) they are not the entire story.[6] A longer historical trajectory that explores the often slow and uneven industrialization of the countryside not only demonstrates the very contingent and contested rise of industrial agriculture but also opens the door to imagining a different kind of agriculture for the future.

This longer historical trajectory allows us to see the various ways interests associated with the sugar beet industry took part in debates about whether it would be possible to make the countryside industrial while also maintaining its democratic underpinning, however real or imagined. These debates included discussions about whether or not the government had any responsibility to balance the interests and well-being of the powerful and the less powerful. During World War I, thousands of farmers pleaded with the federal government to mediate their disputes with the factories and to establish a level playing field where the fruits of their labor could be shared equally with corporate powers. During the 1930s, as the Great Depression descended on the countryside, it looked like the time had finally come for balancing the interests of the companies, the farmers, and the workers. Franklin D. Roosevelt helped push through the Jones-Costigan Act of 1934 and the Sugar Act of 1937, both of which mandated that farmers be paid fair prices, that all sugar beet workers be paid minimum wages, and that no children under the age of fourteen toil in the fields. That the promise of democratizing this industry, and hence the countryside itself, was ultimately not fulfilled should not stop us from exploring the fact that many people envisioned and tried to create a different kind of industrial agriculture than the one that eventually emerged. Neither should it blind us to the importance of recognizing the political strength and clout that corporate agricultural interests managed to amass over the twentieth century.

Finally, the politics of imperialism—and all the contradictory issues that the term raises, including protectionism, free trade, global capitalism, and state power—have only grown more important over the course of the twentieth and twenty-first centuries. In lieu of its historically protectionist policy of fostering domestic industries and protecting American producers, over the last seventy years the United States has largely embraced the free market as a pathway to riches at home and a panacea to the world's political instabilities. Rather than using foreign policy as a way to open up trade abroad, U.S. trade policies are seen as a way to achieve foreign policy objectives by rewarding friends and punishing foes. Somewhat ironically, the protectionist era of the late nineteenth and early twentieth centuries, in which the global economy was patrolled by imperial boundaries and national self interest, has been replaced by a global marketplace that knows no bounds and appears to be beholden only to its own acquisitive logic.

The shift from protectionism to free trade, though clearly envisioned by President Woodrow Wilson, began in earnest in the mid 1930s during Franklin D. Roosevelt's administration. With the selection of Tennessee Senator Cordell Hull as his secretary of state in 1933, Roosevelt helped to initiate a "revolution in U.S. trade policy" that involved wrestling the almost always highly political and contentious tariff battles out of the hands of Congress and into the lap of the presidency.[7] In 1934 Congress passed the Reciprocal Trade Agreement Act, which took the power that Congress has wielded when it came to trade policy and handed it to the president, who was given the right to raise or lower tariff rates by 50 percent.[8] Under the influence of Hull, Roosevelt adopted a policy of trade liberalization that continued to guide the rest of the twentieth century. Since 1934, tariff rates in the United States fell from an average of 45 percent ad valorem to just 8.5 percent by 1973.[9] Though Congress and succeeding presidents have continued to jostle for control over trade policy in the following decades, the free trade mantra has only continued to rise while tariff duties have continued to go in the opposite direction.

The same year that Congress gave Roosevelt the authority to help determine trade policy, it also abrogated the Platt Amendment and passed an act to grant the Philippines its independence. Though these historical developments are not often linked—the trend toward free trade and the devolution of formal empire—together they embody and symbolize the shape of American imperialism over the rest of the twentieth century. Rather than only putting resources into politically dominating other nations, the United States has also looked to the free market to do its political bidding. Confident that the United States would not only be able to compete but also dominate the free market, the United States has searched for ways to access markets abroad while opening its own markets to the world's products. Policy makers believed that economic and cultural imperialism would not only prove to be more flexible and less costly but also more acceptable to a national populace proud of its own anticolonial beginnings. To the chagrin of groups looking to protect the wages and jobs of domestic workers, and to the joy of groups who predict that a world without trade barriers will deliver global peace and harmony, the free market and globalism seem to have won out, at least for the time being.

Strangely, or perhaps not so strange at all considering this industry's very political past, the U.S. sugar industry defied and continues to defy the larger historic trends toward free trade, leading one cynical journalist in 2005 to complain that sugar remains "on the wrong side of history."[10] The 1937 Sugar Act, which was set to expire after three years, instead inaugurated a nearly four-decade period in which domestically produced sugar and preferential colonial sugar enjoyed a nationalized and protected marketplace. Though this era looked like it was finally coming to an end in 1974 when Congress refused to extend the sugar program, this period of relatively freer trade proved very short lived.[11] By the end of the 1970s, the protected marketplace returned, which has continued to the present day. Through a combination of tariffs, foreign and domestic quotas, marketing allotments, government loan programs, and minimum prices for sugar, the protected U.S. sugar beet and sugar cane industries have continued to thrive into the twenty-first century.

Most recently, the domestic sugar industry, "the single largest agricultural donor to political campaigns," has fought against the inclusion of sugar in both the North American Free Trade Agreement and the Dominican Republic–Central American Free Trade Agreement.[12] Once again, as in decades past, the sugar beet and sugar cane industry officials and lobbyists showed up in Washington, testified at hearings, and pursued a vigorous public relations campaign to make sure that their hard-fought protections and largely isolated market would not be disturbed. In both cases, they warned that free trade sugar would not only cost thousands of American jobs and hurt thousands of family farmers, but that any inclusion of sugar in either agreement would set a free trade precedent that would soon destroy their industry. To the dismay of free traders, the sugar industry proved yet again that it could flex its political muscle, gaining concessions in NAFTA that limited the amount of sugar Mexico could export to the United States while also forestalling the full effects of free trade until January 2008.[13] Whether or not the free trade provisions will prove largely negligible to U.S. sugar producers, as NAFTA and DR-CAFTA supporters contend, or open the door to unfair competition, as the sugar industry has predicted, has yet to be determined. What we do know is that at the beginning of the twenty-first century, much like at the beginning of the twentieth, sugar remains a highly political topic, and the sugar industry (cane and beet) remains a powerful and potent force. A sweet tyranny indeed.

Notes

Introduction

1. Louis A. Perez, *The War of 1898: The United States and Cuba in History and Historiography* (Chapel Hill: University of North Carolina Press, 1998), 33.
2. N. H. Stewart, U.S. House of Representatives, Hearings Before Committee on Ways and Means, *Reciprocity with Cuba,* 57th Congress, 1st Session (Washington, D.C.: GPO, 1902), 205.
3. Dan Gutleben, *Sugar Tramp—1954: Michigan* (San Francisco: Bay Cities Duplicating Co., 1955), 146–50.
4. "The Beet Sugar Industry," *Weekly Statistical Sugar Trade Journal* 27.2 (January 1903), 7.
5. *Pigeon Progress,* 25 April 1902 [hereafter *PP*]; *PP,* 2 May 1902.
6. Helen Eichstaedt, *Alla Lizie: A Gripping Narration of the Love and Strength of a German/Russian Woman and her Family as they Survive Pre-Communist Russia and Struggle to Start a New Life in Early Twentieth Century America* (Ann Arbor, Mich.: Kennedy Associates, 1995), 57.
7. For example, see Linda Gordon, "Dorothea Lange: The Photographer as Agricultural Sociologist," *Journal of American History* 93.3 (December 2006): 698–727. For a more critical perspective on Midwestern regional identities, see Andrew R. Clayton and Peter S. Onuf, eds., *The Midwest and the Nation: Rethinking the History of an American Region* (Bloomington: Indiana University Press, 1990) and Andrew R. L. Clayton and Susan E. Gray, eds., *The American Midwest: Essays on Regional Identity* (Bloomington: Indiana University Press, 2001).
8. David B. Danbom, *Born in the Country: A History of Rural America* (Baltimore: Johns Hopkins University Press, 1995), 134.
9. Sidney Mintz, *Sweetness and Power: The Place of Sugar in Modern History* (New

York: Viking, 1985); B. W. Highman, "The Sugar Revolution," *Economic History Review* 53.2 (May 2000): 229.

10. For the sugar statistics, see Bill Albert and Adrian Graves, eds., *Crisis and Change in the International Sugar Economy* (Edinburgh: ISC Press, 1984), 12; Vladimir P. Timoshenko and Boris Swerling, *The World's Sugar: Progress and Policy* (Stanford, Calif.: Stanford University Press, 1957); Bill Albert and Adrian Graves, eds., *The World's Sugar Economy in War and Depression, 1914–1940* (New York: Routledge, 1988).

11. John Franklin Crowell, "The Sugar Situation in the Tropics," *Political Science Quarterly* 14.1 (December 1899): 606–27; C. F. Emerick, "An Analysis of Agricultural Discontent in the United States," *Political Science Quarterly* 12.1 (March 1897): 93–127.

12. Vincent A. Mahler, "Britain, the European Community, and the Developing Commonwealth: Dependence, Interdependence, and the Political Economy of Sugar," *International Organization* 35.3 (1981): 475.

13. Charles Saylor, *Progress of the Beet-Sugar Industry in 1901* (Washington, D.C.: GPO, 1902), 46.

14. Charles Saylor, *Progress of the Beet-Sugar Industry in 1899* (Washington, D.C.: GPO, 1900), 41–42; Saylor, *Progress of the Beet-Sugar Industry in 1901*, 30; Charles Saylor, *Progress of the Beet-Sugar Industry in 1906* (Washington, D.C.: GPO, 1907), 104, 109; Charles Saylor, *Progress of the Beet-Sugar Industry in 1907* (Washington, D.C.: GPO, 1908), 66–68.

15. Quoted in Thomas Bender, *A Nation Among Nations: America's Place in World History* (New York: Hill and Wang, 2006), 12.

16. *Washington Post*, 1 September 1929.

Chapter 1. Rural Industrialization and Imperial Politics

1. Charles Saylor, *Progress of the Beet-Sugar Industry in 1899* (Washington, D.C.: GPO, 1900), 13–14. [hereafter *Progress . . . in 1899*]

2. *Tuscola County Advertiser*, 3 February 1899, found in Clippings File, Michigan Sugar Company Records, Michigan State University Archives, East Lansing.

3. *Pigeon Progress*, 1 August 1902 [hereafter *PP*]; For a ranking of the sugar beet states each year, consult the *Progress of the Beet-Sugar Industry in the United States* (Washington, D.C.: GPO, 1898–1909).

4. Michigan Bureau of Labor and Industrial Statistics, *Nineteenth Annual Report* (Lansing: Wynkoop Hallenbeck Crawford Co., 1902), 6.

5. C. D. Smith, U.S. House of Representatives, Hearings Before Committee On Ways and Means, *Reciprocity with Cuba*, 57th Congress, 1st Session (Washington, D.C.: GPO, 1902), 235.

6. "The Beet Sugar Industry," *Weekly Statistical Sugar Trade Journal* 25.8 (February 1901), 5. [hereafter *STJ*]

7. Brian Page and Richard Walker, "From Settlement to Fordism: The Agro-industrial Revolution in the American Midwest," *Economic Geography* 67 (1991): 281–315;

Deborah Fink, *Cutting into the Meatpacking Line: Workers and Change in the Rural Midwest* (Chapel Hill: University of North Carolina Press, 1997).

8. Charles Saylor, *Special Report on the Beet-Sugar Industry in the United States* (Washington, D.C.: GPO, 1898), 3 and 162. [hereafter *Special Report*]

9. Charles Saylor, *Progress of the Beet-Sugar Industry in 1902* (Washington, D.C.: GPO, 1903), 18. [hereafter *Progress . . . in 1902*]

10. Sugar beet from Europe made up approximately 45 percent of all sugar imports into the United States in 1897. Saylor, *Special Report*, 3.

11. Ibid., 176–77.

12. Ibid., 176.

13. Ibid., 163.

14. Charles Saylor, *Progress of the Beet-Sugar Industry in 1898* (Washington, D.C.: GPO, 1899), 13. [hereafter *Progress . . . in 1898*]

15. In one report, Charles Saylor pointed out that the United States' importation of $122,000,000 of foreign sugar was worth more than the value of the United States' best export—steel—which amounted to $117,319,320. He also pointed out that the nation's total sugar bill of $265,644,000 added up to nearly two-thirds of the total value for U.S. domestic exports. See Saylor, *Progress . . . in 1902*, 18.

16. Ibid., 18.

17. F. W. Taussig, "The United States Tariff Act of 1897," *Economic Journal* 7.28 (December 1897): 592–98; Alfred Eichner, *The Emergence of Oligopoly: Sugar Refining as a Case Study* (Baltimore: Johns Hopkins University Press, 1969), 232. For discussion of foreign policy and the tariff question, see John M. Dobson, *America's Ascent: The United States Becomes a Great Power, 1880–1914* (Dekalb: Northern Illinois University Press, 1978), 110–13; John M. Dobson, *Two Centuries of Tariffs: The Background and Emergence of the United States Trade Commissioner* (Washington, D.C.: GPO, 1976); Thomas J. Heston, *Sweet Subsidy: The Economic and Diplomatic Effects of the United States Sugar Acts, 1934–1974* (New York: Garland, 1987), 41–55; Walter LeFeber, *The Cambridge History of American Foreign Relations: Volume II, The American Search for Opportunity, 1865–1913* (Cambridge, U.K.: Cambridge University Press 1993), 91–95, 105–13, 139–45.

18. William B. Allison, 11 June 1897, *Congressional Record*, 55th Congress, 1st Session, 1674.

19. Edward N. Dingley, 19 July 1897, *Congressional Record*, 55th Congress, 1st Session, 2708.

20. Charles Saylor, *Progress of the Beet-Sugar Industry in 1900* (Washington, D.C.: GPO, 1901), 7. [hereafter *Progress . . . in 1900*]

21. Saylor, *Progress . . . in 1898*, 39; Saylor, *Progress . . . in 1902*, 78.

22. G. W. Shaw, "Conditions Affecting Beet-Sugar Culture in the United States," *Journal of Political Economy* 12.3 (June 1904): 327–38.

23. Hal S. Barron, *Mixed Harvest: The Second Great Transformation in the Rural North, 1870–1930* (Chapel Hill: University of North Carolina Press, 1995), chapters

5 and 6; David Blanke, *Sowing the American Dream: How Consumer Culture Took Root in the Rural Midwest* (Athens: Ohio University Press, 2000).

24. Charles Saylor, "Our American Beet Sugar Industry," *American Sugar Industry and Beet Sugar Gazette* 8 (February 1906), 112. [hereafter *ASI* and *BSG*]

25. Saylor, *Progress . . . in 1899*, 15.

26. Saylor, *Progress . . . 1902*, 17; Saylor, *Progress . . . in 1898*, 24; Charles Saylor, *Progress of the Beet-Sugar Industry in 1900* (Washington, D.C.: GPO, 1901), 11; Saylor, *Progress . . . in 1902*, 16–17; Charles Saylor, *Progress of the Beet-Sugar Industry in 1903* (Washington, D.C.: GPO, 1904), 64, 68, 70–71, 112; Charles Saylor, *Progress of the Beet-Sugar Industry in 1906* (Washington, D.C.: GPO, 1907), 26; Charles Saylor, *Progress of the Beet-Sugar Industry in 1907* (Washington, D.C.: GPO, 1908), 13.

27. For an excellent description of the relationship between urban Chicago and Michigan's hinterlands, see William Cronon, *Nature's Metropolis: Chicago and the Great West* (New York: W.W. Norton and Co., 1991), 148–206; For a detailed discussion of the lumbering industry in Michigan, see Jeremy W. Kilar, *Michigan's Lumbertowns: Lumbermen and Laborers in Saginaw, Bay City, and Muskegon, 1870–1905* (Detroit: Wayne State University Press, 1990).

28. Winter wheat, the state's most popular crop, began to decline after 1899 from two million acres a year to one million acres a year in 1908. Joseph George Duncan, "The Michigan Farmer: A Century of Agricultural Journalism 1843–1943," M.A. thesis, Michigan State College, 1950, 132; The "cheese processing" district at the turn of the century was restricted to relatively few counties, including St. Clair, Kent, Montcalm, and Lapeer. Even fewer Michigan farmers made money by having factories process butter for them. Lew Allen Chase, *Rural Michigan* (New York: MacMillan, 1922), 295–96.

29. Smith, *Reciprocity with Cuba*, 234.

30. This most generous bounty, which was instituted in 1897, was supposed to be only a temporary measure to entice capitalists to invest in sugar factories that cost from $300,000 to $800,000 each, and not a permanent feature of this industry as in Europe. As such, the bounty was scheduled to expire in 1903 once the industry had been established. For a copy of this act, see Michigan, *Fifty-Sixth Annual Report of the Commissioner of the Land Office* (Lansing: Robert Smith Printing Co., 1898), 26–27.

31. *TCA*, 1 November 1901.

32. "The Beet Sugar Industry," *STJ* 24.7 (February 1900): 5; *Alma Record*, 3 January 1902 [hereafter *AR*]; *AR*, 29 January 1904; C. D. Smith and R. C. Kedzie, "Planting Sugar Beets," *Michigan Agricultural College Experiment Station, Special Bulletin* 8 (East Lansing, 1898); C. D. Smith and R. C. Kedzie, "Sugar Beets," *Michigan Agricultural College Experiment Station, Special Bulletin* 10 (East Lansing, 1899); J. D. Towar, "Sugar Beet Experiments, 1901" *Michigan Agricultural College Experiment Station, Special Bulletin* 197 (East Lansing, 1902).

33. Michigan, *Fifty-Sixth Annual Report*, 28–30.

34. Michigan, *Fifty-Seventh Annual Report of the Commissioner of the Land Office* (Lansing: Robert Smith Printing Co., 1899), 16.

35. *PP*, 18 October 1901.

36. Dan Gutleben, *The Sugar Tramp—1954: Michigan* (San Francisco: Bay Cities Duplicating Co., 1955), 2.

37. Ibid., 45–54.

38. *TCA*, 24 February 1899.

39. James Wilson, "Discussion," *Michigan State Farmers' Institutes, Winter of 1901–1902* Bulletin 8 (Agricultural College, Mich.: State Board of Agriculture, 1902), 104.

40. Gutleben, *Sugar Tramp*, 29–30.

41. Michigan, *Fifty-Seventh Annual Report of the Commissioner of the Land Office*, 13–15; Red Books, 1898–1899, Michigan Sugar Company Records, Bentley Historical Library, University of Michigan, Ann Arbor; N. B. Bradley, "Sugar Beets—From the Factory Standpoint," *Michigan State Farmers' Institute, Winter of 1898–99* Bulletin 5 (Agricultural College, Mich.: State Board of Agriculture, 1899), 18–19.

42. Gutleben, *Sugar Tramp*, 29–30, 35, 38–39, 43–45, 50, 54, 61–62, 65; "Michigan," *The Sugar Beet* 19 (July 1898), 64; "Michigan," *The Sugar Beet* (September 1898): 87; "The Beet Sugar Industry," *STJ* 23 (January 1899): 5.

43. Michigan, Census of the State of Michigan, 1894, Vol. I, *Population, Births, Marriages and Deaths* (Lansing: Robert Smith & Co., 1896), 45.

44. *PP*, 8 March 1901; *PP*, 7 June 1901.

45. Gutleben, *Sugar Tramp*, 203–4.

46. The following is a partial list of the cities and towns that boosted for a factory of their own: Bad Axe, Cass City, Vassar, Sault Sainte Marie, Grand Rapids, Traverse City, Mason, Flint, Pinconning, St. Johns, Omer, Pontiac, Ann Arbor, Fowlerville, Caseville, Gaylord, Chesaning, Lapeer, Escorse, Portland, St. Clair, Big Rapids, Harbor Beach, Monroe, Port Austin, Scottsville, Kalkaska, Ishpeming, Cheboygan, Alpena, Gladstone, Ypsilanti, Manistique, Marquette, Houghton, Marinette, Escanaba, Battle Creek, Dundee, Chippewa, Racine, Green Bay, Howell, Muskegon, Orion, Jackson, Ludington, Pigeon, and Breckenridge. For more information, see Saylor, *Progress . . . in 1898*, 49; Charles Saylor, *Progress of the Beet-Sugar Industry in 1901* (Washington, D.C.: GPO, 1902), 28; Saylor, *Progress . . . in 1902*, 111–12; Saylor, *Progress . . . in 1903*, 34; also see "Projects for New Factories," *BSG*, 1898–1904.

47. In early 1899 the *STJ* reported that sugar beet companies had been formed in Port Huron, Jackson, Ludington, and Wayne County. "The Beet Sugar Industry," *STJ* 23.3 (January 1899): 5; "The Beet Sugar Industry," *STJ* 23.4 (January 1899): 5; "The Beet Sugar Industry," *STJ* 23.12 (March 1899): 5; "The Beet Sugar Industry," *STJ* 25.21 (May 1901): 5; "The Beet Sugar Industry," *STJ* 25.42 (October 1901): 5; "The Beet Sugar Industry," *STJ* 26.9 (February 1902): 7; "Projects for New Factories," *BSG* 4 (June 1902): 14.

48. Truman Palmer, *Beet Sugar Industry of the United States* (Washington, D.C.; The United States Beet Sugar Industry, 1913).

49. Michigan, Census of the State of Michigan, 1894, Vol. 2 *Agriculture, Manufactories and Fisheries* (Lansing: Robert Smith & Co., 1896), 522–24.

50. Ibid., 530–35.

51. Michigan Bureau of Labor and Industrial Statistics, *Twenty-Fourth Annual Report* (Lansing: Wynkoop Hallenbeck Crawford Co., 1907).

52. *TCA*, 21 April 1900; *AR*, 18 October 1901; *TCA*, 16 September 1904.

53. Hazel Arnold Trumble, *Sanilac County History, 1834–1934* (Croswell, Mich.: Hazel Arnold Trumble, 1984).

54. Gutleben, *Sugar Tramp*, 5.

55. "No Real Cause for Alarm," *BSG* 4 (October 1902): 216; Smith, *Reciprocity with Cuba*, 235 and 237.

56. Michigan Bureau of Labor and Industrial Statistics, *Nineteenth Annual Report*, 7.

57. Ibid., 6.

58. Sidney Mintz, *Sweetness and Power: The Place of Sugar in Modern History* (New York: Viking, 1985), 185.

59. Roy G. Blakey, *The United States Beet-Sugar Industry and the Tariff* (New York: Longmans, Green and Co., 1912); Percy Bidwell, *Tariff Policy of the United States: A Study of Recent Experience* (New York: Royal Institute of International Affairs, 1933).

60. Herbert Myrick, *A Memorial to the Congress of the United States From the League of Domestic Producers, The Crisis in Agriculture: Being a Statement of the Peril to Domestic Industry, to Agriculture, Labor and Capital* (Chicago and New York: Orange Judd Co., 1900).

61. LaFeber, *The Cambridge History of American Foreign Relations*, 152.

62. Henry T. Oxnard, U.S. Senate, Hearings Before the Committee on Pacific Islands and Puerto Rico, *To Provide a Government for the Island of Puerto Rico and for Other Purposes*, 56th Congress, 1st Session (Washington, D.C.: GPO, 1900), 142. [hereafter *To Provide a Government for the Island of Puerto Rico*]

63. "The American Beet Sugar Manufacturers Association," *BSG* 1 (December 1899): 5.

64. "Business, Not Sentiment, In National Policy," *BSG* 1 (January 1900): 8.

65. "Reject the Treaties!" *BSG* 1 (February 1900): 11. The original quotation is taken from *Gunton's Magazine*, October 1899.

66. Myrick, *A Memorial to the Congress of the United States From the League of Domestic Producers*.

67. Frank Rutter, "The Sugar Question in the United States," *Quarterly Journal of Economics* 17.1 (November 1902): 44–81; Carmen Diana Deere, "Here Come the Yankees! The Rise and Decline of United States Colonies in Cuba," *Hispanic American Historical Review* 78.4 (1998): 729–65.

68. "Tariff Against Dependencies Not Unconstitutional," *BSG* 1 (February 1900): 11–14.

69. Henry T. Oxnard, *To Provide a Government for the Island of Puerto Rico*, 153.

70. Laird Bergad, "Agrarian History of Puerto Rico, 1870–1930," *Latin American Research Review* 13.3 (1978): 74.

71. Oxnard, *To Provide a Government for the Island of Puerto Rico*, 147.

72. Ibid., 164.

73. "FREE SUGAR KILLED," *BSG* 2 (March 1900): 1.

74. Walter L. Wilkins, "United States Indian Policy and the Debate over Philippine Annexation: Implications for the Origins of American Imperialism," *Journal of American History* 66.4 (1980): 810–31; Efren Rivera-Ramos, "The Legal Construction of American Colonialism: The Insular Cases, 1901–1922," *Revista Juridica de la Universidad de Puerto Rico* 65 (1996): 225–328.

75. *Downes v. Bidwell*, 182 U.S., 341–42.

76. LaFeber, *The Cambridge History of American Foreign Relations*, 143–44. Also see John L. Offner, *An Unwanted War: The Diplomacy of the United States and Spain Over Cuba, 1895–1898* (Chapel Hill: University of North Carolina Press, 1992), 189.

77. F. W. Taussig, "The United States Tariff Act of 1897," 594.

78. W. Jett Lauck, "The Political Significance of Reciprocity," *Journal of Political Economy* 12.4 (September 1904): 521.

79. Quoted in Jenks, *Our Cuban Colony*, 133; Stanley Lebergott, "The Returns to U.S. Imperialism, 1890–1929," *Journal of Economic History* 40.2 (June 1980): 229–52.

80. Rutter, "The Sugar Question," 71.

81. W. L. Churchill, *Reciprocity with Cuba*, 472.

82. "Misplaced Sympathy," *BSG* 3 (December 1901): 254–55.

83. "A Presumptuous Child," *BSG* 3 (December 1901): 255.

84. F. R. Hathaway, *Reciprocity with Cuba*, 225.

85. Henry T. Oxnard, *Reciprocity with Cuba*, 173.

86. Harvey W. Wiley, *Reciprocity with Cuba*, 508.

87. "A Premium on Indolence," *BSG* 3 (January 1902): 295.

88. "Save the Farmer and the Manufacturer," *BSG* 3 (November 1901): 221.

89. Henry T. Oxnard, *Reciprocity with Cuba*, 184.

90. N. H. Stewart, *Reciprocity with Cuba*, 210.

91. For example, see the testimony of Col. James D. Hill, *Reciprocity with Cuba*, 259.

92. The testimony was reprinted in the *BSG*. See, H. W. Wiley, "Cane and Beet Sugar," *BSG* 4 (March 1902): 18–21.

93. Ibid., 19.

94. Ibid., 20.

95. H. W. Wiley "Cane and Beet Sugar," *BSG* 4 (July 1902): 142.

96. Stewart, *Reciprocity with Cuba*, 221.

97. "Congress Sacrifices Domestic Sugar in the Interest of Cuban Planters and of the Sugar Trust," *BSG* 5 (November 1903), 389.

98. "The Beet Sugar Industry Must Weather the Storm," *BSG* 5 (December 1903): 410.

99. "Annual Convention of the American Beet Sugar Association," *BSG* 6 (April 1904): 151. On the Philippines and race, see Paul Kramer, *The Blood of Government: Race, Empire, the United States and the Philippines* (Chapel Hill: University of North Carolina Press, 2006).

100. "Mistaken Policy of the President on the Philippine Question," *ASI and BSG* 7 (December 1905): 518.

101. "The American Beet Sugar Industry in 1905," *ASI and BSG* 7 (December 1905): 527.

102. Truman Palmer, U.S. Senate, Hearings Before the Committee on the Philippines, *Revenue for the Philippine Islands,* U.S. Senate, 59th Congress, 1st Session (Washington, D.C.: GPO, 1906), 884; also see "Annual Convention of the American Beet Sugar Association," *BSG* 6 (April 1904): 151.

103. "Annual Convention of the American Beet Sugar Association," *BSG* 6 (April 1904): 151.

104. "The New Menace to the American Sugar Industry," *ASI and BSG* 7 (January 1905): 2.

105. Truman Palmer, "American Sugar Industry and the Philippines," *ASI and BSG* 8 (1906): 535.

106. F. R. Hathaway, *Revenue for the Philippine Islands,* 906.

107. Truman Palmer, *Revenue for the Philippine Islands,* 849.

108. "The Cuban Reciprocity Blunder," *ASI and BSG* 9 (January 1907): 68.

109. Truman Palmer, "American Sugar Industry and the Philippines," *ASI and BSG* 8 (1906): 534.

110. "The New Tariff Act Now in Effect, *ASI and BSG* 11 (August 1909): 324–27; George M. Fisk, "The Payne-Aldrich Tariff," *Political Science Quarterly* 25.1 (March 1910): 35–68.

111. "Memorandum on Recent American Legislation Affecting Philippine Economic Life—I" (Institute of Pacific Relations, American Council) 3.19 (October 1934).

112. Mintz, *Sweetness and Power,* 188.

113. Ibid., 188.

114. Roy G. Blakey, "The Proposed Sugar Tariff," *Political Science Quarterly* 28.2 (June 1913): 236.

115. "FREE SUGAR KILLED," *BSG* 2 (March 1900): 1; "Who Wants Reciprocity?" *BSG* 4 (December 1902): 308; "Congress Sacrifices Domestic Sugar in the Interest of Cuban Planters and the Sugar Trust," *BSG* 5 (November 1903): 389.

116. Roy G. Blakey, "Beet Sugar and the Tariff," *Journal of Political Economy* 21.6 (June 1913): 543.

117. "The Beet Sugar Industry," *STJ* 25.8 (February 1901): 5; "The Beet Sugar Industry," *STJ* 25.7 (February 1901): 5; "From Field and Factory," *BSG* 3 (September 1901): 172.

118. *TCA,* 28 March 1902; "From Field and Factory," *BSG* 6 (April 1904): 138; Gutleben, *Sugar Tramp,* 67.

119. "The Beet Sugar Industry," *STJ* 24.18 (May 1900): 5; "The Beet Sugar Industry,"

STJ 27.16 (April 1903): 5; "From Field and Factory," *ASI and BSG* 6 (November 1904): 412–13; "From Field and Factory," *ASI and BSG* 7 (February 1905): 82; Saylor, *Progress . . . in 1903*, 139–46; Charles Saylor, *Progress of the Beet-Sugar Industry in 1904* (Washington, D.C.: GPO, 1905), 6; Charles Saylor, *Progress of the Beet-Sugar Industry in 1909* (Washington, D.C.: GPO, 1910), 31.

120. "Pineland's Michigan Budget," *The Sugar Beet* 26 (November 1905): 192.
121. *TCA*, 29 December 1905.
122. Charles Saylor, *Reciprocity with Cuba*, 526.

Chapter 2. Contract Farming in Rural Michigan

1. "The American Beet Sugar Manufacturers Association," *Beet Sugar Gazette*, 1 (December 1899): 5. [hereafter *BSG*]
2. W. L. Churchill to Henry Lancashire, Bay City, Mich., 2 February 1900, Box 1, Michigan Sugar Company Records, Bentley Historical Library, University of Michigan, Ann Arbor.
3. For a discussion of capitalism in the countryside, see Steven Hahn and Jonathan Prude, eds. *The Countryside in the Age of Capitalist Transformation: Essays in the Social History of Rural America* (Chapel Hill: University of North Carolina Press, 1985); Alan Kulikoff, "The Transition to Capitalism in Rural America," *William and Mary Quarterly* (January 1989): 120–44; Christopher Clark, *The Roots of Rural Capitalism: Western Massachusetts, 1780–1860* (Ithaca, N.Y.: Cornell University Press, 1990); Victoria Saker Woeste, *The Farmer's Benevolent Trust: Law and Agricultural Cooperation in Industrial America, 1865–1945* (Chapel Hill: University of North Carolina Press, 1998).
4. Lew Allen Chase, *Rural Michigan* (New York: Macmillan, 1922), 235–89.
5. David B. Danbom, *Born in the Country: A History of Rural America* (Baltimore: Johns Hopkins University Press, 1995), 134.
6. Charles Saylor, *Progress of the Beet-Sugar Industry in 1903* (Washington, D.C.: GPO, 1904), 26.
7. U.S. Bureau of the Census, Thirteenth Census of the United States, 1910, Vol. 6, *Agriculture, Reports by States, Alabama-Montana* (Washington, D.C.: GPO, 1913), 767.
8. Richard Illenden Bonner, ed., *Memoirs of Lenawee County Michigan*, Vol. 1 (Madison, Wisc.: Western Historical Association, 1909), 668–69.
9. Joseph George Duncan, "The Michigan Farmer: A Century of Agricultural Journalism, 1843–1943," M.A. thesis, Michigan State College, 1950; Lew Allen Chase, *Rural Michigan*; Bureau of Labor and Industrial Statistics, *Annual Reports* (Lansing: Robert Smith Printing Company, 1898–1907).
10. "Long Term Contracts," *The Sugar Beet* 20 (January 1899): 9.
11. J. W. Cochrane, "Sugar Beets From a Farmer's Standpoint," *Michigan State Farmers' Institutes, Winter of 1900–1901*, Bulletin 7 (Agricultural College, Mich.: State Board of Agriculture, 1901), 30–32.

12. Michigan Bureau of Labor and Industrial Statistics, *Seventeenth Annual Report* (Lansing: Robert Smith Printing Co., 1900), 97.

13. *Alma Record*, 30 March 1900 [hereafter *AR*]; *Pigeon Progress*, 7 June 1901 [hereafter *PP*]; *PP*, 1 August 1902; *Tuscola County Advertiser*, 24 February 1899 [hereafter *TCA*]; *TCA*, 21 December 1900; "From Field and Factory," *BSG* 2 (March 1902): 28; "The Beet Sugar Industry," *Weekly Statistical Sugar Trade Journal* 27.3 (January 1903): 7 [hereafter *STJ*]; *AR*, 23 January 1903.

14. "Take the Advice of Experienced Growers," *BSG* 2 (October 1900): 3; "From Field and Factory," *BSG* 3 (October 1901): 190; J. Y. Clark Orion, "Sugar Beets—From the Farmer's Standpoint," *Michigan State Farmers' Institute, Winter of 1898–1899*, Bulletin 5 (Agricultural College, Mich.: State Board of Education), 15.

15. "Among the Beet Growers," *BSG* 2 (January 1901): 26.

16. "Report of the State Round-Up," *Michigan State Farmers' Institutes, Winter of 1898–1899*, Bulletin 5 (Agricultural College, Mich.: State Board of Education, 1899), 14; "State of Michigan Appoints Sugar Officials," *BSG* 1 (October 1899): 20; "Weighing Beets in Michigan," *BSG* 1 (February 1900): 17; N. B. Bradley, "Sugar Beets—From the Factory Standpoint," *Michigan State Farmers' Institutes, Winter of 1898–1899*, Bulletin 5 (Agricultural College, Mich.: State Board of Education, 1899), 21; J. W. Locke, "Sugar Beet Growing," *Michigan State Farmers' Institutes, Winter of 1898–1899*, Bulletin 5 (Agricultural College, Mich.: State Board of Education, 1899), 175; "From Michigan," *The Sugar Beet* 20 (December 1899): 175.

17. Originally printed in the *Mount Clemens Monitor*, reprinted in "From Field and Factory," *BSG* 3 (September 1901): 176.

18. Originally printed in the *Allegan Gazette*, reprinted in "Field Notes," *BSG* 2 (October 1900): 20.

19. *TCA*, 26 July 1901; *TCA*, 22 May 1903.

20. *TCA*, 30 August 1902; "Communicated," *BSG* 4 (September 1902): 200.

21. "Michigan," *BSG* 4 (December 1902): 285; Charles Saylor, *Progress of the Beet-Sugar Industry in 1900* (Washington, D.C.: GPO, 1901) 46; Charles Saylor, *Progress of the Beet-Sugar Industry in 1902* (Washington, D.C.: GPO, 1903), 131–32; Charles Saylor, *Progress of the Beet-Sugar Industry in 1903* (Washington, D.C.: GPO, 1904), 139–46.

22. "The Beet Sugar Industry," *STJ* 23.43 (October 1899): 5; "Bay City, Mich." *BSG* 1 (August 1899): 26; Michigan, *Fifty-Eighth Annual Report of the Commissioner of the Land Office of the State of Michigan* (Lansing: Wynkoop Hallenbeck Crawford Co., 1900), 16.

23. "The Beet Sugar Industry," *STJ* 23.43 (October 1899): 5; "The Beet Sugar Industry," *STJ* 24.18 (March 1900): 5; "The Beet Sugar Industry," *STJ* 24.20 (May 1900): 5; "The Beet Sugar Industry," *STJ* 24.18 (May 1900): 6.

24. "Sugar Beet Notes," *Louisiana Planter and Sugar Manufacturer* 23 (February 1899); For more on delays, see "Michigan," *The Sugar Beet* 20 (July 1899): 87; "From Michigan," *The Sugar Beet* 20 (December 1899): 175; *TCA*, 3 November 1901; *PP*, 29 November 1901; *TCA*, 13 December 1901; *PP*, 5 December 1902; *AR*, 26 December 1902.

25. "Lessons of the Benton Harbor Failure," *BSG* 3 (September 1901): 153.
26. *TCA*, 7 December 1900.
27. "Beet Sugar in Michigan," *BSG* 2 (November 1900): 13; Michigan, *Fifty-Eighth Annual Report*, 17.
28. "The Beet Sugar Industry," *STJ* 24.14 (April 1900): 5.
29. Michigan, *Seventeenth Annual Report*, 98.
30. "The Beet Sugar Industry," *STJ* 23.36 (September 1898): 5; "The Beet Sugar Industry," *STJ* 24.9 (March 1900): 5.
31. Michigan, *Fifty-Eighth Annual Report*, 16.
32. Special Bicentennial Issue, *Sugar Beet Journal*, 40.1 (Summer/Fall) 1976.
33. "The Beet Sugar Industry," *STJ* 23.52 (December 1899): 5.
34. "Field Notes," *BSG* 1 (February 1900): 26–27; "Field Notes," *BSG* 2 (August 1900): 5.
35. "The Beet Sugar Industry," *STJ* 24.4 (January 1900): 5; "Beet Sugar Notes," *Louisiana Planter and Sugar Manufacturer* 25 (February 1900): 75.
36. "Field Notes," *BSG* 1 (February 1900): 26–27.
37. *New York Times*, 13 December 1899.
38. "The Beet Sugar Industry," *STJ* 24.4 (January 1900): 5; "Weighing Beets in Michigan," *BSG* 1 (February 1900): 17.
39. "The Relation of Factory to Farm in the Beet Sugar Industry," *Michigan State Farmers' Institutes, Winter of 1899–1900*, Bulletin 6 (Agricultural College, Mich.: State Board of Agriculture), 95.
40. Ibid., 95–96.
41. Ibid., 98.
42. "Field Notes," *BSG* 2 (March 1900): 21.
43. W. L. Churchill to Henry Lancashire, Bay City, Michigan, 2 February 1900, Box 1, Michigan Sugar Company Records, Bentley Historical Library, Ann Arbor, Michigan.
44. Ibid.
45. "Beet Sugar Notes," *Louisiana Planter and Sugar Manufacturer* 25 (December 1900): 409.
46. "Offers for the Season of 1900," *BSG* 2 (April 1900): 18.
47. "The Sugar Beet Acreage," *BSG* 1 (June 1899): 6; "The Beet Sugar Industry," *STJ* 23.9 (May 1899): 5.
48. C. D. Smith, "Question Box," *Michigan State Farmers' Institutes, Winter of 1898–1899*, Bulletin 5 (Agricultural College, Mich.: State Board of Education, 1899).
49. "The Beet Sugar Industry," *STJ* 24.51 (December 1900): 5; "Notes of the Campaign," *BSG* 2 (January 1901): 19. For a discussion of the 1900 agreements, see "Offers for the Season of 1900," *BSG* 2 (April 1900): 18.
50. *PP*, 31 January 1902; *PP*, 26 December 1902; *PP*, 23 January 1903; *PP*, 2 January 1903; *PP*, 16 October 1903.

51. Dan Gutleben, *The Sugar Tramp—1945: Michigan* (San Francisco: Bay Cities Duplicating Co., 1954), 56.

52. Michigan Bureau of Labor and Industrial Statistics, *Twenty-Fourth Annual Report* (Lansing: Wynkoop Hallenbeck and Crawford Co., 1907), 8.

53. Ibid., 448.

54. *PP,* 31 January 1902.

55. *AR,* 16 January 1903; "The Beet Sugar Industry," *STJ* 27.4 (January 1903): 7; *TCA,* 13 February 1903.

56. "The Beet Sugar Industry," *STJ* 27.4 (January 1903): 7; "The Beet Sugar Industry," *STJ* 28.35 (August 1904): 5; *AR,* 9 September 1904.

57. "The Beet Sugar Industry," *STJ* 27.2 (January 1903): 7.

58. *TCA,* 23 January 1903; *TCA,* 30 January 1903.

59. "The Beet Sugar Industry," *STJ* 27.1 (January 1903): 9; *AR,* 23 January 1903; *AR,* 24 February 1902.

60. *AR,* 23 January 1903.

61. "From Field and Factory," *BSG* 5 (February 1903): 78; "Soliciting Sugar Beet Acreage," *BSG* 5 (April 1903): 120.

62. "From Field and Factory," *The American Sugar Industry and Beet Sugar Gazette* 6 (December 1904): 432. [hereafter *ASI* and *BSG*]

63. *AR,* 13 December 1901.

64. *AR,* 20 February 1903.

65. *TCA,* 30 January 1903; *TCA,* 2 September 1904.

66. *TCA,* 13 March 1903.

67. "Miscellaneous," *BSG* 5 (April 1903): 151; "The Beet Sugar Industry," *STJ* 27.4 (March 1903): 5.

68. "A Suggestion to Business Men," *BSG* 5 (February 1903): 65.

69. Ibid.

70. *AR,* 6 February 1903.

71. *PP,* 30 January 1903.

72. *PP,* 6 March 1903; *PP,* 23 October 1903; "From Field and Factory," *BSG* 6 (January 1904): 37.

73. *PP,* 24 April 1903.

74. "The Beet Sugar Industry," *STJ* 27.3 (April 1903): 7; "From Field and Factory," *BSG* 5 (June 1903): 214; "From Field and Factory," *BSG* 5 (March 1903): 113; "The Reader's Forum," *BSG* 6 (March 1904): 95.

75. Federal Trade Commission, *Report on the Beet Sugar Industry in the United States* (Washington, D.C.: GPO, 1917), 30.

76. *TCA,* 5 February 1904; *AR,* 11 March 1904.

77. "From Field and Factory," *BSG* 6 (January 1904): 36; "From Field and Factory," *BSG* 6 (December 1904): 432–34.

78. *TCA,* 9 September 1904; *PP,* 9 September 1904; *PP,* 16 September 1904.

79. Michigan Bureau of Labor and Industrial Statistics, *Twenty-Second Annual Report* (Lansing: Wynkoop Hallenbeck Crawford Co., 1905), 414–18.

80. Ibid., 418.

81. *TCA*, 5 October 1906.

82. "From Field and Factory," *BSG* 6 (October 1904): 378; "From Field and Factory," *BSG* 6 (November 1904): 413; "Prizes for Beet Growers," *BSG* 7 (February 1905): 99; *TCA*, 10 November 1905; A. B. Cook, "Making Money from Sugar Beets," *Michigan State Farmers' Institute, Winter of 1905–1906*, Bulletin 12 (Agricultural College, Mich.: State Board of Agriculture, 1906), 41.

83. William M. Doyle, "Capital Structure and the Financial Development of the U.S. Sugar-Refining Industry, 1875–1905," *Journal of Economic History* 60.1 (March 2000): 205–6.

84. "The Beet Sugar Industry," *STJ* 28.34 (August 1904): 5; *PP*, 8 July 1904; *AR*, 8 July 1904.

85. "Merger of Michigan Beet Sugar Factories," *ASI and BSG* 8 (1906): 388.

86. *TCA*, 26 June 1903.

87. "Beet Sugar Possibilities," *ASI and BSG* 8 (1906): 403.

88. Article originally printed in the *Grand Rapids Herald*. Reprinted in "Merger of Michigan Beet Sugar Factories," *ASI and BSG* 8 (1906): 388.

89. "Beet Sugar Possibilities," *ASI and BSG* 8 (1906): 403.

90. Originally printed in *Flint Democrat*. "Beet Sugar Syndicate in Michigan," *ASI and BSG* 8 (1906): 417.

91. "Michigan Sugar Company's Splendid Showing," *ASI and BSG* 10 (June 1908): 225; "Michigan Sugar Company Prosperous," *ASI and BSG* 11 (August 1909): 340.

92. "Sugar History in Michigan," *ASI and BSG* 11 (October 1909): 458–59.

93. "Michigan Sugar Company Reports Profitable Year," *ASI and BSG* 12 (June 1910): 225.

94. Originally in *National Farmer*, Bay City, Michigan. Reprinted in "Gleaned Elsewhere," *The Sugar Beet* 29 (April 1908): 341–42.

95. *AR*, 6 February 1907; *AR*, 20 February 1907; *AR*, 27 February 1907; *PP*, 24 November 1905; *TCA*, 12 January 1906; *TCA*, 26 January 1906; *TCA*, 7 December 1906; *TCA*, 5 July 1907; *TCA*, 13 December 1907.

96. *PP*, 18 November 1910; *PP*, 10 December 1910; *TCA*, 16 December 1910; "Swore Sugar Company Paid Forty Percent," *Michigan Business Farming: The First Crop Reporter and Market Guide Ever Published Solely in the Interest of Those Who Make a Business Tilling the Soil for Profit!* 1 (May 1913): 5. [hereafter *MBF*]

97. *PP*, 10 January 1908.

98. *PP*, 11 January 1907; *PP*, 15 March 1907.

99. *PP*, 11 January 1907.

100. Nathan D. Simpson, "Religious, Social, Educational, and Farmers' Organizations," *Michigan State Farmers' Institute Season of 1912–1913*, Bulletin 19 (Agricultural College, Mich.: State Board of Agriculture, 1913), 43.

101. Lew Allen Chase, *Rural Michigan* (New York: MacMillan, 1922), 341–43.

102. "Editorial—The Decision," *MBF* 1 (October 1912).

103. "Agricultural Economics," *The Gleaner* 17 (November 1911): 8.

104. "Does the Farmer Get the High Price of Sugar," *The Gleaner* 17 (October 1911): 22.

105. "Michigan," *STJ* 34.12 (March 1910): 89; "The Beet Sugar Industry," *STJ* 34.51 (December 1910): 511; "The Beet Sugar Industry," *STJ* 35.3 (January 1911): 29.

106. "Whereas, We . . .," *The Gleaner* 17 (January 1911): 28.

107. Victor C. Woods Sr., *Thoughtful for the Future: A History of the Gleaners* (Detroit: The Gleaner Life Insurance Society), 1993; Lowell K. Dyson, *Farmers' Organizations* (New York: Greenwood Press, 1986), 30–32; (Emphasis in original) "BEET GROWER! TIME TO ACT!" *The Gleaner* 17 (October 1911): 5.

108. "Can the Farmer Afford to Grow Beets?" *The Gleaner* 17 (May 1911): 29; "The Tip—The Farmers' End of the Sugar Beet," *The Gleaner* 18 (June 1912): 6 and 20.

109. *PP*, 2 December 1910.

110. *TCA*, 16 December 1910; *AR*, 1 December 1912, "The Farmer's Forum," *The Gleaner* 17 (February 1911): 37.

111. *PP*, 20 October 1911; *TCA*, 20 October 1911; "The Tip," *The Gleaner* 18 (June 1912): 6.

112. James L. Howell, *History of the Michigan Sugar Company, Caro Michigan*, 1 May 1948, Clipping Files, Sugar Beet, Library of Michigan.

113. "For the Protection of Sugar Beet Growers," *The Gleaner* 17 (March 1911): 39.

114. Annual Report to the Stockholders, 1906–1909, German-American Sugar Company Records, Bay County Historical Society, Bay City, Michigan; "From Field and Factory," *ASI and BSG* 8 (1906): 204.

115. "From Field and Factory," *ASI and BSG* 8 (1906): 122 and 142; "Michigan," *ASI and BSG* 12 (1910): 162.

116. "Auto Displaces Horse in the Beet Sugar Industry in Michigan," *ASI and BSG* 11 (March 1909): 153.

117. "Making Sugar in Michigan," *ASI and BSG* 10 (August 1908): 341.

118. "From Field and Factory," *ASI and BSG* 11 (February 1909): 72.

119. *TCA*, 20 October 1911; *TCA*, 24 November 1911.

120. "Gleaner's Section," *The Gleaner* 17 (May 1911): 27; "The Beet Sugar Industry," *STJ* 35.14 (April 1911): 173.

121. *TCA*, 10 October 1913; "The Beet Sugar Industry," *STJ* 35.13 (March 1911): 133.

122. "Agriculture on a Fifty-Fifty Basis," *GBF* 23 (December 1916): 91.

123. Clipping File, Michigan Sugar Company Records, Michigan State University Archives, East Lansing.

Chapter 3. Family Farms, Child Labor, and Migrant Families

1. Charles Saylor, *Special Report on the Beet-Sugar Industry in the United States* (Washington, D.C.: GPO, 1898), 204.

2. For the local perspective on this labor shortage, see *Pigeon Progress*, 14 June 1902 [hereafter *PP*]; *Tuscola County Advertiser*, 27 March 1903 [hereafter *TCA*]; *PP*, 3 April 1903; *TCA*, 10 July 1903; *PP*, 22 April 1904; *TCA*, 27 May 1904; *TCA*, 9 September 1904; *TCA*, 21 July 1905; *PP*, 28 July 1905; *PP*, 21 September 1906; *PP*, 2 November 1906.

3. L. W. Oviatt, "Points on Labor Saving," *Michigan State Farmers' Institute, Winter of 1904–1905*, Bulletin 11 (Agricultural College, Mich.: State Board of Education, 1905), 13.

4. U.S. Bureau of the Census, Thirteenth Census of the United States, 1910, Vol. 6, *Agriculture, Reports by States, Alabama—Montana* (Washington, D.C.: GPO, 1913), 780.

5. E. A. Goldenweiser, U.S. Department of Agriculture, *Atlas of Agriculture—Part IX Rural Population and Organizations* (Washington, D.C.: GPO, 1919).

6. "Correcting Misapprehensions," *Beet Sugar Gazette* 3 (July 1901): 117 [hereafter *BSG*]; U.S. Industrial Commission, *Reports*, Vol. 10, *Report of the Industrial Commission on Agriculture and Agricultural Labor* (Washington, D.C.: GPO, 1901), 532–33, 546–47, and 574–75. [hereafter *Industrial Commission*]

7. Mary Neth, *Preserving the Family Farm: Women, Community and the Foundations of Agribusiness in the Rural Midwest, 1900–1940* (Baltimore: Johns Hopkins University Press, 1995), chapter 1.

8. Nathan Bradley, U.S. House of Representatives, Hearings Before Committee On Ways and Means, *Reciprocity with Cuba*, 57th Congress, 1st Session (Washington, D.C.: GPO, 1902), 235 and 334.

9. W. L. Churchill, *Reciprocity with Cuba*, 473.

10. *PP*, 18 November 1904; *PP*, 2 December 1904; *PP*, 13 October 1905; *PP*, 10 October 1907; *PP*, 18 October 1907; *PP*, 23 October 1908; *PP*, 30 October 1908; *PP*, 6 November 1908.

11. Originally printed in the *Cadillac News Express*, Cadillac, Michigan, reprinted in "Field and Factory," *BSG* 5 (December 1903): 426.

12. For example, see *AR*, 2 February 1907; *AR*, 20 February 1907; *AR*, 27 February 1907; *AR*, 6 March 1907.

13. *AR*, 6 March 1907.

14. As with most migrant labor populations, it is difficult to precisely estimate the numbers working in the fields. However, federal and state agencies, as well as private reform groups and locals, published reports detailing the figures for specific areas and for specific years. In 1911 the *TCA* reported that 7,500 out of twelve thousand acres of sugar beet in the area were being tended by migrant workers. In 1923, a National Child Labor Committee study of Michigan found that 59 percent of all growers tended their own fields. See Walter W. Armentrout, Sara A. Brown, and Charles E. Gibbons, *Child Labor in the Sugar Beet Fields of Michigan*, Publication No. 310 (New York: National Child Labor Committee, 1923), 13; A 1923 Children's Bureau study estimated that 35 percent of all farmers growing sugar beet tended to their own fields. See U.S. Children's Bureau, *Child Labor and the Work of Mothers*

in the Beet Fields of Colorado and Michigan, Bureau Publication No. 115 (Washington, D.C.: GPO, 1923), 80. Also see Michigan Bureau of Labor and Industrial Statistics, *Twenty-Second Annual Report* (Lansing: Wynkoop Hallenbeck Crawford Co., 1905).

15. Charles Smith, *Industrial Commission*, CI; Saylor, *Progress of the Beet-Sugar Industry in 1899*, (Washington, D.C.: GPO, 1900), 47.

16. "Discussion," *Michigan State Farmers' Institute, Winter of 1898–1899*, Bulletin 5 (Agricultural College, Mich.: State Board of Education, 1899), 18.

17. J. Y. Clark Orion, "Sugar Beets—From the Farmer's Standpoint," *Michigan State Farmers' Institute, Winter of 1898–1899*, 16.

18. C. D. Smith, "Sugar Beets: A Word of Encouragement and a Word of Caution," *Michigan State Farmers' Institute, Winter of 1898–1899*, 22–23.

19. Saylor, *Special Report*, 14.

20. Michigan, *Twenty-Second Annual Report*, 314–48.

21. For a discussion of hired hands, see David E. Schob, *Hired Hands and Plowboys: Farm Labor in the Midwest, 1815–1860* (Urbana: University of Illinois Press, 1975), 254–72; Jon Gjerde, *The Minds of the West: Ethnocultural Evolution in the Rural Middle West, 1830–1917* (Chapel Hill: University of North Carolina Press, 1997), 146–50; Neth, *Preserving the Family Farm*, 79–80.

22. Charles Saylor, *Progress of the Beet-Sugar Industry in the United States in 1900* (Washington, D.C.: GPO, 1901), 19.

23. "Field Notes," *BSG* 1 (June 1899): 21.

24. *AR*, 13 September 1901; J. F. Thissell, "Beet Farming in Michigan," *BSG* 2 (February 1901): 13.

25. For an excellent discussion of the labor padrone system in agriculture, see David Vaught, "An Orchardist's Point of View: Harvest Labor Relations on a California Almond Ranch, 1892–1921," *Agricultural History* 69 (Fall 1995): 563–91; Gunther Peck, "Reinventing Free Labor: Immigrant Padrones and Contract Laborers in North America, 1885–1925," *Journal of American History* 83 (December 1996): 848–71; Cindy Hahamovitch, *The Fruits of Their Labor: Atlantic Coast Farmworkers and the Making of Migrant Poverty, 1870–1945* (Chapel Hill: University of North Carolina Press, 1997), 38–54.

26. Smith, *Industrial Commission*, 574.

27. *PP*, 14 June 1902; "From Field and Factory," *BSG* 3 (August 1901): 143–47.

28. "Field Notes," *BSG* 2 (May 1900): 19–20.

29. *PP*, 27 June 1902.

30. *Lansing State Journal*, 22 July 1903.

31. Smith, *Industrial Commission*, 574.

32. "From Field and Factory," *BSG* 5 (May 1903): 180.

33. Thissell, "Beet Farming in Michigan," 13.

34. "From Field and Factory," *BSG* 5 (May 1903): 180; "The Beet Sugar Industry," *STJ* 27.21 (28 May 1903): 5; Gutleben, *Sugar Tramp*, 131.

35. *PP,* 18 November 1904; *PP,* 2 December 1904; *PP,* 13 October 1905; *PP,* 10 October 1907; *PP,* 18 October 1907; *PP,* 23 October 1908; *PP,* 30 October 1908; *PP,* 6 November 1908.

36. *TCA,* 5 July 1901.

37. *Lansing State Journal,* 22 July 1903.

38. *TCA,* 20 June 1902.

39. *PP,* 27 June 1902; *TCA,* 20 June 1902.

40. "Sugar Beet Colonies for Children," *BSG* 4 (July 1902): 123; "Children in Beet Fields," *BSG* 4 (August 1902): 153.

41. "Field Notes," *BSG* 1 (December 1899): 25.

42. "From Field and Factory," *BSG* 3 (August 1901): 143.

43. Michigan *Twenty-Second Annual Report,* 314–48.

44. "From Field and Factory," *BSG* 3 (August 1901): 147.

45. "Miscellaneous," *BSG* 5 (July 1903): 235.

46. "Don't Monkey with the Sugar Beet," *BSG* 5 (August 1903): 286.

47. R. C. Kedzie, *Industrial Commission,* 547.

48. *Industrial Commission,* CCLXII.

49. L. W. Oviatt, "Economy in Sugar Beet Production," *Michigan State Farmers' Institute, Winter of 1907–08,* Bulletin 14 (Agricultural College, Mich.: State Board of Education, 1908), 82.

50. *Industrial Commission,* 548.

51. "Beet Growing Near Tremont," *BSG* 1 (July 1899): 25; "Crop Reports," *BSG* 2 (July 1900): 16.

52. *Industrial Commission,* 531.

53. Ibid., 494.

54. Hahamovitch, *The Fruits of Their Labor,* 56–57.

55. Charles Saylor, "The Present Status of the American Beet Sugar Industry," *ASI and BSG* 7 (February 1905): 76.

56. Charles Saylor, *Progress of the Beet-Sugar Industry in the United States in 1901* (Washington, D.C.: GPO, 1902), 19. [hereafter *Progress . . . in 1901*]

57. Charles Saylor, *Progress of the Beet-Sugar Industry in 1902* (Washington, D.C.: GPO, 1903), 20–21. [hereafter *Progress . . . in 1902*]

58. R. S. Woodrow, "Soliciting Sugar Beet Acreage," *BSG* 5 (April 1903): 121.

59. David Montgomery, *The Fall of the House of Labor: the Workplace, the State, and American Labor Activism, 1865–1925* (Cambridge, U.K.: Cambridge University Press, 1987), 60; Gunther Peck, *Reinventing Free Labor: Padrones and Immigrant Workers in the North American West, 1880–1930* (Cambridge, U.K.: Cambridge University Press, 2000), 49–81.

60. *PP,* 28 February 1902; *PP,* 15 April 1904; "From Field and Factory," *BSG* (May

1904): 202; *PP*, 1 May 1908; *TCA*, 4 June 1909; *TCA*, 10 June 1910; *PP*, 4 February 1916.

61. Theresa Wolfson, "People Who Go to the Beets," *The American Child* 1 (November 1919), 218.

62. Ibid., 217.

63. "Field Notes," *BSG* 4 (May 1902): 89; Dan Gutleben, *Sugar Tramp—1954: Michigan* (San Francisco: Bay Cities Duplicating Co., 1955) 179; *PP*, 3 January 1902; *PP*, 28 February 1902; "Miscellaneous," *BSG* 5 (December 1903): 426; "The Beet Sugar Industry," *STJ* 27.21 (May 1903): 5; "The Beet Sugar Industry," *STJ* 28.14 (April 1904): 5; "The Beet Sugar Industry," *STJ* 28.21 (May 1904): 5.

64. *PP*, 18 May 1911.

65. *PP*, 11 March 1910.

66. For a local accounting of arrivals and departures of migrant families, see *PP*, 25 April 1902;" *PP*, 2 May 1902; *PP*, 12 December 1902; *PP*, 1 May 1903; *TCA*, 8 May 1903; *PP*, 4 December 1903; *TCA*, 26 February 1904; *TCA*, 13 May 1904; *PP*, 18 November 1904; "Miscellaneous" *ASI and BSG* 6 (November 1904): 416; *TCA*, 5 May 1905; *TCA*, 27 April 1906; *PP*, 24 April 1907; *PP*, 8 May 1907; *PP*, 1 November 1907; *PP*, 22 November 1907; *PP*, 6 November 1908; *TCA*, 30 April 1909; *PP*, 6 May 1910; *PP*, 2 June 1911; *PP*, 17 May 1912; *PP*, 23 May 1913.

67. *PP*, 12 December 1913; *TCA*, 19 December 1913; *TCA*, 24 December 1915.

68. *TCA*, 25 March 1904.

69. For a similar argument, see Peck, "Reinventing Free Labor," 848–71.

70. Armentrout et al., *Child Labor in the Sugar Beet Fields of Michigan*, 44–45.

71. Helen Eichstaedt, *Alla Lizzie: A Gripping Narration of the Love and Strength of a German/Russian Woman and her Family as they Survive Pre-Communist Russia and Struggle to Start a New Life in Early Twentieth Century America* (Ann Arbor, Mich.: Kennedy Associates, 1995), 94.

72. U.S. Children's Bureau, *Child Labor and the Work of Mothers*, 116–17.

73. *PP*, 25 July 1902.

74. Wolfson, "People Who Go to the Beets," 223.

75. *TCA*, 13 April 1906.

76. "Pineland's Michigan Budget," *The Sugar Beet* 26 (September 1905): 156.

77. Richard Sallet, *Russian-German Settlements in the United States* (Fargo: North Dakota Institute for Regional Studies, 1974), 110.

78. Hattie Plum Williams, "A Social History of the Russian German," *University Studies of the University of Nebraska* 16 (July 1916): 7.

79. Ibid., 8.

80. U.S. Bureau of the Census, *Thirteenth Census of the United States Taken in the Year 1910, Vol. 2, Population Reports by States, Alabama—Montana* (Washington, D.C.: GPO, 1913), 932, 936.

81. Eichstaedt, *Alla Lizzie*, 57.

82. Stockholders Report, 1906, German-American Sugar Company Records, Bay County Historical Society, Bay City, Michigan.
83. *TCA*, 20 February 1903.
84. *PP*, 8 November 1901.
85. *PP*, 1 May 1908.
86. Children's Bureau, *Child Labor and the Work of Mothers in the Beet Fields*, 83; For a discussion of race and ethnicity, see James R. Barrett and David Roediger, "Inbetween Peoples: Race, Nationality and the 'New Immigrant' Working Class," *Journal of American Ethnic History* 16 (Spring 1997): 3–44.
87. Wolfson, "People Who Go to the Beets," 222.
88. Armentrout et al., *Child Labor in the Sugar Beet Fields of Michigan*, 49.
89. Ibid., 6.
90. F. W. Taussig, "Beet Sugar and the Tariff," *Quarterly Journal of Economics* 26.2 (February 1912): 203.
91. Frank Tobias Higbie, *Indispensable Outcasts: Hobo Workers and Community in the American Midwest, 1880–1930* (Urbana: University of Illinois Press, 2003).
92. Wolfson, "People Who Go to the Beets," 223.
93. Armentrout et al., *Child Labor in the Sugar Beet Fields of Michigan*, 59.
94. *AR*, 25 May 1901.
95. *PP*, 24 May 1901.
96. Originally printed in the *Sebewaing Blade*, reprinted in *PP*, 24 October 1902. For other accounts of migrant families settling in Michigan, see *PP*, 27 November 1903 and "Miscellaneous," *BSG* 4 (November 1902): 287.
97. *PP*, 2 May 1902.
98. *PP*, 22 May 1903 and *TCA*, 8 May 1903.
99. *PP*, 9 January 1903.
100. *TCA*, 22 July 1904.
101. *TCA*, 29 July 1904; *PP*, 12 November 1909; *PP*, 1 September 1911.
102. *TCA*, 13 September 1907.
103. *PP*, 29 August 1913.
104. Originally printed in the *Sebewaing Blade*. Reprinted in the *PP*, 30 October 1903.
105. *TCA*, 3 October 1913.
106. *TCA*, 5 August 1910.
107. *PP*, 17 November 1911.
108. *PP*, 9 August 1918.
109. *PP*, 3 June 1910.
110. *PP*, 16 August 1912.
111. *Washington Post*, 20 May 1912.
112. *TCA*, 17 May 1912.
113. *TCA*, 24 May 1912.

114. Eichstaedt, *Alla Lizzie*, 57.

115. Jack Galzier and Arthur Wesley Helway, *Ethnicity in Michigan: Issues and Peoples* (East Lansing: Michigan State University Press, 2001), 25–27.

116. The following discussion is based on an analysis of the ninety-nine migrant households in Tuscola County and the 134 migrant households in Huron County listed in the 1910 Federal Manuscript Census Returns. Of the ninety-nine Tuscola County households, fifty lived next to other migrant families. In Huron County, seventy-eight of the 134 migrant households lived next to other migrant families. 1910 U.S. Federal Manuscript Census, Huron County, Sebewaing and Brookfield Townships, T624-649; 1910 U.S. Federal Manuscript Census, Tuscola County, Columbia Township, T624-676.

117. For migrant colonies, see Columbia Township, Tuscola County, and Sebewaing and Brookfield Townships, Huron County; Reymundo Cardenas, "The Mexican in Adrian," *Michigan History* 42 (September 1958): 343.

118. *PP*, 3 June 1910; *TCA*, 19 May 1916; *TCA*, 16 August 1912; *TCA*, 11 October 1912.

119. Eichstaedt, *Alla Lizzie*, 66–67.

120. *PP*, 5 May 1905; *TCA*, 20 November 1914; *TCA*, 15 January 1915.

121. Wolfson, "People Who Go to the Beets," 222; Children's Bureau, *Child Labor and the Work of Mothers*, 81, 114–15.

122. The average number of years migrants traveled to the fields was 4.9. See Armentrout et al., *Child Labor in the Sugar Beet Fields of Michigan*, 32.

123. Children's Bureau, *Child Labor and the Work of Mothers*, 2.

124. Carl Brablec, *Tales From the Headlands* (Roseville, Mich.: Prescott Press, 1971), 23; U.S. Children's Bureau, *Child Labor and the Work of Mothers*, 55.

125. Armentrout et al., *Child Labor in the Sugar Beet Fields of Michigan*, 14 and 32; Sonya Michel, *Children's Interests/Mother's Rights: The Shaping of America's Child Care Policy* (New Haven, Conn.: Yale University Press, 1999), 96.

126. Children's Bureau, *Child Labor and the Work of Mothers*, 111.

127. Ibid., 111.

128. Armentrout et al., *Child Labor in the Sugar Beet Fields of Michigan*, 23; In 1903, three German Russian women gave birth to children while aboard a specially chartered sugar beet train en route from Nebraska to Michigan. *PP*, 22 May 1903.

129. Wolfson, "People Who Go to the Beets," 224.

130. Armentrout et al., *Child Labor in the Sugar Beet Fields of Michigan*, 114.

131. U. S. Children's Bureau, *Child Labor and the Work of Mothers*, 113.

132. Armentrout et al., *Child Labor in the Sugar Beet Fields of Michigan*, 33.

133. U. S. Children's Bureau, *Child Labor and the Work of Mothers*, 113.

134. Wolfson, "People Who Go to the Beets," 221–22.

135. Armentrout et al., *Child Labor in the Sugar Beet Fields of Michigan*, 31–33.

136. Lew Allen Chase, *Rural Michigan* (New York: MacMillan, 1922), 294; John F. Thaden, "Ethnic Settlements in Rural Michigan," *Michigan Quarterly Bulletin* 29

(November 1946): 108; La Vern J. Rippley, "German Russians," *Harvard Encyclopedia of Ethnic Groups,* ed. Stephan Thernstrom (Cambridge, Mass.: Belknap Press of Harvard University, 1980), 427; Sallet, *Russian-German Settlements,* 49–54; Emily Greene Balch, *Our Slavic Citizens* (New York: Charities Publishing Committee, 1910), 320; Thomas Capek, *The Cechs (Bohemians) in American Life: A Study of Their National, Cultural, Political, Social and Religious Life* (New York: Houghton Mifflin Co., 1920), 81; Karen Johnson Freeze, "Czechs," *Harvard Encyclopedia of American Ethnic Groups,* ed. Stephen Thernstrom (Cambridge, Mass.: Belknap Press of Harvard University, 1980), 295; Children's Bureau, *Child Labor and the Work of Mothers,* 83; James M. Anderson and Iva A. Smith, eds., *Ethnic Groups in Michigan,* The Peoples of Michigan, Vol. 2 (Detroit: Ethos Press, 1983).

137. Armentrout et al., *Child Labor in the Sugar Beet Fields of Michigan,* 36; Brablec, *Tales from the Headlands,* 27; Eichstaedt, *Alla Lizzie,* 138, 115, 134, and 140.

138. La Vern Rippley, "The Other Frontier: Rural Germans and the Settlement of America," in *Immigrant America: European Ethnicity in the United States,* ed. Timothy Welch (New York: Garland, 1994); Sallet, *Russian-German Settlements,* 106; Eichstaedt, *Alla Lizzie,* 112, 124–25, 133; Kenneth D. Miller, *The Czecho-Slovak in America* (New York: George H. Doron Co., 1922), 112; Linda Schelbitzki Pickle, *Contented Among Strangers: Rural German-Speaking Women and Their Families in the Nineteenth-Century Midwest* (Urbana: University of Illinois Press, 1996), 133–45; La Vern Rippley, "German Russians," *Harvard Encyclopedia of American Ethnic Groups,* 426; Brablec, *Tales from the Headlands,* 39; Sylvia Kihn McCullough, "Tales from Wolf Creek,'" (M.A. thesis, University of Arizona, 1988), 100 and 250.

139. John F. Thaden, "Ethnic Settlements in Rural Michigan," *Michigan Agricultural Experiment Station Quarterly Bulletin* 29 (November 1946): 111.

140. Nancy Grey Osterud, "Gender and the Transition to Capitalism in Rural America," *Agricultural History* 67 (1993): 25.

Chapter 4. Farmers and the Great War

1. "Subscribe to the Liberty Loan," *The Gleaner* 24 (1 June 1917): 327; "Please Don't Say that You Cannot Buy at Least One Liberty Loan," *The Gleaner and Business Farmer* 25 (April 1918): 151. [hereafter *GBF*]

2. "Gleaners Will Do Their 'Bit,'" *The Gleaner* 24 (July 1917): 358; "Big Time at Richmond," *GBF* 25 (November 1917): 34; "Gleaner Medals Appreciated by Soldier Boys," *GBF* 25 (March 1918): 138.

3. Hugh Thomas, *Cuba: The Pursuit of Freedom* (New York: Harper & Row, 1971), 51.

4. "Soldiers of the Soil," *The Gleaner* 24 (July 1917): 342; "Beet Situation Calls for Federal Intervention: Time has Come for Mr. Hoover to Unseat Sugar Kings and See that Growers Get a Price Based on the Cost of Production," *The Gleaner* 25 (February 1918): 97.

268 · NOTES TO PAGES 98–101

5. Roy G. Blakey, "Sugar Prices and Distribution Under Food Control," *Quarterly Journal of Economics* 32.4 (1918): 569; Vincent Mahler, "The Political Economy of North-South Commodity Bargaining: The Case of the International Sugar Agreement," *International Organization* 38.4 (1984): 713.

6. "Mr. Farmer Gets the Blame, But Little Profit," *GBF* 23 (December 1916): 93.

7. "The Strong Arm," *GBF* 21 (November 1914): 12.

8. "Fat Dividends for Michigan Sugar Company," *Michigan Business Farming* 24 (August 1917): 4. [hereafter *MBF*]

9. *Tuscola County Advertiser*, 5 January 1917 [hereafter *TCA*]; *TCA*, 12 January 1917.

10. "Fat Dividends for Michigan Sugar Company," *MBF* 4 (August 1917): 4.

11. Federal Trade Commission, *Report on the Sugar Beet Industry in the United States*, (Washington, D.C.: GPO, 1917); "Editorial—Tariff and the High Price of Sugar," *GBF* 24 (January 1917), 148.

12. *TCA*, 23 February 1917; *TCA*, 16 February 1917; "What Crop Will I Plant? Asks the Beet Farmer," *GBF* 24 (March 1917): 221; "Flax a Profitable Crop for the Sugar Beet District," *GBF* 24 (April 1917): 247.

13. *TCA*, 12 January 1917.

14. *Pigeon Progress*, 19 January 1917. [hereafter *PP*]

15. *PP*, 5 January 1917.

16. *PP*, 5 January 1917; "No Sugar in the Grower's Tea," *GBF* 23 (December 1916): 91.

17. "No Sugar in the Grower's Tea," 91.

18. "Governor's Intervention Saves the Day for Beet Men," *GBF* 24 (April 1917): 269; "The Sugar Beet Resolution," *GBF* 24 (April 1917): 270; "The Sugar Beet Resolution," *GBF* 24 (May 1917): 294.

19. "Governor's Intervention," 269.

20. Ibid., 269.

21. Ibid., 269.

22. *PP*, 6 April 1917; *Christian Science Monitor*, 31 March 1917, 23. [hereafter *CSM*]

23. *TCA*, 16 April 1917.

24. Ibid.

25. Melvyn Dubofsky, "Abortive Reform: The Wilson Administration and Organized Labor, 1913–1920," in *Work, Community, and Power: The Experience of Labor in Europe and America, 1900–1925*, eds. James E. Cronin and Carmen Sirianni (Philadelphia: Temple University Press): 197–220; David Montgomery, *The Fall of the House of Labor: The Workplace, the State and American Labor Activism, 1865–1925* (Cambridge, U.K.: Cambridge University Press, 1987), 330–411; Joseph A. McCartin, *Labor's Great War: The Struggle for Industrial Democracy and the Origins of Modern American Labor Relations, 1912–1921* (Chapel Hill: University of North Carolina Press, 1997).

26. U.S. Food Administration: Policies and Plans of Operation: Sugar, May 1918, 130-008/31/00, RG 4, U.S. Food Administration, National Archives, College Park, Maryland. [hereafter USFA]

27. Quoted in Leland H. Jenks, *Our Cuban Colony* (New York: Vanguard Press, 1928), 197.

28. Joshua Bernhardt, *Government Control of the Sugar Industry in the United States* (New York: MacMillan, 1920), 21–22. See Robert F. Smith, *The United States and Cuba: Business and Diplomacy, 1917–1960* (New York: Bookman Associates, 1960), 99–104.

29. Smith, *The United States and Cuba*, 99–104.

30. Ibid.

31. Agreement with United States Food Administration, Columbia Sugar Company, Bay City, Michigan, 2 October 1917, 130-008/32/00, Box 4, USFA.

32. William Clinton Mullendore, *History of the United States Food Administration, 1917–1919* (Stanford, Calif.: Stanford University Press, 1941), 178.

33. "The Government Urges Farmers to Boost Sugar Beet Yield," *MBF* 5 (June 1918): 8. [hereafter *MBF*]

34. Bernhardt, *Government Control of the Sugar Industry in the United States*, 25–26.

35. "Inherent Weakness Revealed," *The Gleaner* 25 (November 1917): 23.

36. "Beet Growers Seek More Profits," *Michigan Manufacturers and Financial Record* 21 (January 1918): 33. [hereafter *MMFR*]

37. "Are You Friend or Enemy?" *The Gleaner* 25 (November 1917): 22.

38. "A Case of Robbing Peter to Pay Paul," *The Gleaner* 25 (October 1917): 5–18.

39. "The American Farmer Stands Ready to do His Share: Guarantee Him a Minimum Price," *GBF* 24 (May 1917): 291.

40. "Beet Situation Calls for Federal Intervention," *The Gleaner* 25 (February 1918): 97; "Government Intervention," *MBF* 4 (March 1917): 5; "Investigate Beet Deal—Gratiot County Farmer Believes the Time is Ripe for Beet Growers to Ask Government to Insure Fair Prices," *MBF* 5 (November 1917): 2; *TCA*, 7 December 1917; Joshua Bernhardt, "Government Control of Sugar During the War," *Quarterly Journal of Economics* 33.4 (1919): 677.

41. Lamb, U.S. Food Administration D.C. to George Prescott, 14 January 1918, U.S. Food Administration—Michigan—Federal Food Administration Correspondence 123A-A6 1918-1919 F; Sugar Division Equalization Board, Box 66, RG 4, U.S. Food Administration, National Archives, Great Lakes Region, Chicago, Illinois. [hereafter Great Lakes-USFA]

42. "SUGAR MF'RS OFFER $8 a Ton—Many Beet Growers Refusing to Sign up on that Basis," *MBF* 5 (December 1917): 16; "State Beet Men to Meet—Important Gathering of Michigan Sugar Beet Men," *MBF* 5 (December 1917): 2; *TCA*, 18 January 1918.

43. *PP*, 18 January 1918.

44. "State Beet Men to Meet—Important Gathering of Michigan Sugar Beet Growers to be Held at Saginaw," 2.

45. "Ten Dollar Minimum: State Association in Session at Saginaw Declare For Fifty-Fifty Division of Sugar Profit and Leaves Decision to Food Administration," *MBF* 5 (January 1918): 1.

46. "SUGAR MF'RS OFFER $8 a Ton," 16; "SUGAR MANUFACT'RS OPPOSE $10 BEETS," *MBF* 5 (January 1918), 3.

47. George Prescott to Mr. Lamb, 21 January 1918, F: George Prescott, Box 34, U.S. Food Administration, Federal Food Administrator, General Correspondence (123A-A3) 1918-1919, Great Lakes-USFA.

48. George Prescott to Mr. Lamb, 24 January 1918, F: George Prescott, Box 34, U.S. Food Administration, Federal Food Administrator, General Correspondence (123A-A3) 1918-1919, Great Lakes-USFA.

49. M. J. Bialy, Sec, Treasurer, and Manager to George Prescott, 23 January 1918, F: George Prescott, Box 34, U.S. Food Administration, General Food Administrator, General Correspondence (123A-A3) 1918-1919, Great Lakes-USFA; *TCA*, 1 February 1918.

50. *TCA*, 15 February 1918.

51. *PP*, 18 January 1918; *TCA*, 25 January 1918.

52. "The Sugar Beet Controversy," *MBF* 5 (February 1918): 12.

53. *TCA*, 1 February 1918; George Prescott to Mr. Lamb, 24 January 1918, F: George Prescott, Box 34, Federal Food Administrator, General Correspondence (123A-A3) 1918-1919, Great Lakes-USFA.

54. "Sidelights on the Sugar Beet Industry," *MBF* 5 (February 1918): 4.

55. "Michigan's Sugar Beet Industry's Future," *MBF* 5 (February 1918): 6.

56. "Soldiers of the Soil," *The Gleaner* 24 (July 1917): 342.

57. "Publisher's Announcement," *The Gleaner* 25 (December 1917): 47.

58. "Beet Situation Calls for Federal Intervention, 97.

59. "Sugar Beet Growers Awarded Price of $10 Ton," *MMRF* 21 (February 1918): 21.

60. *TCA*, 8 February 1918.

61. *TCA*, 22 February 1918.

62. *TCA*, 15 February 1918; *TCA*, 22 February 1918.

63. *Wall Street Journal*, 20 February 1918, 8 [hereafter *WSJ*]; *CSM*, 22 February 1918, 11.

64. "Growers Get $10 for Their Sugar Beets," *GBF* 25 (March 1918): 128; *PP*, 15 February 1918.

65. "Sugar Manufacturers Agree to $10 Beets: Organized Growers' Committee Wins Great Victory for Michigan Beet Industry and Pave Way for Biggest and Best Year in its History," *MBF* 5 (February 1918): 1.

66. "Beet Situation Calls for Federal Intervention," *The Gleaner* 25 (February 1918): 97; When the time came for deciding sugar beet prices for the upcoming 1919 season, the sugar companies immediately gave in to the farmers. Hoping to get the farmers to grow more sugar beet and avoid another protracted fight, the manufacturers agreed

to pay the farmers' $10 demand. *TCA,* 29 November 1918; *PP,* 29 November 1918; *PP,* 6 December 1918; "Ten Dollars for the 1919 Beets," *MBF* 7 (November 1918): 4.

67. For a discussion of World War I and postwar farmer organizations, see James H. Shiedler, *Farm Crisis, 1919–1923* (Berkeley: University of California Press, 1957); Murray Benedict, *Farm Policies of the United States, 1790–1950: A Study of Their Origins and Development* (New York: Octagon Books, 1966), 139–89; David B. Danbom, *The Resisted Revolution: Urban America and the Industrialization of Agriculture, 1900–1930* (Ames: Iowa State University Press, 1977), 97–119; John Mark Hansen, *Gaining Access: Congress and the Farm Lobby, 1919–1981* (Chicago: University of Chicago Press, 1991), 1–31; Elisabeth S. Clemens, *The People's Lobby: Organizational Innovation and the Rise of Interest Group Politics in the United States, 1890–1925* (Chicago: University of Chicago Press, 1997).

68. "The Farmers' Nonpartisan League," *Farmers' Open Forum* 2.5 (1 September 1915): 12. [hereafter *FOF*] Also see Elizabeth Sanders, *Roots of Reform: Farmers, Workers, and the American State, 1877–1917* (Chicago: University of Chicago Press, 1999).

69. By affiliating the Gleaner with the FNC, Slocum brought an estimated 150,000 members to the young organization, raising its total membership to an estimated 350,000. (The other organizations adding members included the following groups: American Society of Equity, 100,000 members; Nebraska Farmers' Union, 40,000 members; North Carolina Farmers' Union, 30,000 members; State Granges of Washington, Colorado, Oregon, and Idaho, 30,000 members.); Marquis, "The Radical Minority: Farmers Represented by the Farmers' National Council and Related Bodies," *The Country Gentlemen,* 24 April 1920, 26.

70. "Why a Farmer's War Council Should be Constantly on the Job in Washington," *FOF* 4 (April 1918): 16.

71. "Minimum Prices Only Security for Farmer—Congress Will be Asked to Guarantee Farmers Against Loss on Next Year's Crops by Fixing Prices on Leading Commodities," *MBF* 5 (January 1918): 1.

72. "The Nation Must Back the Farmers' Program of Preparedness," *GBF* 24 (April 1917): 267; "The American Farmer Stands Ready to Do His Share," *The Gleaner* 24 (May 1917): 291; "The Man of the Hour, The American Farmer," *GBF* 24 (May 1917): 313; "Congress Asked to Guarantee Minimum Prices," *GBF* 24 (May 1917): 315.

73. "The Farmer and the War," *FOF* 4 (November 1917): 8; "The Railroad Problem," *FOF* 3 (December 1917): 8; "Making Wealth Patriotic," *FOF* 3 (January 1918): 15; "The Big Things," *FOF* 3 (February 1918): 10; "Farmers' National War Council," *FOF* 3 (March 1918): 16; "Farmers' National Committee on Packing Plants and Allied Industry," *FOF* 4 (September 1918): 11; "Why New Farmer Federation," *FOF* 4 (November 1918): 1.

74. "Some Achievements of the Progressive Farm Organization," *FOF* 4 (September 1918): 16.

75. "In Time of War Prepare for Peace," *FOF* 3 (September 1917): 16.

76. "Why a Farmer's War Council Should be Constantly on the Job in Washington," 16.

77. "The Larger Victory," *FOF* 4 (October 1918): 1.

78. "The Era of Business Farming Now Begins," *The Gleaner* 25 (December 1917): 52.

79. For works on industrial democracy, see James R. Barrett, "Americanization from the Bottom Up: Immigration and the Remaking of the Working Class in the United States, 1880-1930," *Journal of American History* 79 (December 1992): 996-1020; Nelson Lichtenstein and Howell John Harris, eds., *Industrial Democracy in America: The Ambiguous Promise* (Cambridge, U.K.: Cambridge University Press, 1996).

80. "Dairy Industry Problems," *MBF* 6 (December 1918): 4.

81. "Farmers and Reconstruction," *FOF* 4 (December 1918): 16.

82. "The Railroad Problem," 8; "Making Wealth Patriotic," *FOF* 3 (January 1918): 15; "The Big Things," *FOF* (February 1918): 10; "Farmers' National War Council," 16; "Farmers' National Committee on Packing Plants and Allied Industry," 11; "Why New Farmer Federation," 1; Ben Marsh, *Lobbyist for the People: A Record of Fifty Years* (Washington, D.C.: Public Affairs Press, 1953), 50-54.

83. "The Policy and Program of American Farmers," *FOF* 4 (December 1918): 3.

84. U.S. House of Representatives, Hearings Before the Committee on Banking and Currency, *Farm Organizations*, 66th Congress, 3rd Session, 1921 (Washington, D.C.: GPO, 1922), 3-25.

85. *New York Times*, 11 May 1919 [hereafter *NYT*]; *NYT*, 7 March 1920; *NYT*, 30 March 1919; *NYT*, 27 January 1920; *NYT*, 27 February 1920.

86. "The Policy and Program of American Farmers," 1.

87. Marsh, *Lobbyist for the People*, 58.

88. "A National Federation of Farmers," *FOF* 4 (September 1918): 2. For a discussion of the American Farm Bureau Federation, see O. M. Kile, *The Farm Bureau through Three Decades* (Baltimore: Waverly Press, 1948); Theodore Saloutos and John Donald Hicks, *Twentieth-Century Populism: Agricultural Discontent in the Middle West, 1900-1939* (New York: Oxford University Press, 1980), 255-85; Grant McConnell, *The Decline of Agrarian Democracy* (Berkeley: University of California Press, 1953), 44-54; Danbom, *Born in the Country*, 189, 191, 202; Mary Neth, *Preserving the Family Farm: Women, Community, and the Foundations of Agribusiness in the Midwest, 1900-1940* (Baltimore: Johns Hopkins University Press, 1995), 130-46.

89. Danbom, *Born in the Country*, 180-83; Neth, *Preserving the Family Farm*, 132-35; Saloutos and Hicks, *Twentieth-Century Populism*, 258; Shiedler, *Farm Crisis*, 248-54.

90. Shiedler, *Farm Crisis*, 259.

91. "The American Farm Bureau Federation and the FNC," *FOF* 5 (March 1920): 11.

92. "Looking After the Farmer's Business at Washington," *FOF* 5 (May 1920): 1.

93. Stuart A. Rice, *Farmers and Workers in American Politics* (New York: Columbia

University, 1924), 136. Also see "A General Survey of Present-Day Farmers' Organizations," in *Readings in the Economic History of American Agriculture*, ed. Louis Bernard Schmidt and Earle Dudley Ross (New York: MacMillan, 1925).

94. Montgomery, *The Fall of the House of Labor*, 395–464; Alan Dawley, *Struggle for Justice: Social Responsibility and the Liberal State* (Cambridge, Mass.: Harvard University Press, 1991); McCartin, *Labor's Great War*, 173–220; William M. Tuttle Jr., *Race Riot: Chicago in the Red Summer of 1919* (New York: Antheum, 1970); David M. Kennedy, *Over Here: The First World War and American Society* (New York: Oxford University Press, 1980), 258–84.

95. Richard M. Valley, *Radicalism in the States: The Minnesota Farmer-Labor Party and the American Political Economy* (Chicago: University of Chicago Press, 1989).

96. *TCA*, 30 January 1920; "Official Data Reveals Profits of the Sugar Industry—United States Tariff Commission Publishes Cost of Sugar Production from 1918–1919," *MBF* 7 (February 1920): 6.

97. *TCA*, 19 December 1919.

98. "Liberating the Farmer," *Michigan Business Farmer* 7 (May 1920): 13. [hereafter *MBFR*]

99. "Western Beet Growers Present 1920 Contract," *MBF* 7 (January 1920): 4.

100. Ibid.

101. "When Right is Obtained No One is Wronged," *MBF* 7 (January 1920): 1.

102. *PP*, 12 March 1920; *PP*, 12 December 1919.

103. *TCA*, 26 December 1919; *PP*, 12 December 1919; "Farmers Ask for Better Sugar Beet Contract," *MBF* 7 (December 1919): 2; *TCA*, 19 December 1919; "Beet Growers Ask for a 50/50 Split of Profits," *MBF* 7 (December 1919): 3; "Saginaw," *MMFR* 25 (January 1920): 54.

104. "State Farm Bureau Is Now Ready for Business," *MBF* 7 (February 1920): 4.

105. *PP*, 16 January 1920; "Beet Growers Organize Scores of Associations: Farmers Set to Work in Earnest to Organize Sugar Beet Territory," *MBF* 7 (January 1920): 7; *TCA*, 2 January 1920; *TCA*, 20 February 1920; *AR*, 19 February 1920.

106. "Some Facts on the Sugar Beet Situation," *MBF* 7 (January 1920): 20.

107. "All Our Locals are Voting to Stand Behind the Organization," *MBFR* 7 (May 1920): 1.

108. *TCA*, 2 January 1920; *TCA*, 12 March 1920.

109. *PP*, 5 March 1920; *PP*, 12 March 1920; "1,500 Swear Loyalty," *MBF* 7 (March 1920): 9.

110. "Beet Counties Lining Up for Fair Beet Prices," *MBF* 7 (January 1920): 1.

111. "Beet Counties Lining Up for Fair Beet Prices," 1. "Four Thousand Farmers Join Beet Sugar Association—Work of Organizing Sweeps Over Territory Like Wildfire—Enlisting Support of Over 90%," *MBF* 7 (February 1920): 6.

112. *PP*, 2 April 1920.

113. "Hundreds of Sugar Beet Contracts Returned," *MBFR* 7 (March 1920): 12; *PP*, 9 April 1920.

114. *NYT,* 2 January 1920; William John May Jr., *The Great Western Sugarlands: The History of the Great Western Sugar Company and the Economic Development of the Great Plains* (New York: Garland Publishing, 1989), 88–89.

115. "The Sugar Beet Growers Issue Convention Call—Denver, Colo., to Be Scene of First National Convention of Beet Growers to Gain Strength," *MBF* 7 (January 1920): 2; "John Ketchum Chosen President of United States Beet Growers' Federation," *MBF* 7 (February 1920): 6.

116. "Michigan Sugar Men Stand Pat," *MBF* 7 (January 1920): 4; "Beet Growers Turned Down By Manufacturers," *MBF* 7 (January 1920): 10; *PP,* 7 February 1920; *TCA,* 19 March 1920.

117. "Saginaw," *MMFR* 26 (February 1920): 48–49.

118. *AR,* 18 March 1920.

119. *PP,* 12 March 1920; "Sugar Men Take Issue with Farmers' Claims," *MBFR* 7 (April 1920): 7.

120. "Beet Controversy Waxes Warm: Michigan Growers at Odd with Sugar Makers, Threaten Strike," *MMFR* 25 (March 1920): 15–16. "Saginaw," *MMFR* 25 (February 1920): 48–49.

121. "Sugar Men Distort Facts to Deceive Farmers: Statements That Leaders Are Untrue to Cause and That Movement is Failing is Pure Fiction," *MBFR* 7 (April 1920): 6.

122. *PP,* 7 May 1920.

123. *PP,* 14 May 1920.

124. *PP,* 21 May 1920.

125. *PP,* 28 May 1920.

126. "The 'Strike' the Last Resort," *MBFR* 7 (April 1920): 6.

127. "Sugar Beet Growers' Strike is on in Earnest," *MBFR* 7 (March 1920): 9.

128. "Farmers Stand Firm as Beet Fight Nears End," *MBFR* 7 (May 1920): 7.

129. "To Members Farmers' Co-Operative Union, Bay County," *MBFR* 7 (May 1920): 2.

130. "All Our Locals Are Voting to Stand Behind the Organization," *MBFR* 7 (May 1920): 1–2.

131. "Sugar Plants Will Run with Lower Tonnage," *MBFR* 7 (June 1920): 2–3.

132. *PP,* 30 April 1920; *TCA,* 14 May 1920.

133. *TCA,* 14 May 1920; *PP,* 7 May 1920.

134. *TCA,* 14 May 1920; "Lawlessness," *MBFR* 7 (May 1920): 7.

135. "Farmers Stand Firm as Beet Fight Nears End," 7.

136. "Thumb Beet Growers Hold Big Mass Meetings—Final Wind-Up Shows Farmers More Determined than Ever to Stand Against Autocracy of Manufacturers," *MBFR* 7 (May 1920): 6.

137. *NYT,* 23 May 1920.

138. "All Our Locals Are Voting to Stand Behind the Organization," 1–2.

139. "Lawlessness," *MBF* 7 (May 1920): 7.

140. "To Members Farmers' Co-Operative Union, Bay County," 1; "Grit and Loyalty," *MBF* 7 (June 1920): 13.

141. "Sugar Companies Acreage on Poor Land," *MBFR* 7 (July 1920): 7.

142. *AR*, 29 April 1920.

143. "Letter to the Editor—W.B.B. Arenac County," *MBFR* 8 (October 1920): 10.

144. "Beet Acreage Larger Than Ever," *MMFR* 26 (July 1920): 17; "Beet Crop a Record One," *MMFR* 26 (September 1920): 45.

145. "Beet Crop a Record One," 45.

146. *PP,* 8 October 1920; "What the State Farm Bureau is Doing," *MBFR* 8 (October 1920): 14; *PP,* 19 November 1920; *PP,* 31 December 1920.

147. "Editorial—Sugar Prices and Beet Contracts," *MBFR* 8 (October 1920): 12.

148. "Beet Growers to Renew Efforts at Recognition," *MBFR* 7 (August 1920): 2; "Does the Farm Bureau Mean Business?" *MBFR* 7 (July 1920): 10. For criticism of farmer cooperatives, see "Some Facts About the Manufacture of Beet Sugar—Impractical to Operate Small Plants for Extracting Sugar," *MBFR* 8 (December 1920): 6.

149. "Sugar Beet Growers Still Undecided on Course for Coming Season," *MBFR* 8 (December 1920): 3; "Stage is Set for Renewal of Sugar Beet Fight—Michigan State Farm Bureau and Growers Association Prepare Plans for Final Adjustment of Controversy," *MBFR* 8 (October 1920): 3; "State Farm Bureau Takes Up Sugar Beet Fight," *MBFR* 8 (December 1920): 5; "Sugar Beet Growers Reject Manuf's Contracts," *MBFR* 8 (February 1921): 4; *TCA*, 11 February 1921; "Michigan Beet Growers Place United Action With State Farm Bureau," *MBFR* 8 (March 1921): 6.

150. "The State Farm Bureau Makes Good Record," *MBFR* 8 (October 1920): 7.

151. "Confidence," *MBFR* 7 (May 1920): 7.

152. Report of the Secretary, *Michigan State Farm Bureau, Annual Meeting,* Lansing, Michigan, 1921, 14.

153. "Beet Growers Association Distributes Contracts," *MBFR* 8 (12 March 1921): 3; "Contract by Beet Growers Association based on Price of Sugar For the Year," *MBFR* 8 (March 1921): 3; *TCA*, 25 March 1921; "April 16 the Closing Date for Beet Contracts—Beet Association Makes a Final Found-Up Campaign for Beet Acreage," *MBFR* 8 (April 1921): 7; *TCA*, 18 April 1921; "Signed Contracts Pour Into Offices of Beet Growers Association—Reports on Closing Day of Campaign Indicates Growers throughout the State are Signing the Association's Contract," *MBFR* 8 (April 1921): 6.

154. *TCA*, 22 April 1921.

155. *PP,* 6 May 1921; *TCA*, 6 May 1921; "Sugar Manufacturers Refuse to Accept Grower Contracts," *MBFR* 8 (May 1921): 6.

156. Shiedler, *Farm Crisis,* 46.

157. Elizabeth Hoffman and Gary D. Libecap, "Institutional Choice and the Development of U.S. Agricultural Policies in the 1920s," *Journal of Economic History* 51 (June 1991): 397–411.

158. *PP,* 3 March 1922; *TCA,* 7 April 1922.
159. "Letter to the Editor," *MBFR* 10 (February 1923): 14.

Chapter 5. Immigrant Labor and the Guest Worker Program

1. *Pigeon Progress,* 27 July 1917 [hereafter *PP*]; *PP,* 3 August 1917.
2. *PP,* 24 May 1918.
3. *PP,* 13 June 1919.
4. Cindy Hahamovitch, *The Fruits of Their Labor: Atlantic Coast Farmworkers and The Making of Migrant Poverty, 1870–1945* (Chapel Hill: University of North Carolina Press, 1997), 79–112.
5. Ibid., 79.
6. Ibid., 81.
7. Otey M. Scruggs, "The First Mexican Farm Labor Program," *Arizona and the West* 2 (Winter 1960): 319–26; Mark Reisler, *By the Sweat of Their Brow: Mexican Immigrant Labor in the United States, 1900–1940* (Westport, Conn.: Greenwood Press, 1976), 24–48; Neil Foley, *The White Scourge: Mexicans, Blacks, and Poor Whites in Texas Cotton Culture* (Berkeley: University of California Press, 1997), 45–48; David Gutierrez, *Walls and Mirrors: Mexican Americans, Mexican Immigrants and the Politics of Identity* (Berkeley: University of California Press, 1995), 47–53; Steven Stoll, *The Fruits of Natural Advantage: Making the Industrial Countryside in California* (Berkeley: University of California Press, 1998), 150–54.
8. Hahamovitch, *The Fruits of Their Labor,* 79–112.
9. Ibid., 92–93.
10. "Who Will Help Harvest the Crops?" *The Gleaner* 25 (January 1918): 76.
11. Hahamovitch, *The Fruits of Their Labor,* 79–112; Reisler, *By the Sweat of Their Brow,* 24–48; David Vaught, *Cultivating California: Growers, Specialty Crops, and Labor, 1875–1920* (Baltimore: Johns Hopkins University Press, 1999), chapter 5.
12. "Hoover Calls on Farmers and Others to Plant Heavily," *Michigan Manufacturer and Financial Record* 21 (February 1918): 18. [hereafter *MMFR*]
13. "Michigan Farm Labor Situation," *Michigan Business Farming* 5 (February 1918): 10. [hereafter *MBF*]
14. *PP,* 29 June 1917.
15. *Tuscola County Advertiser,* 20 July 1917 [hereafter *TCA*]; *PP,* 28 June 1918; *TCA,* 10 May 1918.
16. *PP,* 17 May 1918; *TCA,* 5 July 1918.
17. *PP,* 4 May 1917; *TCA,* 15 March 1918; *TCA,* 19 April 1918; "U.S. Boy's Working Reserve," *Monthly Review of the Bureau of Labor Statistics* (June 1917): 992; E. V. Wilcox, "The Farmer's Labor Problem," *American Labor Legislation Review* (March 1918): 44–47; Helen D. Fischer, "The Boys, the War, and the Harrow," *Survey* 30 (March 1918): 704–6; A. E. Grantham, "Lessons in Solving Labor Credit and Other Production Problems," *The Annals* (November 1917): 210–23; *U.S. Employment Service Bulletin* (May 1918): 3; C. F. Stoddard, "How the US Employment Service is Mobilizing

Its Workers," *Monthly Review of the Bureau of Labor Statistics* (March 1918): 1245–55; for the headlines, see, *PP,* 4 May 1917; *TCA,* 15 March 1918; "The Camp Bulletin: News and Other things for and About the United States Boys' Working Reserves Boys in the Farm Camps of Michigan," 22 June 1918, found in F: George A. Prescott, Box 34, U.S. Food Administration, Michigan Federal Food Administrator—General Correspondence, 123A-A3, 1918-1919, RG 4, National Archives, Great Lakes Region, Chicago, Illinois.

18. "Mr. Farmer:—Do You Want One of These Young Men?" *The Gleaner* 25 (April 1918): 168.

19. "Plain Facts Plainly Spoken," *The Gleaner* 25 (January 1918): 17.

20. Theresa Wolfson, "People Who Go to the Beets," *The American Child* 1 (November 1919): 223.

21. Ibid., 220.

22. *PP,* 5 January 1917.

23. Wolfson, "People Who Go to the Beets," 226–27.

24. Ibid., 226.

25. *TCA,* 5 September 1919; "Agricultural Workers Industrial Union," *MBF* 5 (December 1917): 2; "Notes and News of the Organization," *MBF* 5 (December 1917): 4; "Agricultural Workers' Industrial Union," *MBF* 5 (May 1918): 3; "Thru the Great Harvest Fields," *MBF* 7 (September 1919): 3; "Four Hundred Delegates Say "Ah, COME ON!" *MBF* 7 (September 1919): 1.

26. "How U.S. Expects to Solve Farm Labor Shortage," *MBF* 5 (April 1918): 5.

27. *TCA,* 22 February 1918.

28. J. A. Harper and W. B. Mandeville, U.S. Senate, Hearings Before Committee on Immigration, *Emergency Immigration Legislation,* 66th Congress, 3rd Session (Washington, D.C.: GPO, 1921), 117–19.

29. "Labor Laws and Regulations: Regulations by the United States Department of Labor for Admission of Mexican Laborers," *Monthly Labor Review* (November 1918): 1416–21.

30. "To Commissioners of Immigration: Inspectors in Charge, and Others Concerned," 6 June 1917, 54261/202, RG 85, National Archives, Washington, D.C. [hereafter INS]

31. *Washington Post,* 1 June 1917. [hereafter *WP*]

32. William B. Wilson to John L. Burnett, 8 June 1917, Immigration Bureau File 54261/202, RG 85, National Archives, Washington, D.C., cited in Reisler, *By The Sweat of Their Brow,* 28.

33. Anthony Caminetti to James L. Slayden, 28 June 1917, 54261/202, INS. Also see Wilcox, "The Farmer's Labor Problem," 44–46.

34. Lawrence Cardoso, *Mexican Emigration to the United States, 1897–1931: Socio-Economic Patterns* (Tucson: University of Arizona Press, 1987), 58–59; Claudio Lomnitz, "Modes of Citizenship in Mexico," in Luis Roniger and Carlos Waisman, eds., *Globality and Multiple Modernities: Comparative North American and Latin*

American Perspectives (Brighton, U.K.: Sussex Academic Press, 2002), 276–77. For a critical perspective on U.S./Mexican relations as well as U.S. empire, see Gilbert G. Gonzalez and Paul Fernandez, *A Century of Chicano History: Empire, Nation, and Migration* (New York: Routledge, 2003) and Gilbert G. Gonzalez, *Culture of Empire: American Writers, Mexico, and Mexican Immigrants, 1880–1930* (Austin: University of Texas Press, 2004).

35. English Translation, Circular Number 2, Official Periodical of the Government of the Free State of Tamaulipas, Ciudad Victoria, 20 March 1918, 54261/2029, INS.

36. *Bulletin From Mexican News Bureau,* 4 April 1918, 54261/202A, INS.

37. Robert Lansing to William B. Wilson, 23 August 1917, 54261/202A, INS.

38. Circular for the Mexican Consuls in the U.S. No. 25, 7 June 1918, 54261/202C, INS; *Wall Street Journal*, 3 July 1918, 7. [hereafter *WSJ*]

39. Robert Lansing to William B. Wilson, 23 August 1917, 54261/202A, INS.

40. Memorandum for the Director General: *In re Obtaining Mexican Labor,* 3 July 1918, 54261/202B, INS.

41. G. H. Harris, Acting Supervising Inspector to Inspector in Charge, Immigration Service, 15 June 1917, 54261/202, INS.

42. Memorandum for the Secretary, from Anthony Caminetti, Commissioner-General, 11 February 1918, 54261/202A, INS.

43. *WSJ*, 21 December 1918, 2; *WP,* 24 December 1918, 6.

44. *Emergency Immigration Legislation,* 709; *WP,* 6 January 1919.

45. *Emergency Immigration Legislation,* 710.

46. Reisler, *By the Sweat of Their Brow,* 34; U.S. Bureau of Labor Statistics, *Monthly Labor Review* 11 (November 1920): 221; *CSM*, 15 April 1920, 5.

47. Reisler, *By the Sweat of Their Brow,* 33.

48. Kathleen Mapes, "A 'Special Class of Labor': Mexican Migrants, Immigration Debate, and Industrial Agriculture in the 1920s," *Labor: Studies in Working Class History of the Americas* 1 (Summer 2004): 65–88.

49. *Christian Science Monitor*, 5 February 1919 [hereafter *CSM*]; *NYT,* 18 April 1920, 6; *WP,* 18 April 1920, 24; *CSM*, 22 April 1920, 2.

50. *WP,* 18 January 1920, 6; *CSM*, 5 March 1920.

51. For a copy of the report, see *Emergency Immigration Legislation,* 64–72.

52. Reisler, *By the Sweat of Their Brow,* 36.

53. *Emergency Immigration Legislation,* 67.

54. Ibid., 67.

55. Ibid., 67.

56. Ibid., 71.

57. *CSM*, 4 September 1920.

58. Artemis to Caminetti, 22 February 1921, 55091/6, INS.

59. For a national perspective, see Gerald B. Breitigam, *NYT,* 20 June 1920.

60. *Adrian Daily Telegraph,* 17 April 1920. [hereafter *ADT*]

61. *ADT,* 17 April 1920.

62. *ADT,* 28 April 1920.
63. Fordney to Caminetti, March 14, 1921, 55091/6, INS.
64. For wage increases, see *PP,* 23 February 1917; *PP,* 15 February 1918.
65. Wolfson, "People Who Go to the Beets," 227; George T. Edson, "Mexicans in Saginaw, Michigan," 1, Carton 1, Detroit Conversations, Paul Taylor Papers, Bancroft Library, University of California, Berkeley. [hereafter PTP]
66. George K. Apple to Inspector in Charge, Immigration Service, Cleveland, Ohio, 3 June 1919, 54261/202G, INS.
67. F. W. Berkshire, Supervising Inspector, to Inspector in Charge, Immigration Service, Cleveland, Ohio, 21 January 1919, 54261/202F, INS.
68. W. B. Rosevear to Truman Palmer, 15 February 1919, 54261/202F, INS.
69. Artemis to Caminetti, 22 February 1921, RG 85, 55091/6, National Archives; Clark to Caminetti, February 3, 1921, 55091/6, INS.
70. Clark to Caminetti, 23 December 1920, 55091/6, INS.
71. Artemis to Caminetti, 22 February 1921, 55091/6, INS.
72. Coe to Caminetti, 21 February 1921, 55091/6, INS.
73. Clark to Caminetti, 3 February 1921, 55091/6, INS; Artemis to Caminetti, 22 February 1921, 55091/6, INS.
74. Coe to Caminetti, 22 February 1921, 55091/6, INS.
75. Inspector in Charge, Port Huron, to Commissioner of Immigration, Montreal, Canada, 22 February 1921, 2118/245, INS.
76. Artemis to Caminetti, 22 February 1921, 55091/6, INS.
77. Francisco Pereda, Consul of Mexico, to William Hale Thompson, Mayor City of Chicago, 25 April 1921, 55091/6, INS.
78. Joe Fordney to Caminetti, 14 March 1921, 55091/6, INS.
79. Assistant Secretary of Immigration to Fordney, 19 March 1921, 55091/6, INS.
80. Coe to Caminetti, 21 February 1921, 55091/6, INS.
81. *Detroit News,* 17 February 1921, F: clippings, Carton 1, Detroit Conversations, PTP.
82. Artemis to Caminetti, 22 February 1921, 55091/6, INS.
83. Annual Report of St. Vincent de Paul of Detroit, 1921, found in Eduard Adam Skendzel, *Detroit's Pioneer Mexicans: A Historical Study of the Mexican Colony in Detroit* (Grand Rapids, Mich.: Littleshield Press, 1980), 11. For a general description of the 1921 repatriation, see Vargas, *Proletarians of the North,* 79–84; Dennis Nodin Valdes, *Al Norte: Agricultural Workers in the Great Lakes Region, 1917–1970* (Austin: University of Texas Press, 1991), 10.

Chapter 6. Mexican Immigrants and Immigration Debate

1. United States, House of Representatives, Committee on Immigration and Naturalization, *Seasonal Agricultural Laborers from Mexico,* 69th Congress, 1st Session, (Washington, D.C.: GPO, 1926) 1. [hereafter *Seasonal Agricultural Laborers*]

2. Roy Orchard Woodruff and Chairman Albert Johnson, *Seasonal Agricultural Laborers*, 273–75.

3. Madison Grant, "America for the Americans," *Forum* 74 (September 1925): 335, quoted in Mark Reisler, *By the Sweat of Their Brow: Mexican Immigrant Labor in the United States, 1900–1940* (Westport, Conn.: Greenwood Press, 1976), 153.

4. While the 1926 and 1928 bills proposed to amend the 1924 Immigration Act to include all of the Western Hemisphere, the 1930 Harris Bill sought to amend the 1924 Immigration Act to include only Mexico. U.S. House of Representatives, Hearings Before the House Committee on Immigration and Naturalization, *Immigration from Countries of the Western Hemisphere*, 70th Congress, 1st Session (Washington, D.C.: GPO, 1928) [hereafter *Immigration from Countries*]; U.S. House of Representatives, Hearings Before the House Committee on Immigration and Naturalization, *Western Hemisphere Immigration*, 71st Congress, 2nd Session (Washington, D.C.: GPO, 1930). [hereafter *Western Hemisphere*]

5. Ian F. Haney Lopez, *White by Law: The Legal Construction of Race* (New York: New York University Press, 1996).

6. For the most thorough monographs on the experiences of Mexicans and Mexican Americans in the Midwest, see Dennis Nodin Valdes, *Al Norte: Agricultural Workers in the Great Lakes Region, 1917–1970* (Austin: University of Texas Press, 1991); Zaragosa Vargas, *Proletarians of the North: A History of Mexican Industrial Workers in Detroit and the Midwest, 1917–1933* (Berkeley: University of California Press, 1993).

7. Harry Austin, *Seasonal Agricultural Laborers*, 251.

8. Woodruff, *Seasonal Agricultural Laborers*, 272.

9. L. J. Dickinson, *Immigration from Countries*, 586.

10. T. S. Crapo, *Immigration from Countries*, 535–36.

11. L. B. Tompkins, *Seasonal Agricultural Laborers*, 177.

12. Woodruff, *Seasonal Agricultural Laborers*, 276.

13. Originally found in U.S. Senate, Committee on Agriculture and Forestry, *Agricultural Labor Supply*, 71st Congress, 2nd Session, (Washington, D.C.: GPO, 1930), 90, cited in Valdes, *Al Norte*, 19.

14. S. R. McLean, *Seasonal Agricultural Laborers*, 182.

15. F. H. Ross, *Immigration from Countries*, 530–31.

16. Woodruff, *Seasonal Agricultural Laborers*, 273.

17. McLean, *Seasonal Agricultural Laborers*, 177–78.

18. Tompkins, *Seasonal Agricultural Laborers*, 176.

19. Woodruff, *Immigration from Countries*, 622.

20. Austin, *Immigration from Countries*, 448.

21. McLean, *Seasonal Agricultural Laborers*, 180–81.

22. Crapo, *Immigration from Countries*, 535.

23. Ibid., 535.

24. Austin, *Western Hemisphere*, 126.

25. Johnson and August Andresen, *Immigration from Countries,* 502.

26. Reisler, *By the Sweat of Their Brow,* 203.

27. Austin, *Immigration from Countries,* 435.

28. T. G. Gallagher, *Western Hemisphere,* 144.

29. Dickinson, *Immigration from Countries,* 585.

30. Mae M. Ngai, "The Architecture of Race in American Immigration Law: A Reexamination of the Immigrant Act of 1924," *Journal of American History* 86 (1999): 67–92.

31. David Gutierrez, *Walls and Mirrors: Mexican Americans, Mexican Immigrants and the Politics of Identity* (Berkeley: University of California Press, 1995), 56.

32. Lawrence Cardoso, *Mexican Emigration to the United States, 1897–1931: Socio-Economic Patterns* (Tucson: University of Arizona Press, 1987), 117–43.

33. Elmer Cornelius Koch, "The Mexican Laborer in the Sugar Beet Fields of the United States," M.A. thesis, University of Illinois, 1927, 26. [hereafter "The Mexican Laborer"]

34. Ad, *La Prensa,* 10 April 1927, F: Clippings, Box 1, Detroit Conversations, Paul Taylor Papers; "Betabeleros Para Michigan," F: Clippings, Box 1, Detroit Conversations, Paul Taylor Papers, Bancroft Library, University of California at Berkeley. [hereafter PTP]

35. "Betabeleros Para Michigan y Ohio," F: Clippings, Box 1, Detroit Conversations, PTP.

36. David Montejano, *Anglos and Mexicans in the Making of Texas, 1836–1986* (Austin: University of Texas Press, 1987), 210–11.

37. George T. Edson, *Mexicans in Our Northcentral States* [1927], Folder 32, Box 13, Paul Taylor Papers, Bancroft Library, University of California at Berkeley, 50 [hereafter *Mexicans in Our Northcentral States*]; Interview, Javier Tovar, 30–31 July 1928, Box 1, Detroit Conversations, PTP.

38. Interview, Mr. Cesario Hernandez, 3 August 1928, Rodrigo's Notes, Carton 12, PTP.

39. Edson, *Mexicans in Our Northcentral States,* 152–53.

40. Koch, "The Mexican Laborer," 42; Edson, *Mexicans in Our Northcentral States,* 162.

41. Interview, Dr. Morris, 2 August 1928, Box 1, Detroit Conversations, PTP; Edson, *Mexicans in Our Northcentral States,* 162; Koch, "The Mexican Laborer," 56.

42. Koch, "The Mexican Laborer," 34; Edson, *Mexicans in Our Northcentral States,* 164–66; *Pigeon Progress,* 18 May 1923 [hereafter *PP*]; *Tuscola County Advertiser,* 18 April 1924 [hereafter *TCA*]; *TCA,* 30 May 1924; *PP,* 6 August 1926; *PP,* 22 April 1927; *TCA,* 27 April 1928.

43. Koch, "The Mexican Laborer," 54.

44. For a copy of a labor contract from 1926, see "Agreement for Hand Labor in Beets," Box 1, Carton 1, Detroit Conversations, PTP; For a copy of the 1927 contract,

see "Michigan Contract—Agreement for Hand Labor in Beets, 1927" in Koch, "The Mexican Laborer," 121.

45. Koch, "The Mexican Laborer," 121.

46. George Edson, "Mexicans in Milwaukee, Wisconsin," Carton 1, Detroit Conversations, PTP.

47. Interview with unnamed employee, 23 September 1928, City Public Employment Office, Carton 1, Detroit Conversations, PTP.

48. Interview, G. Benjamin, 24 July 1928, Carton 1, Box 1, Detroit Conversations, PTP.

49. George Edson, "Mexicans in Saginaw," 5–6, F: Midwest, Carton 1, Detroit Conversations, PTP.

50. Interview, Mrs. Diaz, 16 July 1928, F: Mrs. Jones Notes, Carton 12, PTP.

51. Edson, "Mexicans in Saginaw," 7, F: Midwest, Carton 1, PTP.

52. Interview, Javier Tovar, 30–31 July 1928, Carton 1, Box 1, Detroit Conversations, PTP.

53. F. A. Stilgenbauer, "The Michigan Sugar Beet Industry," *Economic Geography* (October 1927): 491; Edson, *Mexicans in Our Northcentral States*, 142.

54. For example, see *PP*, 15 April 1927; *PP*, 26 October 1928.

55. *PP*, 6 July 1923; *TCA*, 20 June 1924; *PP*, 8 August 1924; *PP*, 29 August 1924; *PP*, 21 August 1925; *PP*, 9 April 1926; *PP*, 3 December 1926; *PP*, 4 February 1927; *PP*, 4 March 1927; *PP*, 15 April 1927; *PP*, 15 July 1927; *TCA*, 15 July 1927; *PP*, 2 September 1924; *PP*, 2 September 1927; *TCA*, 23 September 1927; *PP*, 14 October 1927; *TCA*, 21 October 1927; *TCA*, 30 December 1927; *TCA*, 29 June 1928; *PP*, 17 August 1928; *PP*, 28 September 1928; *TCA*, 28 September 1928; Edson, *Mexicans in Our Northcentral States*, 53.

56. *PP*, 9 September 1924; *PP*, 16 September 1927; *PP*, 23 September 1927; *PP*, 14 September 1928.

57. *PP*, 19 September 1924.

58. *PP*, 16 September 1927; *PP*, 23 September 1927; *PP*, 14 September 1928.

59. Ibid., 44–45.

60. Edson, *Mexicans in Our Northcentral States*, 109–10; Interview, Javier Tovar, 30–31 July 1928, Carton 1, Detroit Conversations, PTP; John Frederick Thaden, *Mexican Beet Workers in Michigan*, Special Bulletin 319 (East Lansing: Michigan State College Experiment Station, 1942), 44–45.

61. Thaden, *Mexican Beet Workers in Michigan*, 44–45.

62. For an excellent description and analysis of Mexican celebrations in the United States, see George J. Sanchez, *Becoming Mexican American: Ethnicity, Culture and Identity in Chicano Los Angeles, 1900–1945* (New York: Oxford University Press, 1993), 108–25.

63. Edson, *Mexicans in Our Northcentral States*, 76; George Edson, "Mexicans in Detroit," Carton 1, PTP.

64. Paul S. Taylor, *Mexican Labor in the United States: Chicago and the Calumet*

Region, University of California Publications in Economics, 7 (Berkeley: University of California Press, 1932), 215.

65. Edson, *Mexicans in Our Northcentral States,* 196.
66. Ibid., 31.
67. George Edson, "Mexicans in Saginaw, Michigan," 13–14, Carton 1, PTP.
68. Interview, Unnamed Mexican, Jones St., 14 July 1928, Box 1, Detroit Conversations, PTP.
69. Taylor, *Mexican Labor in the United States,* 57.
70. Edson, *Mexicans in Our Northcentral States,* 151–55.
71. Interview, Mrs. Larsen, Social Worker and Interpreter, 25 June 1928, Carton 1, Detroit Conversations, PTP.
72. Koch, "The Mexican Laborer," 37.
73. Interview, Dr. Morris, 2 August 1928, Carton 1, Detroit Conversations, PTP.
74. Edson, *Mexicans in Our Northcentral States,* 50.
75. *PP,* 6 August 1926.
76. Interview, Mr. Terrezas, 3 July 1928, Carton 1, Detroit Conversations, PTP.
77. *TCA,* 25 November 1927.
78. George Edson, "Mexicans in Detroit, Michigan," 8–9, Carton 1, Detroit Conversations, PTP.
79. "A Nuestras Amigas de Texas," 1926, F: Clippings, Detroit Conversations, PTP.
80. Edson, *Mexicans in Our Northcentral States,* 24, 37–38.
81. Edson, "Mexicans in Detroit, Michigan," 4, Carton 1, Detroit Conversations, PTP.
82. Edson, *Mexicans in Our Northcentral States,* 2–7.
83. Ibid., 152.
84. Taylor, *Mexican Labor in the United States,* 80–81.
85. Ibid., 82.
86. Ibid., 86.
87. Ibid., 89.
88. Interview, Doorman at Sanger's Biscuit Company, Chicago, Illinois, 12 July 1928, Box 12, C-B Notes, Third Set Incomplete, PTP.
89. Taylor, *Mexican Labor in the United States,* 110.
90. Ibid.
91. Ibid.
92. Ibid., 228.
93. Ibid., 235.
94. Edson, *Mexicans in Our Northcentral States,* 33.
95. Ibid., 211.
96. Ibid., 182.
97. Interview, Miss Baker, International Institute, 19 June 1928, Carton 1, Detroit Conversations, PTP; Interview, Domestic Relations Division, Probation Department,

26 July 1928, Carton 1, Detroit Conversations, PTP; Interview, Public Employment Office, 23 September 1928, Carton 1, Detroit Conversations, PTP.

98. Taylor, *Mexican Labor in the United States,* 131–32.

99. Ibid., 133–69.

100. Zaragosa Vargas, *Proletarians of the North: A History of Mexican Industrial Workers in Detroit and the Midwest, 1917–1933* (Berkeley: University of California Press, 1993), 31–32.

101. Edson, *Mexicans in Our Northcentral States,* 6.

102. Interview, Mrs. Maria Montana, n.d., Carton 1, Detroit Conversations, PTP.

103. Clare Sheridan, "Contested Citizenship: National Identity and the Mexican Immigration Debates of the 1920s," *Journal of American Ethnic History* (Spring 2002): 8; Ericka Lee, "The Chinese Exclusion Example: Race, Immigration, and American Gatekeeping, 1882–1924," *Journal of American Ethnic History* (Spring 2002): 36–62.

104. For a discussion of immigration policy in the years after 1924, see Robert A. Divine, *American Immigration Policy, 1924–1952* (New Haven, Conn.: Yale University Press, 1957); Mark Reisler, *By the Sweat of Their Brow*; Mark Reisler, "Always the Laborer, Never the Citizen: Anglo Perceptions of the Mexican Immigrant during the 1920s," in *Between Two Worlds: Mexican Immigrants in the United States,* ed. David Gutierrez (Wilmington, Del.: Scholarly Resources, 1996), 23–43; Gutierrez, *Walls and Mirrors,* 47–68; Neil Foley, *The White Scourge: Mexicans, Blacks, and Poor Whites in Texas Cotton Culture* (Berkeley: University of California Press, 1997), 40–63; Ngai, "The Architecture of Race in American Immigration Law," 67–92; Cindy Hahamovitch, "'In America Life is Given Away': Jamaican Farmworkers and the Making of Agricultural Immigration Policy," in *The Countryside in the Age of the Modern State: Political Histories of Rural America,* eds. Catherine McNicol Stock and Robert D. Johnston (Ithaca, N.Y.: Cornell University Press, 2001), 134–60.

Chapter 7. Child Labor Reformers and Industrial Agriculture

1. Kriste Lindenmeyer, *"A Right to Childhood": The U.S. Children's Bureau and Child Welfare, 1912–1946* (Urbana: University of Illinois Press, 1997), 128.

2. Walter W. Armentrout, Sara A. Brown, and Charles Gibbons, *Child Labor in the Sugar Beet Fields of Michigan* (New York: National Child Labor Committee, Publication No. 310, 1923); Children's Bureau, *Child Labor and the Work of Mothers in the Beet Fields of Colorado and Michigan,* Bureau Publication Number 115 (Washington, D.C.: GPO, 1923), 122. [hereafter *Child Labor and the Work of Mothers*]

3. "Beet Complex," *The American Child* 5 (June 1923): 2.

4. William Trattner, *Crusade for the Children: a History of the National Child Labor Committee and Child Labor Reform in America* (Chicago: Quadrangle Books, 1970), 145–60; Lindenmeyer, "A Right to Childhood," 111–14.

5. Felix Adler, *Child Labor: A Menace to Civilization* 156 (New York: National Child Labor Committee, 1906), 3.

6. Trattner, *Crusade for the Children*; Robyn Muncy, *Creating a Female Dominion in American Reform, 1890–1935* (Oxford, U.K.: Oxford University Press, 1991), 102–3; Molly Ladd-Taylor, *Mother-Work: Women, Child Welfare, and the State, 1890–1930* (Urbana: University of Illinois Press, 1994), 91–97; Kriste Lindenmeyer, "A Right to Childhood," 108–38; Sonya Michel, *Children's Interests/Mother's Rights: The Shaping of America's Child Care Policy* (New Haven, Conn.: Yale University Press, 1999), 91–109; Anne B. Effland, "Agrarianism and Child Labor Policy for Agriculture," *Agricultural History* 79 (2005): 281–97.

7. Ladd-Taylor, *Mother-Work*, 93–96.

8. Trattner, *Crusade for the Children*, 159.

9. "Word to Readers," *The American Child* 5 (September 1923): 1.

10. Of the Children's Bureau's thirty-one studies of child labor from 1915 to 1930, approximately half focused on "rural employment." Lindenmeyer, *"A Right to Childhood,"* 135.

11. For a discussion of the Country Life movement and rural reform, see David B. Danbom, *The Resisted Revolution: Urban America and the Industrialization of Agriculture, 1900–1930* (Ames: Iowa State University Press, 1979).

12. "Old Witnesses for a New Defense," *The American Child* 8 (June 1926): 1.

13. Christine Stansell, *City of Women: Sex and Class in New York, 1789–1860* (New York: Knopf, 1986), chapter 10; Linda Gordon, *The Great Arizona Orphan Abduction* (Cambridge, Mass.: Harvard University Press, 1999).

14. Charles Gibbons, "What is Rural Child Labor?" *The American Child* 3 (May 1921–February 1922): 171.

15. Owen Lovejoy, "The Country Child and the Social Worker," *The American Child* 8 (June 1926): 3.

16. "Old Witnesses for a New Defense," 1.

17. "Old Clothes," *The American Child* 8 (February 1926): 3.

18. "Old Witnesses for a New Defense," 1.

19. "Your Questions Answered: Agriculture and the Child Labor Amendment," *The American Child* 6 (June 1924): 4.

20. Charles Gibbons, "What is Rural Child Labor?"

21. "Child Labor Myths—II. The Farm," *The American Child* 6 (February 1924): 5.

22. Children's Bureau, *Eleventh Annual Report of the Chief, Children's Bureau To the Secretary of Labor* (Washington, D.C.: GPO, 1923), 14.

23. Nettie McGill, *Child Labor in Agriculture*, Bureau Publication Number 187 (Washington, D.C.: GPO, 1929), 41.

24. Ibid., 3–20.

25. Lovejoy, "The Country Child and the Social Worker," 3.

26. Ibid.

27. "Migratory Child Labor," *The American Child* 8 (July 1926): 7.

28. "Child Labor in Michigan Sugar Beet Fields," *The American Child* 5 (March 1923): 1.

29. Bertram H. Mautner and W. Lewis Abbott, *Child Labor in Agriculture and Farm Life in the Arkansas Valley of Colorado: Based Upon Studies Made During the Summer, Fall, and Winter, 1924* (New York: National Child Labor Committee, 1925), 29; "Work Children Do in Sugar Beet Fields," *The American Child* 5 (February 1923): 3.

30. Children's Bureau, *Child Labor and the Work of Mothers*, 122.

31. McGill, *Child Labor in Agriculture*, 10.

32. Ibid., 35.

33. "Old Witness for a New Defense," 4.

34. Children's Bureau, *Child Labor and the Work of Mothers*, 85–95.

35. U.S. Children's Bureau, *Ninth Annual Report of the Chief, Children's Bureau To the Secretary of Labor* (Washington, D.C.: GPO, 1921), 16.

36. Children's Bureau, *Child Labor and the Work of Mothers*, 76–78.

37. Armentrout et al., *Child Labor in the Sugar Beet Fields*, 30.

38. "What Thanksgiving Day Costs," *The American Child* 4 (November 1922): 4.

39. Armentrout et al., *Child Labor in the Sugar Beet Fields*, 8.

40. Children's Bureau, *Child Labor and the Work of Mothers*, 81.

41. Armentrout et al., *Child Labor in the Sugar Beet Fields*, 23–38, 41.

42. Ibid., 53, 62.

43. Children's Bureau, *Child Labor and the Work of Mothers*, 82.

44. Armentrout et al., *Child Labor in the Sugar Beet Fields*, 30.

45. "Child Labor and Poverty: Both Cause and Effect," *National Child Labor Bulletin* 2 (May 1913): 27.

46. Owen Lovejoy, "The Child Labor Problem in the Sugar Beet Industry," *U.S. Bureau of Labor Statistics Bulletin* 321 (Washington, D.C.: GPO, 3_.

47. Armentrout et al., *Child Labor in the Sugar Beet Fields*, 58.

48. Children's Bureau, *Child Labor and the Work of Mothers*, 23.

49. Ibid., 83.

50. Armentrout et al., *Child Labor in the Sugar Beet Fields*, 23.

51. Ibid., 23.

52. Children's Bureau, *Child Labor and the Work of Mothers*, 107.

53. Ibid., 55.

54. Ibid., 110–11.

55. Sara Brown, "Neglected Children of Migrant Workers," *The Missionary Review of the World* 45 (July 1923): 517.

56. "Child Labor in Michigan Sugar Beet Fields," 1–3.

57. Trattner, *Crusade for the Children*, 153; "Child Labor in Michigan Sugar Beet Fields," 3.

58. Armentrout et al., *Child Labor in the Sugar Beet Fields*, 16.

59. Brown, "Neglected Children of Migrant Workers," 517.
60. Armentrout et al., *Child Labor in the Sugar Beet Fields*, 16.
61. Children's Bureau, *Child Labor and the Work of Mothers*, 89.
62. Ibid., 22, 31.
63. Ibid., 31.
64. Ibid., 26.
65. Armentrout et al., *Child Labor in the Sugar Beet Fields*, 32.
66. Brown, "Neglected Children of Migrant Workers," 517.
67. Armentrout et al., *Child Labor in the Sugar Beet Fields*, 128.
68. Ibid., 14.
69. Ibid., 59.
70. Children's Bureau, *Child Labor and the Work of Mothers*, 106.
71. Ibid., 46.
72. Lovejoy, "The Child Labor Problem in the Beet Sugar Industry," 31.
73. Armentrout et al., *Child Labor in the Sugar Beet Fields*, 7.
74. Children's Bureau, *Child Labor and the Work of Mothers*, 122.
75. Ibid., 121.
76. "Bitter Sweets," *The American Child* 6 (June 1923): 8.
77. Nineteenth Annual Report of the National Child Labor Committee, *The American Child*, January 1924.
78. *Christian Science Monitor*, 13 March 1923. [hereafter *CSM*]
79. *Chicago Daily Tribune*, 3 November 1923 [hereafter *CDT*]; *CDT*, 28 February 1924.
80. *CDT*, 28 February 1924.
81. "Wlad," *The American Child* 5 (September 1923): 1.
82. *Tuscola County Advertiser*, 13 April 1923. [hereafter *TCA*]
83. Ibid.
84. Ibid.
85. Ibid.
86. *Pigeon Progress*, 13 April 1923. [hereafter *PP*]
87. *TCA*, 6 April 1923.
88. "No Small Children Working in Beet Fields," *Michigan Business Farmer* 8 (November 1923): 16. [hereafter *MBFR*]
89. *TCA*, 13 April 1923; "Beet Complex," *The American Child* 5 (June 1923): 2.
90. *PP*, 18 May 1923.
91. *PP*, 4 May 1923.
92. "Are We Guilty?" *MBF* 8 (October 1923): 14.
93. "We have Met the Challenge," *The American Child* 5 (November 1923): 1.
94. *CSM*, 10 May 1924, 4.
95. "Labor and the Legislature in Michigan," *The American Child* 5 (June 1923): 5.
96. "Child Labor in the Beet Fields," *MBFR* 8 (October 1923): 12.

97. *TCA*, 5 October 1923.
98. "Foreigners Use Children in the Beet Fields," *MBFR* 8 (December 1923): 8.
99. "Don't Sign that Sugar Beet Contract," *MBFR* 9 (January 1924): 2.
100. *PP*, 20 February 1925.
101. "In the Name of Child Labor, What Is This?" *MBFR* 9 (October 1924): 2.
102. One of the few exceptions included the article "Democracy?" *The American Child* 8 (January 1926): 6. This article was an excerpt from one that had run in the *Lansing State Journal* in October of the preceding year. In that article, Michigan's population was warned that each year at least five thousand little "brown hands" were coming into the fields to do the kind of work that white farm boys refused to do.

Chapter 8. Remaking Imperialism and the Industrial Countryside

1. T. G. Gallagher, U.S. Senate, Committee on Finance, *Tariff Act of 1929, Schedule 5—Sugar, Molasses, and the Manufacture Of*, 71st Congress, 1st Session, (Washington, D.C.: GPO 1929), 101. [hereafter *Tariff Act of 1929*]

2. Ibid., 103.

3. Grayson L. Kirk, *Philippine Independence: Motives, Problems, and Prospects* (New York: Farrar & Rinehart, 1936), 108; Julian Go and Anne L. Foster, *The American Colonial State in the Philippines: Global Perspectives* (Durham, N.C.: Duke University Press, 2003); H. W. Brands, *Bound to Empire: The United States and the Philippines* (New York: Oxford University Press, 1992); Frank H. Golay, *Face of Empire: United States—Philippine Relations, 1898–1946* (Madison: University of Wisconsin Press, 1998); John Larkin, *Sugar and the Origins of Modern Philippine Society* (Berkeley: University of California Press, 1993).

4. Murray R. Benedict and Oscar C. Stine, *The Agricultural Commodity Programs: Two Decades of Experience* (New York: Twentieth Century Fund, 1956); Van L. Perkins, *Crisis in Agriculture: The AAA and the New Deal, 1933* (Berkeley: University of California Press, 1969); Anthony Badger, *Prosperity Road: The New Deal, Tobacco, and North Carolina* (Chapel Hill: University of North Carolina Press, 1985); Peter Daniel, *Breaking the Land: The Transformation of Cotton, Tobacco, and Rice Cultures Since 1880* (Urbana: University of Illinois Press, 1985), 63–151.

5. *Pigeon Progress*, 27 September 1929 [hereafter *PP*]; *PP*, 30 August 1929; *PP*, 19 September 1929; Michigan farmers planted only 58,355 acres of sugar beet in 1929, just over half the amount they planted in the mid 1920s. C. M. Nicholson, "Head, Grower-Processor Contracts Section, Preliminary Report with Respect to Processor-Grower Relations in the U.S. Sugar Beet Industry," USDA, 1938, 31–32, Folder 2, Box 223, Thaden Papers, Library of Michigan (LOM), Lansing, Michigan. [hereafter Thaden Papers]

6. Thomas J. Heston, *Sweet Subsidy: The Economic and Diplomatic Effects of the United States Sugar Acts, 1934–1937* (New York: Garland, 1987), 62.

7. *PP*, 3 November 1933; "The New Contract," *Field and Factory*, April 1933, 8; Monitor Sugar Company Records, Bay County Archives, Bay City, Michigan.

8. "Our Obligation," *Field and Factory,* September 1934, 2.

9. *PP,* 5 August 1932.

10. Frank Oberst, "Working Together," *Sugar Beet Journal* 1 (October 1935): 5. [hereafter *SBJ*]

11. *Tuscola County Advertiser,* 22 February 1929 [hereafter *TCA*]; *TCA,* 8 March 1929; *TCA,* 21 March 1929; *TCA,* 26 December 1930.

12. *TCA,* 15 February 1929; *PP,* 23 September 1932.

13. For local articles on boosting during the Depression, see *TCA,* 22 February 1929; *TCA,* 1 March 1929; *TCA,* 8 March 1929; *TCA,* 15 March 1929; *TCA,* 21 March 1930; *TCA,* 28 April 1930; *TCA,* 14 November 1930; *TCA,* 21 November 1930; *TCA,* 30 January 1931; *PP,* 16 January 1931; *PP,* 13 November 1931; *PP,* 1 January 1932; *PP,* 19 February 1932; *PP,* 20 May 1932; *PP,* 29 July 1932; *PP,* 9 September 1932; *PP,* 7 October 1932.

14. *History and Operations of the U.S. Sugar Program* (Washington, D.C.: GPO, 1962), 20–21; Heston, *Sweet Subsidy,* 62.

15. *History and Operations,* 21.

16. Heston, *Sweet Subsidy,* 75.

17. Abraham Berglund, "The Tariff Act of 1922," *American Economic Review* 13.1 (March 1923): 14–33.

18. *Wall Street Journal,* 3 January 1929. [hereafter *WSJ*]

19. Resolutions, 11th Annual Meeting of the American Farm Bureau Federation, 1929, reprinted in U.S. Senate, Hearings before the Committee on Territories and Insular Affairs, *Independence for the Philippine Islands,* 71st Congress, 2nd Session (Washington, D.C.: GPO, 1930), 68. [hereafter *Independence for the Philippine Islands*]

20. F. W. Taussig, *The Tariff History of the United States,* eighth revised edition (New York: GP Putnam Sons, 1931), 490–91; *New York Times,* 7 March 1929, 5. [hereafter *NYT*]

21. *NYT,* 22 January 1929.

22. Wilford Eiteman, "The Rise and Decline of Tariff Propaganda," *Quarterly Journal of Economics* 45.1 (November 1930): 32–33; William H. Baldwin, "Pressure Politics and Consumer Interests: The Sugar Issue," *Public Opinion Quarterly* 5.1 (March 1941): 104; Kirk, *Philippine Independence,* 93.

23. *NYT,* 21 January 1929.

24. *NYT,* 12 January 1930.

25. *Tariff Act of 1929,* 63.

26. Cited in *Tariff Act of 1929,* 63.

27. Cited in *Tariff Act of 1929,* 67.

28. Stephen H. Love, *Tariff Act of 1929,* 51.

29. W. R. Ogg, *Tariff Act of 1929,* 7.

30. Ibid., 20.

31. James N. McBride, *Tariff Act of 1929*, 112.
32. Ibid., 117.
33. Fred Crawford, *Tariff Act of 1929*, 433.
34. Ibid., 441.
35. Ibid., 433.
36. *NYT*, 23 January 1929.
37. *Washington Post*, 7 April 1929. [hereafter *WP*]
38. *WP*, 9 February 1930.
39. *WSJ*, 24 January 1929.
40. *WP*, 17 February 1929.
41. *WP*, 1 March 1929.
42. Brands, *Bound to Empire*; Golay, *Face of Empire*.
43. *NYT*, 26 March 1929.
44. *NYT*, 21 April 1929.
45. Mr. Orth, *Independence for the Philippine Islands*, 190.
46. *NYT*, 21 April 1929.
47. *NYT*, 10 January 1930.
48. *WP*, 2 February 1930; *WP*, 9 February 1930.
49. Heston, *Sweet Subsidy*, 78.
50. *History and Operations*, 21.
51. *WSJ*, 5 February 1929.
52. *WSJ*, 5 February 1929.
53. *WSJ*, 12 February 1929.
54. Julian Go, "Chains of Empire: State Building and Political Education in Puerto Rico and the Philippines," in Go and Foster, *The American Colonial State*, 196.
55. *WP*, 16 January 1929.
56. Taussig, *The Tariff History*, 500–504.
57. Whitney Perkins, *Denial of Empire: The United States and Its Dependencies* (Leyden, New York: A.W. Sythoff, 1962).
58. *NYT*, 7 March 1930.
59. Brands, *Bound to Empire*, 151; Golay, *Face of Empire*, 320.
60. U.S. Senate, Hearings before the Committee on Territories and Insular Affairs, *Independence for the Philippines*, 71st Congress, 2nd Session, on S. 204, S. 3108, S.J. Res. 113, S. Res. 199, S. 3379 and S. 3827, May 22 1930 (Washington, D.C.: GPO, 1930), 657–58.
61. Chester H. Gray, *Independence for the Philippine Islands*, 77.
62. Ibid., 100.
63. Frederic Brenckman, *Independence for the Philippine Islands*, 110.
64. W. C. Hushing, *Independence for the Philippine Islands*, 114; See also Mae M. Ngai, *Impossible Subjects: Illegal Aliens and the Making of Modern America* (Princeton, N.J.: Princeton University Press, 2004), 116–20.

65. John Switzer, *Independence for the Philippine Islands*, 378.
66. Ibid., 379.
67. Ibid., 379–80.
68. Fred Cummings, President of the National Beet Growers' Association, testified at the 1932 House hearings. See U.S. House of Representatives, Hearings Before the Committee on Insular Affairs, *Independence for the Philippine Islands*, 72nd Congress, 1st Session (Washington, D.C.: GPO, 1932), 158–64. [hereafter *Independence*]
69. Kirk, *Philippine Independence*, 108.
70. *NYT,* 19 January 1930; *NYT,* 2 February 1930; *WP,* 18 November 1931; *Christian Science Monitor,* 3 June 1930. [hereafter *CSM*]
71. *WSJ,* 1 August 1931.
72. *NYT,* 16 August 1931.
73. *CSM,* 3 June 1930.
74. *NYT,* 15 July 1931.
75. *WSJ,* 1 August 1931.
76. Manuel Roxas, *Independence for the Philippine Islands*, 6–7.
77. Ibid., 16.
78. Reprinted in "Its Friends Oppose Freedom," *NYT,* 4 December 1932.
79. Roxas, *Independence*, 118.
80. For a recounting of the debate and compromises, see Kirk, *Philippine Independence*, 110–20; *NYT,* 23 December 1932.
81. *WP,* 24 December 1932.
82. *WP,* 26 December 1932.
83. Reprinted in Kirk, *Philippine Independence*, 227.
84. Ibid., 227–28.
85. Ibid., 230.
86. Ibid., 121.
87. Brands, *Bound to Empire*, 153.
88. "Memorandum on Recent Legislation Affecting Philippine Economic Life—I," *Memorandum (Institute of Pacific Relations, American Council)* 3.19 (October 1934).
89. *CSM,* 19 December 1932.
90. *NYT,* 24 December 1932; Michael Paul Onorato, "Quezon and Independence: A Reexamination," *Philippine Studies* 37 (1989): 221–31.
91. *NYT,* 23 December 1932.
92. Kirk, *Philippine Independence*, 125.
93. Brands, *Bound to Empire*, 155.
94. Ibid.
95. *NYT,* 15 January 1934.
96. Brands, *Bound to Empire*, 157, footnote 34.
97. Golay, *Face of Empire*, 327.
98. Akira Iriye, *The Cambridge History of American Foreign Relations: The Global-*

izing of America, 1913–1945, Volume II (Cambridge, U.K.: Cambridge University Press, 1993); Steve MacIssac, "The Struggle for Economic Development in the Philippine Commonwealth, 1935–1940," *Philippine Studies* 50.2 (2002): 141–67.

99. Heston, *Sweet Subsidy.*

100. C. R. Whittlesey, "Import Quotas in the United States," *Quarterly Journal of Economics* 52.1 (1937): 37–65; John E. Dalton, "Sugar and Public Opinion," *Public Opinion Quarterly* 2.2 (1938): 287–94.

101. F. W. Taussig, *The Tariff History of the United States,* eighth revised edition (New York: Capricorn Books, 1931), 481–82.

102. *NYT,* 29 June 1933; E. Pendleton Herring, "The Political Context of the Tariff Commission," *Political Science Quarterly* 49.3 (1934): 421–40; *History and Operations,* 21; Heston, *Sweet Subsidy,* 97–101.

103. D. Gale Johnson, *The Sugar Program: Large Costs and Small Benefits* (Washington, D.C.: American Enterprise for Public Policy, 1974), 23.

104. President Roosevelt to Resident Commissioner Bolivar Pagan of Puerto Rico, Concerning the Extension of the 1937 Sugar Act of 1937, 1 December 1941, Box 7, F: Sugar Legislation, Letters, Etc., 1934–1944 170/64/23/02, ASC-Sugar Division Correspondence and Program Records, 1934–1960, RG 145, Farm Service Agency, National Archives, College Park, Maryland. [hereafter FSA]

105. Heston, *Sweet Subsidy,* 75–128.

106. Franklin D. Roosevelt, Message to Congress, U.S. House of Representatives, Hearing Before the Committee on Agriculture, *Include Sugar Beets and Sugarcane as Basic Commodities,* 73rd Congress, 2nd Session (Washington, D.C.: GPO, 1934), 1. [hereafter *Include Sugar Beets*]

107. Charles M. Kearney, U.S. Senate, Hearings Before the Committee On Finance, *To Include Sugar Beets and Sugarcane as Basic Agricultural Commodities Under the Agricultural Adjustment Act,* 73rd Congress, 2nd Session (Washington, D.C.: GPO, 1934), 41. [hereafter *To Include Sugar Beets*]

108. This theme was repeated in industry journals, including Michigan's *SBJ.* For example, see "Editorial," *SBJ* 1 (January 1936): 51; "Editorial," *SBJ* 2 (November 1936): 24.

109. C. R. Oviatt, *To Include Sugar Beets,* 95.

110. Ibid., 155–56.

111. Ibid., 96.

112. Radio Address—The Administration's Sugar Bill, by Edward P. Costigan of Colorado, March 6, 1934—Over the National Broadcasting System, ASC, Sugar Division Correspondence and Program Records, 1934–60, Box 7, F: Sugar Legislation, Letters, etc., 1933–44, 170/64/23/02, FSA.

113. Heston, *Sweet Subsidy,* 107.

114. *NYT,* 5 April 1934; *NYT,* 17 April 1934.

115. Johnson, *The Sugar Program,* 23.

116. Heston, *Sweet Subsidy,* 110, 114.

117. Johnson, *The Sugar Program*, 23.

118. *NYT*, 1 May 1934.

119. Sugar Beets and the Sugar Act, ca. 1940, Box 7, Folder: Sugar Beet Program Dates 1934–41, ASC—Sugar Division Correspondence and Program Records, 1934–60, 170/64/23/02, FSA.

120. USDA—AAA—Continental United States Beet Sugar Regulations, August 1934, ASC—Sugar Division Records, 1934–1960, 170/64/23/02, FSA.

121. USDA—AAA—Continental Beet Sugar Order No 1, 26 July 1934, page 2, ASC—Sugar Division Records, 1934–1960, 170/64/23/02, FSA.

122. Fred L. Crawford to C. J. and Hubert [Crawford] 25 March 1934, cited in Heston, *Sweet Subsidy*, 130.

123. *Adrian Daily Telegraph*, 28 April 1934.

124. "Blissfield Beet Growers Association," Newsletter, 1935, 176/2321, Federal Mediation and Conciliation Service, RG 280, National Archives, College Park, Maryland [hereafter FMCS]; *PP*, 5 April 1935.

125. *TCA*, 19 April 1935.

126. The FU represented the only real alternative to the FB. *PP*, 21 September 1934; 5 October 1934; 18 January 1935; 29 March 1935; 3 April 1936; 7 August 1936.

127. "Editorial," *SBJ* 1.1 (October 1935): 3.

128. Frank Oberst, "Working Together," *SBJ* 1.1 (October 1935): 5.

129. Heston, *Sweet Subsidy*, 130.

130. Heston, *Sweet Subsidy*, 131; Kenneth Finegold, "From Agrarianism to Adjustment: The Politic Origins of New Deal Agricultural Policy," *Politics and Society* 11 (1981): 1–27; Gregory Hooks, "From an Autonomous to a Captured State Agency: The Decline of the New Deal in Agriculture," *American Sociological Review* 55 (February 1990): 29–43.

131. "Editorial," *SBJ* 3 (November 1937): 25.

132. Heston, *Sweet Subsidy*, 200.

133. *PP*, 26 October 1934.

134. *PP*, 2 August 1935.

135. Heston, *Sweet Subsidy*, 202.

136. *TCA*, 19 April 1935; *PP*, 5 April 1935.

137. *Adrian Daily Telegraph*, 28 April 1934.

138. "Blissfield Growers Association," Newsletter, 1935, 176/2321, FMCS.

139. C. M. Nicholson, Head, Grower-Processor Contracts Section, Preliminary Report with Respect to Processor-Grower Relations in the U.S. Sugar Beet Industry, USDA, 1938, 31–32, Folder 2, Box 223, Thaden Papers; *Adrian Daily Times*, 29 September 1934.

Chapter 9. The Politics of Migrant Labor

1. W. H. Davis to Henry Hull, 4 October 1930, 55639/617a, RG 85, National Archives, Washington, D.C.

2. Murray R. Benedict and Oscar C. Stine, *The Agricultural Commodity Programs: Two Decades of Experience* (New York: Twentieth Century Fund, 1956), 295. Devra Weber, *Dark Sweat, White Gold: California Farm Workers, Cotton, and the New Deal* (Berkeley: University of California Press), 112; Cindy Hahamovitch, *The Fruit of Their Labor: Atlantic Coast Farmworkers and the Making of Migrant Poverty, 1870–1945* (Chapel Hill: University of North Carolina Press, 1997), 138–39, 151–52.

3. T. H. Watkins, *The Hungry Years: A Narrative History of the Great Depression in America* (New York: Henry Holt & Company, 1999), 44–45.

4. Lizabeth Cohen, *Making a New Deal: Industrial Workers in Chicago, 1919–1939* (Cambridge, U.K.: Cambridge University Press, 1990); Robert McElvaine, *The Great Depression: America, 1929–1941* (New York: Times Books, 1984).

5. John Hammerstein to Herbert Hoover, 21 July 1929, 55639/616, RG 85, National Archives, Washington, D.C. [hereafter INS]

6. Arthur A. Caulkett to Herbert Hoover, 22 April 1930, 55639/616, INS.

7. Albert Bauaski to the Gentlemen of the Immigration Bureau, 5 September 1930, 55639/616, INS.

8. George J. Sanchez, *Becoming Mexican American: Ethnicity, Culture and Identity in Chicano Los Angeles* (New York: Oxford University Press, 1993), 213.

9. Ibid., 214.

10. Franciso E. Balderrama and Raymond Rodriguez, *Decade of Betrayal: Mexican Repatriation in the 1930s* (Albuquerque: University of New Mexico Press, 1995); Abraham Hoffman, *Unwanted Mexican Americans in the Great Depression: Repatriation Pressures, 1929–1939* (Tucson: University of Arizona Press, 1974); Sanchez, *Becoming Mexican American*, 209–26; Zaragosa Vargas, *Labor Rights and Civil Rights: Mexican American Workers in Twentieth Century America* (Princeton, N.J.: Princeton University Press, 2005), 43–61.

11. *Saginaw Daily News*, 3 September 1931. [hereafter *SDN*]

12. John L. Zurick to Henry Hull, 20 October 1932, 55784/585, INS.

13. *SDN*, 10 October 1932.

14. *SDN*, 11 October 1932.

15. Sanchez, *Becoming Mexican American*, 209–26; also see Humphrey, "Mexican Repatriation from Michigan," *Social Service Review* 15 (September 1941): 497–513.

16. Ignacio Batiza, "To the Mexican Colony," handbill, 13 October 1932, 55784/585, INS; *SDN*, 21 November 1932.

17. Zaragosa Vargas, *Proletarians of the North: A History of Mexican Industrial Workers in Detroit and the Midwest, 1917–1933* (Berkeley: University of California Press, 1992), 178–82.

18. *Detroit Free Press*, 13 November 1932.

19. *SDN*, 23 November 1932.

20. *SDN*, 23 November 1932.

21. Vargas, *Proletarians of the North*, 173.

22. *Detroit Free Press,* 13 November 1932.
23. John L. Zubrick, 28 November 1932, 55784/585, INS.
24. R. W. Gangewere, U.S. Immigration Inspector, to District Director of Immigration, Detroit, Michigan, 29 November 1932, 55784/585, INS.
25. *Pigeon Progress,* 7 October 1932. [hereafter *PP*]
26. "Industrial and Labor Conditions: Labor Conditions in the Sugar-Beet Fields and Some Suggested Remedies," *Monthly Labor Review* 39 (July 1934): 57; "Sugar Beet Field Labor Under the A.A.A.," *Journal of Farm Economics* 19 (May 1937): 645; Kent Hendrickson, "The Sugar-Beet Laborer and the Federal Government: An Episode in the History of the Great Plains in the 1930s," *Great Plains Journal* 3 (Spring 1964): 50.
27. "The Sugar Hearing," *The American Child* 15 (September 1933): 4; "The Price of Beet Sugar," *The American Child* 15 (September 1933): 5.
28. "Minimum Standards for the Employment of Children," *The American Child* 13 (June 1931): 2; "Child Labor in Agriculture," *The American Child* 13 (April 1931): 1; "Migratory Workers," *The American Child* 13 (April 1931): 2; Charles Fountain Willis, "Is Child Labor an Economic Boon?" *The American Child* 13 (April 1931): 5; "Interstate Migratory Conference Acts," *The American Child* 13 (April 1931): 8; "Beet Workers and their Wages," *The American Child* 13 (October 1931): 3; "A New Deal for Children Too!" *The American Child* 15 (April 1933): 2.
29. Franklin Roosevelt to Francis Perkins, Memorandum, "Labor Conditions in the Sugar Beet Fields of the United States," F; Child Labor, Records of the AS and C, Office of Administration, Sugar Division Records, 1936–1952, Box 2, Farm Service Agency, RG 145, National Archives, College Park, Maryland. [hereafter FSA]
30. *New York Times,* 4 January 1934 [hereafter *NYT*]; Thomas J. Heston, *Sweet Subsidy: The Economic and Diplomatic Effects of the United States Sugar Acts, 1934–1974* (New York: Garland, 1987), 95.
31. William Trattner, *Crusade for the Children: a History of the National Child Labor Committee and Child Labor Reform in America* (Chicago: Quadrangle Books, 1970), 209.
32. "Industrial and Labor Conditions," 60.
33. "Children Out of the Beet Fields," *The Survey* 22 (December 1934): 388.
34. *NYT,* 20 April 1934; Heston, *Sweet Subsidy,* 111.
35. For a copy of the labor provisions of the Jones-Costigan Act, see Elizabeth Johnson, *Welfare of Families of Sugar-Beet Laborers: A Study of Child Labor and Its Relation to Family Work, Income, and Living Conditions in 1935* (Washington, D.C.: GPO, 1939), 96–97; Heston, *Sweet Subsidy,* 109.
36. *NYT,* 26 April 1936; *NYT,* 23 November 1936.
37. *NYT,* 2 March 1937.
38. Hahamovitch, *Fruits of Their Labor,* 138–50; Trattner, *Crusade for the Children,* 209.
39. Memorandum to the Administration, n.d., ca. October 1937, William T. Ham

and Joshua Bernhardt, F; Determination of Fair and Reasonable Wage Rates for Harvesting of the 1937 Crop of Sugar Beets Pursuant to the Sugar Act of 1937, Box 16, FSA.

40. Ibid.

41. Ibid.

42. A Memorandum prepared by Florence Brooks, Abuses Connected with the Seasonal Migration of Mexicans to Michigan, February 1, 1943, Folder 10, Box 229, Thaden Papers, Library of Michigan, Lansing, Michigan [hereafter Thaden Papers]. Also see, Heston, *Sweet Subsidy*, 331; "Washington News Notes," *Sugar Beet Journal* 3 (January 1938): 74; *PP*, 6 January 1939.

43. Memorandum for the Administrator, USDA, F; Determination of Fair and Reasonable Wage Rates for Harvesting of the 1937 Crop of Sugar Beets, Pursuant to the Sugar Act of 1937, Box 16, ASC—Sugar Division Correspondence and Program Records, 1934–60, 170/60/23/02, FSA.

44. Stanley White to Dr. J. R., Steelman, 1 November 1937, Re: Sugar Act Hearings in Toledo, on Beet Sugar Wage Rates, 196/139, Federal Mediation and Conciliation Service, RG 280, National Archives, College Park, Maryland. [hereafter FMCS]

45. Heston, *Sweet Subsidy*, 131.

46. Stanley White to Dr. J. R. Steelman, 1 November 1937, Re: Sugar Act Hearings in Toledo on Beet Sugar Wage Rates, 196/139, FMCS.

47. Toledo, Ohio: Sugar Beet Wage Hearing: AAA: February 28, 1938, Reports Stanley V. White to J. R. Steelman, 196/139, 2/27/38, 196/139, FMCS.

48. *PP*, 13 January 1939.

49. Memorandum for the Secretary, H. R. Trolley, Administrator, January 1938, In Regards to the 1937, ASC-Sugar Division Correspondence and Program Records, 1934–1960, 170/64/23/02, F: Determination of Fair and Reasonable Wage Rates for Harvesting of the 1937 Crop of Sugar Beets Pursuant to the Sugar Act of 1937, Box 16, FSA.

50. USDA, Sugar Division, No. 15, (Revised) Issued January 25, 1938, Revision of Determination of Fair and Reasonable Wage Rates for Harvesting of the 1937 Crop of Sugar Beets, Pursuant to the Sugar Act of 1937, ASC, Sugar Division Correspondence and Program Records, 1934–1960, 170/64/23/02, F: Sugar Determinations, Nos. 1–2, Box 7, FSA.

51. Determination of Fair and Reasonable Wage Rates for Harvesting the 1938 Crop, Pursuant to the Sugar Act of 1937, USDA, Sugar Division Publication No. 24, April 4, 1938, ASC, Sugar Division Correspondence and Program Records, 1934–1960, 170/64/23/02, F: Sugar Determinations, Nos. 1–2, Box 7, FSA.

52. Memorandum to the Secretary, Bernhardt to Wallace, March 28, 1939, ASC, Sugar Division Correspondence and Program Records, 1934–1960, 170/54/23/02, F: Determination of Fair and Reasonable Wage Rates for Harvesting of the 1939 Sugar Crop, Pursuant to the 1937 Sugar Beet Act, Box 16, FSA.

53. Memorandum Re: Determination of Fair and Reasonable Wage Rates for Harvesting of the 1939 Sugar Beet Crop, Pursuant, ASC, Sugar Division Correspondence and Program Records, 1934–1960, 170/54/23/02, F: Determination of Fair and Reasonable Wage Rates for the Harvesting the 1939 Sugar Crop, Box 16, FSA.

54. Joshua Bernhardt, Chief, Memorandum to the Secretary, 1940, F: Determination of Fair and Reasonable Wage Rates for Persons Employed in the Production, Cultivation or Harvesting of the 1940 Crop of Sugar Beets Pursuant to the Sugar Act of 1937, ASC, Sugar Division Correspondence and Program Records, 1934–1960, 170/54/23/02, Box 16, FSA; *PP,* 12 April 1940.

55. Michigan Works Projects Administration, Lansing, Michigan, "Migratory Workers in Southwest Michigan," August 12, 1940, Folder 4, Box 225, Thaden Papers.

56. Michigan Works Projects Administration, Lansing, "Migratory Workers in Southwest Michigan," August 12, 1940, Folder 4, Box 225, Thaden Papers.

57. "AAA Memorandum of Information on Sugar Beet Labor Practices, 1938," Folder 7, Box 228, Thaden Papers.

58. USDA, AAA, Michigan Agricultural Conservation Committee, Lansing, Michigan, April 10, 1939, "Re: 1939 Sugar Beet Wages," Folder 5, Box 225, Thaden Papers.

59. Mrs. Agnes Anderson to John E. Dalton, 11 June 1935, ASC, O of ADM, Sugar Division Records, Box 2 F: Corr. 1934–1935, 170/64/15/03, FSA.

60. J. A. Dickey, Head, Production Adjustment Unit, Sugar Section to Mr. R. N. Baldwin, Director of Extension, Michigan State College, East Lansing, 21 June 1935, ASC, O of ADM, Sugar Division Records, Box 2 F: Corr. 1934–1935, 170/64/15/03, FSA.

61. Draft, John E. Dalton to the Bay City Factory District Production Control Association, 20 June 1935, ASC, O of ADM, Sugar Division Records, Box 2 F: Corr. 1934–1935, 170/64/15/03, FSA.

62. C. R. Oviatt to John E. Dalton, Chief, Sugar Section, 18 July 1935, ASC, O of ADM, Sugar Division Records, Box 2 F: Corr. 1934–1935, 170/64/15/03, FSA.

63. Chas. A. Coryell, Monitor Sugar Company to John E. Dalton, Sugar Chief, 21 June 1934, ASC, O of ADM, Sugar Division Records, Box 2 F: Corr. 1934–1935, 170/64/15/03, FSA.

64. Johnson, *Welfare of Families,* 28–36.

65. Ibid., 38–39.

66. Sidney C. Surfin, "Labor Organization in Agricultural America, 1930–1935," *American Journal of Sociology* 43 (1938): 557.

67. Stuart Jamieson, *Labor Unionism in American Agriculture,* Department of Labor Bulletin 836 (Washington, D.C.: GPO, 1945), 383; Surfin, "Labor Organization in Agricultural America, 1930–1935," 557; Memo: "Mexican Village" on Edge of Blissfield, November 15–16, 1939, Folder 3, Box 228, Thaden Papers.

68. "Agreement," 1935, 176/2321, FMCS.

69. "Beet Workers Force Pay Raise," *Rural Worker* 1 (October 1935), Folder: Mid-

west, Z-R-2, Stuart Jamieson Papers, Bancroft Library, University of California at Berkeley. [hereafter SJP]

70. Fred Schmidt to Frances Perkins, May 4, 1935, Postal Telegram, 176/2321, FMCS.

71. J. E. O'Conner to Hugh Kerwin, Preliminary Report of the Commission of Conciliation, Blissfield, Michigan, May 14, 1935, 176/2321, FMCS; J. E. O'Conner to Hugh Kerwin, Re: Agricultural Workers Blissfield Beet Striking, 19 May 1935, 176/2321, FMCS.

72. "Beet Workers Force Pay Raise," *Rural Worker* 1 (October 1935), Folder: Midwest, Z-R-2, SJP; Albert Cotton, "Blissfield Beet Worker Union Wins $5.00 Per Acre Increase—Contract Urged as a Model for Other Groups," *Rural Worker,* Folder: Midwest, Z-R-2, SJP; Fred Schmidt, "Union President Explains the Way to Win Contracts," *Rural Worker* 2 (1936), Folder: Midwest, Z-R-2, SJP.

73. Great Lakes Sugar Company—Growers Contract with Field Workers, 1935, 176/2321, FMCS.

74. "Beet Workers Force Pay Raise," *Rural Worker* 1 (October 1935), Folder: Midwest, Z-R-2, SJP.

75. Johnson, *Welfare of Families,* 61.

76. Ibid., 57.

77. Ibid., 26.

78. Ibid., 58.

79. "Michigan and Ohio Get New Union—AFL to Organize 19 Beet Factory Districts," *Rural Worker* 2 (June 1936), Folder: Midwest, Z-R-2, SJP.

80. "Beet Industry Gets Benefits—Michigan and Ohio Unions Demand Share," *Rural Worker* 2 (1936), Folder: Midwest, Z-R-2, SJP.

81. "Plan Conference in Ohio and Michigan," *Rural Worker* 3 (1937), Folder: Midwest, Z-R-2, SJP.

82. Jamieson, *Labor Unionism,* 384.

83. Ibid., 385.

84. Albert Markva, "Beet Company Lowers Wages," *Rural Worker* 3 (1937), Folder: Midwest, Z-R-2, SJP; Jamieson, *Labor Unionism,* 385.

85. Albert Markva to Frances Perkins, March 1937, 176/2321, FMCS; Albert Markva to J. E. O'Conner, March 1937, 176/2321, FMCS.

86. Dennis Nodin Valdes, *Al Norte: Agricultural Workers in the Great Lakes Region, 1917–1970* (Austin: University of Texas Press, 1991), 45.

87. Jamieson, *Labor Unionism,* 385.

88. J. R. Steelman to Frances Perkins, 20 May 1938, F: Conciliation Reports General Labor Information—USDL Conciliation Services—Washington, D.C., Box 33, General Records of the Department of Labor, RG 174, National Archives, College Park, Maryland.

89. Jamieson, *Labor Unionism,* 385–86.

90. *Adrian Daily Telegraph,* 19 May 1938.

91. *Detroit Free Press,* 20 May 1938; *Adrian Daily Telegraph,* 20 May 1938.

92. *Adrian Daily Telegraph,* 26 May 1938.

93. Jamieson, *Labor Unionism,* 386.

94. Cited in Valdes, *Al Norte,* 46.

95. *TCA,* 1 July 1927.

96. For example, see *PP,* 15 December 1933; *PP,* 11 May 1934; *PP,* 2 April 1937; *PP,* 16 April 1937.

97. "Sugar Beet Field Workers in Michigan," Draft Manuscript, 78, Folder 2, Box 222, Thaden Papers.

98. "Sugar Beet Field Workers in Michigan," Draft Manuscript, 41, Folder 2, Box 222, Thaden Papers.

99. "Sugar Beet Field Workers in Michigan," Draft Manuscript, 78, Folder 2, Box 222, Thaden Papers.

100. Migrant Information for Workers, Home Mission Council of North America, June 1942, Folder 2, Box 227, Thaden Papers.

101. *PP,* 26 March 1937.

102. Carey McWilliams, *Ill Fares the Land: Migrants and Migrant Labor in the United States* (Boston: Little, Brown & Company, 1942), 275.

103. Ibid.

104. Clippings, *Marshall Register,* 29 November 1938, Folder 4, Box 225, Thaden Papers.

105. Ibid.

106. "Sugar Beet Field Workers in Michigan," Draft Manuscript, 20, Folder 2, Box 222, Thaden Papers.

107. "Sugar Beet Field Workers in Michigan," Draft Manuscript, 14, Folder 2, Box 222, Thaden Papers.

108. "Mexican Labor is Championed by State Department," *The Apple Blossom,* 11 December 1937, F: 4, Box 223, Thaden Papers.

109. "Sugar Beet Field Workers in Michigan," Draft Manuscript, 14, Folder 2, Box 222, Thaden Papers.

110. "Sugar Beet Field Workers in Michigan," Draft Manuscript, Folder 2, Box 222, Thaden Papers.

111. "Sugar Beet Field Workers in Michigan," Folder 2, Box 222, Thaden Papers.

112. *PP,* 13 May 1938.

113. "Sugar Beet Field Workers in Michigan," Draft Manuscript, 20–21, Folder 2, Box 222, Thaden Papers.

114. "Sugar Beet Field Workers in Michigan," Draft Manuscript, 20–21, Folder 2, Box 222, Thaden Papers; also see "Sugar Beet Field Workers in Michigan," 68–69, Folder 2, Box 222, Thaden Papers.

115. *PP,* 17 June 1938.

116. Article cited in McWilliams, *Ill Fares the Land*, 279.

117. Albert Bauaski to the Gentlemen of the Immigration Bureau, 5 September 1930, 55639/616, INS.

Epilogue

1. Paul S. Taylor, "Migratory Farm Labor in the United States," *Monthly Labor Review* 44 (March 1937): 537.

2. U.S. House of Representatives, *Hearings Before the Select Committee to Investigate the Interstate Migration of Destitute Citizens*, 76th Congress, 3rd Session, (Washington, D.C.: GPO, 1941), 1145. [hereafter *Interstate Migration*]

3. Ibid., 1149.

4. John DeWilde, Ben Graham, Marguerite Dwan, and Bernard Litwin, *Interstate Migration*, 1235.

5. The most popular recent account of industrial agriculture can be found in Michael Pollen, *The Omnivore's Dilemma: A Natural History of Four Meals* (New York: Penguin Press, 2006).

6. Deborah Fitzgerald, "Eating and Remembering," *Agricultural History* 79.4 (2005): 393–408.

7. Alfred E. Eckes Jr., *Opening America's Market: U.S. Foreign Trade Policy Since 1776* (Chapel Hill: University of North Carolina Press, 1995), 998.

8. Ibid., 141.

9. Ibid., 282.

10. *Washington Post*, 11 May 2005.

11. Vincent A. Mahler, "The Political Economy of North-South Bargaining: The Case of the International Sugar Agreement," *International Organization* 38.4 (1984): 719.

12. "Mighty Lobby is Losing Some Luster," *New York Times*, 3 June 2005.

13. David Orden, "Agricultural Interest Groups and the North American Free Trade Agreement," in *The Political Economy of American Trade Policy*, ed. Anne D. Krueger (Chicago: University of Chicago Press, 1996), 378–79.

Index

Abbott, Grace, 170
Ackerman, C. E., 115, 183
Agricultural Adjustment Act (AAA), 187–88, 205–7, 222–23
agricultural ladder, 6, 63; eastern Europeans and, 92–93, 150, 174–75; Mexicans and 147, 150
Agricultural Workers Union (AWU), 226, 228–32
Allison, William B., 16
Alma Sugar Beet Growers' Association, 45
Alma Sugar Company, 30, 59, 71
Alonzo, Marco, 158
American Beet Sugar Manufacturers' Association, 39
American Farm Bureau Federation (AFBF): competition with Farmers' National Council, 110–11, 121; founding of, 98; promotion of Philippine independence, 198; during tariff debate, 191–92
American Federation of Labor (AFL), 135, 199, 226, 233
Americanization, 76, 93, 122
American Society of Equity (AS of E), 56, 107
American Sugar Refining Company (ASRC), 30, 54, 60
Anderson, Agnes, 227
Andresen, August, 150
Archer Daniels Midland, 244

Atkins, George, 86
Austin, Harry, 146, 151
Ayala, Jesus, 235

Backsher, Paul, 87
Baker, Herbert, 110
Barbee, David Rankin, 12, 194
Batiza, Ingacio L., 218–20
Bauaski, Albert, 217
Bay City Businessmen's Association, 20
Bay City Sugar Company, 31, 68
Beck, P. D., 241
Beet-Sugar Law, 19n30, 49
Benjamin, Charles G., 156
Berger, John, 85
Bernhardt, Joshua, 224–25
Bialy, M. J., 104
Bingham, Hiram, 197, 200
Blissfield Beet Growers Association, 226, 229–31
Bodesiler, Fred, 226
Bohemians, 6, 66, 83, 92
bounties, 3–4, 19, 20
Boutell, Benjamin, 20
Box, John, 144
Boys Working Reserve (Department of Interior), 125–26, 128
Bracero program, 152
Bradley, Nathan, 20, 68, 70
Brenckman, Frederic, 198

Brooks, Florence, 225
Burnett, John L., 129
Bush, George W., 242

Caminetti, Anthony, 129–30, 133–34, 142
cane sugar: as barbaric, 1, 24; cheap labor and, 1, 24–25, 30–31, 34; as competitor to beet sugar, 1, 3–4, 7, 16–17, 32–33, 35–36, 186, 190, 193–99, 202–5; Louisiana and, 4, 25–26; natural advantages of, 31–32; sugar acts and, 207–9; the trust and, 30; during World War I, 101
capitalism, 15; imperialism and, 23, 36–37; industrial agriculture and, 39–40, 46, 57–58, 63, 107–10, 121; as local phenomenon, 39–40
Cardoso, Lawrence, 131
Carr, Arthur, 85–86
Carranza, Venustiano, 130–32
Catholic Church, 234–35
Caulkett, Arthur A., 217
Central Beet Growers' Association, 50
Charlevoix Sugar Company, 52
child labor, 6, 9, 11, 66, 71–75; and Agricultural Adjustment Act, 222; child labor reformers and, 166–68; constitutional debate over, 183–84; farmer critique of, 183–84; farm family use of, 173–78; industrial agriculture and, 167–71, 184; Jones-Costigan Act and, 223; migrant family use of, 175–77; militancy of, 74–75; as philanthropy, 73–74; physical attributes of, 72, 74; press critique of, 179–80; recruitment of urban, 72; state of Michigan investigation into, 180–82; state regulation of, 178–79; sugar acts and, 222–23, 227–28; sugar beet industry defense of, 180–82; town support of, 72–73
Children's Bureau, 91–92, 230; Agricultural Adjustment Act and, 222; critique of farm families, 175; definition of industrial agriculture, 168–70; field investigations of, 173–74; highlighting health risks of child labor, 172–73; neglect of Mexican children, 175, 183; sugar acts and, 227–28; view of migrant fathers, 176–77; view of migrant mothers, 177
Churchill, W. L., 31, 39, 47–48, 69
Circulo de Obreros Catolicos, 154
Clark, John, 139

colonialism: beet sugar and, 7–8, 23, 33, 34–37, 39, 186–87, 191, 207, 213; cane sugar and, 1, 4, 28; as economic burden, 35–36, 187; European, 1, 3, 4, 7–8, 23, 25, 29, 35–36; Philippine independence and, 203
Columbia Sugar Company, 96, 143, 154
Comisiones Honorificas, 156, 158
Committee on Insular Affairs, 199
Committee on Territories and Insular Affairs, 197, 204
company farms, 52–53
ConAgra Foods, 244
Connally, Tom, 193
Constitution, Mexican, 130–32
Constitution, U.S., 26, 186
consul, Mexican, 131, 140, 156–59, 218–19
consul, U.S., 132
consumption, 15–16, 36, 101
Continental Sugar Company, 138–39
contract farming, 2–3, 40–43, 63, 112
contract labor law, 123. See also Foran
Costigan, Edward, 206, 203
Country Life movement, 57, 168
Cranage, Thomas, 20
Crapo, T. S., 146, 149
Crawford, Fred, 193, 221
Cuba: American capitalists in, 24, 28, 196–97; cane sugar competition of, 16–17, 24, 27–33, 39, 186; commercial ties, 35; Jones-Costigan Act, 206; Platt Amendment, 1, 245; sugar acts and, 188, 206–9; tariff debates and, 29–31, 33, 186, 192–94, 196–97; Teller Resolution, 28–29; U.S. Constitution and, 26; during World War I, 101
Culver, Charles, 182–83
Czylowitz, Wlad, 180

Dalton, John E., 227
Danbom, David B., 2–3
Davis, W. E., 215
Detroit Institute of Arts, 219
Detroit Sugar Company, 77
Diaz family, 156
Dickinson, L. J., 146, 151–52
Dieckema, Geret, 182–83
Dillon, Francis J., 233
Dingley, Edward N., 16, 25
Dingley Tariff, 16, 35
Dinwidde Committee, 222, 226

Dinwiddie, Courtney, 222
Doak, William, 217
Dominican Republic-Central American Free Trade Agreement (DR-CAFTA), 246
Downes v. Bidwell (1901), 28

eastern Europeans: assimilation of, 76; conflicts with farmers, 83–85; economic mobility of, 90–91, 95; housing of, 79–81; labor contracts of, 78–79; in migrant colonies, 6, 80, 88–90; newspaper coverage of, 84–88; in other states, 83–84; racialization of, 9, 81, 83; recruitment of to work in fields, 6, 69n14, 77–78, 94; relations with locals, 84–88; role of fathers, 92; role of mothers, 91–92; tragedies of, 86; during World War I, 122, 126–27. *See also* Bohemiains, German Russians, Hungarians, Poles
Edson, George T., 147, 158–60, 162–63
Emigrant Agency Act (1929), 154

Fargett, Joseph, 181
Farm Bureau, (FB/Michigan), 118–20
Farm Bureau/Michigan Sugar Beet Growers' Association (FB/MSBGA), 113, 119–20
farmers: ambivalence about sugar beet industry, 43; calls for state intervention, 103, 107–9; class identity of, 5, 47–48, 53, 58–59, 61, 116–17, 210; commercial agriculture and, 67–68, 93–94; conflicts over control issues, 49–50; dissatisfaction with sugar beet, 44; family labor of, 66–69; frustration with company profits, 56, 98–99; and infighting among, 116–17; patriotic use of rhetoric, 97, 103, 105–6, 108–9, 112; post World War I strikes of, 115–17; southwestern, 128; strikes 9, 48, 51, 53, 59–61; tensions with companies, 44–45, 47, 53–54, 62; town hostility toward, 51–52; union organizing of, 45–47, 50–51, 56–59, 98–99, 113–15, 118–20, 210; World War I militancy, 104–5
Farmers and Manufacturers Beet Sugar Association (F&M), 189, 210–11, 229
Farmers' Clubs, 46, 56
Farmers' National Council (FNC): demands for state intervention, 98, 107–9; overshadowed by AFBF, 110–11, 121; reconstruction plans of, 109–10

Farmers' Union, 113–14, 210
Farm Security Administration (FSA), 224, 241
Federal Trade Commission, 114
fifty-fifty contracts (50/50): Great Depression era and, 188–89, 192, 208, 212–13; World War I era and, 111–12, 114
flat-rate contracts, 50, 53–54, 56, 120, 188
Foran Act, 153
Ford, Sheridan, 99–100

Gallagher, T. G., 151, 186
Garrison, Charles M., 19
German-American Sugar Company, 51, 60, 96
German Russians: as farmers, 92–93; as migrant laborers 2, 66, 75, 80; racialization of, 81–83, 84, 89–90
Germans, 21, 45, 68, 82
Gilbert, Newton, W., 200
Gleaner: cooperative efforts of, 5, 61; founding of, 56; philosophy of, 57–59; support of World War I, 96; during World War I era, 97, 107–8, 113–14
Grange, 46; efforts to organize beet farmers, 113–14, 98–99; as part of the Farmers' National Council, 107; Philippine independence and, 198; tariff debate and, 191
Grant, Madison, 144
Grapes of Wrath, The, 12, 241
Gray, Chester H., 198
Great Britain, 101, 110
Great Depression, 11–12, 215–17, 239
Great Lakes Growers' Employment Corporation, 232
Great Lakes Sugar Company, 212, 230–32
growers. *See* farmers
Guronor, Sluco, 85–86

Hahamovitch, Cindy, 124
Hall, Myron, 181
Ham, William T., 224–25
Hammerstein, John, 217
Hampton, George, 108
Hare-Hawes-Cutting Act, 201–3
Harris, G. H., 133
Harrison, Pat, 191
Hathaway, F. R., 30, 33, 35, 72
Hawaii, 207, 208
Hawes, Harry, 199

Hernandez, Cesario, 154
hired hands, 6, 67, 70–71, 78
Holland-St. Louis Sugar Company, 147–48, 182
Holland Sugar Company, 42, 53
Home of the Friendless Orphanage, 73
Homes Mission Council, 235
Hoover, Herbert: as head of U.S. Food Administration, 101–3, 125; Mexican immigration and 153, 217; Philippine independence and, 198; tariff debate and, 191, 194; veto of Philippine independence act, 202–3
Hopkins, Howard, 132–33
Hornbacker, J. M., 181
House Committee on Immigration and Naturalization, 129
Houston, David, 107
Howard, J. R., 110–11
Hull, Cordell, 245
Hull, Henry, 215, 217
Hull, N. P., 109
Hungarians, 66, 83, 87–90
Hushing, W. C., 199

Illinois Sugar Refining Company, 75
Immigration Act of 1917, 124, 128
Immigration Act of 1921, 164
Immigration Act of 1924, 153. *See also* Johnson-Reed Act
immigration restriction, 10, 123–24, 128
Industrial Commission, 74
industrial democracy, 10, 13, 97, 108–9, 127
Issard, Samuel, 226

Jeffersonian ideals, 108, 135, 150, 171
Johnson, Albert, 143–44, 150–51
Johnson, Elizabeth, 230
Johnson-Reed Act, 143–44, 152, 164. *See also* Immigration Act of 1924
Jones-Costigan Act, 11, 187–88, 205; farm/factory relations and, 209–14; imperial production and, 206–7, 216, 223, 228, 230, 234, 239, 244
Jones, Marvin, 206–7

Kalamazoo Sugar Company, 37
Kearney, Charles M., 207–8
Keating-Owen Act, 167
Kedzie, R. C., 47, 74, 99

Kennedy, Edward, 243
King, William, 196
Kretzler, Antoine, 85
Krogstad, Robert, 236

labor: shortages of, 65–66, 69–71, 123
Lakin, Herbert C., 196
Lancashire, Henry, 47
Lansing, Robert, 132
League of Domestic Producers, 25
Lee, Gilbert H., 39, 52
Lenawee Protective League, 232
Local 19994 (AWU), 228–32
Lopez, Edmund G., 156
Louisiana, 4, 25–26, 29, 31
Love, Stephen H., 192
Lovejoy, Owen, 170, 174, 178, 182
lumber industry, 18–19

Maargraf, Andreas, 31
Marine City Businessmen's Association, 52
Markva, Albert, 226, 231
Martinez, Donaquin, 220
Martini, Henry, 87–88
Maser, Elisabeth Catherine, 80, 88
Mautner, Bertram, 171
McBride, James N., 193
McConnell, Clarence, 219–20
McGill, Nettie, 170, 172
McKenzie, Reverend, 235
McKinley, William, 28, 198
McLean, C. L., 53
McLean, S. R., 147–49
Merchant Beet Company Ltd., 52
Mexican-descent workers: community ties of, 157–58; conflicts with companies, 156; Great Depression and, 215–17; as guest workers, 8, 10; as a health threat, 235–36; housing of, 157; investigation of, 135–36; labor contracts of, 154–56; labor organizing of, 228–30; Michigan Bureau of Labor and Industry and, 236–39; militancy of, 138–40; naturalization and, 158–59; post World War I depression and, 139–41; post World War I repatriation and, 140–42; recruitment of, 122–23, 153–34; resistance to repatriation, 221; response of Mexican state to, 130–32, 135; in the Southwest, 128–29; World War I and, 128–34, 137–38
Mexican Independence Day, 143, 157–58

Mexican Secretary of Foreign Relations, 131
Michigan Agricultural College, 14, 19, 42, 47, 57–58, 62–63, 99
Michigan Agricultural Experiment Station, 14
Michigan Beet Growers' Association (MBGA), 39, 45
Michigan Beet Sugar Manufacturers' Association (MBSMA), 45, 50
Michigan Bureau of Labor and Industry, 14, 22, 42, 44, 47, 236–38
Michigan Commission of Health, 238
Michigan Milk Producers' Association, 109
Michigan State Farmers' Institutes, 20, 47, 48, 65
Michigan State Land Office, 19
Michigan Sugar Beet Growers' Association (MSBGA): defeats of, 61; organizing efforts of, 59, 103, 113–17; philosophy of, 58–59; suspicions toward Michigan Farm Bureau, 118, 120
Michigan Sugar Company: American Sugar Refining Corporation and, 54–56; company farm, 52; conflicts with farmers, 60–61, 106, 114–15; conflicts with other companies and, 48; founding of, 20; Great Depression and, 188; Mexican descent labor and, 106, 114–15, 122, 154–55, 193; migrant labor and, 82, 122, 138–40, 154–55, 193
Michigan Supreme Court, 20, 49
Mintz, Sidney, 12, 23, 36
Monitor Sugar Company, 227
Montano, Maria S., 163
Montgomery, David, 77
Morris, Dr., 154, 159
Mueller, August, 52
Munoz, Joseph, 234
Murphy, Frank, 231
Myrick, Herbert, 25, 27

Napoleonic Wars, 32
National Beet Growers' Association, 208
National Child Labor Committee (NCLC): critique of farm families, 175; critique of industrial agriculture, 184; definition of industrial agriculture, 168–70; field investigations of, 173–74; highlighting health risks of child labor, 172–73; migrant labor and, 78, 83–84, 92; neglect of Mexican labor, 175, 183; role in AAA hearings, 222; view of migrant mothers, 175–76
National Conference of Social Work, 170
National Industrial Recovery Act, 228
National Labor Relations Act, 228
National War Labor Board, 103
Negrette, Jane, 220
New Deal, 11, 187, 206, 214, 216, 222, 228, 234
Non-Partisan League (NPL), 98, 107, 111
North American Free Trade Agreement (NAFTA), 246

Oberst, Frank, 211
Obregon, Alvaro, 135
O'Conner, J. E., 229, 231
Ogg, W. R., 192
Ortiz, Santiago, 156
Osmena, Sergio, 203
Osterud, Nancy Grey, 93
Oviatt, C. R., 208
Owosso Sugar Company, 52, 72, 85
Oxnard, Henry, 27, 30

Palmer, Truman, 34–35, 139
Peck, Gunther, 77
Peninsular Sugar Company, 52, 54, 66
Perkins, Frances, 222, 229, 231–33
Phester, Martin, 87
Philippine-American Chamber of Commerce, 199–200
Philippine Assembly, 36
Philippines: cheap labor and, 192–93; independence debates regarding, 7, 11, 186–87, 198–200, 205, 213; press criticism of independence of, 200, 203; Spanish-American War and, 16–17; Sugar Act and, 207; sugar cane production of, 17, 24–25; sugar imports into United States, 190, 203; tariff debates and, 33–34, 39, 192–93; U.S. Constitution and, 26
Phoenix, George, 218
Pilkington, Robert, 233
Pingree, Hazen S., 46
Platt Amendment, 1, 245
Pobanz, Otto, 115
Poles, 6, 66, 74
Pomerene Act, 167
Prescott, George, 103–6
Price, Thomas, 115
Puerto Rico, 16–17, 24–27, 29, 39, 190, 207

Quezon, Manuel L., 204–5

Reciprocal Trade Agreement Act, 245
repatriation, 10; community support of, 141, 219–20; Great Depression era, 215–16, 218–21; Mexican-descent workers resistance to, 221; Mexican state support of, 218–19; World War I era, 141
Resettlement Administration, 224
Rivera, Diego, 219–20
Rolfs, E. A., 105
Roosevelt, Franklin: Philippine independence and, 204–5; sugar acts and, 11, 187, 207, 223–24, 244; sugar beet labor and, 222–24; trade policy and, 245
Roosevelt, Theodore, 25, 29
Root, Elihu, 29
Ross, F. H., 147
Roxas, Manuel, 201, 203
Ruppal, John, 181
Rust, E. G., 149

Saginaw City Council, 218
Salz, John, 87
Sanilac Sugar Refining Company, 22, 73
Saylor, Charles: labor concerns of, 65, 76; sugar beet boosting of, 4, 13, 15, 17, 38, 41,
Scannell, John J., 183
Schmidt, Fred, 229, 231
scientific agriculture, 17, 108
Sebedie, Alex, 87
Siven, J. C., 71
Sleeper, Albert E., 100
Slocum, Fred, 13
Slocum, Grant, 56–57, 61, 107
Smith, Aura, 201
Smith, C. D., 47, 70, 74
Smoot-Hawley Tariff, 197, 206
Spanish-American War, 1, 7, 16, 23–24, 196
Stanley, White, 225
State Dairy and Food Commission, 59
Steelman, J. R., 232
Stewart, L. R., 181
Stewart, N. H., 1, 31–32, 39
Stimson, Henry L., 194–95, 198, 202
St. Louis Sugar Company, 21
St. Vincent de Paul Society, 141
Sugar Act: child labor prohibitions of, 227–28; extension of, 246; farmers and, 214, 244; Jones-Costigan Act and, 188, 209; labor and, 216, 223–28, 234, 239, 244; labor critique of, 232; sugar production and, 206, 209, 246
Sugar Beet Bill, 59, 62
sugar beet industry, European: colonialism and, 35; expansion of, 3; history of, 31–32; labor in, 75; protectionism and, 3–4, 15–16; during World War I, 98
Sugar Division, 226
Sugar Section, 224, 227
sugar trust, 30, 54–55, 60. *See also* American Sugar Refining Company
Supreme Court, United States, 26, 33, 144, 167, 188
Switzer, John, 199

tariff: creation of U.S. sugar beet industry and, 4, 7; imperial politics and, 11, 25–28, 33–37, 186, 190, 192, 194, 196–97, 206–8; Mexican labor and, 192–93; Philippine independence and, 202; press criticism of sugar industry and, 193–94
Taussig, Frank, 83
Taylor, Paul S., 158–60, 241
Teller, Henry, 28–29
Teller Resolution, 28–29
Tenure and Labor Relations Section, 224
Texas Health Department, 238
Thaden, John F., 93
Thissell, J. F., 51 72
Tompkins, L. B., 148
townspeople: boosterism, 1–2, 8, 13–14, 21n46, 22, 38, 42–43, 55–56, 189, 190, 212; child labor and, 72–73, 182; eastern Europeans and, 80–82, 84–88; farmers and, 51–52, 56, 61, 105; farm family labor and, 69; labor unions and, 232–33; Mexican-descent workers and, 137, 157, 218–20; migrant labor and, 234–38; sugar trust and, 54–55; World War I and, 96
Turner, Frederick Jackson, 8
Twentieth Amendment (proposed child labor), 184
Tyddings, Millard, 204
Tyddings-McDuffie Act, 204–5, 209, 213

United States Beet Sugar Association, 192
United States Sugar Manufacturing Association, 139
U.S. Bureau of Immigration, 133

U.S. Department of Agriculture (USDA): boosterism of, 4, 13–15, 17, 20, 42; critique of cane sugar, 30; farmers and, 57–58; migrant labor and, 65, 70; promotion of migrant family labor, 76; scientific agriculture of, 102; sugar acts and, 211–14, 222–23, 226–28; World War I labor, 124–25, 209

U.S. Department of Labor (USDL): child labor and, 222; Great Depression and, 217; labor strikes and, 229, 233; World War I labor shortages and, 125; World War I temporary labor program of, 10, 123–25, 128–29, 133–35, 137, 139

U.S. Food Administration, 101–3, 125

U.S. Tariff Commission, 206

Vandenburg, Arthur, 196, 209, 223
Van Dorn, Reverend, 234
Vincent, J. Bird., 145, 151
Virgin Islands, 207

Wagner, R. G., 54
Wagner, Robert, 223
Wallace, Henry A., 226
Wallace, W. H., 52, 84, 114
Warner, Fred, 99, 125
Watkings, O. C., 119
Ways and Means Committee, 31, 195

Webster, Arthur J., 218
West Bay City Sugar Company, 47–48, 51, 104
White, Helen, 235
Wiley, H. W., 31–32, 47
Williams, Frances B., 180
Williams, Hattie Plum, 81–82
Wilson, James, 19–20
Wilson, William B., 123, 128–29, 134–35, 142
Wilson, Woodrow, 113, 120, 129
Wisconsin Sugar Company, 54
Wolfson, Theresa, 83
Wolverine Sugar Company, 37, 48
women: as beet weeders, 9, 66, 74, 75
Woodruff, Roy Orchard, 143–44, 147–48, 209
Works Progress Administration, 241
World War I: extension of temporary labor program after, 134–35; federal intervention in farmer/factory conflicts, 10, 97, 102–6, 111; limits of temporary labor program during, 138–39; state of Michigan intervention during, 99–101; sugar company profits during 98–99; temporary labor program during, 128–32

Young, Carl, 182–83

Zagelmeyer, Frank, 20
Zurbick, John L., 218

KATHLEEN MAPES is an associate professor of history at the State University of New York, Geneseo.

THE WORKING CLASS IN AMERICAN HISTORY

Worker City, Company Town: Iron and Cotton-Worker Protest in Troy and Cohoes, New York, 1855–84   *Daniel J. Walkowitz*

Life, Work, and Rebellion in the Coal Fields: The Southern West Virginia Miners, 1880–1922   *David Alan Corbin*

Women and American Socialism, 1870–1920   *Mari Jo Buhle*

Lives of Their Own: Blacks, Italians, and Poles in Pittsburgh, 1900–1960   *John Bodnar, Roger Simon, and Michael P. Weber*

Working-Class America: Essays on Labor, Community, and American Society   *Edited by Michael H. Frisch and Daniel J. Walkowitz*

Eugene V. Debs: Citizen and Socialist   *Nick Salvatore*

American Labor and Immigration History, 1877–1920s: Recent European Research   *Edited by Dirk Hoerder*

Workingmen's Democracy: The Knights of Labor and American Politics   *Leon Fink*

The Electrical Workers: A History of Labor at General Electric and Westinghouse, 1923–60   *Ronald W. Schatz*

The Mechanics of Baltimore: Workers and Politics in the Age of Revolution, 1763–1812   *Charles G. Steffen*

The Practice of Solidarity: American Hat Finishers in the Nineteenth Century   *David Bensman*

The Labor History Reader   *Edited by Daniel J. Leab*

Solidarity and Fragmentation: Working People and Class Consciousness in Detroit, 1875–1900   *Richard Oestreicher*

Counter Cultures: Saleswomen, Managers, and Customers in American Department Stores, 1890–1940   *Susan Porter Benson*

The New England Working Class and the New Labor History   *Edited by Herbert G. Gutman and Donald H. Bell*

Labor Leaders in America   *Edited by Melvyn Dubofsky and Warren Van Tine*

Barons of Labor: The San Francisco Building Trades and Union Power in the Progressive Era   *Michael Kazin*

Gender at Work: The Dynamics of Job Segregation by Sex during World War II   *Ruth Milkman*

Once a Cigar Maker: Men, Women, and Work Culture in American Cigar Factories, 1900–1919   *Patricia A. Cooper*

A Generation of Boomers: The Pattern of Railroad Labor Conflict in Nineteenth-Century America   *Shelton Stromquist*

Work and Community in the Jungle: Chicago's Packinghouse Workers, 1894–1922   *James R. Barrett*

Workers, Managers, and Welfare Capitalism: The Shoeworkers and Tanners of Endicott Johnson, 1890–1950   *Gerald Zahavi*

Men, Women, and Work: Class, Gender, and Protest in the New England Shoe Industry, 1780–1910   *Mary Blewett*

Workers on the Waterfront: Seamen, Longshoremen, and Unionism in the 1930s   *Bruce Nelson*

German Workers in Chicago: A Documentary History of Working-Class Culture from 1850 to World War I   *Edited by Hartmut Keil and John B. Jentz*

On the Line: Essays in the History of Auto Work   *Edited by Nelson Lichtenstein and Stephen Meyer III*

Labor's Flaming Youth: Telephone Operators and Worker Militancy, 1878–1923   *Stephen H. Norwood*

Another Civil War: Labor, Capital, and the State in the Anthracite Regions of Pennsylvania, 1840–68   *Grace Palladino*

Coal, Class, and Color: Blacks in Southern West Virginia, 1915–32   *Joe William Trotter, Jr.*

For Democracy, Workers, and God: Labor Song-Poems and Labor Protest, 1865–95   *Clark D. Halker*

Dishing It Out: Waitresses and Their Unions in the Twentieth Century   *Dorothy Sue Cobble*

The Spirit of 1848: German Immigrants, Labor Conflict, and the Coming of the Civil War   *Bruce Levine*

Working Women of Collar City: Gender, Class, and Community in Troy, New York, 1864–86   *Carole Turbin*

Southern Labor and Black Civil Rights: Organizing Memphis Workers   *Michael K. Honey*

Radicals of the Worst Sort: Laboring Women in Lawrence, Massachusetts, 1860–1912   *Ardis Cameron*

Producers, Proletarians, and Politicians: Workers and Party Politics in Evansville and New Albany, Indiana, 1850–87   *Lawrence M. Lipin*

The New Left and Labor in the 1960s   *Peter B. Levy*

The Making of Western Labor Radicalism: Denver's Organized Workers, 1878–1905   *David Brundage*

In Search of the Working Class: Essays in American Labor History and Political Culture   *Leon Fink*

Lawyers against Labor: From Individual Rights to Corporate Liberalism   *Daniel R. Ernst*

"We Are All Leaders": The Alternative Unionism of the Early 1930s   *Edited by Staughton Lynd*

The Female Economy: The Millinery and Dressmaking Trades, 1860–1930   *Wendy Gamber*

"Negro and White, Unite and Fight!": A Social History of Industrial Unionism in Meatpacking, 1930–90   *Roger Horowitz*

Power at Odds: The 1922 National Railroad Shopmen's Strike   *Colin J. Davis*

The Common Ground of Womanhood: Class, Gender, and Working Girls' Clubs, 1884–1928   *Priscilla Murolo*

Marching Together: Women of the Brotherhood of Sleeping Car Porters   *Melinda Chateauvert*

Down on the Killing Floor: Black and White Workers in Chicago's Packinghouses,
    1904–54   *Rick Halpern*
Labor and Urban Politics: Class Conflict and the Origins of Modern Liberalism
    in Chicago, 1864–97   *Richard Schneirov*
All That Glitters: Class, Conflict, and Community in Cripple Creek   *Elizabeth Jameson*
Waterfront Workers: New Perspectives on Race and Class   *Edited by Calvin Winslow*
Labor Histories: Class, Politics, and the Working-Class Experience   *Edited by
    Eric Arnesen, Julie Greene, and Bruce Laurie*
The Pullman Strike and the Crisis of the 1890s: Essays on Labor and Politics   *Edited
    by Richard Schneirov, Shelton Stromquist, and Nick Salvatore*
AlabamaNorth: African-American Migrants, Community, and Working-Class
    Activism in Cleveland, 1914–45   *Kimberley L. Phillips*
Imagining Internationalism in American and British Labor, 1939–49
    Victor Silverman
William Z. Foster and the Tragedy of American Radicalism   *James R. Barrett*
Colliers across the Sea: A Comparative Study of Class Formation in Scotland and the
    American Midwest, 1830–1924   *John H. M. Laslett*
"Rights, Not Roses": Unions and the Rise of Working-Class Feminism, 1945–80
    Dennis A. Deslippe
Testing the New Deal: The General Textile Strike of 1934 in the American South
    Janet Irons
Hard Work: The Making of Labor History   *Melvyn Dubofsky*
Southern Workers and the Search for Community: Spartanburg County, South
    Carolina   *G. C. Waldrep III*
We Shall Be All: A History of the Industrial Workers of the World (abridged edition)   *Melvyn Dubofsky, ed. Joseph A. McCartin*
Race, Class, and Power in the Alabama Coalfields, 1908–21   *Brian Kelly*
Duquesne and the Rise of Steel Unionism   *James D. Rose*
Anaconda: Labor, Community, and Culture in Montana's Smelter City   *Laurie Mercier*
Bridgeport's Socialist New Deal, 1915–36   *Cecelia Bucki*
Indispensable Outcasts: Hobo Workers and Community in the American Midwest,
    1880–1930   *Frank Tobias Higbie*
After the Strike: A Century of Labor Struggle at Pullman   *Susan Eleanor Hirsch*
Corruption and Reform in the Teamsters Union   *David Witwer*
Waterfront Revolts: New York and London Dockworkers, 1946–61   *Colin J. Davis*
Black Workers' Struggle for Equality in Birmingham   *Horace Huntley and
    David Montgomery*
The Tribe of Black Ulysses: African American Men in the Industrial South
    William P. Jones
City of Clerks: Office and Sales Workers in Philadelphia, 1870–1920
    Jerome P. Bjelopera
Reinventing "The People": The Progressive Movement, the Class Problem, and the
    Origins of Modern Liberalism   *Shelton Stromquist*

Radical Unionism in the Midwest, 1900–1950   *Rosemary Feurer*
Gendering Labor History   *Alice Kessler-Harris*
James P. Cannon and the Origins of the American Revolutionary Left, 1890–1928   *Bryan D. Palmer*
Glass Towns: Industry, Labor, and Political Economy in Appalachia, 1890–1930s   *Ken Fones-Wolf*
Workers and the Wild: Conservation, Consumerism, and Labor in Oregon, 1910–30   *Lawrence M. Lipin*
Wobblies on the Waterfront: Interracial Unionism in Progressive-Era Philadelphia   *Peter Cole*
Red Chicago: American Communism at Its Grassroots, 1928–35   *Randi Storch*
Labor's Cold War: Local Politics in a Global Context   *Edited by Shelton Stromquist*
Bessie Abromowitz Hillman and the Making of the Amalgamated Clothing Workers of America   *Karen Pastorello*
The Great Strikes of 1877   *Edited by David O. Stowell*
Union-Free America: Workers and Antiunion Culture   *Lawrence Richards*
Race against Liberalism: Black Workers and the UAW in Detroit   *David M. Lewis-Colman*
Teachers and Reform: Chicago Public Education, 1929–70   *John F. Lyons*
Upheaval in the Quiet Zone: 1199/SEIU and the Politics of Healthcare Unionism   *Leon Fink and Brian Greenberg*
Shadow of the Racketeer: Scandal in Organized Labor   *David Witwer*
Sweet Tyranny: Migrant Labor, Industrial Agriculture, and Imperial Politics   *Kathleen Mapes*

The University of Illinois Press
is a founding member of the
Association of American University Presses.

Composed in 10.5/13 Adobe Minion Pro
by Celia Shapland
at the University of Illinois Press
Manufactured by Sheridan Books, Inc.

University of Illinois Press
1325 South Oak Street
Champaign, IL 61820-6903
www.press.uillinois.edu